Taste of Home
Holidays
& CELEBRATIONS

TASTE OF HOME BOOKS • RDA ENTHUSIAST BRANDS, LLC • MILWAUKEE, WI

Taste of Home

Reader's digest

A TASTE OF HOME/READER'S DIGEST BOOK

©2015 RDA Enthusiast Brands, LLC, 1610 N. 2nd St., Suite 102, Milwaukee WI 53212-3906. All rights reserved.
Taste of Home and Reader's Digest are registered trademarks of The Reader's Digest Association, Inc.

"Cooking, Caring, Sharing" is a registered trademark of RDA Enthusiast Brands, LLC.

For other *Taste of Home* books and products, visit us at *tasteofhome.com*.

For more Reader's Digest products and information, visit *rd.com* (in the United States) or *rd.ca* (in Canada).

International Standard Book Number: 978-1-61765-416-9
Library of Congress Control Number: 2014957258

Pictured on front cover (clockwise from top left):
Candy Land Garland, page 240; Halloween Chocolate Cookie Pops, page 155; Creamy Pastel Mints, page 57; Garlic Rosemary Turkey, page 186; Frozen Peppermint Torte, page 260; All-American Bacon Cheeseburgers , page 112; Overnight Reindeer Rolls, page 273; and Overnight Cinnamon Rolls, page 273.

Pictured on back cover (clockwise from top left):
Fun Caramel Apples, page 158; Salt-Encrusted Prime Rib, page 292; Marmalade Candied Carrots, page 289; and Melting Snowmen, page 238.

Printed in China.
1 3 5 7 9 10 8 6 4 2

LIKE US
facebook.com/tasteofhome

TWEET US
@tasteofhome

FOLLOW US
pinterest.com/taste_of_home

SHOP WITH US
shoptasteofhome.com

SHARE A RECIPE
tasteofhome.com/submit

Christmas Dinner, page 278

St. Patrick's Day, page 22

Tailgating, page 164

Firework Fun, page 106

Let's Party!

WITH 467 RECIPES, YOU'RE READY TO CELEBRATE ALL YEAR LONG!

There's always time to eat, drink and be merry with **Taste of Home Holidays & Celebrations** at your fingertips! That's because it features 467 recipes worth sharing at backyard barbecues and tailgate picnics as well as Halloween parties and Christmas buffets.

Divided into the four seasons, this amazing collection features recipes, menu ideas, tips and reviews for more than 25 parties, holidays and occasions throughout the year. Hosting a Mother's Day brunch? See page 72. Need a few frosty treats to cool off a Fourth of July bash? Turn to page 106. Looking for some new Thanksgiving Day favorites? Flip to page 176. From Valentine's Day specialties to New Year's Eve party starters, **Holidays & Celebrations** has you covered!

Best of all, these recipes come from family cooks—just like you. These are the tried-and-true dishes they prepare for holidays at their homes, and now they're sharing their secrets with you. The *Taste of Home* Test Kitchen tests and approves each recipe, so you can take comfort knowing everything will turn out perfectly for your own celebration.

So, what are you waiting for? With **Holidays & Celebrations** you have all the recipes you need to make any day worth celebrating!

icons

SLOW COOKER
Recipes marked with this icon free up oven space, travel well and simmer on their own because they're made in a slow cooker.

⑤ INGREDIENTS
With the exception of water, salt, pepper and oil, these dishes call for only a few items, many of which you likely have on hand.

FREEZE IT
With a little planning, you can make these holiday dishes ahead of time and simply store them in your freezer.

❝ These cupcakes were a big hit with the kids and the adults, too! ❞
—TEMILES TASTEOFHOME.COM

Look for **READER RAVES** like this one throughout the cookbook.

Almond Bonbon
Cookies, page 247

Layered Peppermint
Icebox Cake, page 300

Southwest Pulled
Pork, page 35

Tart Cranberry
Quick Bread,
page 154

Boo-Ya Mini
Pizzas, page 166

Breakfast Sausage
Patties, page 277

Raspberry Lemonade
Concentrate, page 90

Mahogany-Glazed
Cornish Hen, page 183

Contents

Glazed Pineapple
Ham, page 47

Rainbow Cake
with Clouds, page 27

Colorful Quinoa Salad, page 58

Berry Breakfast Parfaits, page 75

Spring

IT'S EASY TO CREATE SPRINGTIME CELEBRATIONS AS BRIGHT AS THE SEASON ITSELF. WHETHER YOU'RE SHAKING OFF WINTER'S CHILL WITH A VALENTINE'S DAY PARTY, WATCHING THE BIG GAME ON TV WITH THE GUYS OR HOSTING A COLORFUL EASTER WITH THE PERFECT MENU, LET THE FOLLOWING CHAPTERS PUT A LIGHTHEARTED (AND DELICIOUS) SPRING IN YOUR STEP!

LOTS OF LOVE CHERRY PIES
PAGE 14

Be My Valentine

IT'S TIME TO GIVE JACK FROST THE COLD SHOULDER AND COZY UP WITH YOUR VALENTINE! FROM ROMANTIC DINNERS TO CUTE CLASSROOM TREATS, THE FOLLOWING PAGES ARE PACKED WITH DELIGHTFUL IDEAS THAT BEAT THE CHILL AND WARM HEARTS.

GERRY COFTA'S CHOCOLATE CHERRY TRUFFLES *PAGE 17*

GILDA LESTER'S ORZO TIMBALES WITH FONTINA CHEESE *PAGE 18*

COOKIE CURCI'S BRACIOLE *PAGE 20*

Mozzarella Strawberry Salad
with Chocolate Vinaigrette

Mozzarella Strawberry Salad with Chocolate Vinaigrette

A chocolate salad dressing? How else would you dress a salad on Valentine's Day? Don't let the unusual name and flavor combination confuse you—the salty prosciutto and mellow mozzarella are beautifully balanced with the sweet-tart chocolate balsamic vinegar dressing.
—*TASTE OF HOME* TEST KITCHEN

START TO FINISH: 30 MIN. • **MAKES:** 6 SERVINGS

- 6 **thin slices prosciutto or deli ham, chopped**
- 1 **package (5 ounces) spring mix salad greens**
- 1½ **cups watercress**
- 1 **carton (8 ounces) fresh mozzarella cheese pearls**
- 1½ **cups sliced fresh strawberries**
- ¼ **cup dark chocolate chips**
- ¼ **cup balsamic vinegar**
- ¼ **cup olive oil**
- 1½ **teaspoons honey**
- ¼ **teaspoon salt**
- ⅛ **teaspoon pepper**

1. In a small skillet, cook prosciutto over medium heat until crisp. Remove to paper towels with a slotted spoon; drain and set aside. Divide salad greens and watercress among six salad plates. Arrange cheese, strawberries and prosciutto over greens.
2. In a microwave, melt chocolate; stir until smooth. Whisk in the vinegar, oil, honey, salt and pepper. Drizzle over each salad.

TOP TIP

Go Green!

Spice up salads and sandwiches with the small dark green leaves and edible stems of watercress. Grown in cool-running streams and brooks, it has a pungent flavor that is slightly bitter or peppery. It's available in bunches in the produce aisle of the grocery store.

Berry Mini Cheesecakes

Berry Mini Cheesecakes

There's always room for dessert when these special little bites are on the menu!
—*TASTE OF HOME* TEST KITCHEN

PREP: 20 MIN. • **BAKE:** 15 MIN. + CHILLING
MAKES: 1½ DOZEN

- 1 **cup graham cracker crumbs**
- 3 **tablespoons butter, melted**
- 1 **package (8 ounces) cream cheese, softened**
- ⅓ **cup sugar**
- 1 **teaspoon vanilla extract**
- 1 **egg, lightly beaten**
- 18 **fresh raspberries**

1. Preheat oven to 350°. In a small bowl, combine graham cracker crumbs and butter. Press gently onto the bottom of 18 paper-lined miniature muffin cups. In another small bowl, beat cream cheese, sugar and vanilla until smooth. Add egg; beat on low speed just until combined. Spoon over crusts.
2. Bake 12-14 minutes or until centers are set. Cool 10 minutes before removing cakes from pan to a wire rack to cool completely. Refrigerate at least 1 hour.
3. To serve, remove paper liners; top cheesecakes with raspberries.

⑤ INGREDIENTS

Have a Heart Cupcake

Every now and then we all need a little love! Decorate as many baked cupcakes as you need, following these easy steps.
—*TASTE OF HOME* TEST KITCHEN

PREP: 20 MIN. • **MAKES:** 1 CUPCAKE

- 1 **can (16 ounces) vanilla frosting**
  Aqua blue food coloring or coloring of your choice
  Cupcake of your choice
  Red shoestring licorice, cut into two 3-inch pieces
  Aqua blue colored sugar or color of your choice

1. Tint 3 tablespoons icing with food coloring; set aside. Frost cupcake with white icing.
2. Using a toothpick, draw a heart on the icing. Following the pattern, gently press licorice into frosting to form heart.
3. Fill heart with colored sugar. Pipe colored icing onto curved ends of licorice to hold in place.

White Wine Coq au Vin

Coq au vin is a chicken dish typically made with red wine. This wonderful version calls for white wine instead, and it makes a special dinner for two.
—*TASTE OF HOME* **TEST KITCHEN**

PREP: 25 MIN. • **COOK:** 40 MIN.
MAKES: 2 SERVINGS

- 4 **cups water**
- 1 **cup pearl onions**
- 4 **bacon strips, cut into 1-inch pieces**
- 2 **bone-in chicken breast halves (8 ounces each)**
- ¼ **teaspoon salt**
- ⅛ **teaspoon pepper**
- ¾ **cup sliced fresh mushrooms**
- 2 **garlic cloves, minced**
- 4½ **teaspoons all-purpose flour**
- ¾ **cup chicken broth**
- ¾ **cup white wine or additional chicken broth**
- 1 **bay leaf**
- ½ **teaspoon dried thyme**
  Hot cooked noodles

1. In a large saucepan, bring water to a boil. Add onions; boil 3 minutes. Drain onions and rinse in cold water; peel and set aside.
2. In a large skillet, cook bacon over medium heat until crisp. Using a slotted spoon, remove to paper towels.
3. Sprinkle chicken with salt and pepper. Brown chicken in drippings; remove and keep warm. Add onions and mushrooms to drippings; saute until crisp-tender. Add garlic; cook 1 minute longer.
4. Combine flour and broth; stir into onion mixture. Add the wine, bay leaf and thyme; bring to a boil. Return chicken and bacon to the pan. Reduce heat; cover and simmer 25-30 minutes or until a thermometer reads 170°.
5. Remove chicken and keep warm. Cook sauce over medium heat until slightly thickened. Discard bay leaf. Serve chicken and sauce with noodles.

Double Chocolate Chipotle Cookies

Double Chocolate Chipotle Cookies

One bite tells you that this isn't a typical chocolate cookie. Chipotle and cayenne peppers give these chewy, fudgy delights a yummy twist for Valentine's Day.
—**LISA MEREDITH** ST. PAUL, MN

PREP: 25 MIN. + CHILLING • **BAKE:** 10 MIN./BATCH
MAKES: 1½ DOZEN

- ⅔ **cup butter, softened**
- ½ **cup sugar**
- ½ **cup packed brown sugar**
- 1 **egg**
- 1 **teaspoon vanilla extract**
- ½ **teaspoon minced chipotle pepper in adobo sauce**
- 1 **cup plus 2 tablespoons all-purpose flour**
- ⅓ **cup baking cocoa**
- 1 **teaspoon ground cinnamon**
- ½ **teaspoon salt**
- ½ **teaspoon baking soda**
- ¼ **teaspoon cayenne pepper**
- 3 **milk chocolate candy bars (1.55 ounces each), chopped**
  Confectioners' sugar

1. In a large bowl, cream butter and sugars until light and fluffy. Beat in egg, vanilla and chipotle pepper. Combine flour, cocoa, cinnamon, salt, baking soda and cayenne; gradually add to creamed mixture and mix well. Stir in chopped candy. Chill 1 hour or until dough is easy to handle.
2. Preheat oven to 350°. Roll into 1½-in. balls; place 4 in. apart on ungreased baking sheets. Bake 10-12 minutes or until set. Cool 4 minutes before removing from pans to wire racks. Dust with confectioners' sugar.

❝ Fantastic! I didn't have any chipotle, so instead I added 3 teaspoons cayenne pepper. Everyone loved them. ❞
—**ANNIII** TASTEOFHOME.COM

Red Velvet Whoopie Pies

Everyone gets a kick out of this fun take on the trendy cake. Take a shortcut if you like and use packaged cream cheese frosting for the filling.

—JUDI DEXHEIMER STURGEON BAY, WI

PREP: 40 MIN. • **BAKE:** 10 MIN./BATCH + COOLING
MAKES: 2 DOZEN

- ¾ cup butter, softened
- 1 cup sugar
- 2 eggs
- ½ cup sour cream
- 1 tablespoon red food coloring
- 1½ teaspoons white vinegar
- 1 teaspoon clear vanilla extract
- 2¼ cups all-purpose flour
- ¼ cup baking cocoa
- 2 teaspoons baking powder
- ½ teaspoon salt
- ¼ teaspoon baking soda
- 2 ounces semisweet chocolate, melted and cooled

FILLING
- 1 package (8 ounces) cream cheese, softened
- ½ cup butter, softened
- 2½ cups confectioners' sugar
- 2 teaspoons clear vanilla extract

TOPPINGS
- White baking chips, melted
- Finely chopped pecans

1. Preheat oven to 375°. In a large bowl, cream butter and sugar until light and fluffy. Beat in eggs, sour cream, food coloring, vinegar and vanilla. In another bowl, whisk flour, cocoa, baking powder, salt and baking soda; gradually beat into creamed mixture. Stir in the cooled chocolate.

2. Drop dough by tablespoonfuls 2 in. apart onto parchment paper-lined baking sheets. Bake 8-10 minutes or until edges are set. Cool on pans 2 minutes. Remove to wire racks to cool completely.

3. For filling, in a large bowl, beat cream cheese and butter until fluffy. Beat in confectioners' sugar and vanilla until smooth. Spread filling on bottom of half of cookies; cover with remaining cookies.

4. Drizzle with melted baking chips; sprinkle with pecans. Refrigerate cookies until serving.

FREEZE OPTION *Freeze unfilled cookies in freezer containers. To use, thaw cookies in covered containers. Fill and decorate as directed.*

Red Velvet Whoopie Pies

(5)INGREDIENTS

Shrimp with Basil-Mango Sauce

Instead of serving cold shrimp with cocktail sauce, offer cooked shrimp alongside this simple basil sauce. It's a fun yet fancy first course for two.

—KEN HULME PRESCOTT, AZ

START TO FINISH: 15 MIN. • **MAKES:** 2 SERVINGS

- 1 medium ripe mango or 2 medium peaches, peeled and sliced
- 2 to 4 tablespoons minced fresh basil
- 1 tablespoon lemon juice
- 12 cooked medium shrimp, peeled and deveined
- 1 tablespoon butter
  Basil sprigs, optional

1. In a blender or food processor, combine the mango, basil and lemon juice; cover and process until blended. Pour onto two serving plates; set aside.

2. Skewer two shrimp each onto six 4- to 6-in. metal or soaked wooden skewers, forming a heart shape. Cook in a large skillet in butter over medium-high heat for 4-5 minutes or until shrimp turn pink, turning once. Place skewers over mango sauce. Garnish with sprigs of basil if desired.

Chocolate Cookie Cheesecake

Chocolate Cookie Cheesecake

Both cheesecake lovers and chocolate fans go wild when I present this rich dessert sprinkled with cream-filled cookies. It's always gone in a flash.

—**LISA M. VARNER** EL PASO, TX

PREP: 30 MIN. • **BAKE:** 50 MIN. + CHILLING
MAKES: 12 SERVINGS

- 1½ cups cream-filled chocolate sandwich cookie crumbs (about 16 cookies)
- 3 tablespoons butter, melted
- 4 packages (8 ounces each) cream cheese, softened
- 1 cup sugar
- 1½ cups semisweet chocolate chips, melted and cooled
- 3 teaspoons vanilla extract
- 4 eggs, lightly beaten
- 20 cream-filled chocolate sandwich cookies, coarsely chopped

1. In a small bowl, combine cookie crumbs and butter. Press onto the bottom of a greased 9-in. springform pan. Refrigerate while preparing filling.
2. Preheat oven to 325°. In a large bowl, beat cream cheese and sugar until smooth. Beat in chocolate and vanilla. Add eggs; beat on low speed just until combined. Fold in half of the chopped cookies. Pour batter over crust. Sprinkle with remaining cookies. Place pan on a baking sheet.
3. Bake 50-60 minutes or until center is almost set and top appears dull. Cool on a wire rack 10 minutes.
4. Carefully run a knife around edge of pan to loosen; cool 1 hour longer. Refrigerate overnight. Remove side of pan before serving.

Lemon-Butter New Potatoes

We adore the combination of parsley and spices with a lemony butter sauce in this classic side dish. Serve it alongside nearly any meaty entree.

—**SANDY MCKENZIE** BRAHAM, MN

START TO FINISH: 30 MIN. • **MAKES:** 4 SERVINGS

- 12 small red potatoes
- ⅓ cup butter, cubed
- 3 tablespoons lemon juice
- 1 teaspoon salt
- 1 teaspoon grated lemon peel
- ¼ teaspoon pepper
- ⅛ teaspoon ground nutmeg
- 2 tablespoons minced fresh parsley

1. Peel a strip from around each potato. Place potatoes in a large saucepan and cover with water. Bring to a boil. Reduce heat; cover and cook for 15-20 minutes or just until tender.
2. Meanwhile, in small saucepan, melt butter. Stir in the lemon juice, salt, lemon peel, pepper and nutmeg. Drain potatoes and place in a serving bowl. Pour butter mixture over potatoes; toss gently to coat. Sprinkle with parsley.

Lots of Love Cherry Pies

Become the Queen of Hearts when you prepare these tart-style cherry pies. Made as single servings, they're ideal for a Valentine's dessert or any time you'd like to show a little love.

—**TASTE OF HOME** TEST KITCHEN

PREP: 30 MIN. + CHILLING
BAKE: 15 MIN./BATCH + COOLING
MAKES: 1 DOZEN

- 3¾ cups all-purpose flour
- ¾ teaspoon salt
- 1 cup cold butter, cubed
- ¾ cup shortening
- 9 to 10 tablespoons cold water

FILLING

- ⅓ cup sugar
- ¼ cup water
- 2 tablespoons cornstarch
- 1 tablespoon lemon juice

3 cups fresh or frozen pitted dark
   sweet cherries, thawed, halved
⅛ teaspoon almond extract
1 egg, lightly beaten
   Coarse sugar

1. In a large bowl, combine flour and salt; cut in butter and shortening until crumbly. Gradually add water, tossing with a fork until dough holds together when pressed. Divide dough in half; form each into a disk. Wrap separately in plastic wrap; refrigerate 1 hour or until easy to handle.

2. In a large saucepan, combine sugar, water, cornstarch and lemon juice until smooth. Add cherries. Bring to a boil; cook and stir 1 minute or until thickened. Remove from heat. Stir in extract. Set aside to cool.

3. Preheat oven to 400°. On a lightly floured surface, roll one portion of dough to ⅛-in. thickness. Cut out 12 hearts with a floured 4-in. heart-shaped cookie cutter. Transfer half of the hearts to a parchment-lined baking sheet. Using a floured ¾-in. heart-shaped cookie cutter, cut out small hearts from the remaining hearts. (Discard small hearts or reserve for another use.)

4. Spoon 2 tablespoons cherry mixture onto the center of each solid heart. Brush edges of pastry with egg. Top with cutout hearts; press edges with a fork to seal. Brush tops with egg; sprinkle with the coarse sugar.

5. Bake 15-20 minutes or until crust is golden brown and filling is bubbly. While tarts are baking, repeat with remaining dough and filling.

6. Let pies stand 5 minutes before removing to wire racks. Serve warm.

66 **The crust was so flaky and good! Love the filling, too!** 99
—**KO44** TASTEOFHOME.COM

Lots of Love
Cherry Pies

Hazelnut Pots de Creme

Hazelnut Pots de Creme

White chocolate and toasted ground hazelnuts make a heavenly combination in this rich, silky custard. Guests are sure to rave over the elegant treats served in individual ramekins.

—ELISE LALOR ISSAQUAH, WA

PREP: 30 MIN. • **BAKE:** 25 MIN. + CHILLING
MAKES: 6 SERVINGS

- 2 **cups heavy whipping cream**
- 1 **cup ground hazelnuts, toasted**
- 4 **ounces white baking chocolate, chopped**
- 6 **egg yolks**
- ⅓ **cup sugar**
- 2 **tablespoons hazelnut liqueur, optional**
  Chocolate curls

1. Preheat oven to 325°. In a small saucepan, heat cream, hazelnuts and chocolate until bubbles form around sides of pan and chocolate is melted, stirring occasionally.
2. In a small bowl, whisk egg yolks and sugar. Remove cream mixture from heat; stir a small amount of hot cream mixture into egg mixture. Return all to the pan, stirring constantly. Stir in liqueur if desired. Strain, discarding hazelnuts.
3. Transfer to six 6-oz. ramekins. Place in a baking pan; add 1 in. of boiling water to pan. Bake, uncovered, 25-30 minutes or until centers are just set (mixture will jiggle). Remove ramekins from water bath; cool 10 minutes. Cover and refrigerate at least 2 hours. Garnish servings with chocolate curls.

TOP TIP

Dress It Up!

Chocolate garnishes are a cinch to create for Valentine desserts. Simply use a vegetable peeler to "peel" curls from a solid block of room temperature chocolate, allowing the curls to fall gently onto a plate.

Chocolate Cherry Truffles

My blue ribbon cherry truffles were the delicious result of a kitchen experiment involving a bottle of kirsch I'd received as a gift and some dried cherries I had on hand. Today, they're an annual favorite of family and friends alike.

—GERRY COFTA MILWAUKEE, WI

PREP: 1½ HOURS + STANDING • **MAKES:** 4 DOZEN

- 1 cup finely chopped dried cherries
- ¼ cup cherry brandy
- 11 ounces 53% cacao dark baking chocolate, chopped
- ½ cup heavy whipping cream
- 1 teaspoon cherry extract

COATING

- 4 ounces milk chocolate, chopped
- 4 ounces dark chocolate, chopped
    Melted dark, milk and white chocolate and pearl dust

1. In a small bowl, combine cherries and brandy; cover and let soak for 1 hour or until cherries are softened.

2. Place dark chocolate in a small bowl. In a small saucepan, bring cream just to a boil. Pour over chocolate; whisk until smooth. Stir in extract and soaked cherries with liquid. Cool to room temperature, stirring occasionally. Refrigerate for 1 hour or until firm.

3. Shape into 1-in. balls. Place on baking sheets; cover and refrigerate for at least 1 hour.

4. In a microwave, melt milk chocolate; stir until smooth. Dip half of the balls into milk chocolate, allowing excess to drip off. Place on waxed paper; let stand until set.

5. Melt dark chocolate; stir until smooth. Dip remaining balls into dark chocolate, allowing excess to drip off. Place on waxed paper; let stand until set. Drizzle with melted chocolate and decorate with pearl dust as desired. Store in an airtight container in the refrigerator.

NOTE *Pearl dust is available from Wilton Industries. Call 800-794-5866 or visit www.wilton.com.*

Pork Chops with Honey-Balsamic Glaze

Pork Chops with Honey-Balsamic Glaze

My husband loves pork chops, so I try to find new ways to use them. He calls this quick version "restaurant quality"!

—NICOLE CLAYTON PRESCOTT, AZ

START TO FINISH: 30 MIN.
MAKES: 4 SERVINGS

- 4 bone-in pork loin chops (1 inch thick and 10 ounces each)
- ½ teaspoon crushed red pepper flakes
- ½ teaspoon salt
- ½ teaspoon pepper
- 2 tablespoons olive oil

GLAZE

- ½ cup balsamic vinegar
- ½ cup honey
- 3 green onions, chopped
- 2 garlic cloves, minced
- 1 teaspoon minced fresh rosemary or ¼ teaspoon dried rosemary, crushed
- ⅛ teaspoon salt
- ⅛ teaspoon pepper
- ¼ cup butter, cubed

1. Sprinkle pork chops with pepper flakes, salt and pepper. In a large skillet, heat oil over medium heat. Add pork; cook for 5-7 minutes on each side or until meat reaches desired doneness (for medium-rare, a thermometer should read 145°; medium, 160°). Remove and keep warm.

2. In the same skillet, whisk the vinegar, honey, green onions, garlic, rosemary, salt and pepper; bring to a boil. Reduce heat; simmer, uncovered, for 6-8 minutes or until slightly thickened, stirring occasionally. Remove from the heat; whisk in butter until melted. Serve with pork chops.

Orzo Timbales with Fontina Cheese

Orzo Timbales with Fontina Cheese

Take mac and cheese to a new level using orzo pasta and fontina. With a pop of color from sweet red peppers, these timbales bake in ramekins for individual servings.
—**GILDA LESTER** MILLSBORO, DE

PREP: 20 MIN. • **BAKE:** 30 MIN.
MAKES: 6 SERVINGS

- 1 cup uncooked orzo pasta
- 1½ cups (6 ounces) shredded fontina cheese
- ½ cup finely chopped roasted sweet red peppers
- 1 can (2¼ ounces) sliced ripe olives, drained
- 2 eggs
- 1½ cups 2% milk
- ¼ teaspoon salt
- ⅛ teaspoon ground nutmeg
  Minced fresh parsley, optional

1. Preheat oven to 350°. Cook orzo according to package directions for al dente; drain. Transfer to a bowl. Stir in cheese, peppers and olives. Divide among six greased 10-oz. ramekins or custard cups. Place ramekins on a baking sheet.

2. In a small bowl, whisk eggs, milk, salt and nutmeg; pour over orzo mixture. Bake 30-35 minutes or until golden brown. Let stand 5 minutes before serving. Run a knife around sides of ramekins and invert onto serving plates. If desired, sprinkle with parsley.

⑤ INGREDIENTS

Sweetheart Salad

This speedy salad features convenient salad mix, dried cranberries, bottled salad dressing and purchased honey-roasted almonds. It's wonderful for a romantic dinner for two.
—*TASTE OF HOME* **TEST KITCHEN**

START TO FINISH: 10 MIN.
MAKES: 2 SERVINGS

- 3 cups spring mix salad greens
- ¼ cup dried cranberries
- ¼ cup balsamic vinaigrette
- 2 tablespoons honey-roasted sliced almonds

Divide salad greens and cranberries between two salad plates. Drizzle with vinaigrette and sprinkle with almonds.

⑤ INGREDIENTS

Chocolate-Dipped Strawberry Meringue Roses

Enjoy these cute, kid-friendly treats as is, or crush them into a bowl of strawberries and whipped cream. Readers of my blog, *utry.it*, went nuts when I posted that idea!
—**AMY TONG** ANAHEIM, CA

PREP: 25 MIN. • **BAKE:** 40 MIN. + COOLING
MAKES: 3½ DOZEN

- 3 egg whites
- ¼ cup sugar
- ¼ cup freeze-dried strawberries
- 1 package (3 ounces) strawberry gelatin
- ½ teaspoon vanilla extract, optional
- 1 cup 60% cacao bittersweet chocolate baking chips, melted

1. Place egg whites in a large bowl; let stand at room temperature 30 minutes. Preheat oven to 225°.

2. Place sugar and strawberries in a food processor; process until powdery. Add gelatin; pulse to blend. Beat egg whites on medium speed until foamy, adding vanilla if desired. Gradually add gelatin mixture, 1 tablespoon at a time, beating on high after each addition until sugar is issolved. Continue beating until stiff, glossy peaks form.

3. Cut a small hole in the tip of a pastry bag or in a corner of a food-safe plastic bag; insert a #1M star tip. Transfer meringue to bag. Pipe 2-in. roses 1½ in. apart onto parchment paper-lined baking sheets.

4. Bake 40-45 minutes or until set and dry. Turn off oven (do not open oven door); leave meringues in oven 1½ hours. Remove from oven; cool completely on baking sheets.

5. Remove meringues from paper. Dip bottoms in melted chocolate; allow excess to drip off. Place on waxed paper; let stand until set, about 45 minutes. Store in an airtight container at room temperature.

Chocolate-Dipped
Strawberry Meringue Roses

Braciole

In our family, braciole was served as a special treat for birthdays and holidays. It was Grandma's specialty and the preparation was time consuming. When the meat and sauce were fully cooked, Grandma called us into the kitchen to watch her lift the big roll from the sauce to the cutting board to slice it. The pinwheels of meat, laid side by side on the platter, topped with Grandma's delicious sauce, made a colorful and memorable picture.

—COOKIE CURCI SAN JOSE, CA

PREP: 35 MIN. • **COOK:** 1¼ HOURS
MAKES: 6 SERVINGS

- 1 **beef flank steak (1½ pounds)**
- 4 **tablespoons olive oil, divided**
- ½ **cup soft bread crumbs**
- ½ **cup minced fresh parsley**
- ½ **cup grated Parmesan cheese**
- 2 **garlic cloves, minced**
- 1 **teaspoon dried oregano**
- ½ **teaspoon salt, divided**
- ½ **teaspoon pepper, divided**
- 1 **medium onion, chopped**
- 2 **cans (15 ounces each) tomato sauce**
- ½ **cup water**
- 1 **teaspoon Italian seasoning**
- ½ **teaspoon sugar**
  Hot cooked spaghetti, optional

1. Flatten steak to ½-in. thickness. Rub with 1 tablespoon oil. Combine the bread crumbs, parsley, cheese, garlic, oregano, ¼ teaspoon salt and ¼ teaspoon pepper. Spoon mixture over beef to within 1 in. of edges; press down. Roll beef up jelly-roll style, starting with a long side; tie with kitchen string.

2. In a Dutch oven, brown meat in remaining oil on all sides. Add onion and cook until tender. Stir in the tomato sauce, water, Italian seasoning, sugar and remaining salt and pepper. Bring to a boil. Reduce heat; cover and simmer for 70-80 minutes or until meat is tender.

3. Remove meat from sauce and discard string. Cut into thin slices; serve with sauce and spaghetti if desired.

Mini Chocolate Wafer Cakes

I first made these cute little cakes for a friend when I lived in the dorms at college and had no access to appliances. Little did I know I would be making them 20 years later for my children!

—LARA PENNELL MAULDIN, SC

PREP: 15 MIN. + CHILLING • **MAKES:** 8 SERVINGS

- 1½ **cups heavy whipping cream**
- 3 **tablespoons baking cocoa**
- 2 **tablespoons sugar**
- 1½ **teaspoons vanilla extract**
- 24 **chocolate wafers**
  Chocolate syrup
  Heart-shaped sprinkles

1. In a large bowl, beat the cream, cocoa, sugar and vanilla until soft peaks form. Arrange eight wafers on the bottom of a foil-lined 9-in.-square baking pan. Spoon or pipe about 2 tablespoons cream mixture onto each. Repeat layers twice, making eight stacks. Refrigerate, covered, overnight.

2. To serve, transfer to dessert plates. Drizzle with chocolate syrup; top with sprinkles.

Valentine's Day Snack Mix

Kids of all ages will gobble up this sweet snack mix. Best of all, because it requires no cooking, little ones can help combine all of the ingredients.

—*TASTE OF HOME* TEST KITCHEN

START TO FINISH: 5 MIN. • **MAKES:** 7 CUPS

- 1 **package (12.7 ounces) Valentine's M&M's**
- 1 **can (9¾ ounces) whole cashews**
- 1 **package (8 ounces) yogurt-covered raisins**
- 1 **package (5 ounces) dried cranberries**
- 1 **cup miniature pretzels**
- 1 **cup chocolate bear-shaped crackers**

In a large bowl, combine all ingredients. Store in an airtight container.

❝Really cute idea, lots of color, endless possibilities!❞

—JEANSGIRL
TASTEOFHOME.COM

Mini Chocolate Wafer Cakes

**Honey Pecan &
Goat Cheese Salad**

Walnut Chocolate Hearts

I've been making these cute cookies with Mom since I was a little girl. They're certainly one of my favorites, and they bake up fast.

—**MARIA HULL** BARTLETT, IL

PREP: 30 MIN. + CHILLING
BAKE: 10 MIN./BATCH + COOLING
MAKES: ABOUT 4 DOZEN

  1 **cup butter, cubed**
  ⅔ **cup packed brown sugar**
  1 **teaspoon vanilla extract**
  1 **egg, lightly beaten**
2¼ **cups all-purpose flour**
  ¼ **cup baking cocoa**
  ½ **teaspoon salt**
  ¾ **cup finely chopped walnuts**
TOPPING
1½ **cups semisweet chocolate chips**
  2 **tablespoons shortening**
  ½ **cup ground walnuts**

1. In a large saucepan, combine butter and brown sugar. Cook and stir over medium-low heat until butter is melted. Remove from heat; stir in vanilla. Cool 15 minutes. Stir in egg.
2. Combine flour, cocoa and salt; add to butter mixture. Fold in walnuts. Cover and chill 30 minutes or until dough is easy to handle.
3. Preheat oven to 350°. On a lightly floured surface, roll dough to ¼-in. thickness. Cut with a floured 3-in. heart-shaped cookie cutter. Place 1 in. apart on ungreased baking sheets.
4. Bake 9-10 minutes or until edges are firm. Remove to wire racks to cool.
5. For topping, in a microwave, melt chocolate chips and shortening; stir until smooth. Dip half of each heart into chocolate mixture; allow excess to drip off. Dip edges of dipped side into ground walnuts. Place on waxed paper; let stand until set.

Honey Pecan & Goat Cheese Salad

I was able to toss this entire salad together one time while our pizza was baking. My son loves goat cheese, and he and my wife thought this creation was terrific. It comes together in less than 30 minutes, but it feels very special.

—**GREG FONTENOT** THE WOODLANDS, TX

START TO FINISH: 25 MIN. • **MAKES:** 4 SERVINGS

  ½ **cup chopped pecans**
  2 **teaspoons plus 1 tablespoon honey, divided**
  ⅓ **cup plus 3 tablespoons olive oil, divided**
  2 **tablespoons balsamic vinegar**
  ½ **teaspoon salt**
  ⅛ **teaspoon pepper**
  ¼ **cup all-purpose flour**
  1 **egg, beaten**
  ¾ **cup seasoned bread crumbs**
  8 **ounces fresh goat cheese**
  4 **cups spring mix salad greens**

1. In a shallow microwave-safe dish, combine pecans and 2 teaspoons honey; microwave, uncovered, on high 1½ to 2 minutes or until toasted, stirring twice. Immediately transfer to a waxed paper-lined baking sheet to cool.
2. For dressing, in a small bowl, whisk ⅓ cup oil, vinegar, remaining honey, salt and pepper; set aside.
3. Place flour, egg and bread crumbs in separate shallow bowls. Shape cheese into eight balls; flatten slightly. Coat cheese with flour, then dip in egg and coat with bread crumbs.
4. Heat remaining oil in a large skillet over medium-high heat. Fry cheese 1-2 minutes on each side or until golden brown. Drain on paper towels.
5. Divide salad greens among four plates; top with cheese. Drizzle with dressing and sprinkle with honey pecans.

"This is my favorite cake! Super moist and light!"
—LMCEAC
TASTEOFHOME.COM

MARGE NICOL'S WEARING O' GREEN CAKE *PAGE 28*

St. Patrick's Day Fun

EVERYONE IS IRISH ON ST. PADDY'S DAY! WHETHER YOU'RE AN OFFICIAL IRISHMAN OR JUST ONE FOR THE DAY, ENJOY SOME TRADITIONAL TASTES SURE TO HELP CELEBRATE THE GREEN. FROM STEWS AND BREADS TO BEVERAGES AND DESSERTS, YOUR BUFFET PROMISES TO BE THE BEST IN TOWN.

JAN ALFANO'S FAVORITE IRISH SODA BREAD *PAGE 26*

REBECCA LITTLE'S CREAMY IRISH COFFEE *PAGE 24*

PAM ALLEN'S SUNDAY'S CORNED BEEF *PAGE 24*

⑤ INGREDIENTS

Sunday's Corned Beef

Here's an Irish recipe I have enjoyed for decades. It's so easy to prepare, I make it all year long!

—**PAM ALLEN** LEBANON, PA

PREP: 15 MIN. • **COOK:** 2½ HOURS
MAKES: 16 SERVINGS

- 2 **corned beef briskets with spice packets (3 pounds each)**
- 1 **medium head cabbage, cut into 8 wedges**
- 1 **bottle (2 liters) ginger ale**
- ¼ **cup mixed pickling spices**
- 8 **medium potatoes, peeled and quartered**

1. Discard spice packets from corned beef or save for another use. Place briskets in a Dutch oven; add cabbage. Pour ginger ale over top. Place pickling spices on a double thickness of cheesecloth; bring up corners of cloth and tie with string to form a bag. Add to pan.

2. Bring to a boil. Reduce heat; cover and simmer for 2½ to 3 hours or until meat is tender, adding potatoes during the last 20 minutes of cooking. Discard spice bag.
3. Remove meat and vegetables to a serving platter. Thinly slice brisket across the grain and serve with vegetables.

⑤ INGREDIENTS

Creamy Irish Coffee

My maternal grandma was never a drinker, beyond a glass of champagne at Christmas, but she couldn't resist this Irish coffee.

—**REBECCA LITTLE** PARK RIDGE, IL

START TO FINISH: 10 MIN. • **MAKES:** 4 SERVINGS

- 3 **cups hot strong brewed coffee**
- 4 **ounces Irish cream liqueur**
  Sweetened whipped cream, optional
  Chocolate shavings, optional

Divide coffee and liqueur among four mugs; stir. If desired, top with whipped cream and chocolate shavings.

Blarney Breakfast Bake

I got this recipe from my mom, and I used it when I served an Irish brunch to my neighbors for St. Patrick's Day.

—**KERRY AMUNDSON** OCEAN PARK, WA

PREP: 20 MIN. • **BAKE:** 50 MIN. + STANDING
MAKES: 12 SERVINGS

- 1 **pound bulk pork sausage**
- ½ **pound sliced fresh mushrooms**
- 1 **large onion, chopped**
- 10 **eggs, lightly beaten**
- 3 **cups 2% milk**
- 2 **teaspoons ground mustard**
- 1 **teaspoon salt**
- ½ **teaspoon pepper**
- 6 **cups cubed day-old bread**
- 1 **cup chopped seeded tomatoes**
- 1 **cup (4 ounces) shredded pepper jack cheese**
- 1 **cup (4 ounces) shredded cheddar cheese**

1. Preheat oven to 325°. In a large skillet, cook sausage, mushrooms and onion over medium heat until meat is no longer pink; drain. In a large bowl, whisk the eggs, milk, mustard, salt and pepper.
2. In a greased 13x9-in. baking dish, layer half the bread cubes, tomatoes, cheeses and sausage mixture. Repeat layers. Pour egg mixture over the top.
3. Bake, uncovered, 50-55 minutes or until a knife inserted near the center comes out clean. Let stand 10 minutes before serving.

❝Blarney Breakfast Bake was a dream to make and so delicious! ❞

—**DIANE HIGGINS** TAMPA, FL

Sunday's Corned Beef

Lucky Leprechaun Cookies and Royal Icing

5. Tint small amounts of Royal Icing red, yellow and black. Leave a small amount plain. Tint remaining icing green and orange. Frost leprechauns; decorate with shimmer dust and shamrock sprinkles if desired. For eyes, attach miniature chocolate chips with plain frosting.

NOTE *This recipe may also be used to make shamrock cookies, using 2½-in. or 4-in. cookie cutters. Or, using 3-in. alphabet cookie cutters, cut out the letters for IRISH or any phrase or name. Reduce baking time to 8-10 minutes for both cookies. Yield for shamrocks or letters is about 6 dozen. Edible glitter is available from Wilton Industries, www.wilton.com.*

(5)INGREDIENTS

Royal Icing

This classic decorating icing sets up and dries quickly. It's perfect for Lucky Leprechaun Cookies.

—*TASTE OF HOME* TEST KITCHEN

START TO FINISH: 10 MIN.
MAKES: ABOUT 1 CUP

  2 **cups confectioners' sugar**
  2 **tablespoons plus 2 teaspoons water**
4½ **teaspoons meringue powder**
  ¼ **teaspoon cream of tartar**
    Food coloring, optional

1. In a small bowl, combine the confectioners' sugar, water, meringue powder and cream of tartar; beat on low speed just until combined. Beat on high for 4-5 minutes or until stiff peaks form. Tint with food coloring if desired. Keep unused icing covered at all times with a damp cloth. If necessary, beat again on high speed to restore texture.
2. To decorate, place icing in a pastry bag. For border decorations and dots, use #3 round pastry tip. For small detailed decorations, use #1 or #2 round pastry tip.

NOTE *Use of a coupler ring will allow you to easily change pastry tips for different designs. Meringue powder is available from Wilton Industries, www.wilton.com.*

Lucky Leprechaun Cookies

Let these cute little guys star at your St. Patrick's Day party. They're so fun to make, and no one ever forgets them!

—*TASTE OF HOME* TEST KITCHEN

PREP: 30 MIN. + CHILLING
BAKE: 10 MIN./BATCH + COOLING
MAKES: ABOUT 3 DOZEN

1½ **cups butter, softened**
1½ **cups sugar**
  2 **eggs**
  3 **teaspoons vanilla extract**
  4 **cups all-purpose flour**
  1 **teaspoon baking soda**
  1 **teaspoon cream of tartar**
  1 **teaspoon salt**
  3 **to 4 cups Royal Icing**
    Assorted paste food coloring
    Green shimmer dust or edible glitter, optional
    Green shamrock sprinkles, optional
    Miniature semisweet chocolate chips

1. In a large bowl, cream butter and sugar until light and fluffy. Add eggs, one at a time, beating well after each addition. Beat in vanilla. Combine the flour, baking soda, cream of tartar and salt; gradually add to the creamed mixture. Cover and refrigerate for 30 minutes or until easy to handle.
2. Preheat oven to 350°. On a lightly floured surface, roll out dough to ¼-in. thickness. For leprechauns, cut out dough with lightly floured 5-in. gingerbread boy cookie cutter. If desired, trim body for a thinner shape.
3. For each hat, cut a 1½-in. square and a 1¾x¼-in. brim from dough scraps. Place leprechauns 2 in. apart on ungreased baking sheets. Place hat squares and brims above heads, shaping gently to touch the heads.
4. Bake 10-14 minutes or until edges are lightly browned. Cool 1 minute before carefully removing to wire racks to cool completely.

Mini Reuben
Casseroles

Mini Reuben Casseroles

These creamy individual roast beef casseroles have the classic flavors of a Reuben sandwich.

—*TASTE OF HOME* TEST KITCHEN

PREP: 20 MIN. • **BAKE:** 20 MIN.
MAKES: 4 SERVINGS

- 1 **medium onion, chopped**
- 1 **medium green pepper, chopped**
- 2 **teaspoons olive oil**
- 2 **cups cubed cooked beef roast**
- 1 **can (14 ounces) sauerkraut, rinsed and well drained**
- 1 **can (10¾ ounces) condensed cream of chicken soup, undiluted**
- 1¼ **cups (5 ounces) shredded Swiss cheese, divided**
- ⅓ **cup 2% milk**
- ½ **cup Thousand Island salad dressing**
- 2 **slices rye bread, cubed**
- 1 **tablespoon butter, melted**
- ½ **teaspoon onion powder**

1. Preheat oven to 350°. In a large skillet, saute onion and pepper in oil until tender. Stir in meat, sauerkraut, soup, 1 cup cheese, milk and salad dressing; heat through. Transfer to four greased 10-oz. ramekins or custard cups. Place ramekins on a baking sheet.
2. In a small bowl, toss bread cubes with butter and onion powder. Arrange over tops. Bake, uncovered, 15 minutes. Sprinkle with remaining cheese. Bake 5-10 minutes longer or until the cheese is melted.

Mashed Potatoes 'n' Brussels Sprouts

Tired of eating the same old mashed potatoes? Try this tasty version. These potatoes are fluffy and delicious.

—RAYMONDE HEBERT BERNIER
SAINT-HYACINTHE, QC

PREP: 30 MIN. • **COOK:** 20 MIN.
MAKES: 6-8 SERVINGS

- 3 **pounds potatoes (about 9 medium), peeled and quartered**
- 2 **cups fresh or frozen Brussels sprouts**
- 2 **garlic cloves, peeled**
- ½ **cup half-and-half cream**
- 2 **tablespoons butter**
- 2 **teaspoons chicken bouillon granules**
- 1 **teaspoon salt**
- ¼ **teaspoon dried basil**
- ⅛ **teaspoon pepper**

1. Place potatoes in a large saucepan and cover with water. Bring to a boil. Reduce heat; cover and cook for 15-20 minutes or until tender.
2. Meanwhile, place ½ in. of water and Brussels sprouts in a small saucepan; bring to a boil. Reduce heat; cover and cook for 5 minutes. Add garlic; cook 3-5 minutes longer or until tender.
3. Drain potatoes, sprouts and garlic; cool slightly. Place in a food processor; cover and process for 1-2 minutes. Add the remaining ingredients; cover and process just until blended. Transfer to a serving bowl.

Favorite Irish Soda Bread

My best friend shared this irresistible Irish soda bread. It bakes up high, with a golden brown top and a combination of sweet and savory flavors.

—JAN ALFANO PRESCOTT, AZ

PREP: 20 MIN. • **BAKE:** 45 MIN. + COOLING
MAKES: 1 LOAF (12 WEDGES)

- 3 **cups all-purpose flour**
- ⅔ **cup sugar**
- 3 **teaspoons baking powder**
- 1 **teaspoon salt**
- 1 **teaspoon baking soda**
- 1 **cup raisins**
- 2 **eggs, beaten**
- 1½ **cups buttermilk**
- 1 **tablespoon canola oil**

1. Preheat oven to 350°. In a large bowl, combine first five ingredients. Stir in raisins. Set aside 1 tablespoon beaten egg. In a bowl, combine buttermilk, oil and remaining eggs; stir into flour mixture just until moistened (dough will be sticky). Transfer to a greased 9-in. round baking pan; brush top with reserved egg.
2. Bake 45-50 minutes or until a toothpick inserted near the center comes out clean. Cool 10 minutes before removing from pan to a wire rack to cool. Cut into wedges.

TOP TIP

Color Cues

The Rainbow Cake at far right is both easy and impressive. Simply pipe the rings in this order: red, orange, yellow, green, blue and purple. The photo at right shows the cake before a final layer of white batter is piped over the purple ring, creating the bottom arch of the rainbow.

Rainbow Cake with Clouds

Some cakes stand on their own without icing. For this bright Rainbow Cake, use a little whipped cream to make fluffy clouds.

—JANET TIGCHELAAR JERSEYVILLE, ON

PREP: 30 MIN. • **BAKE:** 40 MIN. + COOLING
MAKES: 16 SERVINGS

- 1 **package white cake mix (regular size)**
  Purple, blue, green, yellow, orange and red paste food coloring
- 1 **cup heavy whipping cream**
- 3 **tablespoons confectioners' sugar**
- ½ **teaspoon vanilla extract**

1. Preheat oven to 325°. Grease and flour a 10-in. fluted tube pan. Prepare cake mix according to package directions. Transfer 1⅓ cups batter to prepared pan; spread evenly. Remove an additional 2 tablespoons of batter to a small bowl and reserve.

2. Divide the remaining batter into six bowls, tinting each with food coloring to make the following: 2 tablespoons purple batter, ¼ cup blue batter, ⅓ cup green batter, ½ cup yellow batter, ⅔ cup orange batter, and the remaining batter red.

3. Fill each of six small food-safe plastic bags with a different color batter. Cut a small hole in a corner of the red batter bag; pipe a wide ring onto white batter to within ½ in. of pan edges. Pipe a ring of orange in the middle of the red ring, leaving some red visible on each side. Repeat by piping remaining colors in the middle of the previous layer, in rainbow color order. (Each ring will be narrower than the previous layer.) Fill a bag with reserved white batter; pipe over purple ring only.

4. Bake 40-45 minutes or until a toothpick inserted into center comes out clean. Cool completely in pan on rack.

5. Remove cake from pan; place on a serving plate. In a bowl, beat whipping cream until it begins to thicken. Add confectioners' sugar and vanilla; beat until soft peaks form. Serve cake with whipped cream clouds.

Rainbow Cake with Clouds

Creamy Chicken Boxty

A savory chicken filling flavored with bacon and leeks is wrapped in tender potato pancakes (boxty). The Irish recipe is light but sure to satisfy.

—*TASTE OF HOME* **TEST KITCHEN**

PREP: 30 MIN. + STANDING
COOK: 10 MIN./BATCH • **MAKES:** 4 SERVINGS

- 1 medium potato, peeled and grated
- 1½ cups fat-free milk
- 1 cup all-purpose flour
- ¾ cup mashed potato (made with fat-free milk)
- ¼ teaspoon salt
- ¼ teaspoon pepper

FILLING

- 2 bacon strips, chopped
- 2 cups sliced fresh mushrooms
- 1 medium leek (white portion only), chopped
- ¼ cup half-and-half cream
- 2 tablespoons all-purpose flour
- ¾ cup fat-free milk
- 2 cups cubed cooked chicken breast
- ¼ teaspoon salt
- ¼ teaspoon pepper

1. Place grated potato in a colander to drain; squeeze to remove excess liquid. Pat dry. In a bowl, combine the grated potato, milk, flour, mashed potato, salt and pepper. Let stand for 20 minutes.

2. Meanwhile, in a large nonstick skillet, cook bacon over medium heat until crisp. Add mushrooms and leek; cook until tender. Gradually add cream. Whisk together flour and milk; add to pan. Bring to a boil. Cook and stir for 2 minutes or until thickened. Stir in the chicken, salt and pepper; heat through. Remove from the heat and keep warm.

3. Coat another large nonstick skillet with cooking spray; heat over medium heat. Pour ¾ cup batter into center of skillet; lift and tilt pan to coat bottom evenly. Cook until top appears dry; turn and cook 2-3 minutes longer. Remove and keep warm. Repeat with remaining batter, coating skillet with cooking spray as needed. Spoon filling onto pancakes.

Wearing O' Green Cake

One bite of this colorful cake and you'll think you've found the pot o' gold at the end of the rainbow. It's the perfect dessert to round out your St. Patrick's Day feast, and it travels well to share with co-workers.

—**MARGE NICOL** SHANNON, IL

PREP: 25 MIN. • **BAKE:** 30 MIN. + COOLING
MAKES: 12-15 SERVINGS

- 1 package white cake mix (regular size)
- 2 packages (3 ounces each) lime gelatin
- 1 cup boiling water
- ½ cup cold water

TOPPING

- 1 cup cold milk
- 1 package (3.4 ounces) instant vanilla pudding mix
- 1 carton (8 ounces) frozen whipped topping, thawed
  Green sprinkles

1. Prepare and bake cake according to package directions, using a greased 13x9-in. baking dish. Cool on a wire rack 1 hour. In a small bowl, dissolve gelatin in boiling water; stir in cold water and set aside.

2. With a meat fork or wooden skewer, poke holes about 2 in. apart into cooled cake. Slowly pour gelatin over cake. Cover and refrigerate.

3. In a large bowl, whisk milk and pudding mix 2 minutes (mixture will be thick). Fold in whipped topping. Spread over cake. Decorate with sprinkles. Cover and refrigerate until serving.

Wearing O' Green Cake

Caraway Rye Dinner Rolls

Caraway seeds give these rye dinner rolls a delicate nutty flavor. Denser than most, the onion-infused buns are ideal for dipping into hearty soups and stews.

—DEBORAH MAKI KAMLOOPS, BC

PREP: 35 MIN. + RISING • **BAKE:** 15 MIN.
MAKES: 1½ DOZEN

- 1¼ cups rye flour
- ½ cup wheat germ
- 2 tablespoons caraway seeds
- 1 package (¼ ounce) active dry yeast
- 1 teaspoon salt
- 3 cups all-purpose flour, divided
- 1 cup 2% milk
- ½ cup water
- 3 tablespoons butter
- 2 tablespoons honey
- ⅓ cup finely chopped onion

EGG WASH
- 1 egg
- 2 teaspoons water

1. In a large bowl, mix the first five ingredients and 1 cup all-purpose flour. In a small saucepan, heat milk, water, butter and honey to 120°-130°. Add to dry ingredients; beat on medium speed 3 minutes. Stir in onion and enough remaining all-purpose flour to form a soft dough (dough will be sticky).

2. Turn dough onto a floured surface; knead until smooth and elastic, about 6-8 minutes. Place in a greased bowl, turning once to grease the top. Cover with plastic wrap and let rise in a warm place until doubled, about 1 hour.

3. Punch down dough. Turn onto a lightly floured surface; divide and shape into 18 balls. Place 2 in. apart on greased baking sheets. Cover with a kitchen towel; let rise in a warm place until almost doubled, about 45 minutes. Preheat oven to 400°.

4. For egg wash, in a small bowl, whisk egg and water; brush over rolls. Bake 11-14 minutes or until lightly browned. Remove to wire racks to cool.

Lamb Stew

Lamb Stew

If you like your stew thick and rich, you've got to try this heartwarming treat from Ireland. My grandmother used to make it for special Sunday meals.

—VICKIE DESOURDY WASHINGTON, NC

PREP: 40 MIN. • **BAKE:** 1½ HOURS
MAKES: 8 SERVINGS (2½ QUARTS)

- 2 pounds lamb stew meat, cut into 1-inch cubes
- 1 tablespoon butter
- 1 tablespoon olive oil
- 1 pound carrots, sliced
- 2 medium onions, thinly sliced
- 2 garlic cloves, minced
- 1½ cups reduced-sodium chicken broth
- 1 bottle (12 ounces) Guinness stout or additional reduced-sodium chicken broth
- 6 medium red potatoes, peeled and cut into 1-inch cubes
- 4 bay leaves
- 2 fresh thyme sprigs
- 2 fresh rosemary sprigs
- 2 teaspoons salt
- 1½ teaspoons pepper
- ¼ cup heavy whipping cream

1. Preheat oven to 325°. In an ovenproof Dutch oven, brown lamb in butter and oil in batches. Remove and keep warm. In the same pan, saute carrots and onions in drippings until crisp-tender. Add garlic; cook 1 minute. Gradually add broth and beer. Stir in lamb, potatoes, bay leaves, thyme, rosemary, salt and pepper.

2. Cover and bake 1½ to 2 hours or until meat and vegetables are tender, stirring every 30 minutes. Discard bay leaves, thyme and rosemary. Stir in whipping cream; heat through.

**DEB LEBLANC'S SOUTHWEST
PULLED PORK** *PAGE 35*

March Madness

IT DOESN'T MATTER IF YOU'RE INTO BASKETBALL OR NOT, THERE ARE PLENTY OF REASONS TO SERVE A HEARTY BUFFET OF "GUY FOOD" THIS SPRING! PERFECT FOR WATCHING THE BIG GAMES ON TV, GREAT FOR MOVIE NIGHTS, AND IDEAL FOR TAILGATES, SLEEPOVERS, SNACK TIME AND MORE, THESE SAVORY BITES ARE SURE TO BE POPULAR WHENEVER YOU SERVE THEM!

RHONDA WILKINSON'S PASTRAMI WRAPS *PAGE 34*

MIKE TCHOU'S PARTY NACHOS *PAGE 32*

LAURIE LACLAIR'S CHILI CHEESE SPREAD *PAGE 34*

Loaded Baked Potato Dip

Loaded Baked Potato Dip

I never thought of using waffle-cut fries as a scoop for dip until a friend of mine did so. They're ideal for my cheesy bacon and chive dip, which tastes just like a baked potato topper. Yum!

—**ELIZABETH KING** DULUTH, MN

START TO FINISH: 10 MIN. • **MAKES:** 2½ CUPS

- 2 cups (16 ounces) reduced-fat sour cream
- 2 cups (8 ounces) shredded reduced-fat cheddar cheese
- 8 center-cut bacon or turkey bacon strips, chopped and cooked
- ⅓ cup minced fresh chives
- 2 teaspoons Louisiana-style hot sauce
  Hot cooked waffle-cut fries

In a small bowl, mix the first five ingredients until blended; refrigerate until serving. Serve with waffle fries.

Marinated Mozzarella

I always come home with an empty container when I bring this dish to a party. It can be made ahead to free up time later. I serve it with party picks for a festive look.

—**PEGGY CAIRO** KENOSHA, WI

PREP: 15 MIN. + MARINATING
MAKES: 8-10 SERVINGS

- ⅓ cup olive oil
- 1 tablespoon chopped oil-packed sun-dried tomatoes
- 1 tablespoon minced fresh parsley
- 1 teaspoon crushed red pepper flakes
- 1 teaspoon dried basil
- 1 teaspoon minced chives
- ¼ teaspoon garlic powder
- 1 pound cubed part-skim mozzarella cheese

1. In a large resealable plastic bag, combine the first seven ingredients; add cheese cubes. Seal bag and turn to coat; refrigerate for at least 30 minutes.
2. Transfer to a serving dish; serve with toothpicks.

Party Nachos

Shredded pork puts a new spin on nachos! Simple to make, these are ideal for most any party or a fun night in with family. Consider a build-your-own nacho bar so guests can choose their toppings.

—**MIKE TCHOU** PEPPER PIKE, OH

START TO FINISH: 20 MIN. • **MAKES:** 12 SERVINGS

- 1 carton (16 ounces) refrigerated fully cooked barbecued shredded pork
- 1 package (12½ ounces) nacho tortilla chips
- 2 cups (8 ounces) shredded Mexican cheese blend
- ½ cup sour cream
- ½ cup salsa
- ½ cup shredded lettuce
- ¼ cup thinly sliced green onions
- ¼ cup sliced ripe olives, optional
- ¼ cup pickled pepper rings, optional

1. Heat pork according to package directions. Place tortilla chips on a large microwave-safe serving plate. Layer with pork and cheese.
2. Microwave, uncovered, on high for 1-2 minutes or until cheese is melted. Top with sour cream, salsa, lettuce and onions. Sprinkle with olives and pepper rings if desired.
NOTE *This recipe was tested in a 1,100-watt microwave.*

TOP TIP

Quick Cleanup

I tried a recipe that called for ¾ cup green onions. Instead of using a knife and messing up a cutting board, I came up with another solution. I found that snipping the onions with a pair of kitchen shears took only a few seconds, and I could snip them right into the dish I was preparing.

—**KRISTY B.** KELOWNA, BC

Sweet & Tangy Barbecue Wings

I came up with this recipe when I got tired of the same old wings. These are baked with onion and garlic, then broiled and basted with a mixture of barbecue sauce, jalapeno peppers and raspberry jam. The sauce is also excellent on grilled pork.

—**SANDRA FISHER** MISSOULA, MT

PREP: 15 MIN. + CHILLING • **BAKE:** 50 MIN.
MAKES: 2½ DOZEN

- ⅔ cup barbecue sauce
- ⅔ cup seedless raspberry jam
- 3 tablespoons finely chopped onion
- 1 to 2 jalapeno peppers, seeded and finely chopped
- 2 teaspoons minced garlic, divided
- 2 teaspoons liquid smoke, optional, divided
- ¼ teaspoon salt
- 15 chicken wings (about 3 pounds)
- 1 small onion, sliced
- 1 cup water

1. In a small bowl, combine barbecue sauce, jam, chopped onion, peppers, 1 teaspoon garlic, 1 teaspoon liquid smoke if desired and salt; mix well. Cover and refrigerate at least 2 hours.

2. Preheat oven to 350°. Cut chicken wings into three sections; discard wing tip section. Place chicken wings in a greased 15x10x1-in. baking pan. Top with sliced onion and remaining garlic. Combine water and remaining liquid smoke if desired; pour over wings. Cover and bake at 30 minutes or until juices run clear.

3. Transfer wings to a greased broiler pan; brush with sauce. Broil 4-6 in. from heat 20-25 minutes, turning and basting every 5 minutes or until wings are well coated.

NOTE *Uncooked chicken wing sections (wingettes) may be substituted for whole chicken wings. Disposable gloves are recommended for cutting hot peppers. Avoid touching your face.*

Sweet & Tangy Barbecue Wings

Pastrami Wraps

Instead of using tortillas, you can simply wrap the meat around the other ingredients and fasten with a toothpick. Either way, these wraps can be sliced and served as appetizers or eaten whole.

—RHONDA WILKINSON LEVITTOWN, PA

START TO FINISH: 20 MIN. • **MAKES:** 4 SERVINGS

- 4 flour tortillas (10 inches), room temperature
- 4 ounces cream cheese, softened
- ¾ cup shredded cheddar cheese
- ¼ cup chopped red onion
- ¼ cup sliced Greek olives
- ½ pound thinly sliced deli pastrami
- 1½ cups fresh baby spinach

Spread tortillas with cream cheese; sprinkle with cheddar cheese, onion and olives. Top with pastrami and spinach. Roll up tightly; secure with toothpicks.

Chili Cheese Spread

Appetizers just don't get much easier than this hearty cheese spread with a refreshing hint of raspberry and lime. I turn to this recipe when unexpected guests drop by.

—LAURIE LACLAIR NORTH RICHLAND HILLS, TX

START TO FINISH: 10 MIN. • **MAKES:** 14 SERVINGS

- 2 packages (8 ounces each) cream cheese, softened
- 1 can (14 ounces) whole-berry cranberry sauce
- 1 can (4 ounces) chopped green chilies, drained
- 1 green onion, sliced
- 1 tablespoon lime juice
- ½ teaspoon garlic salt
- ½ teaspoon cayenne pepper
- ½ teaspoon chili powder
  Assorted crackers

Place cream cheese on a serving plate. In a small bowl, combine the cranberry sauce, green chilies, onion, lime juice and spices. Spoon over cream cheese. Serve with crackers.

SLOW COOKER
Spicy Touchdown Chili

For me, football, cool weather and chili just seem to go together. Whether I'm cheering on the local team on a Friday night or enjoying a Saturday afternoon of Oklahoma Sooner football with some friends, I enjoy serving this chili on game day.

—CHRIS NEAL QUAPAW, OK

PREP: 30 MIN. • **COOK:** 4 HOURS
MAKES: 12 SERVINGS (3 QUARTS)

- 1 pound ground beef
- 1 pound bulk pork sausage
- 2 cans (16 ounces each) kidney beans, rinsed and drained
- 2 cans (15 ounces each) pinto beans, rinsed and drained
- 2 cans (10 ounces each) diced tomatoes with mild green chilies, undrained
- 1 can (14½ ounces) diced tomatoes with onions, undrained
- 1 can (12 ounces) beer
- 6 bacon strips, cooked and crumbled
- 1 small onion, chopped
- ¼ cup chili powder
- ¼ cup chopped pickled jalapeno slices
- 2 teaspoons ground cumin
- 2 garlic cloves, minced
- 1 teaspoon dried basil
- ¾ teaspoon cayenne pepper

1. In a large skillet, cook beef over medium heat 6-8 minutes or until no longer pink, breaking into crumbles; drain. Transfer to a 6-qt. slow cooker. Repeat with sausage.
2. Stir in remaining ingredients. Cook, covered, on low 4-5 hours.

Spicy Touchdown Chili

Meatball Hoagies with Seasoned Fries

Southwest Pulled Pork

I made this on a whim one morning when friends said they would drop in later in the day. The recipe makes a lot of servings so it's great for a party, and the seasonings and green chilies give the meat a spicy kick.

—**DEB LEBLANC** PHILLIPSBURG, KS

PREP: 20 MIN. • **COOK:** 8 HOURS
MAKES: 14 SERVINGS

- 1 boneless pork shoulder butt roast (4 pounds)
- 2 tablespoons chili powder
- 1 tablespoon brown sugar
- 1½ teaspoons ground cumin
- 1 teaspoon salt
- ½ teaspoon pepper
- ½ teaspoon cayenne pepper
- 1 large sweet onion, coarsely chopped
- 2 cans (4 ounces each) chopped green chilies
- 1 cup chicken broth
- 14 kaiser rolls, split

1. Cut roast in half. In a small bowl, combine the chili powder, brown sugar, cumin, salt, pepper and cayenne; rub over meat. Transfer to a 5-qt. slow cooker. Top with onion and chilies. Pour broth around meat.

2. Cover and cook on low for 8-10 hours or until tender. Remove roast; cool slightly. Skim fat from cooking juices. Shred pork with two forks and return to slow cooker; heat through. Serve on rolls.

Meatball Hoagies with Seasoned Fries

Try this fresh take on a classic combo, and you'll have a new game-day staple! Bacon and apricot preserves give the sandwich a sweet-savory twist, and celery salt on the fries is a welcome surprise.

—**TASTE OF HOME** TEST KITCHEN

START TO FINISH: 30 MIN. • **MAKES:** 4 SERVINGS

- 4 cups frozen steak fries
- 1 tablespoon olive oil
- ½ teaspoon seasoned salt
- ¼ teaspoon celery salt
- 1 package (12 ounces) frozen fully cooked Italian meatballs, thawed
- 2 cups barbecue sauce
- ¼ cup apricot preserves
- 4 hoagie buns, split and toasted
- 4 large lettuce leaves
- 3 plum tomatoes, sliced
- 8 ready-to-serve fully cooked bacon strips, warmed
- 8 slices provolone cheese

1. Place steak fries in a single layer in a 15x10x1-in. baking pan. Drizzle with oil; sprinkle with seasonings. Toss to coat. Bake according to package directions.

2. Meanwhile, place meatballs, barbecue sauce and preserves in a large saucepan. Bring to a boil over medium heat; cook and stir 6-8 minutes or until meatballs are heated through.

3. Layer bun bottoms with lettuce, tomatoes, bacon, meatball mixture and cheese; replace tops. Serve with fries.

> " I am a field clerk for a construction company. I fixed these hoagies for the guys and got rave reviews. This is a keeper! "
> —**SKEETER100857** TASTEOFHOME.COM

Sausage & Bean Dip

This is a spin-off of a Mexican dip. The original was wicked good, but I was going through an "I'm-so-over-Mexican-dip" phase and decided to switch it up. Take it to a party. No one else will bring anything like it!
—**MANDY RIVERS** LEXINGTON, SC

PREP: 25 MIN. • **BAKE:** 20 MIN.
MAKES: 16 SERVINGS (¼ CUP EACH)

- 1 pound bulk hot Italian sausage
- 1 medium onion, finely chopped
- 4 garlic cloves, minced
- ½ cup dry white wine or chicken broth
- ½ teaspoon dried oregano
- ¼ teaspoon salt
- ¼ teaspoon dried thyme
- 1 package (8 ounces) cream cheese, softened
- 1 package (6 ounces) fresh baby spinach, coarsely chopped
- 1 can (15 ounces) white kidney or cannellini beans, rinsed and drained
- 1 cup chopped seeded tomatoes
- 1 cup (4 ounces) shredded part-skim mozzarella cheese
- ½ cup shredded Parmesan cheese
   Assorted crackers or toasted French bread baguette slices

1. Preheat oven to 375°. In a large skillet, cook sausage, onion and garlic over medium heat until sausage is no longer pink, breaking up sausage into crumbles; drain. Stir in wine, oregano, salt and thyme. Bring to a boil; cook until liquid is almost evaporated.
2. Add cream cheese; stir until melted. Stir in spinach, beans and tomatoes; cook and stir until spinach is wilted. Transfer to a greased 8-in.-square or 1½-qt. baking dish. Sprinkle with cheeses.
3. Bake 20-25 minutes or until bubbly. Serve with crackers.

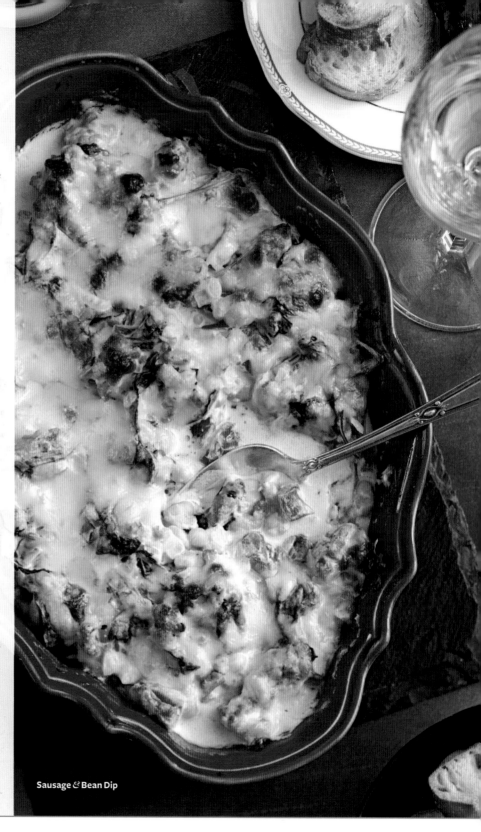

Sausage & Bean Dip

Corn Salsa

Mix up your snack-time routine with colorful Corn Salsa. It's an easy accompaniment to any appetizer buffet, and it's perfect alongside grilled entrees in the summer. It adds a kick of flavor to any party!

—SHIRLEY GLAAB HATTIESBURG, MS

PREP: 20 MIN. + CHILLING • **MAKES:** 5 CUPS

- 3 cups frozen corn, thawed
- 1 can (15 ounces) black beans, rinsed and drained
- 5 green onions, thinly sliced
- 1 medium sweet red pepper, finely chopped
- 1 jalapeno pepper, finely chopped
- ⅓ cup rice vinegar
- 1 tablespoon olive oil
- 1 tablespoon Dijon mustard
- ½ teaspoon salt
- ¼ to ½ teaspoon hot pepper sauce
- ¼ teaspoon pepper
  Dash cayenne pepper
- ⅔ cup minced fresh cilantro

1. In a large bowl, combine the first five ingredients. In another bowl, whisk the vinegar, oil, mustard, salt, pepper sauce, pepper and cayenne. Stir in cilantro. Drizzle over corn mixture and toss to coat.

2. Chill until serving. Serve with your favorite snack chips or grilled meats.

NOTE *Wear disposable gloves when cutting hot peppers; the oils can burn skin. Avoid touching your face.*

Corn Salsa

Meat-atarian Sub

Meat-atarian Sub

When I entered my sandwich in a local contest, the judges said it was "meaty but not overly salty; it's the ultimate football food; it's beautiful!"

—SHANON MAYER EVANSTON, WY

PREP: 20 MIN. • **BAKE:** 25 MIN.
MAKES: 6 SERVINGS

- 1 cup (4 ounces) shredded part-skim mozzarella cheese
- ½ cup grated Parmesan cheese
- ½ cup butter, softened
- ½ cup mayonnaise
- 2 garlic cloves, minced
- 1 teaspoon Italian seasoning
- ¼ teaspoon crushed red pepper flakes
- ¼ teaspoon pepper
- 1 loaf (1 pound) French bread, halved lengthwise
- 1 pound sliced deli ham
- 2 packages (2.1 ounces each) ready-to-serve fully cooked bacon, warmed
- 4 ounces sliced pepperoni
- ½ cup pizza sauce

1. Preheat oven to 350°. In a small bowl, combine first eight ingredients. Spread over cut sides of bread. Layer with ham, bacon, pepperoni and pizza sauce; replace top.

2. Wrap in foil; place on a large baking sheet. Bake 25-30 minutes or until heated through. Cut into slices.

SLOW COOKER
Sweet & Spicy Peanuts

With a caramel-like coating, these crunchy peanuts have a touch of heat from the hot sauce. They make a tasty snack on game day and movie nights, as well as a unique hostess gift.

—TASTE OF HOME TEST KITCHEN

PREP: 10 MIN. • **COOK:** 1½ HOURS + COOLING
MAKES: 4 CUPS

- 3 cups salted peanuts
- ½ cup sugar
- ⅓ cup packed brown sugar
- 2 tablespoons hot water
- 2 tablespoons butter, melted
- 1 tablespoon Sriracha Asian hot chili sauce or hot pepper sauce
- 1 teaspoon chili powder

1. Place peanuts in a greased 1½-qt. slow cooker. In a small bowl, combine the sugars, water, butter, hot sauce and chili powder. Pour over peanuts. Cover and cook on high for 1½ hours, stirring once.

2. Spread on waxed paper to cool. Store in an airtight container.

CHRISSY CLARK'S
GLAZED PINEAPPLE HAM *PAGE 47*

Easter Parade of Food

STEP THINGS UP THIS YEAR WITH AN EASTER MEAL THAT FAMILY AND FRIENDS WILL NEVER FORGET. LIVEN UP MENUS WITH SPRING'S FRESHEST PRODUCE AS WELL AS COMFORTING ENTREES, GOLDEN BAKED GOODS AND MORE. WHAT A TERRIFIC WAY TO USHER IN THE SEASON!

DEANNA MCDONALD'S SPRING GREEN RISOTTO *PAGE 46*

DEB HEALEY'S BACON & CHEDDAR STRATA *PAGE 51*

ROXANNE CHAN'S SPECIAL RADICCHIO-SPINACH SALAD *PAGE 41*

Dilled New Potatoes

Hop, Hop, Hooray!

Kick off Easter with this cute creation. Start with a pancake mix so you can hightail it out of the kitchen in minutes. Don't forget to shape a few flapjacks for ears and feet.

On individual plates, stack the pancakes as seen in the photo. Make a tail with a dollop of whipped cream and shredded coconut. Banana slices and mini chocolate chips make for adorable bunny feet.

⑤ INGREDIENTS
Dilled New Potatoes

With six kids at home, I try to grow as much of our own food as possible, and our big potato patch means easy and affordable meals for much of the year. For this fresh and tasty side dish, I season red potatoes with homegrown dill.
—**JENNIFER FERRIS** BRONSON, MI

START TO FINISH: 25 MIN. • **MAKES:** 8 SERVINGS

- 2 **pounds baby red potatoes (1¾ inches wide, about 24)**
- ¼ **cup butter, melted**
- 2 **tablespoons snipped fresh dill**
- 1 **tablespoon lemon juice**
- 1 **teaspoon salt**
- ½ **teaspoon pepper**

1. Place potatoes in a Dutch oven; add water to cover. Bring to a boil. Reduce heat; cook, uncovered, 15-20 minutes or until tender.
2. Drain; return to pan. Mix remaining ingredients; drizzle over potatoes and toss to coat.

Asparagus with Orange-Ginger Butter

Zesty orange and earthy ginger are the perfect complement to this veggie that has become a springtime staple.
—**LISA FELD** GRAFTON, WI

START TO FINISH: 15 MIN. • **MAKES:** 6 SERVINGS

- 1½ **pounds fresh asparagus, trimmed**
- ½ **cup butter, softened**
- ½ **cup orange marmalade**
- 1 **tablespoon minced crystallized ginger**
- 1 **tablespoon balsamic vinegar**
- 2 **teaspoons grated orange peel**

1. In a large skillet, bring ½ in. of water to a boil. Add asparagus; cover and boil for 3-5 minutes or until crisp-tender. Drain; transfer to a serving platter and keep warm.
2. In a small bowl, beat the butter, marmalade, ginger, vinegar and orange peel until blended. Spoon over asparagus.

Raspberry & White Chocolate Cheesecake

My mom makes this cheesecake a lot because it's so delicious and pretty. She calls it a "go-to" recipe. Someday I'll try to make it myself.

—PEGGY ROOS MINNEAPOLIS, MN

PREP: 40 MIN. • **BAKE:** 1¾ HOURS + CHILLING
MAKES: 16 SERVINGS

- 1 package (10 ounces) frozen sweetened raspberries, thawed
- 1 tablespoon cornstarch

CRUST

- 1 cup all-purpose flour
- 2 tablespoons sugar
- ½ cup cold butter

FILLING

- 4 packages (8 ounces each) cream cheese, softened
- 1½ cups sugar
- 1¼ cups heavy whipping cream
- 2 teaspoons vanilla extract
- 2 eggs, lightly beaten
- 12 ounces white baking chocolate, melted and cooled

1. In a small saucepan, mix raspberries and cornstarch until blended. Bring to a boil; cook and stir 1-2 minutes or until thickened. Press through a fine-mesh strainer into a bowl; discard seeds. Cool completely.

2. Preheat oven to 350°. Place a greased 9x3-in. deep springform pan on a double thickness of heavy-duty foil (about 18 in. square). Wrap foil securely around pan.

3. For crust, in a small bowl, mix flour and sugar. Cut in butter until crumbly. Press onto bottom of prepared pan. Place pan on a baking sheet. Bake for 20-25 minutes or until golden brown. Cool on a wire rack. Reduce oven setting to 325°.

4. For filling, in a large bowl, beat cream cheese and sugar until smooth. Beat in cream and vanilla. Add eggs; beat on low speed just until blended. Stir in cooled chocolate. Pour half of the mixture over crust. Spread with half of the raspberry puree. Top with remaining batter. Drop remaining puree by tablespoonfuls over top. Cut through the batter with a knife to swirl.

5. Place springform pan in a larger baking pan; add 1 in. of hot water to larger pan. Bake 1¾ to 2 hours or until edge of cheesecake is set and golden. (Center of cheesecake will jiggle when moved.) Remove springform pan from water bath. Cool cheesecake on a wire rack for 10 minutes. Loosen cheesecake from pan with a knife; remove foil. Cool 1 hour longer. Refrigerate overnight. Remove rim from pan.

Special Radicchio-Spinach Salad

Enjoy a spicy-sweet salad when you mix mint, chipotle pepper and honey together in this tasty, change-of-pace favorite.

—ROXANNE CHAN ALBANY, CA

START TO FINISH: 20 MIN.
MAKES: 12 SERVINGS

- 6 cups fresh baby spinach
- 1 head radicchio, torn
- 2 cups fresh raspberries
- ½ cup raisins
- ¼ cup pine nuts, toasted
- ¼ cup thinly sliced red onion
- ¼ cup minced fresh mint
- 3 tablespoons lime juice
- 2 tablespoons olive oil
- 2 teaspoons honey
- 1½ to 3 teaspoons chopped chipotle pepper in adobo sauce
- ¼ teaspoon salt
- ½ cup crumbled feta cheese

In a large salad bowl, combine the first seven ingredients. In a small saucepan, combine the lime juice, oil, honey, chipotle pepper and salt. Cook and stir until blended and heated through. Immediately pour over salad; toss to coat. Sprinkle with cheese.

Raspberry & White Chocolate Cheesecake

" Amazing! I used whatever apples I had on hand. Best pie crust I've ever had. *"*
—STACEY JOHNSTON TASTEOFHOME.COM

Berry-Apple-Rhubarb Pie

Berry-Apple-Rhubarb Pie

I make this family favorite every year for a get-together at my sister's home, where the recipe is known as "Uncle Mike's pie." I use berries, apples and rhubarb I grow myself.
—**MICHAEL POWERS** NEW BALTIMORE, VA

PREP: 30 MIN. + CHILLING
BAKE: 65 MIN. + COOLING • **MAKES:** 8 SERVINGS

- 2⅔ **cups all-purpose flour**
- 1 **teaspoon salt**
- 1 **cup butter-flavored shortening**
- 6 **to 8 tablespoons cold water**

FILLING

- 2 **cups thinly sliced peeled tart apples**
- 1 **tablespoon lemon juice**
- 1 **teaspoon vanilla extract**
- 1 **cup halved fresh strawberries**
- 1 **cup fresh blueberries**
- 1 **cup fresh raspberries**
- 1 **cup fresh blackberries**
- 1 **cup sliced fresh or frozen rhubarb**
- ⅓ **cup all-purpose flour**
- 1 **teaspoon ground allspice**
- 1 **teaspoon ground cinnamon**
- 1½ **cups plus 1 teaspoon sugar, divided**
- 2 **tablespoons butter**
- 1 **tablespoon 2% milk**

1. In a large bowl, combine flour and salt; cut in shortening until crumbly. Gradually add water, tossing with a fork until dough forms a ball. Divide dough in half so that one portion is slightly larger than the other; wrap each in plastic wrap. Refrigerate 30 minutes or until dough is easy to handle.

2. Preheat oven to 400°. On a lightly floured surface, roll out larger portion of dough to fit a 9-in. deep-dish pie plate. Transfer pastry to pie plate.

3. In a large bowl, toss apples with lemon juice and vanilla; add berries and rhubarb. Combine flour, allspice, cinnamon and 1½ cups sugar; add to apple mixture and toss gently to coat. Spoon into crust; dot with butter.

4. Roll out remaining pastry; make a lattice crust. Trim, seal and flute edges. Brush milk over lattice top. Sprinkle with remaining sugar.

5. Bake 15 minutes. Reduce heat to 350°; bake 50-60 minutes longer or until crust is golden brown and filling is bubbly. Cover edges with foil during the last 15 minutes to prevent overbrowning if necessary. Cool on a wire rack.

NOTE *If using frozen rhubarb, measure rhubarb while still frozen, then thaw completely. Drain in a colander, but do not press liquid out.*

Creamed Garden Potatoes and Peas

New potatoes and peas are treated to a creamy sauce for this special spring side.

—**JANE UPHOFF** CUNNINGHAM, KS

START TO FINISH: 25 MIN. • **MAKES:** 12 SERVINGS

- 2   **pounds small red potatoes, quartered**
- 3   **cups fresh or frozen peas**
- 1   **cup water**
- 2   **tablespoons chopped onion**
- 2   **tablespoons butter**
- 3   **tablespoons plus 1 teaspoon all-purpose flour**
- 1½ **teaspoons salt**
- ¼   **teaspoon pepper**
- 2   **cups 2% milk**
- 1   **cup half-and-half cream**

1. Place potatoes in a large saucepan and cover with water. Bring to a boil. Reduce heat; cover and simmer for 8-12 minutes or until tender. Drain.

2. Meanwhile, place peas and water in a small saucepan. Bring to a boil. Reduce heat; cover and simmer for 3-5 minutes or until tender. Drain.

3. In a large saucepan, saute onion in butter until tender. Stir in the flour, salt and pepper until blended; gradually add milk and cream. Bring to a boil; cook and stir for 2 minutes or until thickened. Stir in potatoes and peas; heat through.

Easter Bunny Breads

Easter Bunny Breads

These cute bunny breads are a must at our house during the Easter season. Kids of all ages love the chocolate surprise inside.

—**MOLLY HURD** NEWCASTLE, WA

PREP: 25 MIN. + RISING
BAKE: 15 MIN. + COOLING • **MAKES:** 8 SERVINGS

- 2   **packages (¼ ounce each) active dry yeast**
- 1   **cup warm water (110° to 115°)**
- 1   **cup warm 2% milk (110° to 115°)**
- 2   **tablespoons sugar**
- 2   **tablespoons canola oil**
- 1   **egg**
- 1   **teaspoon salt**
- 5½ **to 6½ cups all-purpose flour**
- 16 **small milk chocolate eggs**

ICING
- 1   **tablespoon confectioners' sugar**
- ¼   **teaspoon water**
- 1   **drop red food coloring**

1. In a large bowl, dissolve yeast in warm water. Add milk, sugar, oil, egg, salt and 4 cups flour. Beat on medium speed for 3 minutes, until smooth. Stir in enough remaining flour to form a soft dough (dough will be sticky).

2. Turn onto a floured surface; knead until smooth and elastic, about 6-8 minutes. Place in a greased bowl, turning once to grease top. Cover and let rise in a warm place until doubled, about 1 hour.

3. Preheat oven to 400°. Punch dough down. For each bunny, shape a 3-in. ball for the body; press a chocolate egg into each ball. Shape dough around egg so it is completely covered. For each head, shape a 2-in. ball; press a chocolate egg into each. Shape dough around egg so it is completely covered. Add a 1-in. ball for the tail and two 2x¾-in. pieces for ears.

4. Place bunnies 2 in. apart on greased baking sheets. Bake 12-15 minutes or until golden brown. Carefully remove from pans to wire racks to cool.

5. For icing, in a small bowl, combine confectioners' sugar and water; tint pink with red food coloring. With a small new paintbrush, paint a nose and whiskers on each bunny.

Roasted Carrots with Thyme

⑤ INGREDIENTS

Roasted Carrots with Thyme

Cutting the carrots lengthwise makes this dish look extra pretty.
—**DEIRDRE COX** KANSAS CITY, MO

START TO FINISH: 30 MIN.
MAKES: 4 SERVINGS

- 1 **pound medium carrots, halved lengthwise**
- 2 **teaspoons minced fresh thyme or ½ teaspoon dried thyme**
- 2 **teaspoons canola oil**
- 1 **teaspoon honey**
- ¼ **teaspoon salt**

Preheat oven to 400°. Place carrots in a greased 15x10x1-in. baking pan. In a small bowl, mix thyme, oil, honey and salt; brush over carrots. Roast 20-25 minutes or until tender.

Easter Egg Bread

I've made this treat for more than 20 years. Colored hard-cooked eggs baked in the dough give the sweet bread an Easter appearance, but you can leave the eggs out to enjoy the bread anytime. The festive loaf is great with ham.
—**HEATHER DURANTE** WELLSBURG, WV

PREP: 55 MIN. + RISING
BAKE: 25 MIN. + COOLING
MAKES: 1 LOAF (16 SLICES)

- ½ **cup sugar**
- 2 **packages (¼ ounce each) active dry yeast**
- 1 **to 2 teaspoons ground cardamom**
- 1 **teaspoon salt**
- 6 **to 6½ cups all-purpose flour, divided**
- 1½ **cups whole milk**
- 6 **tablespoons butter, cubed**
- 4 **eggs**
- 3 **to 6 hard-cooked eggs, unpeeled**
  Assorted food coloring
  Canola oil
- 2 **tablespoons water**

1. In a large bowl, mix sugar, yeast, cardamom, salt and 2 cups flour. In a small saucepan, heat milk and butter to 120°-130°. Add to dry ingredients; beat on medium speed 2 minutes. Add 3 eggs; beat on high 2 minutes. Stir in enough remaining flour to form a soft dough (dough will be sticky).

2. Turn dough onto a floured surface; knead until smooth and elastic, about 6-8 minutes. Place in a greased bowl, turning once to grease the top. Cover with plastic wrap and let rise in a warm place until doubled, about 45 minutes.

3. Meanwhile, dye hard-cooked eggs with food coloring following package directions. Let eggs stand until they are completely dry.

4. Punch down dough. Turn onto a lightly floured surface; divide into thirds. Roll each portion into a 24-in. rope. Place ropes on a greased baking sheet and braid. Bring ends together to form a ring. Pinch ends to seal. Lightly coat dyed eggs with oil; arrange on braid, tucking them carefully between ropes.

5. Cover with a kitchen towel; let rise in a warm place until doubled, about 20 minutes. Preheat oven to 375°.

6. In a bowl, whisk remaining egg and water; gently brush over dough, avoiding eggs. Bake 25-30 minutes or until golden brown. Remove from pan to a wire rack to cool. Refrigerate leftovers.

TOP TIP

Coloring Eggs

If coloring eggs for Easter, return them to the refrigerator after they've been dyed. Don't let hard-cooked eggs stand at room temperature for more than 2 hours. If you plan on using hard-cooked eggs as decorations, cook extra for eating and discard the eggs on display. Don't eat any colored eggs that have cracked. Either throw them out immediately or use them for display and then discard.

Lemon-Raspberry Streusel Cake

Lemon-Raspberry Streusel Cake

Buttery almond streusel tops the luscious, raspberry-studded lemon cream in these very special bars. They're fresh enough for spring, but just as well received in summer and even during cooler months. What a great treat for potlucks or luncheons.

—**JEANNE HOLT** MENDOTA HEIGHTS, MN

PREP: 25 MIN. • **BAKE:** 35 MIN. + COOLING
MAKES: 24 SERVINGS

- ⅓ cup shortening
- ⅓ cup butter, softened
- 1¼ cups sugar
- 3 eggs
- ½ teaspoon almond extract
- 2¼ cups all-purpose flour
- 1¼ teaspoons baking powder
- ½ teaspoon salt
- 1 package (8 ounces) cream cheese, softened
- ½ cup lemon curd
- ½ cup seedless raspberry jam
- 1 cup fresh raspberries

STREUSEL
- ⅔ cup all-purpose flour
- ⅓ cup sugar
- ⅓ cup sliced almonds, finely chopped
- ¼ cup cold butter

ICING
- 1 cup confectioners' sugar
- 4 teaspoons lemon juice

1. Preheat oven to 350°. In a large bowl, cream shortening, butter and sugar until light and fluffy. Beat in eggs and extract. Combine flour, baking powder and salt; gradually add to creamed mixture and mix well. Set aside 1 cup batter.
2. Spread remaining batter into a greased 13x9-in. baking pan. Combine cream cheese and lemon curd; spoon over batter. In a small bowl, beat jam; stir in raspberries. Drop by tablespoonfuls over lemon mixture. Drop reserved batter by tablespoonfuls over top.
3. For streusel, in a small bowl, combine flour, sugar and almonds. Cut in butter until crumbly. Sprinkle over batter.
4. Bake 35-40 minutes or until a toothpick inserted into the center comes out clean. Cool on a wire rack.
5. Combine icing ingredients; drizzle over cake.

Spring Green Risotto

Once a week, I create a new recipe for my blog, *An Officer and a Vegan*. I first made this risotto when I needed something cheerful and comforting. It's fantastic with asparagus, zucchini or summer squash, but use whatever veggies are in season.

—**DEANNA MCDONALD** KALAMAZOO, MI

PREP: 15 MIN. • **COOK:** 30 MIN.
MAKES: 8 SERVINGS

- 1 carton (32 ounces) vegetable stock
- 1 to 1½ cups water
- 1 tablespoon olive oil
- 2 cups sliced fresh mushrooms
- 1 medium onion, chopped
- 1½ cups uncooked arborio rice
- 2 garlic cloves, minced
- ½ cup white wine or additional vegetable stock
- 1 teaspoon dried thyme
- 3 cups fresh baby spinach
- 1 cup frozen peas
- 3 tablespoons grated Parmesan cheese
- 1 tablespoon red wine vinegar
- ½ teaspoon salt
- ¼ teaspoon pepper

1. In a large saucepan, bring stock and water to a simmer; keep hot. In a Dutch oven, heat oil over medium-high heat. Add mushrooms and onion; cook and stir 5-7 minutes or until tender. Add rice and garlic; cook and stir 1-2 minutes or until rice is coated.
2. Stir in wine and thyme. Reduce heat to maintain a simmer; cook and stir until wine is absorbed. Add hot stock mixture, ½ cup at a time, cooking and stirring until stock has been absorbed after each addition, until rice is tender but firm to the bite and risotto is creamy. Stir in spinach, peas, cheese, vinegar, salt and pepper; heat through. Serve immediately.

Glazed Pineapple Ham

This was the first time I ever baked a ham for a holiday, and I was so happy with how crispy and succulent it turned out. It's going to be a new tradition.

—**CHRISSY CLARK** BOISE, ID

PREP: 15 MIN. • **BAKE:** 2¼ HOURS + STANDING
MAKES: 20 SERVINGS

- 1 **fully cooked bone-in ham (7 to 9 pounds)**
  Whole cloves

GLAZE/SAUCE

- 2 **tablespoons cornstarch**
- ¼ **cup cold water**
- 2½ **cups packed dark brown sugar, divided**
- 1 **can (20 ounces) unsweetened crushed pineapple, undrained**
- ¼ **cup lemon juice**
- 2 **tablespoons Dijon mustard**
- ¼ **teaspoon salt**
- 1 **cup packed light brown sugar**

1. Preheat oven to 325°. Place ham on a rack in a shallow roasting pan. Using a sharp knife, score surface of ham with ¼-in.-deep cuts in a diamond pattern; insert a clove into each diamond. Cover and bake 2 to 2½ hours or until a thermometer reaches 130°.

2. Meanwhile, in a large saucepan, dissolve cornstarch in water; stir in 2 cups dark brown sugar, pineapple, lemon juice, mustard and salt. Bring to a boil; cook and stir 1-2 minutes or until slightly thickened. Reserve 2 cups for sauce; keep warm.

3. Remove ham from oven. Increase oven setting to 425°. Pour remaining pineapple mixture over ham. In a small bowl, mix light brown sugar and the remaining dark brown sugar; spread over ham.

4. Bake ham, uncovered, 10-15 minutes longer or until a thermometer reads 140°. Serve with reserved sauce.

Roasted Leg of Lamb

⑤ INGREDIENTS

Roasted Leg of Lamb

Rubbing rosemary, garlic and onion into this delectable lamb roast takes flavor to a whole new level.

—**SUZY HORVATH** MILWAUKIE, OR

PREP: 10 MIN. • **BAKE:** 2 HOURS + STANDING
MAKES: 8 SERVINGS

- ⅓ **cup olive oil**
- ¼ **cup minced fresh rosemary**
- ¼ **cup finely chopped onion**
- 4 **garlic cloves, minced**
- ½ **teaspoon salt**
- ¼ **teaspoon pepper**
- 1 **bone-in leg of lamb (5 to 6 pounds), trimmed**

1. Preheat oven to 325°. Combine the oil, rosemary, onion, garlic, salt and pepper; rub over lamb. Place fat side up on a rack in a shallow roasting pan.

2. Bake, uncovered, 2 to 2½ hours or until meat reaches desired doneness (for medium-rare, a thermometer should read 145°; medium, 160°; well-done, 170°), basting occasionally with pan juices. Let roast stand 15 minutes before slicing.

Glazed Pineapple Ham

Lemony Almond-Feta Green Beans

When you find a vegetable recipe that commands second helpings, it's worth sharing. I made these green beans for a dinner party, and that's exactly what happened. I like to use haricot verts, the skinny type of green bean.

—SAMANTHA BOWMAN HOUSTON, TX

START TO FINISH: 30 MIN.
MAKES: 6 SERVINGS

- 1 **pound fresh green beans, trimmed**
- 2 **tablespoons butter**
- 1 **small onion, halved and sliced**
- 3 **garlic cloves, sliced**
- ½ **cup sliced almonds**
- 1 **teaspoon grated lemon peel**
- 3 **tablespoons lemon juice**
- ¼ **teaspoon salt**
- ⅛ **teaspoon pepper**
- ½ **cup crumbled feta cheese**

1. In a large saucepan, bring 4 cups water to a boil. Add green beans; cook, uncovered, for 4-5 minutes or until beans turn bright green. Remove beans and drop immediately into ice water. Drain and pat dry.

2. In a large skillet, heat butter over medium heat. Add onion; cook and stir 6-8 minutes or until tender. Add garlic; cook 1 minute longer.

3. Add green beans and almonds; cook and stir 3-4 minutes or until beans are crisp-tender. Sprinkle with lemon peel, lemon juice, salt and pepper; toss to combine. Top with cheese.

Lemony Almond-Feta Green Beans

Slow Cooker Ham & Eggs

SLOW COOKER

Slow Cooker Ham & Eggs

This dish is great anytime of the year, but I love serving it on holiday mornings. It's basically a hands-free recipe that helps me create a fun meal for family.
—**ANDREA SCHAAK** JORDAN, MN

PREP: 15 MIN. • **COOK:** 3 HOURS
MAKES: 6 SERVINGS

- 6 eggs
- 1 cup biscuit/baking mix
- ⅔ cup 2% milk
- ⅓ cup sour cream
- 2 tablespoons minced fresh parsley
- 2 garlic cloves, minced
- ½ teaspoon salt
- ½ teaspoon pepper
- 1 cup cubed fully cooked ham
- 1 cup (4 ounces) shredded Swiss cheese
- 1 small onion, finely chopped
- ⅓ cup shredded Parmesan cheese

1. In a large bowl, whisk the first eight ingredients until blended; stir in remaining ingredients. Pour into a greased 3- or 4-qt. slow cooker.
2. Cook, covered, on low 3-4 hours or until eggs are set. Cut into wedges.

Easter Egg Sugar Cookies

Although they take some time to decorate, I enjoy giving these cookies to friends and family. You can use the recipe for Christmas cookies as well.
—**ALISON BENKE** CHETWYND, BC

PREP: 30 MIN. • **BAKE:** 15 MIN.
MAKES: ABOUT 4½ DOZEN

- 1 cup butter, softened
- 1¼ cups sugar
- 3 eggs
- 1 teaspoon vanilla extract
- ½ teaspoon almond extract
- 3½ cups all-purpose flour
- 1 teaspoon baking powder
- ½ teaspoon salt
  ICING
- 2 cups confectioners' sugar
- 1 tablespoon meringue powder
- ¼ cup warm water
- ½ teaspoon almond extract
  Liquid food coloring
  Pastel organdy ribbon (¼ inch wide), cut into 12-inch lengths, optional

1. In a large bowl, cream butter and sugar until light and fluffy. Add eggs, one at a time, beating well after each addition. Beat in extracts. Combine flour, baking powder and salt; gradually add to creamed mixture. Cover and refrigerate 1 hour or until easy to handle.
2. Preheat oven to 375°. On a lightly floured surface, roll out dough to ¼-in. thickness. Cut with a floured 2½-in. egg-shaped cookie cutter. Place 1 in. apart on lightly greased baking sheets. Make a hole for a ribbon by pressing a plastic straw ½-in. from the top of each cookie if desired.
3. Bake 8-10 minutes or until lightly browned. Remove to wire racks to cool.
4. For icing, sift confectioners' sugar and meringue powder into a large bowl. Add water and extract; beat on low speed until blended. Beat on high 5 minutes.
5. Fill a pastry or plastic bag with 1 cup of icing; cut a small hole in the corner of the bag. Outline each cookie with icing. Tint remaining icing with food coloring if desired. Add water, a few drops at a time, until mixture is thin enough to flow smoothly. Fill in the center space of each cookie, allowing the icing to spread to the outline. Let dry overnight.
6. Decorate with remaining icing. Store in airtight containers. Thread ribbon through holes, tie ends in a bow and hang on an Easter tree if desired.
NOTE *You may substitute 1 tablespoon meringue powder with 3 tablespoons plus ½ teaspoon water for the 2 egg whites.*

Easter Egg Sugar Cookies

International Potato Cake

Over the years, I've made this potato cake with lamb, ham and hard salami. It's a perfect side for a spring event.
—**JUDY BATSON** TAMPA, FL

PREP: 40 MIN. • **BAKE:** 35 MIN. + COOLING
MAKES: 12 SERVINGS

- ¼ cup seasoned bread crumbs
- 3 pounds potatoes (about 9 medium), peeled and cubed
- ½ cup heavy whipping cream
- ¼ cup butter, cubed
- 3 eggs, beaten
- 1 teaspoon Greek seasoning
- ¼ teaspoon garlic salt
- ¼ teaspoon lemon-pepper seasoning
- ¼ pound thinly sliced fontina cheese
- ¼ pound thinly sliced hard salami, coarsely chopped

TOPPING

- ⅓ cup grated Parmesan cheese
- 1 tablespoon seasoned bread crumbs
- 1 tablespoon butter, melted

1. Sprinkle bread crumbs onto the bottom of a greased 9-in. springform pan; set aside.
2. Place potatoes in a large saucepan and cover with water. Bring to a boil. Reduce heat; cover and simmer 10-15 minutes or until tender. Drain; transfer to a large bowl. Mash potatoes with cream, butter, eggs and seasonings.
3. Preheat oven to 350°. Spoon half the potatoes into prepared pan. Layer with cheese and salami; top with remaining potatoes. Combine topping ingredients; spoon over potatoes.
4. Cover and bake 30 minutes. Uncover; bake 5-10 minutes longer or until topping is golden brown and a thermometer reads 160°. Cool on a wire rack for 10 minutes. Carefully run a knife around edge of pan to loosen; remove sides of pan. Serve warm.

⑤ INGREDIENTS SLOW COOKER
Cherry Balsamic Pork Loin

After having a wonderful cherry Brie topping from a local market, I just knew I had to create one for pork. If you're really crazy about cherries, add even more to the slow cooker.
—**SUSAN STETZEL** GAINESVILLE, NY

PREP: 20 MIN. • **COOK:** 3 HOURS + STANDING
MAKES: 8 SERVINGS (1⅓ CUPS SAUCE)

- 1 boneless pork loin roast (3 to 4 pounds)
- 1 teaspoon salt
- ½ teaspoon pepper
- 1 tablespoon canola oil
- ¾ cup cherry preserves
- ½ cup dried cherries
- ⅓ cup balsamic vinegar
- ¼ cup packed brown sugar

1. Sprinkle roast with salt and pepper. In a large skillet, heat oil over medium-high heat. Brown roast on all sides.
2. Transfer to a 6-qt. slow cooker. In a bowl, mix preserves, cherries, vinegar and brown sugar until blended; pour over roast. Cook, covered, on low 3-4 hours or until tender (a thermometer inserted in pork should read at least 145°).
3. Remove roast from slow cooker; tent with foil. Let stand 15 minutes before slicing. Skim fat from cooking juices. Serve pork with sauce.

TOP TIP

Don't Flip Your Lid!

Slow cookers lock in steam to help cook food. So unless the recipe instructs you to stir in or add ingredients, do not lift the lid while the food is simmering. Every time you sneak a peek, the food will take longer to cook.

Cherry Balsamic Pork Loin

Raspberry-Rhubarb
Coffee Cake

Raspberry-Rhubarb Coffee Cake

Sweet raspberries and tart rhubarb are perfect partners in this classic coffee cake. For a mid-morning snack, I enjoy a piece alongside a glass of milk.
—**CAROL ROSS** ANCHORAGE, AK

PREP: 30 MIN. • **BAKE:** 1 HOUR + COOLING
MAKES: 12 SERVINGS

- 1 **cup sugar**
- ⅓ **cup cornstarch**
- 3 **cups chopped fresh or frozen rhubarb**
- 1 **cup fresh or frozen raspberries, mashed**
- 2 **teaspoons lemon juice**

BATTER

- ¾ **cup butter-flavored shortening**
- 1½ **cups sugar**
- 3 **eggs**
- 3 **cups all-purpose flour**
- 1½ **teaspoons baking powder**
- ¾ **teaspoon baking soda**
- 1½ **cups (12 ounces) sour cream**

TOPPING

- ½ **cup all-purpose flour**
- ½ **cup sugar**
- ½ **cup quick-cooking oats**
- ½ **teaspoon ground cinnamon**
- ¼ **cup cold butter, cubed**
- ½ **cup flaked coconut**
- ½ **cup chopped walnuts**

1. In a large saucepan, combine sugar and cornstarch; stir in rhubarb and raspberries. Bring to a boil over medium heat; cook 2 minutes or until thickened, stirring constantly. Remove from heat. Stir in lemon juice. Cool slightly.

2. Preheat oven to 350°. In a large bowl, cream shortening and sugar until light and fluffy. Beat in eggs. Combine flour, baking powder and baking soda; add to creamed mixture alternately with the sour cream.

3. Spread two-thirds of the batter into a greased 13x9-in. baking dish. Top with rhubarb mixture. Drop remaining batter by tablespoonfuls over filling.

4. In a small bowl, combine flour, sugar, oats and cinnamon. Cut in butter until crumbly. Stir in coconut and walnuts. Sprinkle over batter.

5. Bake 60-65 minutes or until a toothpick inserted in the center comes out clean. Cool on a wire rack.

Bacon & Cheddar Strata

Because it's assembled the night before, this no-fuss breakfast casserole is ready to pop into the oven when you wake up. We enjoy it for special brunches and breakfasts.
—**DEB HEALEY** COLD LAKE, AB

PREP: 20 MIN. + CHILLING • **BAKE:** 45 MIN.
MAKES: 10 SERVINGS

- 1 **pound bacon strips**
- 1 **medium sweet red pepper, finely chopped**
- 8 **green onions, thinly sliced**
- ½ **cup chopped oil-packed sun-dried tomatoes**
- 8 **slices white bread, cubed**
- 2 **cups (8 ounces) shredded cheddar cheese**
- 6 **eggs, lightly beaten**
- 1½ **cups 2% milk**
- ¼ **cup mayonnaise**
- ½ **teaspoon salt**
- ¼ **teaspoon ground mustard**
- ⅛ **teaspoon pepper**

1. In a large skillet, cook bacon in batches until crisp; drain on paper towels. Crumble into a small bowl. Add red pepper, onions and tomatoes. In a greased 13x9-in. baking dish, layer half of the bread, bacon mixture and cheese. Top with remaining bread and bacon mixture.

2. In another bowl, combine eggs, milk, mayonnaise and seasonings. Pour over top. Sprinkle with remaining cheese. Cover and refrigerate overnight.

3. Remove from the refrigerator 30 minutes before baking. Preheat oven to 350°. Bake, covered, 40 minutes. Uncover and bake 5-10 minutes or until a knife inserted near center comes out clean. Let stand 5 minutes before cutting.

LORI HENRY'S PASTEL
TEA COOKIES *PAGE 57*

Spring Showers

HOSTING A BABY SHOWER? MAYBE YOU HAVE A FRIEND ABOUT TO WALK DOWN THE AISLE OR YOU'RE ORGANIZING A LADIES' LUNCHEON? PERHAPS YOU SIMPLY NEED A DISH TO PASS AT A CHURCH POTLUCK. TURN HERE TO DISCOVER HOW EASY IT IS TO SHOWER A LOVED ONE WITH A SPECIALTY THAT SHOWCASES THE SEASON'S FINEST FLAVORS.

PATTERSON WATKINS' LAYERED GREEK DIP *PAGE 57*

SHARON SKILDUM'S HEARTY CHICKEN LASAGNA *PAGE 58*

TRISHA KRUSE'S CHICKEN SALAD PARTY SANDWICHES *PAGE 60*

Bride and Groom Cupcakes

HOW-TO

Making the Top Hat and Bouquet

Top hat: Spoon a circle of chocolate onto waxed paper. Place a chocolate-dipped marshmallow on the circle's center. Let stand until all chocolate is set.

Bouquet: Pipe bouquet stems onto waxed paper. Immediately attach sprinkles to the stems. Let the bouquets stand until set.

Bride and Groom Cupcakes

Who doesn't love a bite of cake? Bake the cupcakes a month ahead and freeze. Prep the accessories two days ahead and store at room temperature in an airtight container. Frost and decorate the day of the shower.
—*TASTE OF HOME* TEST KITCHEN

PREP: 1½ HOURS • **BAKE:** 20 MIN. + COOLING
MAKES: 2 DOZEN

- 1 **package strawberry or yellow cake mix (regular size)**

FROSTING
- 1 **cup shortening**
- 1 **cup butter, softened**
- 8 **cups confectioners' sugar**
- 7 **to 8 tablespoons 2% milk, divided**
- 2 **teaspoons clear vanilla extract**
- ½ **cup baking cocoa**
- 2 **teaspoons grated lemon peel**
- ½ **teaspoon lemon extract**

DECORATIONS
- 1 **cup dark chocolate candy coating disks, melted**
- ½ **cup vanilla candy coating disks, melted**
- 1 **large marshmallow**
- ½ **cup green candy coating disks, melted**
  White pearl dragees, flower sprinkles, white edible glitter and colored sugar
  Small piece of tulle

1. Prepare and bake cake batter according to package directions for cupcakes. Cool completely.
2. In a large bowl, beat shortening and butter until light and fluffy. Add the confectioners' sugar, 6 tablespoons milk and vanilla; beat until smooth.
3. Transfer half of the frosting to another bowl; add baking cocoa and 1-2 tablespoons remaining milk to achieve desired consistency. Add lemon peel and extract to remaining frosting.
4. Using melted chocolate, pipe 12 bow ties onto waxed paper. For bride's crown, pipe a 1¼-in. ring with melted vanilla coating. Arrange dragees onto ring.
5. For groom's hat, spoon a ½-teaspoon round of melted chocolate onto waxed paper into a 1¾-in. circle. Cut a ¼-in. slice from the top of marshmallow. Dip marshmallow in chocolate coating and place in the center of chocolate round.
6. Using melted green coating, pipe 12 bouquet stems onto waxed paper. Immediately attach flower sprinkles. Let decorations stand until set.
7. Pipe lemon frosting onto half of the cupcakes and chocolate frosting onto remaining cupcakes. For the bride, add crown to the top of a lemon-frosted cupcake and attach a piece of tulle for veil; add a bouquet and sprinkle with white glitter.
8. For groom, add top hat to the top of a chocolate-frosted cupcake. Attach a bow tie and pearl dragees for buttons.
9. Decorate remaining cupcakes with bouquets, bow ties, dragees, glitter and colored sugar as desired.

⑤INGREDIENTS

Lemony Cooler

This refreshing drink looks like it takes a while to mix, but it's so easy! I also like to make my own ice cubes by adding a half-cup lemon juice and a mint sprig to 4 cups water.
—**BONNIE HAWKINS** ELKHORN, WI

PREP: 15 MIN. + CHILLING
MAKES: 8 SERVINGS (2 QUARTS)

- 3 **cups white grape juice**
- ½ **cup sugar**
- ½ **cup lemon juice**
- 1 **bottle (1 liter) club soda, chilled**
  Ice cubes
  Assorted fresh fruit, optional

1. In a pitcher, combine the grape juice, sugar and lemon juice; stir until sugar is dissolved. Refrigerate until chilled.
2. Just before serving, stir in club soda. Serve over ice. Garnish with fruit if desired.

⑤INGREDIENTS

Shrimp Salad Appetizers

This refreshing hors d'oeuvre has gained a big following since a friend shared her family recipe with me. Even little ones like it!
—**SOLIE KIMBLE** KANATA, ON

START TO FINISH: 15 MIN. • **MAKES:** 2 DOZEN

- 1 **pound peeled and deveined cooked shrimp, chopped**
- 1 **can (6 ounces) lump crabmeat, drained**
- 2 **celery ribs, finely chopped**
- ¼ **cup Dijon-mayonnaise blend**
- 24 **Belgian endive leaves (3-4 heads) or small butterhead lettuce leaves**

In a large bowl, combine shrimp, crab and celery. Add mayonnaise blend; toss to coat. To serve, top each leaf with about 2 tablespoons shrimp mixture.

Lemony Cooler

Mediterranean
Cobb Salad

Mediterranean Cobb Salad

I'm a huge fan of taking classic dishes and adding some flair to them. I also like to change up heavier dishes, like the classic Cobb salad. I've traded out typical chicken for crunchy falafel that's just as satisfying.

—**JENNIFER TIDWELL** FAIR OAKS, CA

PREP: 1 HOUR • **COOK:** 5 MIN./BATCH
MAKES: 10 SERVINGS

- 1 package (6 ounces) falafel mix
- ½ cup sour cream or plain yogurt
- ¼ cup chopped seeded peeled cucumber
- ¼ cup 2% milk
- 1 teaspoon minced fresh parsley
- ¼ teaspoon salt
- 4 cups torn romaine
- 4 cups fresh baby spinach
- 3 hard-cooked eggs, chopped
- 2 medium tomatoes, seeded and finely chopped
- 1 medium ripe avocado, peeled and finely chopped
- ¾ cup crumbled feta cheese
- 8 bacon strips, cooked and crumbled
- ½ cup pitted Greek olives, finely chopped

1. Prepare and cook falafel according to package directions. When cool enough to handle, crumble or coarsely chop falafel.
2. In a small bowl, mix sour cream, cucumber, milk, parsley and salt. In a large bowl, combine romaine and spinach; transfer to a platter. Arrange crumbled falafel and remaining ingredients over greens. Drizzle with dressing.

Layered Greek Dip

This Greek-style layered dip uses purchased hummus for quick preparation.

—**PATTERSON WATKINS** PHILADELPHIA, PA

START TO FINISH: 15 MIN. • **MAKES:** 20 SERVINGS

- 2½ cups roasted garlic hummus
- ¾ cup chopped roasted sweet red peppers
- 1 cup fresh baby spinach, coarsely chopped
- 3 tablespoons lemon juice
- 2 tablespoons olive oil
- 2 tablespoons coarsely chopped fresh basil
- 1 tablespoon coarsely chopped fresh mint
- ½ cup crumbled feta cheese
- ½ cup Greek olives, sliced
- ¼ cup chopped red onion
  Assorted fresh vegetables or baked pita chips

1. Spread hummus onto a 12-in. round serving platter; top with roasted peppers.
2. In a small bowl, combine the spinach, lemon juice, oil, basil and mint. Using a slotted spoon, spread spinach mixture over peppers. Top with cheese, olives and onion. Serve with vegetables or chips.

Mini Crab Tarts

Crisp phyllo tart shells are heavenly with this warm, rich, creamy crab filling.

—**LINDA STEMEN** MONROEVILLE, IN

START TO FINISH: 25 MIN.
MAKES: 30 APPETIZERS

- 2 packages (1.9 ounces each) frozen miniature phyllo tart shells
- 1 egg
- ¼ cup 2% milk
- ¼ cup mayonnaise
- 1 tablespoon all-purpose flour
- ⅛ teaspoon salt
- 1 can (6 ounces) lump crabmeat, drained
- 2 tablespoons shredded Monterey Jack cheese
- 1 tablespoon chopped green onion
  Thinly sliced green onions, optional

1. Preheat oven to 375°. Place tart shells in an ungreased 15x10x1-in. baking pan. In a small bowl, whisk egg, milk, mayonnaise, flour and salt until smooth. Stir in crab, cheese and chopped onion. Spoon into tart shells.
2. Bake 9-11 minutes or until set. Garnish with sliced onions if desired. Serve warm.

Pastel Tea Cookies

These glazed sugar cookies are perfect for nibbling between sips at a shower, tea party or graduation celebration.

—**LORI HENRY** ELKHART, IN

PREP: 1 HOUR + CHILLING
BAKE: 10 MIN./BATCH + STANDING
MAKES: 4 DOZEN

- 1 cup butter, softened
- ⅔ cup sugar
- 1 egg
- 1 teaspoon vanilla extract
- 2½ cups all-purpose flour
- ½ teaspoon salt
- 1¼ cups confectioners' sugar
- 2 teaspoons meringue powder
- 5 teaspoons water
  Pastel food coloring

1. In a large bowl, cream butter and sugar until light and fluffy. Beat in egg and vanilla. Combine flour and salt; gradually add to creamed mixture. Cover and refrigerate 1-2 hours until dough is easy to handle.
2. Preheat oven to 350°. On a lightly floured surface, roll out dough to ⅛-in. thickness. Cut with floured 2½-in. butterfly or flower cookie cutters. Place 1 in. apart on ungreased baking sheets.
3. Bake 8-10 minutes or until edges are lightly browned. Remove cookies to wire racks to cool.
4. For glaze, in a small bowl, combine confectioners' sugar and meringue powder; stir in water until smooth. Divide among small bowls; tint pastel colors. Spread over cookies; let stand until set.

⑤ INGREDIENTS
Creamy Pastel Mints

These mints are so easy to put together, and fun to share. I make them for all sorts of occasions, from baby showers to birthday parties. Simply use different cookie cutters depending on the holiday, season or celebration at hand.

—**JANICE BRADY** SEATTLE, WA

PREP: 40 MIN. • **MAKES:** ABOUT 5 DOZEN

- 3 ounces (6 tablespoons) cream cheese
- ¼ to ½ teaspoon peppermint extract
  Red food coloring
- 3 cups confectioners' sugar

1. Place cream cheese in a bowl; let stand at room temperature to soften slightly. Stir in extract until blended. Tint mixture pink or red as desired. Gradually mix in half of the confectioners' sugar.
2. On a work surface, knead in remaining confectioners' sugar until mixture is smooth.
3. Divide mixture into three portions; roll each to ¼-in. thickness. (Flour or additional confectioners' sugar is not necessary for rolling.)
4. Cut candy with a 1-in. heart-shaped cookie cutter. Store between layers of waxed paper in an airtight container in the refrigerator.

Creamy Pastel Mints

Hearty Chicken Lasagna

Give this good-for-you lasagna a try. The lean chicken is a nice change of pace from the Italian sausage or ground beef traditionally used in lasagna.

—SHARON SKILDUM MAPLE GROVE, MN

PREP: 50 MIN. • **BAKE:** 40 MIN. + STANDING
MAKES: 12 SERVINGS

- 12 lasagna noodles
- 2 cans (14½ ounces each) diced tomatoes, drained
- 3 cans (6 ounces each) tomato paste
- 2 cups sliced fresh mushrooms
- ⅓ cup chopped onion
- 4½ teaspoons dried basil
- 1¾ teaspoons salt, divided
- ⅛ teaspoon garlic powder
- 4 cups shredded cooked chicken
- 2 eggs, lightly beaten
- 4 cups (32 ounces) 2% cottage cheese
- ¾ cup grated Parmesan cheese
- ½ cup minced fresh parsley
- ¾ teaspoon pepper
- 3 cups (12 ounces) shredded part-skim mozzarella cheese

1. Cook noodles according to package directions. Meanwhile, in a large saucepan, combine tomatoes, tomato paste, mushrooms, onion, basil, ¾ teaspoon salt and garlic powder. Bring to a boil. Reduce heat; cover and simmer 25 minutes to allow flavors to blend. Add chicken; heat through.

2. Preheat oven to 375°. In a large bowl, combine eggs, cottage cheese, Parmesan cheese, parsley, pepper and remaining 1 teaspoon salt.

3. Drain noodles. Place four noodles in a 13x9-in. baking dish coated with cooking spray. Layer with a third of the cheese mixture, chicken mixture and mozzarella cheese. Repeat layers twice.

4. Cover and bake 30 minutes. Uncover; bake 10-15 minutes longer or until bubbly and top is lightly browned. Let stand 15 minutes before cutting.

Colorful
Quinoa Salad

Colorful Quinoa Salad

My youngest daughter recently learned she has to avoid gluten, dairy and eggs, which gave me a new challenge in the kitchen. I put this dish together as a side we could all share. We love the leftovers, too.

—CATHERINE TURNBULL BURLINGTON, ON

PREP: 30 MIN. + COOLING • **MAKES:** 8 SERVINGS

- 2 cups water
- 1 cup quinoa, rinsed
- 2 cups fresh baby spinach, thinly sliced
- 1 cup grape tomatoes, halved
- 1 medium cucumber, seeded and chopped
- 1 medium sweet orange pepper, chopped
- 1 medium sweet yellow pepper, chopped
- 2 green onions, chopped

DRESSING

- 3 tablespoons lime juice
- 2 tablespoons olive oil
- 4 teaspoons honey
- 1 tablespoon grated lime peel
- 2 teaspoons minced fresh gingerroot
- ¼ teaspoon salt

1. In a large saucepan, bring water to a boil. Add quinoa. Reduce heat; simmer, covered, 12-15 minutes or until liquid is absorbed. Remove from heat; fluff with a fork. Transfer to a large bowl; cool completely.

2. Stir spinach, tomatoes, cucumber, peppers and green onions into quinoa. In a small bowl, whisk dressing ingredients until blended. Drizzle over quinoa mixture; toss to coat. Refrigerate salad until serving.

TOP TIP

Get to Know Quinoa

Quinoa (pronounced "KEEN-wah") is a seed from a plant related to spinach and chard. Packed with protein, it offers a mild taste and fluffy texture, and it can be used in a variety of dishes. Look for quinoa in the rice or grains aisle of the supermarket. Store uncooked quinoa in a cool, dry place. Always rinse it under cool water before using it in a recipe.

Sunshine Cake

I brought this cake to the county fair and took home a ribbon! For a quicker lemon filling, use a cup of prepared lemon curd from a jar.

—**LEAH WILL** BEL AIRE, KS

PREP: 1 HOUR + CHILLING
BAKE: 25 MIN. + COOLING • **MAKES:** 16 SERVINGS

- 1 **cup butter, softened**
- 1⅔ **cups sugar**
- 4 **eggs**
- 1½ **teaspoons vanilla extract**
- 1½ **teaspoons each grated lemon, orange and lime peel**
- 2¾ **cups all-purpose flour**
- 3 **teaspoons baking powder**
- ¾ **teaspoon salt**
- 1 **cup 2% milk**

FILLING
- ½ **cup sugar**
- ¼ **cup cornstarch**
- ¼ **teaspoon salt**
- ¾ **cup water**
- 2 **egg yolks**
- 2 **tablespoons butter**
- ⅓ **cup lemon juice**

FROSTING
- ½ **cup butter, softened**
- 3¾ **cups confectioners' sugar**
- ¼ **cup light corn syrup**
- 3 **tablespoons orange juice**
- 1 **teaspoon vanilla extract**
- ½ **teaspoon grated orange peel**
  Dash salt
- 3 **drops yellow food coloring**
- 1 **drop red food coloring**
  Assorted lollipops, unwrapped

1. Preheat oven to 350°. Line bottom of a greased 15x10x1-in. jelly-roll pan with parchment paper; grease paper.

2. In a large bowl, cream butter and sugar until light and fluffy. Add eggs, one at a time, beating well after each addition. Beat in vanilla and citrus peels. In another bowl, whisk flour, baking powder and salt; add to creamed mixture alternately with milk, beating well after each addition.

3. Transfer to prepared pan. Bake 25-30 minutes or until a toothpick inserted into center comes out clean. Cool in pan 5 minutes before removing to a wire rack; remove paper. Cool completely.

4. For filling, in a small saucepan, combine sugar, cornstarch and salt. Whisk in water. Cook and stir over medium heat until thickened and bubbly. Remove from heat.

5. In a small bowl, whisk a small amount of hot mixture into egg yolks; return all to pan, whisking constantly. Bring to a gentle boil; cook and stir 2 minutes. Remove from heat. Stir in butter. Gently stir in lemon juice. Press plastic wrap onto surface of filling; cool slightly. Refrigerate until cold.

6. For frosting, in a large bowl, cream butter until fluffy. Beat in confectioners' sugar, corn syrup, orange juice, vanilla, orange peel and salt until smooth. Tint orange with yellow and red food coloring.

7. Trim edges of cake; cut crosswise into thirds. Place one third on a serving plate; spread with half of the filling. Repeat layers. Top with remaining cake. Frost top and sides of cake. Insert lollipops in top for flowers. Refrigerate leftovers.

TO MAKE WINDOW BOX CAKE *Press wafer cookies against sides of cake. Tie two shoestring licorice pieces together, and wrap and tie strands around box. For flowers, cut Fruit Roll-Ups with flower-shaped cutters. Sandwich two cutouts around lollipops, moistening edges with water. For stems and leaves, insert drinking straws in cake. Top with lollipop flowers. Cut leaves from green licorice twists and insert into cake.*

Sunshine
Cake

Chicken Salad Party Sandwiches

Chicken Salad Party Sandwiches

My quick chicken salad arrives at the party chilled in a plastic container. When it's time to set out the food, I stir in the pecans and assemble the sandwiches. They're great for buffet-style potlucks. You can also serve the salad dolloped over greens, wrapped in flour tortillas or simply on its own!

—**TRISHA KRUSE** EAGLE, ID

START TO FINISH: 20 MIN.
MAKES: 15 SERVINGS

- 4 **cups cubed cooked chicken breast**
- 1½ **cups dried cranberries**
- 2 **celery ribs, finely chopped**
- 2 **green onions, thinly sliced**
- ¼ **cup chopped sweet pickles**
- 1 **cup fat-free mayonnaise**
- ½ **teaspoon curry powder**
- ¼ **teaspoon coarsely ground pepper**
- ½ **cup chopped pecans, toasted**
- 15 **whole wheat dinner rolls**
    Torn leaf lettuce
    Frilled toothpicks, optional

1. In a large bowl, combine the first five ingredients. In a small bowl, combine the mayonnaise, curry and pepper. Add to the chicken mixture; toss to coat. Chill until serving.

2. Stir pecans into chicken salad. Serve on rolls lined with lettuce. Secure with toothpicks if desired.

❝ Just the kind of recipe I was looking for. It's for a do-ahead sandwich tray to serve after a concert. ❞

—**DOLLARGIRL**
TASTEOFHOME.COM

Key Lime Bites

These cookies actually taste better the day after you bake them. Key limes don't provide much peel, so sometimes I cheat and use regular limes for the grated peel.
—**JONI LARSEN** WELLINGTON, UT

PREP: 20 MIN. • **BAKE:** 10 MIN./BATCH + STANDING
MAKES: 2½ DOZEN

- 1 **cup butter, softened**
- ¼ **cup confectioners' sugar**
- 2 **teaspoons Key lime juice**
- 2 **teaspoons grated Key lime peel**
- 2 **cups all-purpose flour**
- ¼ **teaspoon salt**
- ½ **cup chopped macadamia nuts**

ICING

- 2 **cups confectioners' sugar**
- ¼ **cup Key lime juice**
- 1 **teaspoon grated Key lime peel**

1. Preheat oven to 400°. In a large bowl, cream butter and confectioners' sugar until light and fluffy. Beat in lime juice and peel. Combine flour and salt; gradually add to creamed mixture and mix well. Stir in nuts.
2. Shape into 1-in. balls. Place 2 in. apart on ungreased baking sheets; flatten slightly.
3. Bake 8-10 minutes or until bottoms are lightly browned. Remove to wire racks to cool completely.
4. In a small bowl, combine icing ingredients. Dip cookies in icing; allow excess to drip off. Place on a wire rack; let stand until set. Store in an airtight container.

Olive Caprese Salad

Key Lime Bites

Olive Caprese Salad

When heirloom tomatoes arrive, combine them with red onions, green olives and a surprising twist: star anise.
—**JULIE MERRIMAN** SEATTLE, WA

PREP: 35 MIN. • **COOK:** 5 MIN. + MARINATING
MAKES: 10 SERVINGS

- 1 **cup plus 2 tablespoons red wine vinegar, divided**
- ½ **cup sugar**
- 1 **whole star anise**
- ¾ **cup thinly sliced red onion (about ½ medium)**
- 2 **pounds medium heirloom tomatoes, cut into wedges**
- 2 **cups heirloom cherry tomatoes, halved**
- 1 **cup pitted green olives, halved**
- 8 **ounces fresh mozzarella cheese, sliced and halved**
- 1 **tablespoon each minced fresh basil, tarragon, mint and cilantro**
- 1 **serrano pepper, thinly sliced**
- ¼ **cup olive oil**
- 2 **tablespoons lime juice**
- 1½ **teaspoons grated lime peel**
- ¼ **teaspoon salt, optional**

1. In a small saucepan, combine 1 cup vinegar, sugar and star anise. Bring to a boil, stirring to dissolve sugar. Remove from the heat. Cool slightly; stir in onion. Let stand for 30 minutes.
2. In a large bowl, combine the tomatoes, olives, cheese, herbs and serrano pepper. Remove star anise from onion mixture; drain onion, reserving 2 tablespoons marinade. (Discard remaining marinade or save for another use.) Add onion to tomato mixture.
3. In a small bowl, whisk the oil, lime juice and peel and remaining vinegar; pour over tomato mixture. Drizzle with reserved marinade; toss gently to coat. Season with salt if desired. Serve immediately.
NOTE *Wear disposable gloves when cutting hot peppers; the oils can burn skin. Avoid touching your face.*

Fresh Fruit Combo

Sausage Spinach Pasta Bake

I've sometimes swapped in other meats, such as chicken sausage, veal or ground pork, and added in summer squash, zucchini, green beans and mushrooms, depending on what's in season. Also, fresh herbs add a lot to the dish.

—**KIM FORNI** LACONIA, NH

PREP: 35 MIN. • **BAKE:** 25 MIN.
MAKES: 10 SERVINGS

- 1 package (16 ounces) whole wheat spiral pasta
- 1 pound Italian turkey sausage links, casings removed
- 1 medium onion, chopped
- 5 garlic cloves, minced
- 1 can (28 ounces) crushed tomatoes
- 1 can (14½ ounces) diced tomatoes, undrained
- 1 teaspoon dried oregano
- 1 teaspoon dried basil
- ¼ teaspoon pepper
- 1 package (10 ounces) frozen chopped spinach, thawed and squeezed dry
- ½ cup half-and-half cream
- 2 cups (8 ounces) shredded part-skim mozzarella cheese
- ½ cup grated Parmesan cheese

1. Preheat oven to 350°. Cook pasta according to package directions.
2. Meanwhile, in a large skillet, cook turkey and onion over medium heat until meat is no longer pink. Add garlic. Cook 1 minute longer; drain. Stir in tomatoes, oregano, basil and pepper. Bring to a boil. Reduce heat; simmer, uncovered, for 10 minutes.
3. Drain pasta; stir into turkey mixture. Add spinach and cream; heat through. Transfer to a 13x9-in. baking dish coated with cooking spray. Sprinkle with cheeses. Bake, uncovered, 25-30 minutes or until golden brown.

Fresh Fruit Combo

My simple fruit bowl has enough variety to satisfy even picky eaters.

—**JULIE STERCHI** CAMPBELLSVILLE, KY

PREP: 20 MIN. • **MAKES:** 10 SERVINGS

- 2 cups cubed fresh pineapple
- 2 medium oranges, peeled and chopped
- 3 kiwifruit, peeled and sliced
- 1 cup sliced fresh strawberries
- 1 cup halved seedless red grapes
- 2 medium firm bananas, sliced
- 1 large red apple, cubed
- 1 cup fresh or frozen blueberries
- 1 cup fresh or canned pitted dark sweet cherries

In a large bowl, combine the first five ingredients; refrigerate until serving. To serve, fold in bananas, apple, blueberries and cherries.

Citrus Champagne Sparkler

Here's a festive beverage to use when toasting the bride at her shower.

—**SHARON TIPTON** WINTER GARDEN, FL

START TO FINISH: 10 MIN. • **MAKES:** 11 SERVINGS

- 1¼ cups orange juice
- ⅓ cup orange liqueur
- ⅓ cup brandy
- ¼ cup sugar
- ¼ cup lemon juice
- ¼ cup unsweetened pineapple juice
- 6 cups chilled champagne

In a pitcher, combine the first six ingredients, stirring until sugar is dissolved. Pour ¼ cup into each champagne flute or wine glass. Top with champagne.

TOP TIP

Make Flavored Ice Cubes for Showers

Flavored ice cubes make party punches look special. I freeze mint sprigs, a few basil leaves or lemon zest in regular ice cubes, then drop a few cubes in each glass. I also make pink lemonade ice cubes with maraschino cherries in the center.
—**BETTY PUTZMEISTER** EL CAJON, CA

Sausage Spinach Pasta Bake

"Made this for friends, and it got rave reviews all around."

—DELICIOUSLYRESOURCEFUL_GINA
TASTEOFHOME.COM

NANETTE HILTON'S
HOMEMADE GUACAMOLE *PAGE 70*

Cinco de Mayo

OLE! WHETHER YOU'RE LOOKING TO CELEBRATE MEXICAN CULTURE OR SIMPLY WISH TO SPICE UP YOUR DINNER ROUTINE, LET THIS CHAPTER HELP. FROM FIERY APPETIZERS AND REFRESHING BEVERAGES TO EASY ENTREES AND CHANGE-OF-PACE DESSERTS, YOU'LL FIND EVERYTHING YOU NEED FOR A NO-FUSS FIESTA RIGHT HERE!

NANCY BUCHANAN'S MARGARITA GRANITA WITH SPICY SHRIMP *PAGE 67*

CHRISTINA BREMSON'S CERVEZA MARGARITAS *PAGE 70*

MARY ANNE MCWHIRTER'S SOPAIPILLAS *PAGE 68*

Horchata

Horchata

This popular mixture of ground rice and almonds is accented with a hint of lime for a tasty change-of-pace beverage. Use more or less water for a thinner or creamier drink.
—*TASTE OF HOME* **TEST KITCHEN**

PREP: 5 MIN. + STANDING • **PROCESS:** 10 MIN.
MAKES: 6 SERVINGS

- ¾ **cup uncooked long grain rice**
- 2 **cups blanched almonds**
- 1 **cinnamon stick (3 inches)**
- 1½ **teaspoons grated lime peel**
- 4 **cups hot water**
- 1 **cup sugar**
- 1 **cup cold water**
   Ground cinnamon, optional
   Lime wedges, optional

1. Place rice in a blender; cover and process 2-3 minutes or until very fine. Transfer to a large bowl; add almonds, cinnamon stick, lime peel and hot water. Let stand, covered, at room temperature 8 hours.

2. Discard cinnamon stick. Transfer rice mixture to a blender; cover and process 3-4 minutes or until smooth. Add sugar; process until sugar is dissolved.

3. Place a strainer over a pitcher; line with double-layered cheesecloth. Pour rice mixture over cheesecloth; using a ladle, press mixture through strainer.

4. Stir in cold water. Serve over ice. If desired, sprinkle with cinnamon and serve with lime wedges.

" I love horchata! I used it over cereal but left out the lime. "
—AMYSMESS
TASTEOFHOME.COM

Mango-Pineapple Chicken Tacos

Margarita Granita with Spicy Shrimp

While tinkering and tuning up recipes for my spring menu, I came up with a snazzy little appetizer that's perfect for Cinco de Mayo. It features two of my all-time favorites: shrimp and margaritas!

—**NANCY BUCHANAN** COSTA MESA, CA

PREP: 20 MIN. + FREEZING • **GRILL:** 5 MIN.
MAKES: 8 SERVINGS

- 1 **cup water**
- ½ **cup sugar**
- ½ **cup lime juice**
- 3 **tablespoons tequila**
- 3 **tablespoons Triple Sec**
- 4½ **teaspoons grated lime peel, divided**
- 1 **teaspoon ground cumin**
- 1 **teaspoon smoked paprika**
- 1 **teaspoon ground oregano**
- ½ **teaspoon salt**
- ¼ **teaspoon ground chipotle pepper**
- 16 **uncooked medium shrimp, peeled and deveined**

1. In a large saucepan, bring water and sugar to a boil. Cook and stir until sugar is dissolved. Remove from heat; stir in lime juice, tequila, Triple Sec and 3 teaspoons lime peel.
2. Transfer to an 11x7-in. dish; cool to room temperature. Freeze 1 hour; stir with a fork. Freeze 4-5 hours longer or until completely frozen, stirring every 30 minutes.
3. In a small bowl, combine cumin, paprika, oregano, salt and chipotle pepper; add shrimp, tossing to coat. Thread two shrimp onto each of eight soaked wooden appetizer skewers.
4. Moisten a paper towel with cooking oil; using long-handled tongs, lightly rub grill rack to coat. Grill shrimp, covered, over medium heat or broil 4 in. from heat 3-4 minutes on each side or until shrimp turn pink.
5. Stir granita with a fork just before serving; spoon into small glasses. Top with remaining lime peel; serve with skewered shrimp.

FREEZE IT **SLOW COOKER**
Mango-Pineapple Chicken Tacos

I lived in the Caribbean as a child, and the fresh tropical fruits in this slow-cooked chicken bring me back to my childhood. What a wonderful dinner!

—**LISSA NELSON** PROVO, UT

PREP: 25 MIN. • **COOK:** 5 HOURS
MAKES: 16 SERVINGS

- 2 **medium mangoes, peeled and chopped**
- 1½ **cups cubed fresh pineapple or canned pineapple chunks, drained**
- 2 **medium tomatoes, chopped**
- 1 **medium red onion, finely chopped**
- 2 **small Anaheim peppers, seeded and chopped**
- 2 **green onions, finely chopped**
- 1 **tablespoon lime juice**
- 1 **teaspoon sugar**
- 4 **pounds bone-in chicken breast halves, skin removed**
- 3 **teaspoons salt**
- ¼ **cup packed brown sugar**
- 32 **taco shells, warmed**
- ¼ **cup minced fresh cilantro**

1. In a large bowl, combine the first eight ingredients. Place chicken in a 6-qt. slow cooker; sprinkle with salt and brown sugar. Top with mango mixture. Cover and cook on low for 5-6 hours or until chicken is tender.
2. Remove chicken; cool slightly. Strain cooking juices, reserving mango mixture and ½ cup juices. Discard remaining juices. When cool enough to handle, remove chicken meat from bones; discard bones.
3. Shred chicken with two forks. Return chicken, reserved mango mixture and cooking juices to slow cooker; heat through. Serve in taco shells; sprinkle with cilantro.
FREEZE OPTION *Freeze cooled meat mixture in freezer containers. To use, partially thaw in refrigerator overnight. Heat through in a saucepan, stirring occasionally and adding a little broth if necessary.*

Zesty Salsa Verde

Zesty Salsa Verde

Last year was the first time I had ever grown tomatillos. They were so abundant that I had enough to eat, give away and freeze for future gatherings. What I didn't expect was how well the salsa would freeze.
—**KIM BANICK** SALEM, OR

PREP: 15 MIN. • **BAKE:** 35 MIN. • **MAKES:** 2 CUPS

- 2 **pounds medium tomatillos (about 16), husks removed and halved**
- 2 **large sweet onions, coarsely chopped (about 4 cups)**
- 2 **serrano peppers, seeded and chopped**
- 6 **garlic cloves, peeled and halved**
- ¼ **cup olive oil**
- ⅓ **to ½ cup water**
- ½ **cup chopped fresh cilantro**
- 2 **tablespoons lime juice**
- 1 **teaspoon salt**

1. Preheat oven to 425°. In a large bowl, toss tomatillos, onions, peppers and garlic with oil. Divide mixture between two 15x10x1-in. baking pans. Roast 35-40 minutes or until lightly browned, stirring occasionally. Cool slightly.
2. Process mixture in a food processor until smooth, adding water to reach desired consistency. Add remaining ingredients; pulse just until combined.
NOTE *Wear disposable gloves when cutting hot peppers; the oils can burn skin. Avoid touching your face.*
FREEZE OPTION *Freeze cooled salsa in freezer containers. To use, thaw completely in refrigerator.*

Pastelitos de Boda

In Mexico, these rich cookies are called Little Wedding Cakes, and they are usually served with hot chocolate. Having moved from the Midwest to a location that's closer to Mexico, I've enjoyed trying authentic recipes. These treats are a sharp departure from the Iowa favorites I grew up with!
—**TERRI LINS** SAN DIEGO, CA

PREP: 20 MIN. + CHILLING • **BAKE:** 15 MIN./BATCH
MAKES: ABOUT 3 DOZEN

- ¾ **cup butter, softened**
- ½ **cup confectioners' sugar**
- 2 **teaspoons vanilla**
- 2 **cups sifted all-purpose flour**
- ¼ **teaspoon salt**
- 1 **cup finely chopped walnuts**
- ¼ **cup heavy whipping cream**
  Additional confectioners' sugar

1. In a large bowl, cream butter and sugar until light and fluffy; add vanilla. Combine flour, salt and nuts; gradually add to creamed mixture and mix well. Add cream; knead lightly.
2. Shape into a roll 2½ in. in diameter. Wrap in plastic wrap. Refrigerate several hours or overnight.
3. Preheat oven to 375°. Unwrap and cut into ¼-in. slices. Place 2 in. apart on ungreased baking sheets. Bake 15 minutes or until delicately browned around edges. Remove to wire rack.
4. While warm, roll in additional confectioners' sugar.

Pastelitos de Boda

Sopaipillas

Light, crispy pastry puffs, sopaipillas are a sweet way to round out a spicy meal. They make a nice cool-weather dessert when they're served warm and topped with a little honey, sugar or even a drizzle of warm chocolate sauce.
—**MARY ANNE MCWHIRTER** PEARLAND, TX

PREP: 15 MIN. + STANDING • **COOK:** 25 MIN.
MAKES: 6-8 SERVINGS

- 1 **cup all-purpose flour**
- 1½ **teaspoons baking powder**
- ¼ **teaspoon salt**
- 1 **tablespoon shortening**
- ⅓ **cup warm water**
  Oil for deep-fat frying
  Honey, optional
  Confectioners' sugar, optional

1. In a large bowl, combine flour, baking powder and salt. Cut in shortening until mixture resembles fine crumbs. Gradually add water, tossing with a fork until a loose ball forms (dough will be crumbly).
2. On a lightly floured surface, knead the dough for 3 minutes or until smooth. Cover and let rest for 10 minutes. Roll out into a 12x10-in. rectangle. Cut into 12 squares with a knife or cut into 12 circles using a round biscuit cutter.
3. In a deep-fat fryer, heat 2 in. of oil to 375°. Fry sopaipillas for 1-2 minutes on each side. Drain on paper towels; keep warm.
4. Serve with honey and/or dust with confectioners' sugar if desired.

❝ One of the best sopaipillas recipes I have tried in years—will make again. ❞
—**LINDA_SUE**
TASTEOFHOME.COM

Beefy Taco Dip

Everyone loves taco dip! This version is a combination of several different recipes I received from friends. I experimented until I came up with my favorite. It's always a hit, no matter where I take it!

—FAYE PARKER BEDFORD, NS

PREP: 25 MIN. + CHILLING
COOK: 5 MIN. + COOLING
MAKES: 16-20 SERVINGS

- 1 package (8 ounces) cream cheese, softened
- 1 cup (8 ounces) sour cream
- ¾ cup mayonnaise
- 1 pound ground beef
- 1 envelope taco seasoning
- 1 can (8 ounces) tomato sauce
- 2 cups (8 ounces) shredded cheddar or Mexican cheese blend
- 4 cups shredded lettuce
- 2 medium tomatoes, diced
- 1 small onion, diced
- 1 medium green pepper, diced
  Tortilla chips

1. In a small bowl, beat the cream cheese, sour cream and mayonnaise until smooth. Spread on a 12- to 14-in. pizza pan or serving dish. Refrigerate for 1 hour.

2. In a saucepan over medium heat, brown beef; drain. Add taco seasoning and tomato sauce; cook and stir for 5 minutes. Cool completely. Spread over cream cheese layer. Refrigerate.

3. Just before serving, sprinkle with cheese, lettuce, tomatoes, onion and green pepper. Serve with chips.

Beefy
Taco Dip

Cerveza Margaritas

One sip of this refreshing drink and you'll picture sand, sea and blue skies that stretch for miles. It's like a vacation in a glass, and you can mix it up in moments. What are you waiting for? Give it a try!
—**CHRISTINA BREMSON** PARKVILLE, MO

START TO FINISH: 10 MIN. • **MAKES:** 5 SERVINGS

Lime slices and kosher salt, optional
1 can (12 ounces) lemon-lime soda, chilled
1 bottle (12 ounces) beer
1 can (12 ounces) frozen limeade concentrate, thawed
¾ cup tequila
Crushed ice

1. If desired, use lime slices to moisten the rims of five margarita or cocktail glasses. Sprinkle salt on a plate; dip rims in salt. Set glasses aside.
2. In a pitcher, combine the soda, beer, limeade concentrate and tequila. Serve in prepared glasses over crushed ice.

Homemade Guacamole

My daughters sometimes call this "five-finger" guacamole to remember that it is made with only five ingredients. It's so simple and so tasty!
—**NANETTE HILTON** LAS VEGAS, NV

START TO FINISH: 10 MIN. • **MAKES:** 2 CUPS

3 medium ripe avocados, peeled and cubed
¼ cup finely chopped onion
¼ cup minced fresh cilantro
2 tablespoons lime juice
⅛ teaspoon salt
Tortilla chips

In a small bowl, mash avocados with a fork. Stir in onion, cilantro, lime juice and salt. Serve with chips.

Marinated Steak & Pepper Fajitas

Marinated Steak & Pepper Fajitas

These are the best fajitas ever, and a much healthier version of the typically pan-fried fajitas you find in restaurants. I also like to serve them in flatbread instead of tortillas.
—**ERIN MICHNIACKI** MANHATTAN, KS

PREP: 25 MIN. + MARINATING • **GRILL:** 20 MIN.
MAKES: 8 SERVINGS

½ cup tequila or reduced-sodium beef broth
½ cup lime juice
4 garlic cloves, sliced
1 teaspoon grated lime peel
1 teaspoon chili powder
¾ teaspoon salt
¾ teaspoon pepper
4 poblano peppers or medium sweet red peppers, halved and seeded
4 jalapeno peppers, halved and seeded
1 large sweet onion, cut crosswise into ¾-inch-thick slices
1½ pounds beef skirt steaks or flank steak
8 whole wheat tortillas (8 inches), warmed
½ cup shredded Mexican cheese blend

1. In a small bowl, whisk the first seven ingredients until blended. Divide marinade between two large resealable plastic bags. Add peppers and onion to one bag; seal bag and turn gently to coat. Cut skirt steaks in half and add to the second bag; seal bag and turn to coat. Refrigerate vegetables and beef 8 hours or overnight.
2. Drain vegetables and beef, discarding marinade. Grill onion and poblanos, covered, over medium heat 4-6 minutes on each side or until tender. Grill jalapenos 2-3 minutes on each side or until crisp-tender. Grill steaks, covered, over medium heat 4-6 minutes on each side or until meat reaches desired doneness (for medium-rare, a meat thermometer should read 145°; medium, 160°; well-done, 170°). Let steaks stand for 5 minutes.
3. Cut peppers into strips; coarsely chop onion. Thinly slice steaks across the grain. Serve vegetables and beef on tortillas; top with cheese.
NOTE *Wear disposable gloves when cutting hot peppers; the oils can burn skin. Avoid touching your face.*

Chicken Mole

If you're not familiar with mole, don't be afraid to try this versatile Mexican sauce. I love sharing the recipe because it's a good, simple introduction to mole.

—**DARLENE MORRIS** FRANKLINTON, LA

PREP: 25 MIN. • **COOK:** 6 HOURS
MAKES: 12 SERVINGS

- 12 **bone-in chicken thighs (about 4½ pounds), skin removed**
- 1 **teaspoon salt**

MOLE SAUCE

- 1 **can (28 ounces) whole tomatoes, drained**
- 1 **medium onion, chopped**
- 2 **dried ancho chilies, stems and seeds removed**
- ½ **cup sliced almonds, toasted**
- ¼ **cup raisins**
- 3 **ounces bittersweet chocolate, chopped**
- 3 **tablespoons olive oil**
- 1 **chipotle pepper in adobo sauce**
- 3 **garlic cloves, peeled and halved**
- ¾ **teaspoon ground cumin**
- ½ **teaspoon ground cinnamon**
  Fresh cilantro leaves, optional

1. Sprinkle chicken with salt; place in a 5- or 6-qt. slow cooker. Place the tomatoes, onion, chilies, almonds, raisins, chocolate, oil, chipotle pepper, garlic, cumin and cinnamon in a food processor; cover and process until blended. Pour over chicken.

2. Cover and cook on low for 6-8 hours or until chicken is tender; skim fat. Serve chicken with sauce and sprinkle with cilantro if desired.

FREEZE OPTION *Cool chicken in mole sauce. Freeze in freezer containers. To use, partially thaw in refrigerator overnight. Heat slowly in a covered skillet or Dutch oven until a thermometer inserted into chicken reads 165°, stirring occasionally and adding a little water if necessary.*

TOP TIP

Give Mole a Try

The delicious Mexican sauce, mole (pronounced "MOH-lay"), typically contains tomatoes, chilies and/or peppers and a bit of chocolate. It is often served with chicken.

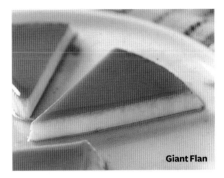
Giant Flan

Giant Flan

When I host a Mexican-themed meal, I often serve this authentic dessert. I appreciate the make-ahead convenience, and guests love the cool, creamy texture.

—**NANETTE HILTON** LAS VEGAS, NV

PREP: 30 MIN. • **BAKE:** 35 MIN. + CHILLING
MAKES: 8 SERVINGS

- 2 **cups sugar, divided**
- 3½ **cups whole milk**
- 6 **eggs**
- ½ **teaspoon salt**
- 3 **teaspoons vanilla extract**

1. In a heavy saucepan over medium-low heat, cook 1 cup sugar until melted, about 20 minutes. Do not stir. Reduce heat to low; cook 5 minutes or until syrup is golden brown, stirring occasionally. Quickly pour into an ungreased shallow 10-in. round baking dish, tilting to coat bottom of dish. Place the dish in a large baking pan; let stand 10 minutes. Preheat oven to 325°.

2. In a large saucepan, heat milk until bubbles form around sides of pan. Remove from heat. In a large bowl, whisk eggs, salt and remaining sugar. Stir 1 cup warm milk into egg mixture; return all to the pan and mix well. Stir in vanilla. Slowly pour into prepared baking dish.

3. Add ¾ in. hot water to the large baking pan. Bake 35-40 minutes or until center is just set (mixture will jiggle). Remove flan to a wire rack; cool 1 hour. Chill overnight. Run a knife around edge to loosen; invert onto a rimmed serving dish.

Chicken Mole

AGNES WARD'S
ITALIAN OMELET *PAGE 76*

Just for Mom

HOORAY FOR MOM! GIVE MOM THE DAY OFF AND WHIP UP ANY OF THESE IMPRESSIVE DISHES IN HER HONOR. WHETHER YOU DECIDE TO SURPRISE HER WITH A SCRUMPTIOUS BRUNCH, LUNCH OR DINNER, THIS SECTION WILL HAVE YOU COVERED...AND GIVE MOM THE SURPRISE OF HER LIFE!

JESSIE SARRAZIN'S GRAPEFRUIT MIMOSA *PAGE 77*

TAHNIA FOX'S GRILLED TERIYAKI PORK TENDERLOIN *PAGE 77*

CHARIS O'CONNELL'S BEST LIME TART *PAGE 74*

Orange Ricotta Pancakes

These popular pancakes are likely to spark a craving. For a different twist, switch the citrus ingredient to lime or lemon juice.

—BREHAN KOHL ANCHORAGE, AK

START TO FINISH: 30 MIN.
MAKES: 12 PANCAKES

- 1½ cups all-purpose flour
- 3 tablespoons sugar
- 1½ teaspoons baking powder
- ½ teaspoon baking soda
- ¼ teaspoon salt
- 1 egg
- 1 cup part-skim ricotta cheese
- ¾ cup 2% milk
- ½ teaspoon grated orange peel
- ½ cup orange juice
- ¼ cup butter, melted
- ½ teaspoon vanilla extract
  Maple syrup and confectioners' sugar

1. In a bowl, whisk the first five ingredients. In another bowl, whisk egg, cheese, milk, orange peel, orange juice, melted butter and vanilla until blended. Add to dry ingredients; stir just until moistened.

2. Lightly grease a griddle; heat over medium heat. Pour batter by ¼ cupfuls onto griddle. Cook until bubbles on top begin to pop and bottoms are golden brown. Turn; cook until second side is golden brown. Serve with syrup and confectioners' sugar.

Orange Ricotta Pancakes

Best Lime Tart

Best Lime Tart

This treat is the perfect balance between tart and sweet, and the almonds in the crust are just wonderful. This is one of our all-time favorite desserts. Enjoy!

—CHARIS O'CONNELL MOHNTON, PA

PREP: 35 MIN. • **BAKE:** 15 MIN. + CHILLING
MAKES: 12 SERVINGS

- 1¼ cups graham cracker crumbs
- 5 tablespoons butter, melted
- ¼ cup ground almonds
- 3 tablespoons sugar

FILLING
- 4 egg yolks
- 1 can (14 ounces) sweetened condensed milk
- ½ cup lime juice
- 2 teaspoons grated lime peel

TOPPING
- ½ cup heavy whipping cream
- 1 tablespoon sugar
- ½ cup sour cream
- 1 teaspoon grated lime peel
  Fresh raspberries and lime wedges

1. Preheat oven to 325°. In a small bowl, combine cracker crumbs, butter, almonds and sugar. Press onto the bottom and up the sides of a greased 9-in. tart pan. Bake 15-18 minutes or until edges are lightly browned.

2. In a large bowl, whisk egg yolks, milk, lime juice and peel. Pour over crust. Bake 12-14 minutes or until center is almost set. Cool on a wire rack. Refrigerate at least 2 hours.

3. In a bowl, beat cream until it begins to thicken. Add sugar; beat until stiff peaks form. Fold in sour cream and grated lime peel. Spread over tart. Garnish with raspberries and lime wedges.

❝ If you don't make this tart, you don't know what you're missing. ❞

—HARLEYDANA
TASTEOFHOME.COM

Berry Breakfast Parfaits

Planning to host a brunch but short on time? My quick, delicious and beautiful parfaits are the perfect solution. Feel free to mix and match your favorite berries.
—**LISA SPEER** PALM BEACH, FL

START TO FINISH: 20 MIN. • **MAKES:** 8 SERVINGS

6½ **cups frozen unsweetened raspberries**
¼ **cup packed brown sugar**
¼ **cup orange juice**
2 **tablespoons cornstarch**
½ **teaspoon grated orange peel**
2 **cups fresh blueberries**
2 **cups fresh blackberries**
2 **cups granola**
4 **cups vanilla Greek yogurt**
 Additional brown sugar, optional

1. Place raspberries and brown sugar in a blender; cover and process until pureed. Press through a sieve; discard seeds.
2. In a small saucepan, combine the raspberry puree, orange juice, cornstarch and orange peel. Cook and stir over medium heat until thickened and bubbly. Reduce heat to low; cook and stir 2 minutes longer. Remove from the heat; cool.
3. In eight parfait glasses, layer half of the raspberry sauce, berries, granola and yogurt. Repeat layers. Sprinkle with additional brown sugar if desired. Serve immediately.

Berry Breakfast Parfaits

TOP TIP

Best of the Berries

Blueberries have been a longtime favorite with families from coast to coast. When purchasing blueberries, look for those that are firm, dry, plump and smooth-skinned and relatively free from leaves and stems. Berries should be deep purple-blue to blue-black; reddish berries aren't ripe, but may be used in baked goods.

New York-Style
Cheesecake
Mousse

New York-Style Cheesecake Mousse

This cheesecake mousse actually tastes better after chilling overnight. Once chilled, it can be covered with plastic wrap and refrigerated for up to 3 days.

—CAROLINE WAMELINK
CLEVELAND HEIGHTS, OH

PREP: 20 MIN. + CHILLING • **MAKES:** 12 SERVINGS

- 1 **package (8 ounces) cream cheese, softened**
- ½ **cup confectioners' sugar**
- 1½ **teaspoons vanilla extract**
- ½ **teaspoon grated lemon peel**
- ¾ **cup heavy whipping cream, whipped**
- ½ **cup graham cracker crumbs**
- 4 **teaspoons sugar**
- 2 **tablespoons butter, melted**
  Sliced fresh strawberries, optional

1. In a large bowl, beat cream cheese, confectioners' sugar, vanilla and lemon peel until fluffy. Fold in whipped cream. Divide among 12 dessert dishes. Cover and refrigerate at least 2 hours.
2. Meanwhile, preheat oven to 375°. Combine cracker crumbs and sugar in a small bowl; add butter and mix well. Press to a ¼-in. thickness on an ungreased baking sheet. Bake 10-12 minutes or until lightly browned. Cool completely.
3. Just before serving, crumble graham cracker mixture; sprinkle over mousse. Top with strawberries if desired.

Italian Omelet

Savory and special, this tasty omelet with classic pizza flavors will be a hit with all those who taste it. It's fun to make and eat.
—AGNES WARD STRATFORD, ON

START TO FINISH: 20 MIN. • **MAKES:** 1 SERVING.

- ¾ **cup sliced fresh mushrooms**
- 2 **tablespoons chopped onion**
- 2 **teaspoons olive oil**
- 1 **tablespoon butter**
- 3 **eggs**
- 3 **tablespoons water**
- ⅛ **teaspoon salt**
- ⅛ **teaspoon pepper**
- ¼ **cup shredded part-skim mozzarella cheese**
- ¼ **cup marinara sauce or spaghetti sauce, warmed**

1. In a small nonstick skillet, saute mushrooms and onion in oil until tender. Remove from skillet and set aside.
2. In the same skillet, melt butter over medium-high heat. Whisk the eggs, water, salt and pepper; add mixture to skillet (mixture should set immediately at edges). As eggs set, push cooked edges toward the center, letting uncooked portion flow underneath. When the eggs are set, spoon mushroom mixture on one side and sprinkle with cheese; fold other side over filling. Slide omelet onto a plate. Serve with marinara sauce.

Chicken Salad with Dijon Vinaigrette

I find myself turning to this quick and easy chicken salad for many weeknight dinners. It's the perfect combination of crunchy and salty. Try it any time of day.
—LYNNE KEAST MONTE SERENO, CA

START TO FINISH: 15 MIN. • **MAKES:** 8 SERVINGS

- 2 **tablespoons champagne vinegar or rice vinegar**
- 4 **teaspoons Dijon mustard**
- ¼ **teaspoon salt**
- ¼ **teaspoon pepper**
- ¼ **cup olive oil**
- 10 **cups torn Bibb or Boston lettuce**
- 1 **rotisserie chicken, skin removed, shredded**
- ⅓ **cup crumbled blue cheese**
- ½ **cup sliced almonds, optional**

1. In a small bowl, whisk vinegar, mustard, salt and pepper. Gradually whisk in oil until blended.
2. In a large bowl, combine lettuce, chicken, cheese and, if desired, almonds. Drizzle with vinaigrette; toss to coat.

Chicken Salad with
Dijon Vinaigrette

Fresh Green Beans & Garlic

Fresh Green Beans & Garlic

I am a firm believer that fresh is best. I developed this recipe to take advantage of our garden veggies. It really shows off the full flavor of the green beans.
—**CAROL MAYER** SPARTA, IL

START TO FINISH: 25 MIN. • **MAKES:** 8 SERVINGS

- 2 **tablespoons canola oil**
- 2 **tablespoons butter**
- 4 **garlic cloves, sliced**
- 2 **pounds fresh green beans**
- 1 **cup reduced-sodium chicken broth**
- ½ **teaspoon salt**
- ¼ **teaspoon pepper**

1. In a Dutch oven, heat oil and butter over medium-high heat. Add garlic; cook and stir 45-60 seconds or until golden. Using a slotted spoon, remove garlic from pan; reserve. Add green beans to pan; cook and stir 4-5 minutes or until crisp-tender.
2. Stir in broth, salt and pepper. Bring to a boil. Reduce heat; simmer, uncovered, 8-10 minutes or just until beans are tender and broth is almost evaporated, stirring occasionally. Stir in the reserved garlic.

Grapefruit Mimosa

Add a splash of color to your brunch table with this lovely rosy mimosa. It has a fantastic sweet-tart taste.
—**JESSIE SARRAZIN** LIVINGSTON, MT

START TO FINISH: 5 MIN. • **MAKES:** 1 SERVING

- 1 **tablespoon red coarse sugar**
- ½ **ounce raspberry liqueur**
- 2 **ounces ruby red grapefruit juice**
- 2 **ounces champagne**
  Grapefruit twist

1. Sprinkle sugar on a plate. Moisten the rim of a champagne flute with water; hold glass upside down and dip the rim into sugar.
2. Pour the raspberry liqueur and grapefruit juice into the glass; top with champagne. Garnish with a grapefruit twist.
NOTE *To make a batch of mimosas (12 servings), slowly pour one bottle (750 ml) chilled champagne into a pitcher. Stir in 3 cups cranberry juice and ¾ cup raspberry liqueur.*

Grilled Teriyaki Pork Tenderloin

Pork tenderloin is treated to a mustard-and-teriyaki sauce marinade, then dressed up with sliced green onion. It makes for an elegant and scrumptious entree whether served in spring or summer.
—**TAHNIA FOX** TRENTON, MI

PREP: 10 MIN. + MARINATING • **GRILL:** 25 MIN.
MAKES: 4 SERVINGS

- ¾ **cup honey mustard**
- ¾ **cup teriyaki marinade**
- 1 **pork tenderloin (1 pound)**
- 2 **garlic cloves, minced**
- 1 **green onion, chopped**

1. In a small bowl, combine mustard and teriyaki marinade; pour 1 cup into a large resealable plastic bag. Add pork and garlic; seal bag and turn to coat. Refrigerate 6 hours or overnight. Cover and refrigerate remaining marinade.
2. Prepare grill for indirect heat using a drip pan. Moisten a paper towel with cooking oil; using long-handled tongs, rub on grill rack to coat lightly. Drain and discard marinade from pork.
3. Place pork over drip pan and grill, covered, over indirect medium-hot heat for 25-40 minutes or until meat reaches desired doneness (for medium-rare, a thermometer should read 145°; medium, 160°), basting with reserved marinade and turning occasionally. Let stand 5 minutes before slicing. Sprinkle with green onion.

Grilled Teriyaki Pork Tenderloin

DAVID DAHLMAN'S BANANA CRUNCH MIX *PAGE 84*

Graduation Party

SCHOOL'S OUT—LET'S PARTY! WHIPPING UP A GRADUATION DAY FEAST IS A SNAP WITH THE SIMPLE RECIPES FOUND HERE. WITH A BIT OF PLANNING, YOU'LL HAVE NO TROUBLE ATTENDING THE CEREMONY AND HOSTING A PARTY TO HONOR THE GRADUATE ON THE SAME DAY.

KELLY WILLIAMS' HAM 'N' CHEESE BISCUIT STACKS *PAGE 81*

SHERRI FROHLICH'S CONGRATULATIONS SENIORS CAKE *PAGE 84*

ANGELA HOWLAND'S LIME FRUIT SALAD *PAGE 82*

Turkey Focaccia Club

Turkey Focaccia Club

This sandwich is pure heaven thanks to the change-of-pace mayo. It's delicious any day of the year!

—**JUDY WILSON** SUN CITY WEST, AZ

START TO FINISH: 20 MIN. • **MAKES:** 4 SERVINGS

- ½ cup mayonnaise
- ½ cup whole-berry cranberry sauce
- 2 tablespoons chopped pecans, toasted
- 2 tablespoons Dijon mustard
- 1 tablespoon honey
- 1 loaf (8 ounces) focaccia bread
- 3 lettuce leaves
- ½ pound thinly sliced cooked turkey
- ¼ pound sliced Gouda cheese
- 8 slices tomato
- 6 bacon strips, cooked

In a small bowl, mix the first five ingredients until blended. Using a long serrated knife, cut focaccia horizontally in half. Spread cut sides with mayonnaise mixture. Layer bottom half with lettuce, turkey, cheese, tomato and bacon; replace bread top. Cut into wedges.

NOTE *To toast nuts, spread in a 15x10-in. baking pan. Bake at 350° for 5-10 minutes or until lightly browned, stirring occasionally. Or, spread in a dry nonstick skillet and heat over low heat until lightly browned, stirring occasionally.*

❝This is one of my family's favorite sandwiches! Thank you Judy Wilson for sharing the recipe.❞

—**SRTW** TASTEOFHOME.COM

Ham 'n' Cheese Biscuit Stacks

These finger sandwiches are pretty enough for the gals and hearty enough for the guys. Try them at your next spring get-together.
—**KELLY WILLIAMS** FORKED RIVER, NJ

PREP: 1 HOUR • **BAKE:** 10 MIN. + COOLING
MAKES: 40 APPETIZERS

- 2 **tubes (12 ounces each) refrigerated buttermilk biscuits**
- ¾ **cup stone-ground mustard, divided**
- ½ **cup butter, softened**
- ¼ **cup chopped green onions**
- ¼ **cup mayonnaise**
- ¼ **cup honey**
- 10 **thick slices deli ham**
- 10 **slices Swiss cheese**
- 2½ **cups shredded romaine**
- 40 **frilled toothpicks**
- 20 **pitted ripe olives, drained and patted dry**
- 20 **pimiento-stuffed olives, drained and patted dry**

1. Preheat oven to 400°. Cut each biscuit in half, forming half circles. Place 2 in. apart on ungreased baking sheets. Spread each with ½ teaspoon mustard. Bake 8-10 minutes or until golden brown. Remove from pans to wire racks to cool.
2. In a small bowl, combine butter and onions. In another bowl, combine mayonnaise, honey and remaining mustard. Cut each slice of ham into four rectangles; cut each slice of cheese into four triangles.
3. Split each biscuit in half; spread bottom halves with butter mixture. Layer with one ham piece, one cheese piece and 1 tablespoon romaine on each biscuit bottom.
4. Spread mustard mixture on cut side of biscuit tops; place over romaine. Thread toothpicks through olives; insert into stacks. Refrigerate leftovers.

Southwestern Nachos

SLOW COOKER
Southwestern Nachos

Guests will go crazy when you serve two heaping pans of this cheesy nacho casserole featuring tender chunks of pork. You don't need to worry about filling the chip bowl... the tortilla chips are conveniently baked right in the dish!
—**KELLY BYLER** GOSHEN, IN

PREP: 40 MIN. • **COOK:** 7¼ HOURS
MAKES: 30 SERVINGS

- 2 **boneless whole pork loin roasts (3½ pounds each)**
- 1 **cup unsweetened apple juice**
- 6 **garlic cloves, minced**
- 1 **teaspoon salt**
- 1 **teaspoon liquid smoke, optional**
- 2½ **cups barbecue sauce, divided**
- ⅓ **cup packed brown sugar**
- 2 **tablespoons honey**
- 1 **package (10 ounces) tortilla chip scoops**
- 1½ **cups frozen corn**
- 1 **can (15 ounces) black beans, rinsed and drained**
- 1 **medium tomato, seeded and chopped**
- 1 **medium red onion, chopped**
- ⅓ **cup minced fresh cilantro**
- 1 **jalapeno pepper, seeded and chopped**
- 2 **teaspoons lime juice**
- 1 **package (16 ounces) process cheese (Velveeta), cubed**
- 2 **tablespoons 2% milk**

1. Cut each roast in half; place in two 5-qt. slow cookers. Combine apple juice, garlic, salt and liquid smoke if desired; pour over meat. Cover and cook on low 7-8 hours or until tender.
2. Preheat oven to 375°. Shred pork with two forks; place in a very large bowl. Stir in 2 cups barbecue sauce, brown sugar and honey. Divide tortilla chips between two greased 13x9-in. baking dishes; top with pork mixture. Combine corn, beans, tomato, onion, cilantro, jalapeno and lime juice; spoon over pork mixture. Bake, uncovered, 15-20 minutes or until heated through.
3. Meanwhile, in a small saucepan, melt cheese with milk. Drizzle cheese sauce and remaining barbecue sauce over the nachos.
NOTE *Wear disposable gloves when cutting hot peppers; the oils can burn skin. Avoid touching your face.*

Brownie Graduation Caps

Brownie Graduation Caps

Guests will flock to these chocolaty caps. The tasty treats are a snap to assemble by topping brownie cupcakes with mortarboards made from chocolate-covered graham cookies. A red licorice tassel adds a fast finishing touch.

—*TASTE OF HOME* TEST KITCHEN

PREP: 55 MIN. • **BAKE:** 25 MIN./BATCH + COOLING
MAKES: 4 DOZEN

- 1 **package fudge brownie mix (13x9-in. pan size)**
- 48 **fudge graham cookies or graham cracker halves**
- 1 **cup chocolate frosting**
- 48 **pieces red shoestring licorice**
- 48 **Skittles bite-size candies**

1. Preheat oven to 350°. Prepare brownie batter according to package directions for cakelike brownies. Fill paper-lined miniature muffin cups two-thirds full. Bake 21-24 minutes. Cool 10 minutes before removing from pans to wire racks to cool completely (remove the paper liners while the cupcakes are still warm).

2. Slice ⅛ in. from the top of each cupcake to level. Invert cupcakes; attach a cookie to each with a small amount of frosting. For tassels, place a licorice piece and a candy on top of each cookie, attaching with frosting. Let stand until set.

Honey-Citrus Chicken Kabobs

It takes only 30 minutes to marinate the chicken for these tangy lemon-lime skewers. They are easy to assemble and grill, and fun to eat!

—**AMANDA MILLS** AUSTIN, TX

PREP: 15 MIN. + MARINATING • **GRILL:** 10 MIN.
MAKES: 4 SERVINGS

- ½ **cup lime juice**
- ½ **cup lemon juice**
- ½ **cup honey**
- 1 **garlic clove, minced**
- 1 **pound boneless skinless chicken breasts, cut into 1-inch cubes**
- 1 **each medium green, sweet red and yellow pepper, cut into 1-inch pieces**

1. In a small bowl, combine the lime juice, lemon juice, honey and garlic. Pour 1¼ cups into a large resealable plastic bag; add chicken. Seal bag and turn to coat; refrigerate for at least 30 minutes. Cover and refrigerate the remaining marinade for basting.

2. Drain and discard marinade. On eight metal or soaked wooden skewers, alternately thread chicken and peppers.

3. Moisten a paper towel with cooking oil; using long-handled tongs, rub it lightly on the grill rack to coat.

4. Grill, covered, over medium-hot heat or broil 4 in. from the heat for 8-10 minutes or until chicken is no longer pink, turning and basting frequently with reserved marinade.

Lime Fruit Salad

Looking for a fast, colorful side to round out any meal? My refreshing fruit salad is pure perfection!

—**ANGELA HOWLAND** HAYNESVILLE, ME

START TO FINISH: 20 MIN.
MAKES: 10 SERVINGS

- ¾ **cup sugar**
- ¼ **cup water**
- ¼ **cup plus 3 tablespoons lime juice**
- 2 **cups cubed fresh pineapple**
- 2 **cups sliced fresh strawberries**
- 2 **cups chopped peeled kiwifruit**
- 2 **cups seedless red grapes, halved**

1. In a small saucepan, bring sugar and water to a boil over medium heat. Remove from the heat; cool completely. Stir in lime juice.

2. In a large bowl, combine the fruit. Drizzle with syrup and toss gently to coat.

Honey-Citrus Chicken Kabobs

Loaded Potato Salad

Graduation Punch

Enjoyed for more than 30 years in our family, this was the punch my mom served when I graduated from high school. And I made it when my own kids graduated!
—**DEBRA WAGGONER** GRAND ISLAND, NE

PREP: 15 MIN. + COOLING • **MAKES:** 3¾ GALLONS

- 1½ **cups sugar**
- 8 **quarts water, divided**
- 4 **envelopes unsweetened strawberry Kool-Aid mix**
- 3 **cans (6 ounces each) frozen orange juice concentrate, thawed**
- 2¼ **cups thawed lemonade concentrate**
- 2 **cans (46 ounces each) unsweetened pineapple juice**
- 2 **liters ginger ale, chilled**

1. In a large saucepan, combine sugar and 2 qts. water. Cook and stir over medium heat until sugar is dissolved. Remove from the heat; stir in Kool-Aid mix. Cool completely.
2. Just before serving, divide the syrup between two large containers or punch bowls; add the concentrates, pineapple juice and remaining water to each. Stir in ginger ale.

Graduation Punch

Loaded Potato Salad

Get a load of this: Sour cream, bacon, shredded cheddar, green onions and more come together to give you all the richness of restaurant potato skins at your next picnic.
—**MONIQUE BOULANGER** GREENWOOD, NS

PREP: 30 MIN. + CHILLING • **MAKES:** 8 SERVINGS

- 2 **pounds red potatoes, quartered**
- ½ **pound bacon strips, chopped**
- ½ **cup mayonnaise**
- ¼ **cup creamy Caesar salad dressing**
- ¼ **cup ranch salad dressing**
- 3 **tablespoons sour cream**
- 1 **tablespoon Dijon mustard**
- 3 **green onions, chopped**
- ¼ **cup shredded cheddar cheese**
  Coarsely ground pepper, optional

1. Place potatoes in a large saucepan and cover with water. Bring to a boil. Reduce heat; cover and cook 15-20 minutes or until tender.
2. Meanwhile, cook bacon in a large skillet over medium heat, until crisp. Remove to paper towels; drain, reserving 3 tablespoons drippings.
3. Drain potatoes and place in a large bowl. Add bacon and reserved drippings; toss to coat. Refrigerate until chilled.
4. Whisk the mayonnaise, dressings, sour cream and mustard in a small bowl. Pour over potato mixture; toss to coat. Stir in onions and cheese. Sprinkle with pepper if desired.

Nutty Caramel Ice Cream Cake

Tuck this dessert in the freezer for one of those anytime celebrations. This caramel, butter pecan and almond version is our favorite, but try it with other ice cream flavors as well.

—**DAVID STELZL** WAXHAW, NC

PREP: 30 MIN. + FREEZING • **MAKES:** 16 SERVINGS

- 4 **cups crushed pecan shortbread cookies (about 52 cookies)**
- ¼ **cup butter, melted**
- 6 **cups butter pecan ice cream, softened**
- 1 **carton (8 ounces) frozen whipped topping, thawed**
- ¾ **cup slivered almonds, toasted**
- ¾ **cup milk chocolate English toffee bits**
- ¼ **cup caramel sundae syrup**

1. In a large bowl, combine cookie crumbs and butter. Press 2 cups onto the bottom of a greased 9-in. springform pan. Spoon half of the ice cream into the prepared pan. Freeze for 20 minutes.
2. Repeat layers with remaining cookie crumbs and ice cream. Spread with whipped topping. Sprinkle with almonds and toffee bits.
3. Cover and freeze overnight or until firm. May be frozen for up to 2 months.
TO USE FROZEN CAKE *Remove from the freezer 10 minutes before serving. Drizzle with syrup.*

TOP TIP

Simple Solution

To soften ice cream for recipes, simply let it stand at room temperature for 10-15 minutes or set it in the refrigerator 20-30 minutes before using. Ice cream can also be softened in the microwave at 30% power for about 30 seconds.

Congratulations Seniors Cake

Banana Crunch Mix

Bananas Foster is one of my favorite desserts, so I thought that a crunchy, snackable version would be a hit. It's heated in the microwave and takes just a few minutes to make.

—**DAVID DAHLMAN** CHATSWORTH, CA

PREP: 10 MIN. • **COOK:** 5 MIN. + COOLING
MAKES: 2½ QUARTS

- 3 **cups Honey Nut Chex**
- 3 **cups Cinnamon Chex**
- 2¼ **cups pecan halves**
- 1½ **cups dried banana chips**
- ⅓ **cup butter, cubed**
- ⅓ **cup packed brown sugar**
- ½ **teaspoon ground cinnamon**
- ½ **teaspoon banana extract**
- ½ **teaspoon rum extract**

1. In a large microwave-safe bowl, combine cereals, pecans and banana chips. In a small microwave-safe bowl, combine the butter, brown sugar and cinnamon. Microwave, uncovered, on high for 2 minutes, stirring once. Stir in extracts; pour over cereal mixture and toss to coat.
2. Cook, uncovered, on high for 3 minutes, stirring after each minute.

Spread onto waxed paper to cool. Store in an airtight container.
NOTE *This recipe was tested in a 1,100-watt microwave.*

---

5 INGREDIENTS

Congratulations Seniors Cake

I decorated a special cake for my son's high school graduation. Each of the frosted figures had hair color and details to resemble his friends.

—**SHERRI FROHLICH** BENTON, AR

PREP: 1 HOUR • **BAKE:** 45 MIN. + COOLING
MAKES: 15-20 SERVINGS

- 1 **package yellow cake mix (regular size)**
- 4 **cups vanilla frosting**
  Paste food coloring in colors of your choice

1. Prepare cake batter and bake according to package directions, using a greased 13x9-in. baking pan. Cool 10 minutes before removing from pan to a wire rack to cool completely.
2. Level top of cake; place on a serving platter. Tint frosting desired colors; spread over top and sides of cake. Pipe a shell border, caps, gowns and desired message.

Viva Panzanella

Add some white beans, and suddenly the traditional Italian bread and tomato salad is filling enough to stand on its own. Here's a great way to use fresh tomatoes from the garden or farmers market.

—**PATRICIA LEVENSON** SANTA ANA, CA

PREP: 40 MIN. • **MAKES:** 6 SERVINGS

- ¾ **pound sourdough bread, cubed (about 8 cups)**
- 2 **tablespoons olive oil**
- 2½ **pounds tomatoes (about 8 medium), chopped**
- 1 **can (15 ounces) white kidney or cannellini beans, rinsed and drained**
- 1 **can (14 ounces) water-packed artichoke hearts, rinsed, drained and quartered**
- 1 **cup thinly sliced roasted sweet red peppers**
- ½ **cup fresh basil leaves, thinly sliced**
- ⅓ **cup thinly sliced red onion**
- ¼ **cup Greek olives, quartered**
- 3 **tablespoons capers, drained**

DRESSING

- ¼ **cup balsamic vinegar**
- 3 **tablespoons minced fresh parsley**
- 3 **tablespoons olive oil**
- 3 **tablespoons lemon juice**
- 2 **tablespoons white wine vinegar**
- 3 **teaspoons minced fresh thyme or 1 teaspoon dried thyme**
- 1½ **teaspoons minced fresh marjoram or ½ teaspoon dried marjoram**
- 1½ **teaspoons minced fresh oregano or ½ teaspoon dried oregano**
- 1 **garlic clove, minced**

1. Preheat oven to 450°. In a large bowl, toss bread with oil and transfer to a baking sheet. Bake 8-10 minutes or until golden brown. Cool to room temperature.
2. In a large bowl, combine tomatoes, beans, artichokes, peppers, basil, onion, olives, capers and bread.
3. In a small bowl, whisk dressing ingredients. Drizzle over salad and toss to coat. Serve immediately.

Cheese & Pepperoni Pizza Dip

⑤ INGREDIENTS

Cheese & Pepperoni Pizza Dip

I wanted to use up a few ingredients in my fridge, so I threw this together. I was pleasantly surprised when it tasted better than my favorite takeout pizza. It is so easy: Just warm up the crust, then cut it up for dipping in the pizza sauce.

—**JULIE PUDERBAUGH** BERWICK, PA

START TO FINISH: 25 MIN.
MAKES: ABOUT 2 CUPS

- **Prebaked 12-inch pizza crust**
- 1 **cup roasted garlic and Parmesan spaghetti sauce**
- 1½ **cups shredded part-skim mozzarella cheese**
- 4 **slices Muenster cheese, cut into thin strips**
- 20 **slices pepperoni, chopped**
- **Dried oregano, optional**

1. Preheat oven to 350°. Place pizza crust on an ungreased baking sheet; bake 9-12 minutes or until heated through.
2. Meanwhile, in a small saucepan, heat spaghetti sauce over medium-low heat. Add cheeses and pepperoni. Cook and stir until cheeses are melted and sauce is heated through; sprinkle with oregano, if desired.
3. Cut pizza crust into 1½-in. strips; serve warm with sauce.

Viva Panzanella

Hawaiian Beef Sliders

Cool Beans Salad

Beans and rice together make a complete protein. So, depending on the serving size, this colorful dish could be a side or a meatless entree. The basmati rice adds a unique flavor and the dressing gives it a bit of a tang.

—JANELLE LEE APPLETON, WI

START TO FINISH: 20 MIN.
MAKES: 6 SERVINGS

- 3 **cups cooked basmati rice**
- 1 **can (16 ounces) kidney beans, rinsed and drained**
- 1 **can (15 ounces) black beans, rinsed and drained**
- 1½ **cups frozen corn, thawed**
- 4 **green onions, sliced**
- 1 **small sweet red pepper, chopped**
- ¼ **cup minced fresh cilantro**

DRESSING
- ½ **cup olive oil**
- ¼ **cup red wine vinegar**
- 1 **tablespoon sugar**
- 1 **garlic clove, minced**
- 1 **teaspoon salt**
- 1 **teaspoon ground cumin**
- 1 **teaspoon chili powder**
- ¼ **teaspoon pepper**

In a large bowl, combine the first seven ingredients. In a small bowl, whisk the dressing ingredients; pour over salad and toss to coat. Chill until serving.

Cool Beans Salad

Hawaiian Beef Sliders

Sweet and savory with just a hint of heat, these dynamite burgers are packed with flavor. Pineapple and bacon may sound like an unusual combination, but you'll find they're the perfect match.

—MARY RELYEA CANASTOTA, NY

PREP: 30 MIN. + MARINATING • **GRILL:** 10 MIN.
MAKES: 6 SERVINGS

- 1 **can (20 ounces) unsweetened crushed pineapple, divided**
- 1 **teaspoon pepper**
- ¼ **teaspoon salt**
- 1½ **pounds lean ground beef (90% lean)**
- ¼ **cup reduced-sodium soy sauce**
- 2 **tablespoons ketchup**
- 1 **tablespoon white vinegar**
- 2 **garlic cloves, minced**
- ¼ **teaspoon crushed red pepper flakes**
- 18 **miniature whole wheat buns**
  Baby spinach leaves
- 3 **center-cut bacon strips, cooked and crumbled**
  Sliced jalapeno peppers, optional

1. Drain pineapple, reserving juice and 1½ cups pineapple (save remaining pineapple for another use). In a large bowl, combine ¾ cup reserved crushed pineapple, pepper and salt. Crumble beef over mixture and mix well. Shape into 18 patties; place in two 11x7-in. dishes.
2. In a small bowl, combine soy sauce, ketchup, vinegar, garlic, pepper flakes and reserved pineapple juice. Pour half of marinade into each dish; cover and refrigerate 1 hour, turning patties once.
3. Drain and discard marinade. Moisten a paper towel with cooking oil; using long-handled tongs, coat grill rack lightly.
4. Grill patties, covered, over medium heat or broil 4 in. from heat 4-5 minutes on each side or until a thermometer reads 160° and juices run clear.
5. Grill buns, uncovered, 1-2 minutes or until toasted. Serve burgers on buns with spinach, remaining pineapple, bacon and jalapeno peppers if desired.
NOTE *If miniature whole wheat buns are not available in your area, you can also use whole wheat hot dog buns cut into thirds.*

Smoked Salmon Deviled Eggs

Flaky salmon and creamy sauce go so well over hard-boiled eggs. Drizzle the sauce or serve it on the side; it's great either way.

—MARINELA DRAGAN PORTLAND, OR

START TO FINISH: 40 MIN.
MAKES: 32 APPETIZERS

- 16 **hard-cooked eggs**
- 4 **ounces cream cheese, softened**
- ⅓ **cup mayonnaise**
- 2 **tablespoons snipped fresh dill**
- 1 **tablespoon capers, drained and finely chopped**
- 1 **tablespoon lemon juice**
- 1 **teaspoon horseradish sauce**
- 1 **teaspoon prepared mustard**
- ½ **teaspoon freshly ground pepper**
- ¾ **cup flaked smoked salmon fillet**

SAUCE

- 1 **cup mayonnaise**
- ¼ **cup plus 2 tablespoons ketchup**
- 1 **tablespoon horseradish sauce**
- 1 **tablespoon prepared mustard**
- ¼ **cup flaked smoked salmon fillets, optional**

1. Cut eggs lengthwise in half. Remove yolks, reserving whites. In a small bowl, mash yolks. Mix in cream cheese, mayonnaise, dill, capers, lemon juice, horseradish sauce, mustard and pepper. Fold in salmon. Spoon into egg whites. Refrigerate, covered, until serving.

2. For sauce, in a small bowl, mix mayonnaise, ketchup, horseradish sauce and mustard. If desired, top eggs with salmon; serve with the sauce.

Smoked Salmon Deviled Eggs

ANDREA REYNOLDS' CORN
WITH CILANTRO-LIME BUTTER *PAGE 92*

Memorial Day Cookout

FINALLY...IT'S TIME TO FIRE UP THE GRILL AND START SIZZLING! KICK OFF BARBECUE SEASON WITH BACKYARD FAVORITES YOU'LL COME TO RELY ON—FROM SPRING THROUGH SUMMER. INVITE THE WHOLE GANG OVER TO ENJOY A CHARBROILED FEAST.

SUE GRONHOLZ'S PATRIOTIC GELATIN SALAD *PAGE 95*

***TASTE OF HOME*'S RASPBERRY LEMONADE CONCENTRATE** *PAGE 90*

BETH ROYALS' GRILLED SIRLOIN KABOBS WITH PEACH SALSA *PAGE 94*

Raspberry Lemonade Concentrate

⑤ INGREDIENTS

Raspberry Lemonade Concentrate

Here's a concentrate that allows you to enjoy a refreshing summer beverage any time of year. Sweet raspberries balance the tartness of the lemons.
—*TASTE OF HOME* TEST KITCHEN

PREP: 30 MIN. • **PROCESS:** 10 MIN.
MAKES: 5 PINTS (4 SERVINGS EACH)

- **4 pounds fresh raspberries (about 14 cups)**
- **6 cups sugar**
- **4 cups lemon juice**
  Chilled tonic water or ginger ale
  Ice cubes

1. Place raspberries in a food processor; cover and process until blended. Strain raspberries, reserving juice. Discard seeds. Place juice in a Dutch oven; stir in sugar and lemon juice. Heat over medium-high heat to 190°. Do not boil.

2. Remove from heat; skim off foam. Carefully ladle hot mixture into five hot 1-pint jars, leaving ¼-in. headspace. Wipe rims of jars; screw on bands until fingertip tight.

3. Place jars into canner simmering water, ensuring that they are completely covered with water. Bring to a boil; process for 10 minutes. Remove jars and cool.

TO USE CONCENTRATE *Mix 1 pint concentrate with 1 pint tonic water. Serve over ice.*

TOP TIP

Swift Substitute

Frozen unsweetened raspberries can be substituted for fresh without any change in a particular recipe. Thaw three 12-ounce bags of raspberries to substitute for 3 to 4 cups fresh raspberries called for in a recipe.

Jalapenos with Olive-Cream Filling

Whenever we need something for a get-together, we take these jalapenos.

—KRISTAL & SEAN PETERSON WALKER, LA

START TO FINISH: 25 MIN.
MAKES: 32 APPETIZERS

- 1 **package (8 ounces) cream cheese, softened**
- ¼ **cup chopped pimiento-stuffed olives**
- 2 **tablespoons olive juice**
- 16 **large jalapeno peppers, halved lengthwise and seeded**

In a small bowl, combine the cream cheese, olives and olive juice. Spoon about 2 teaspoons into each jalapeno half. Serve immediately or refrigerate.
NOTE *Wear disposable gloves when cutting hot peppers; the oils can burn skin. Avoid touching your face.*

Flag Cake

This Stars and Stripes cake is sure to light up any patriotic celebration.

—TASTE OF HOME TEST KITCHEN

PREP: 1½ HOURS + CHILLING
BAKE: 35 MIN. + COOLING • **MAKES:** 15 SERVINGS

- 1 **package French vanilla cake mix (regular size)**
- 1 **cup buttermilk**
- ⅓ **cup canola oil**
- 4 **eggs**

FILLING
- 1 **package (3 ounces) berry blue gelatin**
- 1½ **cups boiling water, divided**
- 1 **cup cold water, divided**
  Ice cubes
- 1 **package (3 ounces) strawberry gelatin**
- ⅔ **cup finely chopped fresh strawberries**
- ¼ **cup fresh blueberries**

FROSTING
- ¾ **cup butter, softened**
- 2 **cups confectioners' sugar**
- 1 **tablespoon 2% milk**
- 1 **jar (7 ounces) marshmallow creme**

Flag Cake

1. Preheat oven to 350°. Line a 13x9-in. baking pan with waxed paper and grease the paper; set aside. In a large bowl, combine first four ingredients; beat on low speed 30 seconds. Beat on medium 2 minutes. Pour into prepared pan.
2. Bake 35-40 minutes or until a toothpick inserted into the center comes out clean. Cool 10 minutes before removing cake from pan to a wire rack.
3. Transfer cooled cake to a covered cake board. Using a small knife, cut out a 5x4-in. rectangle (½ in. deep) in the top left corner of cake, leaving a ½-in. border along edges of cake. For red stripes, cut out ½-in. wide rows (½ in. deep), leaving a ½-in. border. Using a fork, carefully remove cut-out cake pieces.
4. In a small bowl, dissolve berry blue gelatin in ¾ cup boiling water. Pour ½ cup cold water into a 2-cup measuring cup; add enough ice cubes to measure 1¼ cups. Stir into gelatin until slightly thickened. Scoop out and discard any remaining ice cubes. Repeat, making strawberry gelatin.

5. In a small bowl, combine strawberries and 1 cup strawberry gelatin. In another bowl, combine blueberries and 1 cup blue gelatin. Refrigerate 20 minutes or just until soft-set. (Save remaining gelatin for another use.)
6. Stir gelatin mixtures. Slowly pour blueberry mixture into rectangle; spoon strawberry mixture into stripes.
7. In a large bowl, beat butter until fluffy; beat in confectioners' sugar and milk until smooth. Add marshmallow creme; beat well until light and fluffy. Spread 1 cup frosting over sides and top edge of cake. Refrigerate remaining frosting 20 minutes.
8. Cut a small hole in the corner of pastry or plastic bag; insert a large star tip. Fill the bag with remaining frosting. Pipe frosting in between rows of strawberry gelatin and around edges of cake. Refrigerate 1-2 hours or until gelatin is set.

Dill Garden Salad

Dill Garden Salad

I love to cut up whatever fresh vegetables I have on hand and toss them with this delicious dressing and fresh dill. This salad shows up on our table several times a week during warm weather.

—**BETHANY WEAVER** MIDDLEBURG, PA

START TO FINISH: 15 MIN.
MAKES: 6 SERVINGS

- 3 **cups chopped English cucumbers**
- 1 **large tomato, seeded and cut into ½-inch pieces**
- 1 **small sweet red pepper, chopped**
- 2 **tablespoons chopped sweet onion**
- 3 **tablespoons reduced-fat mayonnaise**
- 4 **teaspoons olive oil**
- 2 **teaspoons sugar**
- 2 **teaspoons rice vinegar**
- ½ **teaspoon salt**
- ¼ **teaspoon garlic powder**
- ¼ **teaspoon pepper**
- 2½ **teaspoons snipped fresh dill**

In a large bowl, combine cucumbers, tomato, red pepper and onion. In a small bowl, whisk mayonnaise, oil, sugar, vinegar, salt, garlic powder and pepper until blended. Stir in dill. Spoon dressing over salad; toss to coat.

SLOW COOKER 🍲

Very Best Barbecue Beef Sandwiches

Simple and so good, this recipe is sure to be a hit with all of your friends. These sweet and tangy barbecue beef sandwiches definitely live up to their name.

—*TASTE OF HOME* TEST KITCHEN

PREP: 20 MIN. • **COOK:** 8 HOURS
MAKES: 12 SERVINGS

- 1 **boneless beef chuck roast (3 to 4 pounds)**
- 1½ **cups ketchup**
- 1 **small onion, finely chopped**
- ¼ **cup packed brown sugar**
- ¼ **cup red wine vinegar**
- 1 **tablespoon Dijon mustard**
- 1 **tablespoon Worcestershire sauce**
- 2 **garlic cloves, minced**
- ½ **teaspoon salt**
- ¼ **teaspoon celery seed**
- ¼ **teaspoon paprika**
- ¼ **teaspoon pepper**
- 2 **tablespoons cornstarch**
- 2 **tablespoons cold water**
- 12 **kaiser rolls, split**
  Dill pickle slices, optional

1. Cut roast in half. Place in a 5-qt. slow cooker. In a small bowl, combine the ketchup, onion, brown sugar, vinegar, mustard, Worcestershire sauce, garlic, salt, celery seed, paprika and pepper; pour over roast. Cover and cook on low for 8-10 hours or until meat is tender.
2. Remove meat. Skim fat from cooking juices; transfer to a large saucepan. Bring to a boil. Combine cornstarch and water until smooth; gradually stir into juices. Return to a boil; cook and stir for 2 minutes or until thickened.
3. When meat is cool enough to handle, shred with two forks. Return to slow cooker and stir in sauce mixture; heat through. Serve on rolls with pickle slices if desired.

⑤INGREDIENTS

Corn with Cilantro-Lime Butter

I created a lime butter especially for grilled corn, and I love to add a little fresh cilantro.

—**ANDREA REYNOLDS** WESTLAKE, OH

PREP: 15 MIN. + CHILLING • **GRILL:** 15 MIN.
MAKES: 12 SERVINGS

- ½ **cup butter, softened**
- ¼ **cup minced fresh cilantro**
- 1 **tablespoon lime juice**
- 1½ **teaspoons grated lime peel**
- 12 **medium ears sweet corn, husks removed**
  Grated cotija cheese, optional

1. In a small bowl, mix butter, cilantro, lime juice and lime peel. Shape into a log; wrap in plastic wrap. Refrigerate for 30 minutes or until firm. Wrap each ear of corn with a piece of heavy-duty foil (about 14 in. square).
2. Grill corn, covered, over medium heat 15-20 minutes or until tender, turning occasionally. Meanwhile, cut lime butter into 12 slices. Remove corn from grill. Carefully open foil, allowing steam to escape. Serve corn with butter and, if desired, cheese.

❝ What a great addition to my recipe file! The lime butter is so good. What it does to corn is amazing. I will not have corn without this lime butter! ❞

—**BUTTERMILK MAID** TASTEOFHOME.COM

Sage Shrimp Skewers

This is such a simple and unique grill recipe. And with just four ingredients, it's very easy to increase the amounts for a crowd.

—**LACEY KIRSCH** VANCOUVER, WA

START TO FINISH: 20 MIN.
MAKES: 10 APPETIZERS

- 10 **bacon strips**
- 10 **uncooked jumbo shrimp, peeled and deveined**
- 1 **tablespoon olive oil**
- 10 **fresh sage leaves**

1. In a large skillet, cook bacon over medium heat until partially cooked but not crisp. Remove to paper towels to drain.
2. Sprinkle shrimp with oil. Place a sage leaf on each shrimp; wrap with a strip of bacon. Thread shrimp onto two metal or soaked wooden skewers.
3. Moisten a paper towel with cooking oil; using long-handled tongs, lightly rub the grill rack to coat. Grill skewers, covered, over medium heat or broil 4 in. from the heat for 2-3 minutes on each side or until shrimp turn pink.

Cherry-Chocolate Pudgy Pie

Here's a gooey treat that's just right for campfires and backyard barbecues.

—*TASTE OF HOME* TEST KITCHEN

START TO FINISH: 10 MIN.
MAKES: 1 SERVING

- 2 **slices white bread**
- 3 **tablespoons cherry pie filling**
- 1 **tablespoon chopped almonds**
- 1 **tablespoon semisweet chocolate chunks**
- 1 **teaspoon sugar**

1. Place one slice of bread in a greased sandwich iron. Spread with pie filling; sprinkle with almonds, chocolate chunks and sugar. Top with remaining bread slice. Close iron.

2. Cook over a hot campfire for 1 to 1½ minutes or until golden brown, turning occasionally.

Triple Berry Salsa

Blueberries are so nutritious, low in calories and packed with vitamin C, fiber and disease-fighting antioxidants. This chunky salsa is a fresh, flavorful blend of berries and veggies and would be great over grilled chicken, too.

—**RAYMONDE BOURGEOIS** SWASTIKA, ON

START TO FINISH: 20 MIN.
MAKES: 22 SERVINGS (¼ CUP EACH)

- 1½ **cups fresh blueberries**
- ¾ **cup chopped fresh strawberries**
- ¾ **cup fresh raspberries**
- 1 **medium tomato, seeded and chopped**
- 1 **small sweet yellow pepper, chopped**
- ¼ **cup finely chopped red onion**
- ¼ **cup minced fresh cilantro**
- 1 **jalapeno pepper, seeded and minced**
- 2 **green onions, chopped**
- 1 **tablespoon cider vinegar**
- 1 **tablespoon olive oil**
- 2 **teaspoons lime juice**
- 2 **teaspoons orange juice**
- 1 **teaspoon honey**
- ¼ **teaspoon salt**
  Baked tortilla chip scoops

In a large bowl, combine the first nine ingredients. In a small bowl, whisk the next six ingredients. Drizzle over salsa; toss to coat. Chill until serving. Serve with chips.
NOTE *Wear disposable gloves when cutting hot peppers; the oils can burn skin. Avoid touching your face.*

Triple Berry Salsa

Grilled Sirloin
Kabobs with
Peach Salsa

⑤INGREDIENTS

Grilled Sirloin Kabobs with Peach Salsa

Finding a new way to cook with salsa is just one of the perks of this quick and easy dish. Peaches, peach preserves and peach salsa star in these beef kabobs with a blend of hot and sweet flavors.

—BETH ROYALS RICHMOND, VA

START TO FINISH: 25 MIN.
MAKES: 6 SERVINGS

- 3 tablespoons peach preserves
- 1 tablespoon finely chopped seeded jalapeno pepper
- 1 beef top sirloin steak (1½ pounds), cut into 1-inch cubes
- ½ teaspoon salt
- ¼ teaspoon pepper
- 3 medium peaches, cut into sixths
- 1½ cups peach salsa

1. In a small bowl, mix preserves and jalapeno. Season beef with salt and pepper. Alternately thread beef and peaches onto six metal or soaked wooden skewers.

2. Moisten a paper towel with cooking oil; using long-handled tongs, rub on grill rack to coat lightly. Grill kabobs, covered, over medium heat or broil 4 in. from heat 6-8 minutes or until beef reaches desired doneness, turning occasionally. Remove from grill; brush with preserves mixture. Serve with salsa.

Patriotic Gelatin Salad

Patriotic Gelatin Salad

Almost as spectacular as the fireworks, this lovely salad makes quite a "bang" at patriotic celebrations. It's exciting to serve, and friends and family love the cool fruity and creamy layers.

—SUE GRONHOLZ
BEAVER DAM, WI

PREP: 20 MIN. + CHILLING
MAKES: 16 SERVINGS

- 2 **packages (3 ounces each) berry blue gelatin**
- 2 **packages (3 ounces each) strawberry gelatin**
- 4 **cups boiling water, divided**
- 2½ **cups cold water, divided**
- 2 **envelopes unflavored gelatin**
- 2 **cups milk**
- 1 **cup sugar**
- 2 **cups (16 ounces) sour cream**
- 2 **teaspoons vanilla extract**

1. In four separate bowls, dissolve each package of gelatin in 1 cup boiling water. Add ½ cup cold water to each and stir. Pour one bowl of blue gelatin into a 10-in. fluted tube pan coated with cooking spray; chill until almost set, about 30 minutes.

2. Set other three bowls of gelatin aside at room temperature. Soften unflavored gelatin in remaining cold water; let stand 5 minutes.

3. Heat milk in a saucepan over medium heat just below boiling. Stir in softened gelatin and sugar until sugar is dissolved. Remove from heat; stir in sour cream and vanilla until smooth. When blue gelatin in pan is almost set, carefully spoon 1½ cups sour cream mixture over it. Chill until almost set, about 30 minutes.

4. Carefully spoon one bowl of strawberry gelatin over cream layer. Chill until almost set. Carefully spoon 1½ cups cream mixture over the strawberry layer. Chill until almost set. Repeat, adding layers of blue gelatin, cream mixture and strawberry gelatin, chilling in between each. Chill several hours or overnight.

NOTE *This recipe takes time to prepare since each layer must be set before the next layer is added.*

Mediterranean Tortellini Salad

One of my childhood friends moved to Italy 20 years ago. During a recent visit to see her, I enjoyed a scrumptious salad made with tortellini and fresh vegetables. Here's my re-creation.

—KELLY MAPES FORT COLLINS, CO

START TO FINISH: 30 MIN. • **MAKES:** 6 SERVINGS

- 1 **package (19 ounces) frozen cheese tortellini**
- 1 **package (14 ounces) smoked turkey sausage, sliced**
- ¾ **cup prepared pesto**
- 2 **cups fresh baby spinach, chopped**
- 2 **cups sliced baby portobello mushrooms**
- 1 **can (15 ounces) white kidney or cannellini beans, rinsed and drained**
- 1 **cup roasted sweet red peppers, chopped**
- 1 **cup (4 ounces) crumbled feta cheese**
- ¼ **cup pitted Greek olives, sliced**

1. Cook tortellini according to package directions.

2. Meanwhile, in a large nonstick skillet coated with cooking spray, cook and stir sausage over medium heat 6-7 minutes or until lightly browned. Transfer to a large bowl.

3. Drain tortellini; add to sausage. Stir in pesto. Add remaining ingredients; toss to combine. Serve warm or refrigerate until chilled.

Mediterranean Tortellini Salad

Lemon Blueberry Shortcakes

Lemon Blueberry Shortcakes

Who wouldn't smile if this dessert was placed in front of them? Cute, cool and lemony, this shortcake is the perfect summer's day treat!

—JACKIE PRESSINGER STUART, FL

PREP: 25 MIN. + FREEZING • **BAKE:** 10 MIN.
MAKES: 10 SERVINGS

- 1 pint vanilla ice cream
- 3 tablespoons sweetened lemonade drink mix
- 2 cups all-purpose flour
- 6 tablespoons sugar
- 2 teaspoons baking powder
- 2 teaspoons poppy seeds
- 1½ teaspoons grated lemon peel
- ½ teaspoon salt
- ¼ cup cold butter, cubed
- 1 egg
- ½ cup heavy whipping cream
- ¼ cup frozen unsweetened blueberries
  Confectioners' sugar

1. In a small bowl, combine ice cream and drink mix; cover and freeze for at least 1 hour.

2. Preheat oven to 400°. In a large bowl, combine flour, sugar, baking powder, poppy seeds, lemon peel and salt. Cut in butter until mixture resembles coarse crumbs. Whisk egg and cream; stir into dry ingredients just until moistened. Stir in blueberries.

3. Turn onto a lightly floured surface; knead 8-10 times. Pat dough into a ¾-in. thickness; cut into 10 cakes with a floured 3-in. star-shaped cutter.

4. Place 2 in. apart on a greased baking sheet. Bake 8-10 minutes or until golden brown around edges.

5. To assemble, split cakes in half. Place cake bottoms on dessert plates. Top each bottom layer with a scant ¼ cup of ice cream mixture. Replace shortcake tops. Sprinkle with confectioners' sugar.

Smoky Garlic and Spice Chicken

A soy sauce-based marinade gives my moist, crispy chicken a rich flavor. It's a great way to usher in spring and get the grill flaming once again.

—TINA REPAK MIRILOVICH JOHNSTOWN, PA

PREP: 20 MIN. + MARINATING
GRILL: 1 HR + STANDING
MAKES: 4 SERVINGS

- ⅓ cup reduced-sodium soy sauce
- 3 tablespoons lime juice
- 6 garlic cloves, minced
- 1 tablespoon olive oil
- 1 tablespoon ground cumin
- 1 teaspoon paprika
- ½ teaspoon dried oregano
- ½ teaspoon pepper
- 1 broiler/fryer chicken (3 to 4 pounds), split in half lengthwise

1. In a large resealable plastic bag, combine first eight ingredients. Add chicken; seal bag and turn to coat. Refrigerate 8 hours or overnight.

2. Drain and discard marinade. Moisten a paper towel with cooking oil; using long-handled tongs, rub on the grill rack to coat lightly. Prepare grill for indirect heat, using a drip pan.

3. Place chicken cut side down over drip pan and grill, covered, over indirect medium heat 1 to 1¼ hours or until a thermometer reads 170-175°, turning occasionally. Let stand 10 minutes before carving.

Smoky Garlic and Spice Chicken

Grilled Pound Cake with Warm Amaretto Bananas

Banana, butter and caramel flavors go so well together. I add a little sweet almond liqueur, such as amaretto, and a bit of lemon juice to take this grilled dessert to a new taste level.

—CAROL TRAUPMAN-CARR
BREINIGSVILLE, PA

START TO FINISH: 25 MIN. **• MAKES:** 4 SERVINGS

- 4 **teaspoons butter, divided**
- 2 **large bananas, cut into ¼-inch slices**
- 2 **tablespoons brown sugar**
- 1 **tablespoon amaretto**
- 1 **teaspoon lemon juice**
- 4 **slices pound cake (about 1 inch thick)**
  Sweetened whipped cream and
     toasted sliced almonds, optional

1. Melt 2 teaspoons butter; drizzle over a double thickness of heavy-duty foil (about 10 in. square). Place bananas on foil; top with brown sugar, amaretto and lemon juice. Dot with remaining butter. Fold foil around mixture and seal tightly.

2. Grill, covered, over medium heat for 8-10 minutes or until heated through. Grill pound cake for 1-2 minutes on each side or until lightly browned. Open foil packets carefully, allowing steam to escape. Spoon bananas over pound cake; top with whipped cream and almonds if desired.

NOTE *To toast nuts, spread in a 15x10x1-in. baking pan. Bake at 350° for 5-10 minutes or until lightly browned, stirring occasionally. Or, spread in a dry nonstick skillet and heat over low heat until lightly browned, stirring occasionally.*

TOP TIP

Banana Basics

If bananas are too green, place in a paper bag until ripe. Adding an apple to the bag will speed the process. Store ripe bananas at room temperature.

Grilled Pound Cake with Warm Amaretto Bananas

**Crisp & Spicy
Cucumber Salad, page 136**

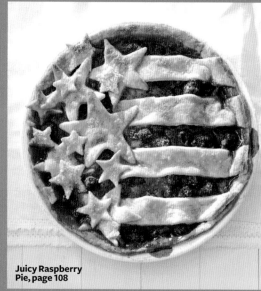

**Juicy Raspberry
Pie, page 108**

Caramelized Apple
Hand Pies, page 125

Carolina-Style Pork
Barbecue, page 133

Summer

IT'S SUMMER! IT'S TIME TO KICK BACK, RELAX AND
ENJOY EASY-BREEZY DAYS. BACKYARD BARBECUES,
INDEPENDENCE DAY FIREWORKS, BLOCK
PARTIES AND MORE MAKE THIS A GREAT SEASON
FOR CELEBRATING. TURN HERE FOR ALL THE
CHARBROILED FAVORITES, REFRESHING SALADS
AND FROSTY DESSERTS THAT MAKE THE DOG DAYS
OF SUMMER OH-SO-DELICIOUS.

KENNY FISHER'S SOUTHWEST
STEAK & POTATOES *PAGE 103*

Just for Dad

IT'S DAD'S DAY! HONOR THE BIG GUY WITH ALL OF HIS HEARTY FAVORITES. FROM BARBECUED RIBS AND JUICY STEAKS TO CORN ON THE COB AND CHERRY COBBLER, THE RECIPES HERE WILL MAKE THIS HIS MOST-DELICIOUS FATHER'S DAY YET.

STEVE MARINO'S GLAZED BBQ RIBS *PAGE 105*

KATHY VONKORFF'S HERBED CORN *PAGE 105*

NOREEN MEYER'S MAKE-AHEAD HEARTY SIX-LAYER SALAD *PAGE 104*

Grilled Mushrooms

[5] INGREDIENTS
Grilled Mushrooms

Mushrooms cooked over hot coals always taste good, but this easy recipe makes them taste fantastic.

—**MELANIE KNOLL** MARSHALLTOWN, IA

START TO FINISH: 15 MIN. • **MAKES:** 4 SERVINGS

- ½ pound medium fresh mushrooms
- ¼ cup butter, melted
- ½ teaspoon dill weed
- ½ teaspoon garlic salt

1. Thread mushrooms on four metal or soaked wooden skewers. Combine butter, dill and garlic salt; brush over mushrooms.
2. Grill over medium-high heat for 10-15 minutes or until tender, basting and turning every 5 minutes.

Beer Cheese

I like to serve this zesty cheese spread with crackers and veggie dippers. It's great to take along on summer picnics.

—**PAT WARTMAN** BETHLEHEM, PA

PREP: 30 MIN. + CHILLING • **MAKES:** 3 CUPS

- ⅓ cup beer or nonalcoholic beer
- 4 ounces cream cheese, cubed
- 3 ounces crumbled blue cheese
- ¼ cup Dijon mustard
- 2 tablespoons grated onion
- ½ to 1 teaspoon hot pepper sauce
- 1 garlic clove, minced
- 3 cups (12 ounces) shredded cheddar cheese
  Assorted crackers

1. In a small saucepan, bring beer to a boil. Remove from the heat and cool to room temperature.
2. In a food processor, combine the beer, cream cheese, blue cheese, mustard, onion, pepper sauce and garlic. Add cheddar cheese; cover and process until well blended. Transfer to a bowl. Cover and refrigerate overnight.
3. Let cheese stand at room temperature for 30 minutes before serving. Serve with crackers.

Cherry Cobbler Bars

Craving an oven-fresh fruit cobbler? This cheery twist on the classic treat is old-fashioned comfort food at its finest. The cherries peeking out of the topping make it a pretty addition to any spread. Feel free to use any flavor pie filling to suit your taste.
—**MARY BOGE** RED BOILING SPRINGS, TN

PREP: 20 MIN. • **BAKE:** 30 MIN. + COOLING
MAKES: 2 DOZEN

- 1 **cup butter, softened**
- 1¾ **cups sugar**
- 4 **eggs**
- 1 **teaspoon vanilla extract**
- 3 **cups all-purpose flour**
- 1½ **teaspoons baking powder**
- ¼ **teaspoon salt**
- 1 **can (21 ounces) cherry pie filling**

ICING
- ½ **cup confectioners' sugar**
- 1 **tablespoon milk**
- ⅛ **teaspoon vanilla extract**

1. Preheat oven to 350°. In a large bowl, cream butter and sugar. Add eggs, one at a time, beating well after each addition. Stir in vanilla. Combine flour, baking powder and salt; add to creamed mixture.
2. Spread 3 cups of batter into an ungreased 15x10x1-in. baking pan. Spread the pie filling over batter. Drop remaining batter by teaspoonfuls over the top.
3. Bake 30-35 minutes or until a toothpick inserted into the center comes out clean. Cool on a wire rack. Combine confectioners' sugar, milk and vanilla; stir until smooth. Drizzle over bars.

> 66 **My family loved these bars! LOVE!** 99
> —RUBYINMAN726
> TASTEOFHOME.COM

Southwest Steak & Potatoes

Southwest Steak & Potatoes

Bold seasonings give meat and potatoes a savory Southwestern twist. Feel free to adjust the heat factor by using more or less chili powder.
—**KENNY FISHER** CIRCLEVILLE, OH

START TO FINISH: 30 MIN. • **MAKES:** 4 SERVINGS

- 4 **medium Yukon Gold potatoes**
- 2 **teaspoons cider vinegar**
- 1 **teaspoon Worcestershire sauce**
- 1 **beef top round steak (1 inch thick and about 1½ pounds)**
- 1 **tablespoon brown sugar**
- 1 **tablespoon chili powder**
- 1½ **teaspoons ground cumin**
- 1 **teaspoon garlic powder**
- 1 **teaspoon salt, divided**
- ⅛ **teaspoon cayenne pepper**
- ⅛ **teaspoon pepper**

1. Pierce potatoes; place on a microwave-safe plate. Microwave, uncovered, on high 4-5 minutes or until almost tender, turning once. Cool slightly.
2. Meanwhile, mix vinegar and Worcestershire sauce; brush over steak. Mix brown sugar, chili powder, cumin, garlic powder, ½ teaspoon salt and cayenne until blended; sprinkle over both sides of steak.
3. Cut potatoes into ½-in. slices. Sprinkle with pepper and remaining salt. Grill potatoes and steak, covered, over medium heat for 12-17 minutes or until potatoes are tender and a thermometer inserted into beef reads 145° for medium-rare, turning occasionally.
4. Cut steak into thin slices. Serve with potatoes.

New England Iced Tea

While growing up in Massachusetts, I spent summers with my family at our cottage. The clam bakes on the beach would also include these cocktails for the adults.

—ANN LIEBERGEN BROOKFIELD, WI

START TO FINISH: 10 MIN. • **MAKES:** 1 SERVING

- 2 **tablespoons sugar**
- 1 **ounce vodka**
- 1 **ounce light rum**
- 1 **ounce gin**
- 1 **ounce Triple Sec**
- 1 **ounce lime juice**
- 1 **ounce tequila**
- 1 **to 1½ cups ice cubes**
- 2 **ounces cranberry juice**
  Lemon slice, optional

1. In a mixing glass or tumbler, combine the sugar, vodka, rum, gin, Triple Sec, lime juice and tequila; stir until sugar is dissolved.

2. Place ice in a highball glass; pour in the sugar mixture. Top with cranberry juice. Garnish with lemon if desired.

LONG ISLAND ICED TEA *Substitute cola for the cranberry juice.*

New England Iced Tea

Make-Ahead Hearty Six-Layer Salad

Make-Ahead Hearty Six-Layer Salad

This salad is an all-time favorite. I reach for the recipe whenever I need a dish to pass. Best of all, it can be assembled a day early.

—NOREEN MEYER MADISON, WI

PREP: 20 MIN. + CHILLING • **MAKES:** 12 SERVINGS

- 1½ **cups uncooked small pasta shells**
- 1 **tablespoon vegetable oil**
- 3 **cups shredded lettuce**
- 3 **hard-cooked eggs, sliced**
- ¼ **teaspoon salt**
- ⅛ **teaspoon pepper**
- 2 **cups shredded cooked chicken breast**
- 1 **package (10 ounces) frozen peas, thawed**

DRESSING
- 1 **cup mayonnaise**
- ¼ **cup sour cream**
- 2 **green onions, chopped**
- 2 **teaspoons Dijon mustard**

TOPPINGS
- 1 **cup (4 ounces) shredded Colby or Monterey Jack cheese**
- 2 **tablespoons minced fresh parsley**

1. Cook pasta according to package directions; drain and rinse with cold water. Drizzle with oil and toss to coat.

2. Place the lettuce in a 2½-qt. glass serving bowl; top with pasta and eggs. Sprinkle with salt and pepper. Layer with chicken and peas. In a small bowl, mix dressing ingredients until blended; spread over top. Refrigerate, covered, for several hours or overnight.

3. Just before serving, sprinkle with cheese and parsley.

❝ This salad was served at bridge club last night. It was great! ❞

—DIANEPRICE1 TASTEOFHOME.COM

Glazed BBQ Ribs

After trying a fruit salad at a backyard barbecue, I wanted to make a rib sauce that tasted just as sweet. Everyone loves the raspberry-red wine combo.
—**STEVE MARINO** NUTLEY, NJ

PREP: 2 HOURS • **BROIL:** 10 MIN.
MAKES: 4 SERVINGS

 - 4 **pounds pork baby back ribs**
 - ½ **cup olive oil**
 - 2 **teaspoons salt**
 - 2 **teaspoons pepper**
 - 1 **bottle (18 ounces) barbecue sauce**
 - 1 **cup seedless raspberry preserves**
 - ¼ **cup dry red wine**
 - ½ **teaspoon onion powder**
 - ½ **teaspoon cayenne pepper**

1. Preheat oven to 325°. Place ribs in a shallow roasting pan, bone side down. In a small bowl, mix oil, salt and pepper; rub over ribs. Bake, covered, 1½ to 2 hours or until tender; drain.
2. In another bowl, mix remaining ingredients; reserve ¾ cup for serving with ribs. Brush some of the remaining sauce over ribs. Bake, uncovered, 25-30 minutes or until ribs are glazed, basting occasionally with additional sauce.
3. Preheat broiler. Transfer ribs to a broiler pan, bone side down. Broil 4-5 in. from heat 8-10 minutes or until browned. Serve with reserved sauce.

Herbed Corn

My husband and I agreed that the original recipe for this corn needed a little jazzing up, so I added thyme and cayenne pepper to suit our tastes. Now the side dish makes a regular appearance on our grill.
—**KATHY VONKORFF**
NORTH COLLEGE HILL, OH

START TO FINISH: 30 MIN.
MAKES: 8 SERVINGS

 - ½ **cup butter, softened**
 - 2 **tablespoons minced fresh parsley**
 - 2 **tablespoons minced fresh chives**
 - 1 **teaspoon dried thyme**
 - ½ **teaspoon salt**
 - ½ **teaspoon cayenne pepper**
 - 8 **ears sweet corn, husked**

1. In a small bowl, beat the first six ingredients until blended. Spread 1 tablespoon mixture over each ear of corn.
2. Wrap corn individually in heavy-duty foil. Grill corn, covered, over medium heat 10-15 minutes or until tender, turning occasionally.
3. Open foil carefully to allow steam to escape before serving.

Maple Vegetable Medley

Brushed with a mild maple glaze before being grilled, these veggies are the hit of summer. They go well with any entree.
—**LORRAINE CALAND** SHUNIAH, ON

PREP: 20 MIN. • **GRILL:** 25 MIN.
MAKES: 8 SERVINGS

 - ⅓ **cup balsamic vinegar**
 - ⅓ **cup maple syrup**
 - 1 **large red onion**
 - 1 **pound fresh asparagus, trimmed**
 - 1 **pound baby carrots**
 - 2 **medium zucchini, cut lengthwise into thirds and seeded**
 - 1 **medium sweet red pepper, cut into 8 pieces**
 - 1 **medium sweet yellow pepper, cut into 8 pieces**
 - 2 **tablespoons olive oil**
 - 1 **tablespoon minced fresh thyme or 1 teaspoon dried thyme**
 - ½ **teaspoon salt**
 - ½ **teaspoon pepper**

1. For glaze, in a small saucepan, bring vinegar and syrup to a boil. Reduce heat; cook and stir over medium heat for 6-8 minutes or until thickened. Remove from the heat; set aside.
2. Cut onion into eight wedges to ½ in. of the bottom. Place onion, asparagus, carrots, zucchini and peppers in a large bowl. Drizzle with oil and sprinkle with seasonings; toss to coat.
3. Moisten a paper towel with cooking oil; using long-handled tongs, rub on grill rack to coat lightly. Arrange vegetables on rack.
4. Grill, covered, over medium heat or broil 4 in. from heat 10 minutes on each side. Brush vegetables with half of the glaze; grill 5-8 minutes longer or until crisp-tender. Before serving, brush with remaining glaze.

Glazed BBQ Ribs

ERIN GLASS' FIRECRACKER CUPCAKES *PAGE 110*

Firework Fun

WHETHER YOU'RE HOSTING AN INDEPENDENCE DAY PARTY, NEED A DISH TO PASS AT A BARBECUE OR PACKING UP A FEW NIBBLES TO ENJOY DURING THE FIREWORKS, YOU'RE SURE TO FIND SUCCESS HERE. FROM SIMPLE SNACK MIXES TO GRILLED STANDBYS, YOU CAN'T GO WRONG WITH THESE SUMMERTIME CLASSICS.

TINA REPAK MIRILOVICH'S GRILLED CHEESE & TOMATO FLATBREADS *PAGE 111*

KAREN BERNER'S JUICY RASPBERRY PIE *PAGE 108*

JACKIE BURNS' ALL-AMERICAN BACON CHEESEBURGERS *PAGE 112*

Juicy Raspberry Pie

Red, White & Blue Bites

JULY 4TH LAYERED DRINKS

All you need for these colorful beverages is cranberry-apple juice, white pina colada juice and blue low-cal Gatorade. The secret is in the sugar content. Start with the cranberry juice. Then fill the glass with ice. Next slowly pour in the pina colada juice and the blue G2 Gatorade. With a little bit of patience and lots of ice, you can really wow a crowd.
—KATRINA BAHL
INKATRINASKITCHEN.COM

SMOKE BALLS

We love fireworks, so I created these sweet treats with doughnut holes (truffles work, too). Dip in melted candy coating, top with colored sugar and sprinkles, and poke in a licorice lace. Cotton candy "smoke" is the finishing touch.
—NORENE COX PARTYPINCHING.COM

Juicy Raspberry Pie

This pie is packed with raspberry flavor! Have some fun with the top pie pastry and punch out star shapes for a festive look.
—KAREN BERNER MILWAUKEE, WI

PREP: 35 MIN. + CHILLING
BAKE: 55 MIN. + COOLING • **MAKES:** 8 SERVINGS

- 2½ **cups all-purpose flour**
- ½ **teaspoon salt**
- ⅔ **cup cold unsalted butter, cubed**
- ⅓ **cup shortening**
- 6 **to 10 tablespoons ice water**

FILLING
- 5 **cups fresh raspberries**
- 2 **teaspoons lemon juice**
- ¼ **teaspoon almond extract**
- 1 **cup sugar**
- ⅓ **cup all-purpose flour**
- 1 **teaspoon ground cinnamon**

SUGAR TOPPING
- 1 **teaspoon sugar**
- ¼ **teaspoon ground cinnamon**
- 1 **tablespoon 2% milk**

1. In a large bowl, mix flour and salt; cut in butter and shortening until crumbly. Gradually add ice water, tossing with a fork until dough holds together when pressed. Divide dough in half. Shape each into a disk; wrap in plastic wrap. Refrigerate 1 hour or overnight.
2. Preheat oven to 375°. For filling, place raspberries in a large bowl; drizzle with lemon juice and almond extract. In a small bowl, mix sugar, flour and cinnamon. Sprinkle over raspberries and toss gently to coat.
3. On a lightly floured surface, roll one half of dough to a ⅛-in.-thick circle; transfer to a 9-in. pie plate. Trim pastry even with rim. Add filling.
4. Roll remaining dough to a ⅛-in.-thick circle; cut out stars or other shapes using cookie cutters. Place top pastry over filling. Trim, seal and flute edge. If desired, decorate top with cutouts.
5. Bake 40 minutes. For topping, mix sugar and cinnamon. Brush top of pie with milk; sprinkle with sugar mixture. Bake 15-20 minutes longer or until crust is golden brown and filling is bubbly. Cool on a wire rack.

Deviled Eggs with Bacon

These yummy deviled eggs went over so well at our summer cookouts, I started making them for holiday dinners as well. Everyone likes the crunchy addition of crumbled bacon.
—BARBARA REID MOUNDS, OK

START TO FINISH: 30 MIN. • **MAKES:** 2 DOZEN

- 12 **hard-cooked eggs**
- ⅓ **cup mayonnaise**
- 3 **bacon strips, cooked and crumbled**
- 3 **tablespoons finely chopped red onion**
- 3 **tablespoons sweet pickle relish**
- ¼ **teaspoon smoked paprika**

Cut eggs in half lengthwise. Remove yolks; set whites aside. In a small bowl, mash yolks. Add the mayonnaise, bacon, onion and relish; mix well. Stuff into egg whites. Refrigerate until serving. Sprinkle with paprika.

Bacon & Egg Potato Salad

Bacon & Egg Potato Salad

Vinegar and lemon juice add a slightly tangy taste to this creamy potato salad. It's wonderful with baked beans and barbecue.
—**MELISSA DAVIES** CLERMONT, FL

PREP: 15 MIN. • **COOK:** 25 MIN. + CHILLING
MAKES: 8 SERVINGS

- 6 **cups cubed red potatoes (about 2½ pounds)**
- 4 **hard-cooked eggs, sliced**
- 1 **small onion, chopped**
- 4 **bacon strips, cooked and crumbled**
- 1 **tablespoon minced fresh parsley**
- 1 **cup mayonnaise**
- 2 **tablespoons dill pickle relish**
- 3 **to 5 teaspoons prepared mustard**
- 1 **tablespoon white vinegar**
- 1 **tablespoon lemon juice**
- ½ **teaspoon salt**
- ½ **teaspoon celery seed**
- ½ **teaspoon dill weed**
- ½ **teaspoon pepper**

1. Place potatoes in a Dutch oven; cover with water. Bring to a boil. Reduce heat; cover and cook for 10-15 minutes or until tender. Drain and cool.

2. Place potatoes in a large bowl. Add the eggs, onion, bacon and parsley. In a small bowl, combine the mayonnaise, relish, mustard, vinegar, lemon juice and seasonings. Pour over potato mixture and toss gently to coat. Refrigerate until chilled.

Lemony Grilled Chicken

Lemon juice, onions and garlic add tangy flavor to this classic main course.
—**MIKE SCHULZ** TAWAS CITY, MI

PREP: 20 MIN. + MARINATING • **GRILL:** 30 MIN.
MAKES: 8 SERVINGS

- 1 **cup olive oil**
- ⅔ **cup lemon juice**
- 6 **garlic cloves, minced**
- 1 **teaspoon salt**
- ½ **teaspoon pepper**
- 2 **medium onions, chopped**
- 8 **chicken drumsticks (2 pounds)**
- 8 **bone-in chicken thighs (2 pounds)**

1. In a small bowl, whisk the first five ingredients until blended; stir in onions. Pour 1½ cups marinade into a large resealable plastic bag. Add chicken; seal bag and turn to coat. Refrigerate overnight. Cover and refrigerate remaining marinade.

2. Prepare grill for indirect heat. Drain chicken, discarding marinade in bag. Place chicken on grill rack, skin side up. Grill, covered, over indirect medium heat 15 minutes. Turn; grill 15-20 minutes longer or until a thermometer reads 170°-175°, basting occasionally with reserved marinade.

" I really enjoyed this. I added 1 tablespoon Italian seasoning. It added a little extra oomph! "
—**TSUOP** TASTEOFHOME.COM

Lemony Grilled Chicken

Firecracker Cupcakes

These no-fuss treats are so much fun to make with kids, and they put a spark in Fourth of July parties. You can tint the whipped topping red and blue to make the frosting festive, too.

—**ERIN GLASS** WHITE HALL, MD

START TO FINISH: 30 MIN. • **MAKES:** 2 DOZEN

- 5 pieces red pull-and-peel licorice
- 6 drops red food coloring
- 1 cup flaked coconut, divided
- 4 drops blue food coloring
- 1 carton (12 ounces) frozen whipped topping, thawed
- 24 cupcakes of your choice
  Assorted red and blue sprinkles, optional

1. Cut each licorice twist into five pieces; pull apart one end of each to make firecracker fuses. Set aside.

2. In a resealable plastic bag, combine ¼ teaspoon water and red food coloring; add ½ cup coconut. Seal bag and shake to tint coconut. In another bag, combine ¼ teaspoon water and blue food coloring; add remaining coconut. Seal bag and shake to tint.

3. Spread whipped topping over cupcakes; decorate with coconut or sprinkles as desired. Insert firecracker fuses into tops. Refrigerate until serving.

Garden Veg Salsa

Firecracker Cupcakes

Garden Veg Salsa

We love this salsa made mostly with fresh garden vegetables. It's healthy, and you can easily adjust the ingredients to suit your own tastes.

—**DAWN GILSON** DENMARK, WI

PREP: 20 MIN. • **MAKES:** 6 CUPS

- 3 large tomatoes, chopped
- 1 cup chopped cucumber
- 1 medium sweet yellow or red pepper, chopped
- ¾ cup chopped zucchini
- 1 small red onion, finely chopped
- ½ cup chopped fresh cilantro
- 1 jalapeno pepper, seeded and finely chopped
- 2 tablespoons olive oil
- 1 tablespoon white vinegar
- ¾ teaspoon pepper
- ½ teaspoon salt
- ½ teaspoon ground cumin
  Tortilla chips

In a large bowl, combine all ingredients; toss to combine. Refrigerate, covered, until serving. Serve with chips.

NOTE *Wear disposable gloves when cutting hot peppers; the oils can burn skin. Avoid touching your face.*

66 This salsa is awesome! So good we ate it as a side dish without the tortilla chips. 99

—WITTWER
TASTEOFHOME.COM

Crisp and Nutty Mix

On those busy days when you're running on the track or running to class, this mixture of dried fruit, cereal, nuts and more is the ultimate combination for munching.

—**MIKE TCHOU** PEPPER PIKE, OH

START TO FINISH: 20 MIN. • **MAKES:** 2 QUARTS

- 1 cup Wheat Chex
- 1 cup Multi Grain Cheerios
- 1 cup reduced-fat Triscuits, broken
- 1 cup yogurt-covered pretzels
- ½ cup blanched almonds
- ½ cup dried apples, chopped
- ½ cup dried banana chips
- ½ cup dried blueberries
- ½ cup salted cashews
- ½ cup dark chocolate M&M's
- ⅓ cup finely shredded unsweetened coconut
- ⅓ cup sunflower kernels
- ⅓ cup salted pumpkin seeds or pepitas

In a large bowl, combine all ingredients. Store in an airtight container.

NOTE *Look for unsweetened coconut in the baking or health food section.*

Minted Fruit Salad

Filled with the season's best and freshest fruit, this salad shouts "summer." The hint of mint adds a refreshing note to the colorful compote.

—**EDIE DESPAIN** LOGAN, UT

PREP: 20 MIN. + COOLING • **MAKES:** 6 SERVINGS

- 1 cup unsweetened apple juice
- 2 tablespoons honey
- 4 teaspoons finely chopped crystallized ginger
- 4 teaspoons lemon juice
- 4 cups cantaloupe balls
- 1 cup sliced fresh strawberries
- 1 cup fresh blueberries
- 2 teaspoons chopped fresh mint leaves

1. In a small saucepan, combine the apple juice, honey, ginger and lemon juice. Bring to a boil over medium-high heat. Cook and stir for 2 minutes or until mixture is reduced to ¾ cup. Remove from the heat. Cool.

2. In a serving bowl, combine the cantaloupe, strawberries, blueberries and mint. Drizzle with cooled apple juice mixture; gently toss to coat.

Grilled Cheese & Tomato Flatbreads

This is a combination of grilled pizza and a cheesy flatbread recipe I discovered years ago. It's a great appetizer or main dish.

—**TINA REPAK MIRILOVICH** JOHNSTOWN, PA

PREP: 30 MIN. • **GRILL:** 5 MIN.
MAKES: 2 FLATBREADS (12 SERVINGS EACH)

- 1 package (8 ounces) cream cheese, softened
- ⅔ cup grated Parmesan cheese, divided
- 2 tablespoons minced fresh parsley, divided
- 1 tablespoon minced chives
- 2 garlic cloves, minced
- ½ teaspoon minced fresh thyme
- ¼ teaspoon salt
- ¼ teaspoon pepper
- 1 tube (13.8 ounces) refrigerated pizza crust
- 2 tablespoons olive oil
- 3 medium tomatoes, thinly sliced

1. In a small bowl, beat the cream cheese, ⅓ cup Parmesan cheese, 1 tablespoon parsley, chives, garlic, thyme, salt and pepper until blended.

2. Unroll pizza crust and cut in half. On a lightly floured surface, roll out each portion into a 12x6-in. rectangle; brush each side with oil. Grill, covered, over medium heat for 1-2 minutes or until bottoms are lightly browned. Remove from the grill.

3. Spread grilled sides with cheese mixture. Sprinkle with remaining Parmesan cheese; top with tomatoes. Return to the grill. Cover and cook for 2-3 minutes or until crust is lightly browned and cheese is melted, rotating halfway through cooking to ensure an evenly browned crust. Sprinkle with remaining parsley.

Crisp and Nutty Mix

All-American Bacon Cheeseburgers

> 66 Tried this recipe during the 4th of July weekend, they were fantastic! 99
> —VKRUZIN
> TASTEOFHOME.COM

All-American Bacon Cheeseburgers

Where can you get a juicy bacon cheeseburger that is so superior to drive-thru fare? Right in your backyard with this delicious recipe.

—**JACKIE BURNS** KETTLE FALLS, WA

START TO FINISH: 30 MIN. • **MAKES:** 4 SERVINGS

- 2 tablespoons finely chopped onion
- 2 tablespoons ketchup
- 1 garlic clove, minced
- 1 teaspoon sugar
- 1 teaspoon Worcestershire sauce
- 1 teaspoon steak sauce
- ¼ teaspoon cider vinegar
- 1 pound ground beef
- 4 slices sharp cheddar cheese
- 4 hamburger buns, split and toasted
- 8 cooked bacon strips
  Optional toppings: lettuce leaves and tomato, onion and pickle slices

1. In a large bowl, combine the first seven ingredients. Crumble beef over mixture and mix well. Shape into four patties.

2. Grill burgers, covered, over medium heat or broil 3 in. from the heat for 4-7 minutes on each side or until a thermometer reads 160° and juices run clear. Top with cheese. Grill 1 minute longer or until cheese is melted. Serve on buns with bacon and toppings of your choice.

TOP TIP

Hamburger Hints

Hamburgers are one of the easiest entrees to prepare. To keep burgers moist, first combine the filling ingredients, then add the meat and mix just until combined. Overmixing can cause the burgers to be dense and heavy. Ground sirloin makes the leanest burgers, then ground round, ground chuck and, lastly, ground beef.

Patriotic Pops

My kids love homemade ice pops, and I love knowing that the ones we make are good for them. We whip up a big batch with multiple flavors so they have many choices, but these patriotic red, white and blue ones are always a favorite!

—SHANNON CARINO FRISCO, TX

PREP: 15 MIN. + FREEZING • **MAKES:** 1 DOZEN

- 1¼ **cups sliced fresh strawberries, divided**
- 1¾ **cups (14 ounces) vanilla yogurt, divided**
- 1¼ **cups fresh or frozen blueberries, divided**
- 12 **freezer pop molds or 12 paper cups (3 ounces each) and wooden pop sticks**

1. In a blender, combine 1 cup strawberries and 2 tablespoons yogurt; cover and process until blended. Transfer to a bowl. Chop remaining strawberries; stir into strawberry mixture.

2. In same blender, combine 1 cup blueberries and 2 tablespoons yogurt; cover and process until blended. Stir in remaining blueberries.

3. Layer 1 tablespoon strawberry mixture, 2 tablespoons yogurt and 1 tablespoon blueberry mixture in each of 12 molds or paper cups. Top molds with holders. If using cups, top with foil and insert sticks through foil. Freeze until firm.

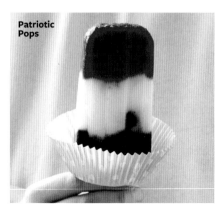

Patriotic Pops

Three-Bean Salad

Three-Bean Salad

Herbs and cayenne pepper provide the fantastic flavor in my marinated salad featuring fresh veggies and canned beans.

—CAROL TUCKER WOOSTER, OH

PREP: 20 MIN. + CHILLING • **MAKES:** 8 SERVINGS

- 1 **can (15½ ounces) great northern beans, rinsed and drained**
- 1 **can (15 ounces) garbanzo beans or chickpeas, rinsed and drained**
- 1 **can (15 ounces) black beans, rinsed and drained**
- 1 **medium tomato, chopped**
- 1 **medium onion, chopped**
- 1 **celery rib, chopped**
- ⅓ **cup each chopped green, sweet red and yellow pepper**
- ½ **cup water**
- 3 **tablespoons minced fresh basil or 1 tablespoon dried basil**
- 2 **tablespoons minced fresh parsley**
- 2 **tablespoons lemon juice**
- 2 **tablespoons olive oil**
- 1½ **teaspoons minced fresh oregano or ½ teaspoon dried oregano**
- ½ **teaspoon salt**
- ½ **teaspoon pepper**
- ¼ **teaspoon cayenne pepper**

In a large bowl, combine the beans, tomato, onion, celery and peppers. In a small bowl, whisk the remaining ingredients; gently stir into bean mixture. Cover and refrigerate for 4 hours, stirring occasionally.

DEVON DELANEY'S CHILI-RUBBED STEAK & BREAD SALAD *PAGE 121*

Pool Party

WHO'S READY FOR A POOL PARTY? BEAT THE HEAT, AND THE KITCHEN CLOCK, WITH THE FOLLOWING DISHES JUST PERFECT FOR POOLSIDE FUN. SERVE UP SPECIALTY BEVERAGES, REFRESHING SALADS OR FROZEN DESSERTS FOR GUARANTEED FUN IN THE SUN.

STACEY JOHNSON'S FRESH MOZZARELLA SANDWICHES *PAGE 119*

MELISSA MILLWOOD'S FROZEN KEY LIME DELIGHT *PAGE 118*

PAMELA VITTI KNOWLES' PINEAPPLE RUM PUNCH *PAGE 116*

Pineapple Rum Punch

I created this with my favorite Bahamian juices. I got the inspiration for it from other Bahama punches I have sampled.

—**PAMELA VITTI KNOWLES**
HENDERSONVILLE, NC

PREP: 10 MIN. • **MAKES:** 12 SERVINGS

- 3½ cups unsweetened pineapple juice
- 1½ cups orange juice
- 1 cup coconut water
- 1 cup coconut rum
- 1 cup orange peach mango juice
- 1 cup dark rum
- ¼ cup Key lime juice
- 3 tablespoons Campari liqueur or grenadine syrup

In a pitcher, combine all ingredients. Serve over ice.

---

⑤ INGREDIENTS

Simple Lemon Fruit Dip

My husband's a construction worker, and this is a great treat to put in his lunch with whatever fresh fruit he wants. It keeps all week in the fridge.

—**MEGAN WILKINSON** MORGAN, UT

START TO FINISH: 5 MIN. • **MAKES:** 1⅔ CUPS

- 1 cup cold milk
- 1 package (3.4 ounces) instant lemon pudding mix
- 1 cup (8 ounces) sour cream
  Assorted fresh fruit

In a small bowl, whisk milk and pudding mix for 2 minutes (mixture will be thick). Whisk in sour cream. Chill until serving. Serve with fruit.

> ❝ Lemon fruit dip is simple and easy to make and tastes so good! ❞
>
> —TKARINAS
> TASTEOFHOME.COM

Strawberry-Chicken Pasta Salad

Strawberry-Chicken Pasta Salad

When I figured out how to re-create this restaurant dish at home, my family was so excited. For a different spin, use raspberries or peaches instead of strawberries.

—**JANE OZMENT** PURCELL, OK

PREP: 25 MIN. • **GRILL:** 15 MIN.
MAKES: 4 SERVINGS

- ½ cup sliced fresh strawberries
- 1 tablespoon sugar
- 1 tablespoon balsamic vinegar
- ½ teaspoon salt, divided
- ¼ teaspoon pepper, divided
- 3 tablespoons olive oil
- 4 boneless skinless chicken breast halves (6 ounces each)

ASSEMBLY

- 1 package (10 ounces) hearts of romaine salad mix
- 1 cup cooked gemelli or spiral pasta
- 1 small red onion, halved and thinly sliced
- 1 cup sliced fresh strawberries
- ½ cup glazed pecans

1. Place strawberries, sugar, vinegar, ¼ teaspoon salt and ⅛ teaspoon pepper in a blender; cover and process until smooth. While processing, gradually add oil in a steady stream. Refrigerate until serving.

2. Moisten a paper towel with cooking oil; using long-handled tongs, rub on grill rack to coat lightly. Sprinkle chicken with remaining salt and pepper; grill, covered, over medium heat 6-8 minutes on each side or until a thermometer reads 165°.

3. Cut chicken into slices. Divide salad mix among four plates; top with pasta, onion, chicken and strawberries. Drizzle with vinaigrette; sprinkle with pecans.

Watermelon Salsa

I threw this together after an overzealous trip to the farmers market! My family loved it from the first bite. You can serve it right away, but the best flavor is achieved by letting the salsa rest in the refrigerator for a few hours.

—ANDREA HEYART AUBREY, TX

START TO FINISH: 25 MIN.
MAKES: 15 SERVINGS (⅓ CUP EACH)

- ¼ **cup lime juice**
- 3 **tablespoons brown sugar**
- 2 **tablespoons cider vinegar**
- 1 **tablespoon honey**
- ¼ **teaspoon salt**
- 3 **cups seeded chopped watermelon**
- 1 **medium cucumber, seeded and chopped**
- 1 **small red onion, finely chopped**
- 2 **jalapeno peppers, seeded and finely chopped**
- ¼ **cup finely chopped sweet yellow pepper**
- ¼ **cup minced fresh cilantro**
- 2 **tablespoons minced fresh basil**

In a large bowl, combine the first five ingredients. Add remaining ingredients; toss to combine. Refrigerate, covered, until serving. If necessary, drain salsa before serving.

Watermelon Salsa

Ladyfinger Ice Cream Cake

FREEZE IT
Ladyfinger Ice Cream Cake

No one will believe how easy it was to create this show-stopping cake. On a hot summer day, it will melt all resistance to dessert—one cool, creamy slice at a time.

—BARBARA MCCALLEY ALLISON PARK, PA

PREP: 25 MIN. + FREEZING • **MAKES:** 16 SERVINGS

- 2 **packages (3 ounces each) ladyfingers, split**
- 3 **cups vanilla ice cream, softened**
- 1 **jar (16 ounces) hot fudge ice cream topping**
- 1 **package (8 ounces) toffee bits**
- 3 **cups chocolate ice cream, softened**
- 3 **cups coffee ice cream, softened**

1. Arrange ladyfingers around the edge and on the bottom of a 9-in. springform pan coated with cooking spray.
2. Spoon vanilla ice cream into prepared pan. Top with a third of the ice cream topping and toffee bits. Freeze for 20 minutes. Repeat layers, using chocolate and coffee ice cream (pan will be full). Freeze overnight or until firm.

Garden-Fresh
Chef Salad

FREEZE IT

Frozen Key Lime Delight

Nothing hits the spot quite like this sublime Key lime dessert.

—MELISSA MILLWOOD LYMAN, SC

PREP: 50 MIN. • **BAKE:** 25 MIN. + FREEZING
MAKES: 8 SERVINGS

- 1 cup all-purpose flour
- ½ cup salted cashews, chopped
- ½ cup flaked coconut
- ¼ cup packed light brown sugar
- ½ cup butter, melted
- 2 cups heavy whipping cream
- 1½ cups sweetened condensed milk
- 1 cup Key lime juice
- 3 teaspoons grated Key lime peel
- 1 teaspoon vanilla extract
  Whipped cream and Key lime slices

1. Preheat oven to 350°. In a small bowl, combine flour, cashews, coconut and brown sugar. Stir in butter. Sprinkle into a greased 15x10x1-in. baking pan. Bake 20-25 minutes or until golden brown, stirring once. Cool on a wire rack.
2. Meanwhile, in a large bowl, combine cream, milk, lime juice, peel and vanilla. Refrigerate until chilled.
3. Fill cylinder of ice cream freezer two-thirds full; freeze according to the manufacturer's directions.
4. Sprinkle half the cashew mixture into an ungreased 11x7-in. dish. Spread ice cream over top; sprinkle with remaining cashew mixture. Cover and freeze 4 hours or until firm. Garnish servings with whipped cream and lime slices.

Frozen Key
Lime Delight

Garden-Fresh Chef Salad

For a good part of the year, I can use my garden's produce when I make this cool salad. In spring, it's salad mix and radishes, and in summer, we have tomatoes, cabbage and carrots. What a great feeling!

—EVELYN GUBERNATH BUCYRUS, OH

START TO FINISH: 25 MIN. • **MAKES:** 6 SERVINGS

- 6 cups spring mix salad greens
- 2 medium tomatoes, coarsely chopped
- 6 hard-cooked eggs, coarsely chopped
- 3 slices deli turkey, cut into thin strips
- 3 slices deli ham, cut into thin strips
- ½ cup shredded cabbage
- 4 green onions, sliced
- 4 fresh baby carrots, sliced
- 4 radishes, thinly sliced
- ¼ teaspoon garlic powder
- ¼ teaspoon pepper
- ½ cup reduced-fat Thousand Island salad dressing or dressing of your choice

In a large bowl, combine the first nine ingredients. Sprinkle with garlic powder and pepper; toss to coat. Serve with salad dressing.

⑤INGREDIENTS

Smooth Sweet Tea

A pinch of baking soda eliminates bitterness in this smooth and easy-to-sip tea. It has just the right amount of sugar so it's not overly sweet. Try it and see!

—KELSEYLOUISE TASTEOFHOME.COM

PREP: 15 MIN. + CHILLING • **MAKES:** 7 SERVINGS

- 2 cups water
- 6 individual black tea bags
- ⅛ teaspoon baking soda
- ⅔ cup sugar
- 6 cups cold water

1. In a small saucepan, bring 2 cups of water to a boil. Remove from the heat; add tea bags. Cover and steep for 10 minutes. Discard tea bags.
2. Sprinkle baking soda into a 2-qt. pitcher. Transfer tea to pitcher; stir in sugar. Add cold water. Refrigerate tea until chilled.

Rainbow Spritzer

Layers of colorful fruit submerged in a fizzy, sweet beverage make this a kid-friendly sipper that gets two thumbs up.
—**WENDY HERR** O'FALLON, MO

START TO FINISH: 20 MIN. • **MAKES:** 4 SERVINGS

- ½ cup fresh blueberries
- ½ cup chopped peeled kiwifruit
- ½ cup chopped fresh pineapple
- ½ cup sliced fresh strawberries or fresh raspberries
- 1 cup chilled ginger ale
- ½ cup chilled unsweetened pineapple juice
- ½ cup chilled lemonade

In four tall glasses, layer blueberries, kiwi, pineapple and strawberries. In a 2-cup glass measure or small pitcher, mix remaining ingredients; pour over fruit. Serve immediately.

Fresh Mozzarella Sandwiches

We love this fast, fresh sandwich, especially when it's too warm to turn on the oven. I like to pair it with a fruity white wine and pasta salad or fancy potato chips. We often add avocado to the sandwiches and in the summer, use fresh Walla Walla onions.
—**STACEY JOHNSON** TACOMA, WA

START TO FINISH: 15 MIN. • **MAKES:** 4 SERVINGS

- 8 slices sourdough bread, toasted
- ¼ cup wasabi mayonnaise
- ½ pound fresh mozzarella cheese, sliced
- 2 medium tomatoes, sliced
- 4 thin slices sweet onion
- 8 fresh basil leaves

Spread toast with mayonnaise. On four slices, layer with cheese, tomatoes, onion and basil; top with remaining toast.

Rainbow Spritzer

Cobb Salad

Cobb Salad

Made on the fly by Hollywood restaurateur Bob Cobb in 1937, the Cobb salad now is a world-famous American dish. Here's a fresh take, with all the original appeal and an extra-special presentation.
—*TASTE OF HOME* TEST KITCHEN

START TO FINISH: 40 MIN.
MAKES: 6 SERVINGS (1¼ CUPS DRESSING)

- ¼ cup red wine vinegar
- 2 teaspoons salt
- 1 teaspoon lemon juice
- 1 small garlic clove, minced
- ¾ teaspoon coarsely ground pepper
- ¾ teaspoon Worcestershire sauce
- ¼ teaspoon sugar
- ¼ teaspoon ground mustard
- ¾ cup canola oil
- ¼ cup olive oil

SALAD

- 6½ cups torn romaine
- 2½ cups torn curly endive
- 1 bunch watercress (4 ounces), trimmed, divided

- 2 cooked chicken breasts, chopped
- 2 medium tomatoes, seeded and chopped
- 1 medium ripe avocado, peeled and chopped
- 3 hard-cooked eggs, chopped
- ½ cup crumbled blue or Roquefort cheese
- 6 bacon strips, cooked and crumbled
- 2 tablespoons minced fresh chives

1. In a blender, combine the first eight ingredients. While processing, gradually add canola and olive oils in a steady stream.

2. In a large bowl, combine romaine, endive and half of the watercress; toss lightly. Transfer to a serving platter. Arrange the chicken, tomatoes, avocado, eggs, cheese and bacon over the greens; sprinkle with chives. Top with remaining watercress. Cover and chill until serving.

3. To serve, drizzle 1 cup dressing over salad. Serve with remaining dressing if desired.

Sunshine Cupcakes

Cute, easy and fun, these cheery lemon cupcakes will bring smiles all summer long.
—*TASTE OF HOME* TEST KITCHEN

PREP: 20 MIN. • **BAKE:** 20 MIN. + COOLING
MAKES: 2 DOZEN

- 1 package lemon cake mix (regular size)
- 1 can (16 ounces) vanilla frosting
  Yellow food coloring
  Miniature semisweet chocolate chips, red shoestring licorice and candy corn

1. Prepare cake batter mix according to package directions for cupcakes; cool completely.

2. In a small bowl, tint frosting yellow. Frost cupcakes. Press two chocolate chips into each cupcake for eyes. For mouths, cut licorice into 1-in. pieces; bent slightly to curve. Press one licorice piece into each cupcake. Add candy corn around edges of cupcakes.

Sunshine Cupcakes

Chili-Rubbed Steak & Bread Salad

We love skirt steak in our house. To make it a meal, I created a ranch-inspired bread salad with the best flavor combinations—creamy, tangy, sweet and fresh.
—**DEVON DELANEY** WESTPORT, CT

PREP: 35 MIN. + STANDING • **GRILL:** 15 MIN.
MAKES: 6 SERVINGS

- 2 **teaspoons chili powder**
- 2 **teaspoons brown sugar**
- ½ **teaspoon salt**
- ½ **teaspoon pepper**
- 1 **beef top sirloin steak (1 inch thick and 1¼ pounds)**
- 2 **cups cubed multigrain bread**
- 2 **tablespoons olive oil**
- 1 **cup ranch salad dressing**
- 2 **tablespoons finely grated horseradish**
- 1 **tablespoon prepared mustard**
- 3 **large tomatoes, cut into 1-inch pieces**
- 1 **medium cucumber, cut into 1-inch pieces**
- 1 **small red onion, halved and thinly sliced**

1. Mix chili powder, brown sugar, salt and pepper; rub over steak. Let stand for 15 minutes.

2. Meanwhile, toss bread cubes with oil. In a large skillet, toast bread over medium heat 8-10 minutes or until crisp and lightly browned, stirring frequently. In a small bowl, whisk salad dressing, horseradish and mustard.

3. Grill steak, covered, over medium heat or broil 4 in. from heat 6-8 minutes on each side or until meat reaches desired doneness (for medium-rare, a thermometer should read 145°; medium, 160°; well-done, 170°). Let stand for 5 minutes.

4. In a large bowl, combine tomatoes, cucumber, onion and toasted bread. Add ½ cup dressing mixture; toss to coat. Slice steak; serve with salad and the remaining dressing.

Loaded Grilled Chicken Sandwich

Loaded Grilled Chicken Sandwich

I threw these ingredients together on a whim, and the sandwich turned out so well, I surprised myself! If you're in a rush, microwave the bacon. Just cover it with a white paper towel to keep the grease from splattering too much.
—**DANA YORK** KENNEWICK, WA

START TO FINISH: 30 MIN. • **MAKES:** 4 SERVINGS

- 4 **boneless skinless chicken breast halves (4 ounces each)**
- 2 **teaspoons Italian salad dressing mix**
- 4 **slices pepper jack cheese**
- 4 **ciabatta or kaiser rolls, split**
- 2 **tablespoons mayonnaise**
- ¾ **teaspoon Dijon mustard**
- 4 **cooked bacon strips, halved**
- 4 **slices tomato**
- ½ **medium ripe avocado, peeled and thinly sliced**
- ½ **pound deli coleslaw (about 1 cup)**

1. Pound chicken with a meat mallet to flatten slightly; sprinkle both sides with dressing mix. Moisten a paper towel with cooking oil; using long-handled tongs, rub on grill rack to coat lightly.

2. Grill chicken, covered, over medium heat or broil 4 in. from heat 4-6 minutes on each side or until a thermometer reads 165°. Place cheese on chicken; grill, covered, 1-2 minutes longer or until cheese is melted. Meanwhile, grill rolls, cut side down, 1-2 minutes or until toasted.

3. Mix mayonnaise and mustard; spread on roll tops. Layer roll bottoms with chicken, bacon, tomato, avocado and coleslaw. Replace tops.

TOP TIP

Keeping Cool by the Pool

Hosting a pool party is a snap. Remember to keep the menu light and refreshing with salads and salsas. Hand-held bites such as sandwiches, kabobs and tacos are also a hit. You might want to make bottled water available to guests in case the temperature climbs during the get-together.

SUZANNE BANFIELD'S
JERSEY-STYLE HOT DOGS *PAGE 128*

Block Party

HIT THE STREETS—FOR A BLOCK PARTY, THAT IS! SUMMER IS A GREAT TIME TO GET TOGETHER WITH NEIGHBORS AND HAVE A LITTLE FUN. THE FOODS THAT FOLLOW MAKE WONDERFUL CONTRIBUTIONS TO OUTDOOR EVENTS BECAUSE THEY TRAVEL WELL AND PLEASE A VARIETY OF TASTES. LET THE GOOD TIMES ROLL!

RITA COMBS' TUSCAN BURGERS WITH PESTO MAYO *PAGE 126*

ANGELA SMITH'S LAYERED GRILLED CORN SALAD *PAGE 127*

LISA LINVILLE'S COLA HOT WINGS *PAGE 126*

Cowboy Baked Beans

Baked beans are a perennial favorite at block parties. My recipe uses a variety of beans and has a great smoky taste. You could even serve them in a slow cooker.
—**JOE SHERWOOD** TRYON, NE

PREP: 25 MIN. • **BAKE:** 50 MIN
MAKES: 12 SERVINGS (¾ CUP EACH)

- 1 **pound ground beef**
- 1 **pound bacon, cooked and crumbled**
- 2 **cups barbecue sauce**
- 1 **can (16 ounces) butter beans, rinsed and drained**
- 1 **can (15¾ ounces) pork and beans**
- 1 **can (15½ ounces) navy beans, rinsed and drained**
- 1 **can (15 ounces) black beans, rinsed and drained**
- 2 **medium onions, chopped**
- ¼ **cup packed brown sugar**
- ¼ **cup molasses**
- 2 **tablespoons balsamic vinegar**
- 2 **teaspoons ground mustard**
- 2 **teaspoons Worcestershire sauce**
- 1 **teaspoon salt**
- 1 **teaspoon garlic powder**
- 1 **teaspoon pepper**

Preheat oven to 350°. In a Dutch oven, cook beef over medium heat until no longer pink; drain. Stir in the remaining ingredients. Transfer to a greased 13x9-in. baking dish. Bake, uncovered, 50-60 minutes or until heated through.

Cowboy Baked Beans

Green Flop Jell-O

⑤ INGREDIENTS
Green Flop Jell-O

Get ready for fluffy lemon-lime goodness. Try it with any flavor gelatin.
—**MICHELLE GAUER** SPICER, MN

PREP: 15 MIN. + CHILLING
MAKES: 16 SERVINGS (¾ CUP EACH)

- 2 **cups lemon-lime soda**
- 2 **packages (3 ounces each) lime gelatin**
- 6 **ounces cream cheese, softened**
- 2 **cups lemon-lime soda, chilled**
- 1 **carton (12 ounces) frozen whipped topping, thawed**

1. Microwave 2 cups soda on high for 1-2 minutes or until hot. Place hot soda and gelatin in a blender; cover and process until gelatin is dissolved. Add cream cheese; process until blended.
2. Transfer to a large bowl; stir in chilled soda. Whisk in whipped topping. Pour into a 3-qt. trifle bowl or glass bowl. Refrigerate, covered, for 4 hours or until firm.

White Wine Sangria

Lime, kumquats and two kinds of oranges infuse this quick and easy cocktail with an unforgettable citrus flair.
—**JOYCE MOYNIHAN** LAKEVILLE, MN

PREP: 10 MIN. + CHILLING
MAKES: 18 SERVINGS (3½ QUARTS)

- 3 **bottles (750 milliliters each) white wine**
- 1½ **cups brandy**
- ¾ **cup orange liqueur**
- ½ **cup sugar**
- 1 **large navel orange, sliced**
- 1 **medium blood orange, sliced**
- 3 **kumquats, sliced**
- 1 **medium lime, sliced**

In a large pitcher, combine wine, brandy and liqueur. Stir in sugar until dissolved. Add remaining ingredients. Refrigerate 1 hour before serving. Serve over ice.

Caramelized Apple Hand Pies

Caramelized apples are tucked in a handheld pie that no one expects you to share!

—EDWINA GADSBY HAYDEN, ID

PREP: 25 MIN. + COOLING • **BAKE:** 20 MIN.
MAKES: 8 SERVINGS

- 2 **tablespoons unsalted butter**
- 3 **medium apples, peeled and finely chopped**
- ⅓ **cup packed brown sugar**
- ½ **teaspoon cornstarch**
- ⅛ **teaspoon ground cinnamon**
- 1 **teaspoon lemon juice**
- ½ **teaspoon vanilla extract**
- 1 **package (14.1 ounces) refrigerated pie pastry**

TOPPING
- ¼ **cup coarse sugar**
- 1 **teaspoon ground cinnamon**
- 3 **tablespoons unsalted butter, melted**
  Vanilla ice cream, optional

1. In a large skillet, heat butter over medium heat. Add apples; cook and stir 5 minutes. Mix brown sugar, cornstarch and cinnamon; add to apples. Cook and stir 7-8 minutes longer or until apples begin to soften and caramelize. Remove from heat; stir in lemon juice and vanilla. Cool completely.

2. Preheat oven to 400°. On a lightly floured surface, unroll pastry sheets. Roll to ⅛-in. thickness; cut four 5-in. circles from each sheet. Place about 3 tablespoons filling on one half of each circle. Moisten pastry edges with water. Fold pastry over filling. Press edges with a fork to seal or, if desired, pinch edges to seal and flute.

3. Transfer to greased baking sheets. Prick tops of pastry with a fork. Bake 20-25 minutes or until golden brown. Remove from pans to wire racks.

4. For topping, mix sugar and cinnamon. Brush pies with melted butter; sprinkle with cinnamon-sugar. Serve warm or at room temperature. If desired, top with ice cream.

Caramelized Apple Hand Pies

Cola Hot Wings

These delectable wings are so easy to make, and they offer year-round versatility, from summer cookouts to autumn tailgates. My husband likes them so much he'll stand out in the snow to grill them!
—**LISA LINVILLE** RANDOLPH, NE

PREP: 15 MIN. • **GRILL:** 40 MIN.
MAKES: ABOUT 2½ DOZEN

- 3 **pounds chicken wings**
- 1 **cup Louisiana-style hot sauce**
- 1 **can (12 ounces) cola**
- 1 **tablespoon soy sauce**
- ¼ **teaspoon cayenne pepper**
- ¼ **teaspoon pepper**
  Blue cheese salad dressing

1. Cut chicken wings into three sections; discard wing tip sections. In a small bowl, combine hot sauce, cola, soy sauce, cayenne and pepper.
2. Prepare grill for indirect heat, using a drip pan. Moisten a paper towel with cooking oil; using long-handled tongs, rub on grill rack to coat lightly. Grill chicken wings, covered, over indirect medium heat 10 minutes. Grill 30-40 minutes longer, turning occasionally and basting frequently with sauce until wings are nicely glazed. Serve with salad dressing.
NOTE *Uncooked chicken wing sections (wingettes) may be substituted for whole chicken wings.*

TOP TIP

Basting Secret

When you are grilling lots of chicken wings for a block party, barbecue or other outdoor get-together, speed up the basting process by putting the sauce in a spray bottle. Simply spray the sauce on the wings as they cook. This works best with thin sauces.
—**ANGELA ROSTER**
GREENBACKVILLE, VA

Tuscan Burgers with Pesto Mayo

Tuscan Burgers with Pesto Mayo

Everyone needs to bring their appetite when you serve these man-size burgers. They have a bit of Italy in them with the use of pancetta, pesto and mozzarella cheese. Double or triple the recipe for crowds.
—**RITA COMBS** VALDOSTA, GA

PREP: 25 MIN. • **GRILL:** 20 MIN.
MAKES: 4 SERVINGS

- ¼ **cup mayonnaise**
- ¼ **cup prepared pesto, divided**
- 3 **ounces sliced pancetta, finely chopped**
- ¼ **teaspoon pepper**
- ⅛ **teaspoon kosher salt**
- 1 **pound ground beef**
- 1 **small red onion, cut into 4 slices**
- 1 **large tomato, cut into 4 slices**
- 1 **tablespoon olive oil**
- 8 **ounces fresh mozzarella cheese, cut into 4 slices**
- 4 **Italian rolls, split**
- 1 **cup fresh arugula or fresh baby spinach**

1. In a small bowl, combine mayonnaise and 2 tablespoons pesto; cover and chill until serving. In a large bowl, combine the pancetta, pepper, salt and remaining pesto. Crumble beef over mixture and mix well. Shape into four patties.
2. Brush onion and tomato slices with oil. Grill onion over medium heat for 4-6 minutes on each side or until crisp-tender. Grill tomato for 1-2 minutes on each side or until lightly browned.
3. Grill burgers, covered, over medium heat for 5-7 minutes on each side or until a thermometer reads 160° and juices run clear. Top burgers with mozzarella cheese. Grill 1 minute longer or until cheese is melted. Spread cut sides of rolls with pesto mayonnaise; top with burgers, onion, tomato and arugula.

Cowabunga Root Beer Cupcakes

I developed these cupcakes for my daughter's first birthday, and got a lot of requests for the recipe. What a great way to dress up a boxed mix!

—**MINDY CARSWELL** WALKER, MI

PREP: 10 MIN. • **BAKE:** 15 MIN. + COOLING
MAKES: 24 SERVINGS

- 1 package butter recipe golden cake mix (regular size)
- 4 teaspoons root beer concentrate, divided
- 1 carton (12 ounces) frozen whipped topping, thawed
   Vanilla ice cream, optional

1. Prepare and bake cupcakes according to the package directions, adding 2 teaspoons root beer concentrate when mixing batter. Remove to wire racks to cool completely.
2. In a small bowl, mix whipped topping and remaining root beer concentrate until blended; spread over cupcakes. Serve with ice cream if desired.
NOTE *This recipe was tested with McCormick root beer concentrate.*

Layered Grilled Corn Salad

This has been a go-to dish for me throughout the years. It's great as a side or can be served in lettuce cups, along with warm crusty bread, for a light lunch.

—**ANGELA SMITH** BLUFFTON, SC

PREP: 15 MIN. + CHILLING • **GRILL:** 10 MIN.
MAKES: 10 SERVINGS

- 10 medium ears sweet corn, husks removed
- ¼ cup olive oil
- 1 teaspoon salt
- ¾ teaspoon coarsely ground pepper
- ¾ teaspoon crushed red pepper flakes
- 2 large tomatoes, finely chopped
- 1 medium red onion, thinly sliced
- 12 fresh basil leaves, thinly sliced
- 1 cup zesty Italian salad dressing

1. Brush corn with oil. Grill corn, covered, over medium heat 10-12 minutes or until lightly browned and tender, turning occasionally. Cool slightly.
2. Cut corn from cobs; transfer to a small bowl. Stir in salt, pepper and pepper flakes. In a 2-qt. glass bowl, layer a third of each of the following: corn, tomatoes, onion and basil. Repeat layers twice. Pour dressing over top; refrigerate at least 1 hour.

Tomatillo Salsa

Tomatillo Salsa

Dare to deviate from tomato salsa and try this tomatillo-based version for a deliciously addictive change of pace. It's fantastic on its own with tortilla chips or served as a condiment alongside a variety of meats.

—**LORI KOSTECKI** WAUSAU, WI

START TO FINISH: 20 MIN. • **MAKES:** 2¼ CUPS

- 8 tomatillos, husks removed
- 1 medium tomato, quartered
- 1 small onion, cut into chunks
- 1 jalapeno pepper, seeded
- 3 tablespoons fresh cilantro leaves
- 3 garlic cloves, peeled
- 1 tablespoon lime juice
- ½ teaspoon salt
- ¼ teaspoon ground cumin
- ⅛ teaspoon pepper
   Tortilla chips

1. In a large saucepan, bring 4 cups water to a boil. Add tomatillos. Reduce heat; simmer, uncovered, for 5 minutes. Drain.
2. Place the tomatillos, tomato, onion, jalapeno, cilantro, garlic, lime juice and seasonings in a food processor. Cover and process until blended. Serve with chips.
NOTE *Wear disposable gloves when cutting hot peppers; the oils can burn skin. Avoid touching your face.*

Cowabunga Root Beer Cupcakes

Jersey-Style Hot Dogs

Jersey-Style Hot Dogs

I grew up in northern New Jersey where this way of eating hot dogs was created. My husband never had them as a kid, but has come to love them even more than I do. The combination of ingredients and flavors is simple, but just right!

—**SUZANNE BANFIELD** BASKING RIDGE, NJ

PREP: 20 MIN. • **GRILL:** 40 MIN.
MAKES: 12 SERVINGS
(10 CUPS POTATO MIXTURE)

- 6 medium Yukon Gold potatoes (about 3 pounds), halved and thinly sliced
- 3 large sweet red peppers, thinly sliced
- 3 large onions, peeled, halved and thinly sliced
- ⅓ cup olive oil
- 6 garlic cloves, minced
- 3 teaspoons salt
- 1½ teaspoons pepper
- 12 bun-length beef hot dogs
- 12 hot dog buns, split

1. In a large bowl, combine potatoes, red peppers and onions. In a small bowl, mix oil, garlic, salt and pepper; add to potato mixture and toss to coat.

2. Transfer to two 13x9-in. disposable foil pans; cover with foil. Place pans on grill rack over medium heat; cook, covered, 30-35 minutes or until potatoes are tender. Remove from heat.

3. Grill hot dogs, covered, over medium heat 7-9 minutes or until heated through, turning occasionally. Place buns on grill, cut side down; grill until lightly toasted. Place hot dogs and potato mixture in buns. Serve with remaining potato mixture.

Backyard Red Potato Salad

Here's a potato salad that has no mayo so it's great for outdoor get-togethers, plus it looks just as good as it tastes.
—**HOLLY BAUER** WEST BEND, WI

PREP: 25 MIN. • **GRILL:** 10 MIN.
MAKES: 9 SERVINGS

- 2½ pounds small red potatoes
- 1 medium onion, cut into ½-inch slices
- ½ cup olive oil, divided
- 1 teaspoon salt, divided
- ½ teaspoon pepper, divided
- 3 tablespoons balsamic vinegar
- 2 tablespoons lemon juice
- 1 tablespoon Dijon mustard
- 2 teaspoons sugar
- 2 garlic cloves, minced
- ¼ cup minced fresh tarragon

1. Place potatoes in a large saucepan and cover with water. Bring to a boil. Reduce heat; cover and cook for 10 minutes. Drain; cool slightly. Cut each in half.
2. In a large bowl, combine the potatoes, onion, ¼ cup oil, ½ teaspoon salt and ¼ teaspoon pepper; toss to coat. Arrange vegetables, cut side down, on a grilling grid; place on a grill rack. Grill, covered, over medium heat for 8-10 minutes or until vegetables are tender and lightly browned, turning occasionally. Chop onion. Place onion and potatoes in bowl.
3. In a small bowl, whisk the vinegar, lemon juice, mustard, sugar, garlic and remaining oil, salt and pepper. Add to potato mixture; toss to coat. Sprinkle with tarragon. Serve warm or at room temperature. Refrigerate leftovers.
NOTE *If you do not have a grilling grid, use a disposable foil pan. Poke holes in the bottom of the pan with a meat fork to allow any liquid to drain.*

Caramel-Mocha Ice Cream Dessert

FREEZE IT
Caramel-Mocha Ice Cream Dessert

You can use any kind of ice cream in this frosty dessert! I personally suggest changing it up by substituting chocolate and vanilla for coffee and dulce de leche.
—**SCARLETT ELROD** NEWNAN, GA

PREP: 45 MIN. + FREEZING • **MAKES:** 20 SERVINGS

- 10 whole graham crackers
- 1 cup butter, cubed
- 1 cup packed brown sugar
- 1 cup chopped pecans

FILLING

- 1 quart dulce de leche ice cream, softened
- 1 jar (16 ounces) hot fudge ice cream topping, warmed
- 1 quart coffee ice cream, softened
- 1½ cups heavy whipping cream
- ⅓ cup coffee liqueur
  Chocolate curls

1. Preheat oven to 350°. Arrange crackers in a single layer in a greased 15x10x1-in. baking pan. In a large saucepan, melt butter over medium heat. Stir in brown sugar. Bring to a gentle boil; cook and stir for 2 minutes. Remove from the heat and stir in pecans. Pour over crackers; spread to cover crackers.
2. Bake 8-10 minutes or until bubbly. Remove to a wire rack to cool completely.
3. Crush cracker mixture into coarse crumbs; sprinkle half into an ungreased 13x9-in. dish. Spread with dulce de leche ice cream. Cover and freeze for 1 hour or until firm.
4. Drizzle with ice cream topping and sprinkle with remaining crumb mixture. Cover and freeze 30 minutes or until ice cream topping is set.
5. Spread with coffee ice cream; freeze. In a small bowl, beat cream until stiff peaks form. Fold in coffee liqueur. Spread over top of dessert. Cover and freeze 4 hours or until firm.
6. Remove from freezer 15 minutes before serving. Garnish dessert with chocolate curls.

❝Fantastic! I hate mayo so most potato salad recipes are out. I took this to a pig roast, and by the time I got to it, it was almost gone!❞
—**OLENAL** TASTEOFHOME.COM

TAMMY DAVIS'
TEXAS TABBOULEH *PAGE 132*

Family Reunion Picnic

IT'S IMPORTANT TO MAKE TIME FOR FAMILY, SO WHY NOT RECONNECT DURING A FAMILY REUNION? GATHER RELATIVES FROM ACROSS THE COUNTRY AND CELEBRATE WITH LAUGHTER, HUGS AND PLENTY OF STICK-TO-YOUR-RIBS SUMMERTIME FAVORITES.

CAROL FARNSWORTH'S PINA COLADA FRUIT SALAD *PAGE 135*

DENISE WHEELER'S PEANUT BUTTER-HAZELNUT BROWNIES *PAGE 134*

JANET HYNES' BAJA CHICKEN & SLAW SLIDERS *PAGE 135*

Summer Caviar

Summer Caviar

Who is ready to party? I love the fresh flavors, colors and convenience of this dish.
—**ELLEN FINGER** LANCASTER, PA

START TO FINISH: 25 MIN. • **MAKES:** 8 CUPS

- 2 **cans (15 ounces each) black beans, rinsed and drained**
- 2 **medium tomatoes, seeded and chopped**
- 1½ **cups frozen corn, thawed**
- 1 **medium ripe avocado, peeled and cubed**
- 1 **can (8 ounces) unsweetened pineapple chunks, drained and quartered**
- 1 **medium sweet orange pepper, chopped**
- 6 **green onions, thinly sliced**
- ½ **cup minced fresh cilantro**
- ⅓ **cup lime juice**
- 2 **tablespoons olive oil**
- 2 **tablespoons honey**
- ½ **teaspoon salt**
- ⅛ **teaspoon cayenne pepper**
  Baked tortilla chip scoops

1. In a large bowl, combine the first eight ingredients.
2. In a small bowl, whisk the lime juice, oil, honey, salt and cayenne. Pour over bean mixture; toss to coat. Serve with baked chips.

---

⑤ INGREDIENTS

Orange Lemonade

This juice is a favorite at our place. I'll often double the batch to share.
—**WENDY MASTERS** GRAND VALLEY, ON

PREP: 20 MIN. + COOLING • **MAKES:** 12 SERVINGS

- 1¾ **cups sugar**
- 2½ **cups water**
- 1½ **cups lemon juice (about 8 lemons)**
- 1½ **cups orange juice (about 5 oranges)**
- 2 **tablespoons grated lemon peel**
- 2 **tablespoons grated orange peel**
  Water

1. In a medium saucepan, combine sugar and water. Cook over medium heat until sugar is dissolved. Cool.
2. Add juices and peel to cooled sugar syrup. Cover and let stand at room temperature 1 hour. Strain syrup; cover and refrigerate.
3. To serve, fill glasses or pitcher with equal amounts of fruit syrup and water. Add ice and serve.

---

⑤ INGREDIENTS

Cheese-Stuffed Jalapenos

We make these several times throughout the summer. With gooey cheese and salty bacon, these jalapenos are irresistible!
—**BRUCE HAHNE** ACWORTH, GA

START TO FINISH: 30 MIN. • **MAKES:** 2½ DOZEN

- 8 **ounces Monterey Jack cheese, cut into 2-inch x ½-inch x ¼-inch strips**
- 15 **jalapeno peppers, halved lengthwise and seeded**
- ¼ **cup dry bread crumbs**
- ¼ **cup real bacon bits**

1. Place a cheese strip in each pepper half; sprinkle with bread crumbs and bacon bits.
2. Grill peppers, covered, over medium-hot heat for 4-6 minutes or until peppers are tender and the cheese is melted. Serve warm.
NOTE *Wear disposable gloves when cutting hot peppers; the oils can burn skin. Avoid touching your face.*

Texas Tabbouleh

This crowd-pleasing salad reminds me of traditional pico de gallo. It's always a pretty, popular dish at our gatherings.
—**TAMMY DAVIS** ARLINGTON, VA

PREP: 40 MIN. + CHILLING • **MAKES:** 10 SERVINGS

- 1 **cup bulgur**
- 2 **cups boiling water**
- 3 **medium tomatoes, chopped**
- 1 **cup finely chopped red onion**
- 2 **green onions, thinly sliced**
- ½ **cup chopped sweet red pepper**
- ½ **cup chopped green pepper**
- 2 **jalapeno peppers, seeded and chopped**
- ½ **cup fresh cilantro leaves, chopped**
- ¼ **cup lime juice**
- 3 **tablespoons canola oil**
- 2 **garlic cloves, minced**
- ¼ **teaspoon salt**
- ¼ **teaspoon coarsely ground pepper**
- 1 **can (15 ounces) black beans, rinsed and drained**
- 1 **cup (4 ounces) crumbled queso fresco or feta cheese**

1. Place bulgur in a bowl; stir in boiling water. Let stand, covered, 30 minutes or until bulgur is tender and most of the liquid is absorbed. Drain well, pressing out excess water. Cool completely.
2. Stir in tomatoes, onions, peppers, cilantro, lime juice, oil and seasonings. Add beans; toss to combine. Refrigerate, covered, at least 30 minutes. Top with crumbled cheese.
NOTE *Wear disposable gloves when cutting hot peppers; the oils can burn skin. Avoid touching your face.*

Carolina-Style Pork Barbecue

I am originally from North Carolina, where swine are divine, and this recipe for the slow cooker is a family favorite. My husband swears my authentic Carolina 'cue is the best BBQ he has ever eaten!

—KATHRYN RANSOM WILLIAMS SPARKS, NV

PREP: 30 MIN. • **COOK:** 6 HOURS
MAKES: 14 SERVINGS

- 1 **boneless pork shoulder butt roast (4 to 5 pounds)**
- 2 **tablespoons brown sugar**
- 2 **teaspoons salt**
- 1 **teaspoon paprika**
- ½ **teaspoon pepper**
- 2 **medium onions, quartered**
- ¾ **cup cider vinegar**
- 4 **teaspoons Worcestershire sauce**
- 1 **tablespoon sugar**
- 1 **tablespoon crushed red pepper flakes**
- 1 **teaspoon garlic salt**
- 1 **teaspoon ground mustard**
- ½ **teaspoon cayenne pepper**
- 14 **hamburger buns, split**
- 1¾ **pounds deli coleslaw**

1. Cut roast into quarters. Mix brown sugar, salt, paprika and pepper; rub over meat. Place meat and onions in a 5-qt. slow cooker.

2. In a small bowl, whisk vinegar, Worcestershire sauce, sugar and seasonings; pour over roast. Cook, covered, on low 6-8 hours or until meat is tender.

3. Remove roast; cool slightly. Reserve 1½ cups cooking juices; discard the remaining juices. Skim fat from reserved juices. Shred the pork with two forks. Return pork and reserved juices to slow cooker; heat through. Serve on buns with coleslaw.

Loaded-Up Pretzel Cookies

Loaded-Up Pretzel Cookies

Coconut, M&M's and salty, crunchy pretzels make these cookies unlike any you've ever tasted! No one can resist them.

—JACKIE RUCKWARDT COTTAGE GROVE, OR

PREP: 20 MIN. • **BAKE:** 15 MIN./BATCH
MAKES: 2 DOZEN

- 1 **cup butter, softened**
- 1 **cup sugar**
- 1 **cup packed brown sugar**
- 2 **eggs**
- 2 **teaspoons vanilla extract**
- 2½ **cups all-purpose flour**
- 1 **teaspoon baking powder**
- 1 **teaspoon baking soda**
- 1 **teaspoon salt**
- 2 **cups miniature pretzels, broken**
- 1½ **cups flaked coconut**
- 1½ **cups milk chocolate M&M's**

1. Preheat oven to 350°. In a large bowl, cream butter and sugars until light and fluffy. Beat in eggs and vanilla. In another bowl, whisk flour, baking powder, baking soda and salt; gradually beat into creamed mixture. Stir in remaining ingredients.

2. Shape ¼ cupfuls of dough into balls; place 3 in. apart on ungreased baking sheets. Bake 12-14 minutes or until golden brown. Remove from pans to wire racks to cool.

Carolina-Style Pork Barbecue

Peanut Butter-Hazelnut Brownies

Over the years I'd been adding this and that to my basic brownie recipe—and then I came up with this one. What a fun twist on a brownie!

—DENISE WHEELER NEWAYGO, MI

PREP: 20 MIN. • **BAKE:** 35 MIN. + COOLING
MAKES: 2 DOZEN

- 1 **cup butter, softened**
- 2 **cups sugar**
- 4 **eggs**
- 2 **teaspoons vanilla extract**
- 1 **cup all-purpose flour**
- ¾ **cup baking cocoa**
- ½ **teaspoon baking powder**
  Dash salt
- 1½ **cups coarsely crushed malted milk balls**
- ½ **cup creamy peanut butter**
- ½ **cup Nutella**

1. Preheat oven to 350°. In a large bowl, cream butter and sugar until light and fluffy. Add eggs, one at a time, beating well after each addition. Beat in vanilla. Combine the flour, cocoa, baking powder and salt; gradually add to creamed mixture. Fold in malted milk balls.

2. Spread into a greased 13x9-in. baking pan. In a small microwave-safe bowl, combine peanut butter and Nutella; cover and microwave at 50% power for 1-2 minutes or until smooth, stirring twice. Drizzle over batter; cut through batter with a knife to swirl.

3. Bake 35-40 minutes or until a toothpick inserted near the center comes out clean (do not overbake). Cool on a wire rack.

Peanut Butter - Hazelnut Brownies

Pina Colada Fruit Salad

Pina Colada Fruit Salad

Give the gang a taste of the tropics on warm summer days with this refreshing fruit blend. For a little extra punch, you might add a splash of coconut rum.

—CAROL FARNSWORTH GREENWOOD, IN

START TO FINISH: 15 MIN. **• MAKES:** 9 SERVINGS

- 1½ cups green grapes
- 1½ cups seedless red grapes
- 1½ cups fresh blueberries
- 1½ cups halved fresh strawberries
- 1 can (8 ounces) pineapple chunks, drained
- ½ cup fresh raspberries
- 1 can (10 ounces) frozen non-alcoholic pina colada mix, thawed
- ½ cup sugar
- ½ cup pineapple-orange juice
- ⅛ teaspoon almond extract
- ⅛ teaspoon coconut extract

In a serving bowl, combine the first six ingredients. In a small bowl, whisk the pina colada mix, sugar, juice and extracts until sugar is dissolved. Pour over fruit; toss to coat. Refrigerate until serving.

Baja Chicken & Slaw Sliders

With their flavorful sauce and colorful, crunchy slaw, these hand-held sandwiches command attention from partygoers.

—JANET HYNES MOUNT PLEASANT, WI

PREP: 30 MIN. **• GRILL:** 10 MIN.
MAKES: 8 SERVINGS

- ¼ cup reduced-fat sour cream
- ½ teaspoon grated lime peel
- ¼ teaspoon lime juice

SLAW

- 1 cup broccoli coleslaw mix
- 2 tablespoons finely chopped sweet red pepper
- 2 tablespoons finely chopped sweet onion
- 2 tablespoons minced fresh cilantro
- 2 teaspoons finely chopped seeded jalapeno pepper
- 2 teaspoons lime juice
- 1 teaspoon sugar

SLIDERS

- 4 boneless skinless chicken breast halves (4 ounces each)
- ½ teaspoon ground cumin
- ½ teaspoon chili powder
- ¼ teaspoon salt
- ¼ teaspoon coarsely ground pepper
- 8 Hawaiian sweet rolls, split
- 8 small lettuce leaves
- 8 slices tomato

1. In a small bowl, combine sour cream, lime peel and lime juice. In another small bowl, combine slaw ingredients. Chill sauce and slaw until serving.

2. Cut each chicken breast in half widthwise; flatten to ½-in. thickness. Sprinkle with seasonings.

3. Moisten a paper towel with cooking oil; using long-handled tongs, rub on grill rack to coat lightly. Grill chicken, covered, over medium heat or broil 4 in. from heat 4 to 7 minutes on each side or until no longer pink.

4. Grill rolls, cut sides down, 30-60 seconds or until toasted. Serve chicken on rolls with lettuce, tomato, sauce and slaw.

NOTE *Wear disposable gloves when cutting hot peppers; the oils can burn skin. Avoid touching your face.*

Smokin' Hot Deviled Eggs

Nearly everybody loves deviled eggs, and this variation has a nice kick. You can't go wrong bringing these to a family reunion.

—JAN ROBERTS SAN PEDRO, CA

START TO FINISH: 20 MIN. **• MAKES:** 2 DOZEN

- 12 hard-cooked eggs
- ½ cup mayonnaise
- 3 chipotle peppers in adobo sauce, finely chopped
- 1 tablespoon capers, drained
- 1 tablespoon stone-ground mustard
- ¼ teaspoon salt
- ¼ teaspoon white pepper
  Minced fresh cilantro

Cut eggs in half lengthwise. Remove yolks; set whites aside. In a small bowl, mash yolks. Add the mayonnaise, chipotle peppers, capers, mustard, salt and white pepper; mix well. Stuff or pipe into egg whites. Refrigerate until serving. Sprinkle with cilantro.

> "You won't find a more flavorful slider out there! The combination of the citrus and chicken is great. It is so YUMMY!"
> **—RANDCBRUNS** TASTEOFHOME.COM

"I made this for a lunch party, and everyone raved about it."

—PINFOX TASTEOFHOME.COM

Crisp & Spicy Cucumber Salad

Sweet-hot Asian flavors using rice vinegar, sesame oil and cayenne will light up everyone's taste buds! Double the recipe for large crowds.

—ALIVIA DOCKERY PARKER, CO

PREP: 25 MIN. + MARINATING
MAKES: 6 SERVINGS

2 small English cucumbers, thinly sliced
2 medium carrots, thinly sliced
1 large sweet red pepper, julienned
½ medium red onion, thinly sliced
2 green onions, sliced
½ serrano or jalapeno pepper, seeded and thinly sliced, optional

MARINADE

⅓ cup sugar
⅓ cup rice vinegar
⅓ cup water
1 teaspoon each salt, garlic powder and pepper
1 teaspoon sesame oil
1 teaspoon reduced-sodium soy sauce
1 small garlic clove, minced
½ teaspoon minced fresh gingerroot
¼ teaspoon cayenne pepper, optional
Optional toppings: minced fresh cilantro, chopped peanuts and additional sliced green onion

1. In a large bowl, combine the first six ingredients. In a small bowl, mix marinade ingredients, stirring to dissolve sugar. Pour over vegetables; toss to combine. Refrigerate, covered, for 30 minutes or overnight.
2. Serve with a slotted spoon. If desired, sprinkle with toppings.
NOTE *Wear disposable gloves when cutting hot peppers; the oils can burn skin. Avoid touching your face.*

Crisp & Spicy Cucumber Salad

Garden Vegetable Pasta Salad

Pot of S'mores

Mom's easy Dutch oven version of the popular camping treat is so good and gooey. The hardest part is waiting for the treats to cool so you can devour them. Yum!
—**JUNE DRESS** MERIDIAN, ID

START TO FINISH: 25 MIN. • **MAKES:** 12 SERVINGS

- 1   **package (14½ ounces) whole graham crackers, crushed**
- ½   **cup butter, melted**
- 1   **can (14 ounces) sweetened condensed milk**
- 2   **cups (12 ounces) semisweet chocolate chips**
- 1   **cup butterscotch chips**
- 2   **cups miniature marshmallows**

1. Prepare grill or campfire for low heat, using 16-18 charcoal briquettes or large wood chips.
2. Line a Dutch oven with heavy-duty aluminum foil. Combine cracker crumbs and butter; press onto the bottom of the pan. Pour milk over crust and sprinkle with chocolate and butterscotch chips. Top with marshmallows.
3. Cover Dutch oven. When briquettes or wood chips are covered with white ash, place Dutch oven directly on top of six of them. Using long-handled tongs, place remaining briquettes on pan cover.
4. Cook for 15 minutes or until chips are melted. To check for doneness, use the tongs to carefully lift the cover.

Garden Vegetable Pasta Salad

To super-size a grilled veggie dish, I added pasta. To give the salad a Mediterranean flair, I tossed in some olives and feta cheese.
—**TINA REPAK MIRILOVICH** JOHNSTOWN, PA

PREP: 40 MIN. • **GRILL:** 10 MIN.
MAKES: 26 SERVINGS (¾ CUP EACH)

- 1   **pound fusilli or pasta of your choice**
- 2   **medium eggplant**
- 2   **medium zucchini**
- 2   **medium yellow summer squash**
- 1   **large red onion, cut into ½-inch slices**
- 1   **medium sweet red pepper, cut in half and seeds removed**
- ¼   **cup olive oil**
- ½   **teaspoon salt**
- ¼   **teaspoon pepper**
- 3   **plum tomatoes, chopped**
- 1½ **cups (6 ounces) crumbled feta cheese**
- 2   **cans (2¼ ounces each) sliced ripe olives, drained**
- 2   **tablespoons minced fresh parsley**

PARMESAN VINAIGRETTE
- ¾   **cup olive oil**
- ⅓   **cup grated Parmesan cheese**
- ⅓   **cup white wine vinegar**
- 3   **tablespoons lemon juice**
- 1   **teaspoon sugar**
- 1   **garlic clove, minced**
- 1   **teaspoon salt**
- ½   **teaspoon dried oregano**
- ½   **teaspoon pepper**

1. Cook pasta according to package directions; drain and rinse in cold water. Place in a large bowl and set aside.
2. Meanwhile, cut the eggplant, zucchini and summer squash lengthwise into ¾-in.-thick slices. Brush the eggplant, zucchini, summer squash, red onion and red pepper with oil; sprinkle with salt and pepper. Grill vegetables, covered, over medium heat for 4-6 minutes on each side or until crisp-tender. When cool enough to handle, cut into cubes.
3. Add the tomatoes, feta cheese, olives, parsley and grilled vegetables to the pasta. In a small bowl, whisk the vinaigrette ingredients. Pour over salad; toss to coat. Cover and refrigerate until serving.

Pot of S'mores

**Classic French
Onion Soup, page 179**

**Fun Caramel
Apples, page 158**

Saucy Grilled Baby Back Ribs, page 147

Make-Ahead Butterhorns, page 178

Autumn

AS FALL BREEZES BEGIN TO BLOW, CONSIDER HOSTING A HEARTWARMING GET-TOGETHER THAT'S SURE TO CREATE COMFY MEMORIES FOR THE CHILLY MONTHS AHEAD. WHETHER THE SEASON FINDS YOU BAKING UP A GOLDEN TREAT, HOSTING A SPOOKY HALLOWEEN PARTY OR CREATING THE PERFECT THANKSGIVING MENU, THIS POPULAR SECTION PROMISES TO BE A DELICIOUS REMINDER OF THE FLAVORS THAT AUTUMN BRINGS.

GINA MYHILL-JONES' MEAT
LOVERS' SNACK MIX *PAGE 148*

Time to Tailgate

THESE DAYS, HAVING A PICNIC IN THE STADIUM PARKING LOT BEFORE A FOOTBALL OR BASEBALL GAME IS NEARLY AS IMPORTANT AS THE GAME ITSELF! FROM BURGERS AND BRATS TO SALADS AND SNACKS, NOTHING IS OUT OF BOUNDS WHEN IT COMES TO TAILGATING. CAN'T MAKE THE GAME? SIMPLY SERVE UP A FEW OF THESE FALL FAVORITES AT HOME!

JEANNE HOLT'S BAJA BEAN SALAD *PAGE 146*

STACEY NERNESS' FAMOUS BBQ CHICKEN *PAGE 149*

JOAN SCHOENHERR'S BBQ BACON BURGERS *PAGE 148*

Grilled Beer Brats with Kraut

Grilled Beer Brats with Kraut

My son invited a dozen of his buddies to his 21st birthday bonfire. These brats, with an incredible topping, were fabulous!

—**KEELEY WEBER** STERLING HEIGHTS, MI

PREP: 45 MIN. • **GRILL:** 35 MIN.
MAKES: 12 SERVINGS

- 6 bacon strips, chopped
- 1 large onion, chopped
- 1 medium apple, peeled and thinly sliced
- 2 garlic cloves, minced
- 1 can (14 ounces) sauerkraut, rinsed and well drained
- 3 tablespoons spicy brown mustard
- 1 tablespoon brown sugar
- 12 uncooked bratwurst links
- 1 bottle (12 ounces) dark beer
- 12 hoagie buns, split

1. In a large skillet, cook bacon over medium heat until crisp, stirring occasionally. Remove with a slotted spoon; drain on paper towels.

2. Cook and stir onion in bacon drippings until softened. Reduce heat to medium-low; cook 15-20 minutes or until deep golden brown, stirring occasionally. Add apple and garlic; cook 2 minutes longer. Stir in sauerkraut, mustard, brown sugar and cooked bacon.

3. Transfer to a 13x9-in. disposable foil pan. Arrange bratwurst over top. Pour beer over bratwurst. Place pan on grill rack over medium heat; cook, covered, 30-35 minutes or until sausages are no longer pink. Remove pan from heat.

4. Remove bratwurst and return to grill. Grill, covered, 2-3 minutes on each side or until browned. Serve on buns with sauerkraut mixture.

> 66 I made this twice for different groups and it was a hit. 99
>
> —BUTCHER2BOY
> TASTEOFHOME.COM

Deli-Style Potato Salad

Deli-Style Potato Salad

My grandmother inspired me to cook, and I loved going to her house for Sunday dinner. She passed her cooking skills down, and today my mom and I still like to make her potato salad.

—**SALLY MINER** EL MIRAGE, AZ

PREP: 25 MIN. • **COOK:** 20 MIN. + CHILLING
MAKES: 8 SERVINGS

- 1 **pound potatoes, peeled and cubed**
- 6 **hard-cooked eggs**
- 8 **whole baby dill pickles, sliced**
- 1 **small onion, chopped**
- 4 **radishes, sliced**

DRESSING

- 1 **cup Miracle Whip**
- 1 **tablespoon 2% milk**
- 1 **teaspoon prepared mustard**
- ½ **teaspoon dill pickle juice**
- ¼ **teaspoon sugar**
- ¼ **teaspoon salt**
- ¼ **teaspoon pepper**
  Paprika, optional

1. Place potatoes in a large saucepan and cover with water. Bring to a boil. Reduce heat; cover and cook for 10-15 minutes or until tender. Drain and set aside to cool.
2. Coarsely chop four eggs. In a large bowl, combine the chopped eggs, pickles, onion and radishes; add potatoes. In a small bowl, combine the Miracle Whip, milk, mustard, pickle juice, sugar, salt and pepper. Pour over potato mixture; stir to combine.
3. Slice remaining eggs and arrange over salad; sprinkle with paprika if desired. Cover potato salad and refrigerate for 4 hours before serving.

Icebox Honey Cookies

If you're looking for a no-fuss cookie that travels well, here's the answer! Not only are the treats perfect to take on the road and contribute to bake sales, the honey and lemon combination is delicious!

—**KRISTI GLEASON** FLOWER MOUND, TX

PREP: 20 MIN. + CHILLING • **BAKE:** 15 MIN./BATCH
MAKES: 8 DOZEN

- 1½ **cups shortening**
- 2 **cups packed brown sugar**
- 2 **eggs**
- ½ **cup honey**
- 1 **teaspoon lemon extract**
- 4½ **cups all-purpose flour**
- 2 **teaspoons baking soda**
- 2 **teaspoons baking powder**
- 1 **teaspoon salt**
- 1 **teaspoon ground cinnamon**

1. In a large bowl, cream shortening and brown sugar until light and fluffy. Add eggs, one at a time, beating well after each addition. Beat in honey and extract. Combine the remaining ingredients; gradually add to creamed mixture and mix well.
2. Shape into two 12-in. rolls; wrap each in plastic wrap. Refrigerate 2 hours or until firm.
3. Preheat oven to 325°. Unwrap and cut into ¼-in. slices. Place 1 in. apart on ungreased baking sheets. Bake for 12-14 minutes or until golden brown. Remove to wire racks to cool.

❝ Yum! These cookies are so soft and taste so good! I love the little hint of cinnamon both in the baking process and in the taste. ❞

—**JENNTATS** TASTEOFHOME.COM

Five-Chip Cookies

With peanut butter, oats and five kinds of chips, these cookies make a hearty snack that appeals to everyone. I sometimes double the recipe to share with my friends and neighbors.

—SHARON HEDSTROM MINNETONKA, MN

START TO FINISH: 25 MIN. • **MAKES:** 4½ DOZEN

- 1 **cup butter, softened**
- 1 **cup peanut butter**
- 1 **cup sugar**
- ⅔ **cup packed brown sugar**
- 2 **eggs**
- 1 **teaspoon vanilla extract**
- 2 **cups all-purpose flour**
- 1 **cup old-fashioned oats**
- 2 **teaspoons baking soda**
- ½ **teaspoon salt**
- ⅔ **cup each milk chocolate chips, semisweet chocolate chips, peanut butter chips, white baking chips and butterscotch chips**

1. Preheat oven to 350°. In a large bowl, cream butter, peanut butter and sugars until light and fluffy. Add eggs, one at a time, beating well after each addition. Beat in vanilla. Combine flour, oats, baking soda and salt; gradually add to creamed mixture and mix well. Stir in the chips.
2. Drop by rounded tablespoonfuls 2 in. apart onto ungreased baking sheets. Bake for 10-12 minutes or until lightly browned. Cool 1 minute before removing to wire racks.
NOTE *Reduced-fat peanut butter is not recommended for this recipe.*

TOP TIP

Beat a Sticky Situation

I like to wipe a bit of vegetable oil inside my measuring cup when I'm making peanut butter or molasses cookies. This keeps the sticky ingredients from clinging to the cup, making cleanup a snap.
—LYNN HAYES ST. JOHN, NB

Antipasto Picnic Salad

Antipasto Picnic Salad

You can't go wrong with my tempting blend of meats, veggies and pasta at your tailgate. The recipe goes together in no time, serves a crowd and tastes just as good at room temperature as it does chilled. If you're expecting a smaller group, simply halve the recipe to accommodate your number of party-goers.

—MICHELE LARSON BADEN, PA

PREP: 30 MIN. • **COOK:** 15 MIN.
MAKES: 25 SERVINGS (1 CUP EACH)

- 1 **package (16 ounces) medium pasta shells**
- 2 **jars (16 ounces each) giardiniera**
- 1 **pound fresh broccoli florets**
- ½ **pound cubed part-skim mozzarella cheese**
- ½ **pound hard salami, cubed**
- ½ **pound deli ham, cubed**
- 2 **packages (3½ ounces each) sliced pepperoni, halved**
- 1 **large green pepper, cut into chunks**
- 1 **can (6 ounces) pitted ripe olives, drained**

DRESSING

- ½ **cup olive oil**
- ¼ **cup red wine vinegar**
- 2 **tablespoons lemon juice**
- 1 **teaspoon Italian seasoning**
- 1 **teaspoon coarsely ground pepper**
- ½ **teaspoon salt**

1. Cook pasta according to package directions. Meanwhile, drain the giardiniera, reserving ¾ cup liquid. In a large bowl, combine the giardiniera, broccoli, mozzarella, salami, ham, pepperoni, green pepper and olives. Drain pasta and rinse in cold water; stir into meat mixture.
2. For dressing, in a small bowl, whisk the oil, vinegar, lemon juice, Italian seasoning, pepper, salt and reserved giardiniera liquid. Pour over salad and toss to coat. Refrigerate until serving.
NOTE *Giardiniera, a pickled vegetable mixture, is available in mild and hot varieties and can be found in the Italian or pickle section of your grocery store.*

Soft Beer Pretzels

What goes together better than beer and pretzels? Not much that I can think of! That's why I put them together into one delicious recipe. I'm always looking for new ways to combine fun flavors, and this pretzel was a delicious success.
—**ALYSSA WILHITE** WHITEHOUSE, TX

PREP: 1 HOUR + RISING • **BAKE:** 10 MIN.
MAKES: 8 PRETZELS

- 1 bottle (12 ounces) amber beer or nonalcoholic beer
- 1 package (¼ ounce) active dry yeast
- 2 tablespoons unsalted butter, melted
- 2 tablespoons sugar
- 1½ teaspoons salt
- 4 to 4½ cups all-purpose flour
- 10 cups water
- ⅔ cup baking soda

TOPPING
- 1 egg yolk
- 1 tablespoon water
  Coarse salt

1. In a small saucepan, heat the beer to 110°-115°; remove from heat. Stir in yeast until dissolved. In a large bowl, combine butter, sugar, 1½ teaspoons salt, yeast mixture and 3 cups flour; beat on medium speed until smooth. Stir in enough remaining flour to form a soft dough (dough will be sticky).

2. Turn dough onto a floured surface; knead until smooth and elastic, about 6-8 minutes. Place in a greased bowl, turning once to grease the top. Cover with plastic wrap and let rise in a warm place until doubled, about 1 hour.

3. Preheat the oven to 425°. Punch the dough down. Turn onto a lightly floured surface; divide and shape into eight balls. Roll each into a 24-in. rope. Curve ends of each rope to form a circle; twist ends once and lay over opposite side of circle, pinching ends to seal.

4. In a Dutch oven, bring water and baking soda to a boil. Drop pretzels, two at a time, into boiling water. Cook 30 seconds. Remove with a slotted spoon; drain well on paper towels.

5. Place 2 in. apart on greased baking sheets. In a small bowl, whisk egg yolk and water; brush over pretzels. Sprinkle with coarse salt. Bake 10-12 minutes or until golden brown. Remove from pans to a wire rack to cool.

FREEZE OPTION *Freeze cooled pretzels in resealable plastic freezer bags. To use, thaw pretzels at room temperature or, if desired, microwave each pretzel on high 20-30 seconds or until heated through.*

Mandarin Salsa

Here, mandarin oranges meet cilantro, jalapeno and onion for an impressive and colorful combination.
—**YVONNE OPP** GREENVILLE, PA

START TO FINISH: 25 MIN. • **MAKES:** 4 CUPS

- 5 plum tomatoes, chopped
- 1 large sweet onion, chopped
- 2 jalapeno peppers, seeded and chopped
- 2 tablespoons sugar
- 2 tablespoons minced fresh cilantro
- 2 tablespoons lime juice
- 1 teaspoon salt
- 1 teaspoon minced garlic
- 1 can (15 ounces) mandarin oranges, drained
  Tortilla chips

In a small bowl, combine the first eight ingredients. Stir in mandarin oranges. Chill until serving. Drain before serving if necessary. Serve with tortilla chips.
NOTE *Wear disposable gloves when cutting hot peppers. Avoid touching your face.*

Soft Beer Pretzels

❝ Fresh salsa where oranges temper the heat—very good! Kids loved it! ❞
—HOMEMADEWITHLOVE
TASTEOFHOME.COM

Crunchy Cool Coleslaw

Crunchy Cool Coleslaw

I created my own version of a restaurant favorite so I could enjoy it at home. I think it's a pretty close match! I love that this coleslaw doesn't require mayo, so it's great for tailgates, picnics and the like.
—**ELAINE HOFFMANN** SANTA ANA, CA

START TO FINISH: 30 MIN. • **MAKES:** 16 SERVINGS

- 2 packages (16 ounces each) coleslaw mix
- 2 medium Honeycrisp apples, julienned
- 1 large carrot, shredded
- ¾ cup chopped red onion
- ½ cup chopped green pepper
- ½ cup cider vinegar
- ⅓ cup canola oil
- 1½ teaspoons sugar
- ½ teaspoon celery seed
- ½ teaspoon salt
- ½ cup coarsely chopped dry roasted peanuts or cashews

1. In a large bowl, combine the first five ingredients. In a small bowl, whisk the vinegar, oil, sugar, celery seed and salt.
2. Just before serving, pour dressing over salad; toss to coat. Sprinkle with peanuts or cashews.

Baja Bean Salad

The bright, fresh flavors of lime, jalapeno and cilantro really bring my Baja Bean Salad to life. Best of all, it travels well since the dressing is made with vinegar and oil.
—**JEANNE HOLT** MENDOTA HEIGHTS, MN

PREP: 30 MIN. + CHILLING
MAKES: 12 SERVINGS (¾ CUP EACH)

- 1 pound cut fresh green beans
- 1 can (15 ounces) black beans, rinsed and drained
- 1 can (15 ounces) garbanzo beans or chickpeas, rinsed and drained
- 1 can (14½ ounces) cut wax beans, drained
- 1 cup julienned peeled jicama
- 1 medium sweet red pepper, finely chopped
- 4 green onions, thinly sliced
- 2 tablespoons finely chopped seeded jalapeno pepper
- ⅓ cup sugar
- ⅓ cup cider vinegar
- ¼ cup canola oil
- 2 tablespoons lime juice
- 2 tablespoons minced fresh cilantro
- ½ teaspoon salt
- ¼ teaspoon pepper

1. In a large saucepan, bring 5 cups water to a boil. Add green beans; cover and cook for 4-6 minutes or until crisp-tender. Drain and immediately place beans in ice water. Drain and pat dry.
2. In a large bowl, combine the black beans, garbanzo beans, wax beans, jicama, red pepper, onions, jalapeno and green beans.
3. In a small bowl, whisk the sugar, vinegar, oil, lime juice, cilantro, salt and pepper. Pour over salad; toss to coat. Cover and refrigerate for 1 hour before serving. Serve with a slotted spoon.
NOTE *Wear disposable gloves when cutting hot peppers; the oils can burn skin. Avoid touching your face.*

Spicy Gazpacho Salad

I turned the ingredients for a cool and refreshing soup into a salad with the addition of greens. Add more or less hot sauce to vary the heat in the dish.
—**DONNA MARIE RYAN** TOPSFIELD, MA

PREP: 25 MIN. + CHILLING • **MAKES:** 10 SERVINGS

- 3 cups chopped and seeded tomatoes
- 1 medium cucumber, seeded and chopped
- 1 medium green pepper, chopped
- 4 green onions, chopped
- 1 celery rib, thinly sliced
- 1 tomatillo, husk removed, seeded and chopped
- ½ cup red wine vinaigrette
- 2 tablespoons lemon juice
- 2 tablespoons Worcestershire sauce
- 2 garlic cloves, minced
- 1 teaspoon coarsely ground pepper
- 1 teaspoon hot pepper sauce
- ½ teaspoon kosher salt
- 1 bunch romaine, torn

1. In a large bowl, combine the first six ingredients. In a small bowl, whisk the vinaigrette, lemon juice, Worcestershire sauce, garlic, pepper, pepper sauce and salt. Pour over tomato mixture; toss to coat. Cover and refrigerate for 4 hours.
2. Just before serving, place romaine in a large serving bowl. Top with vegetable mixture and toss to combine.

Spicy Gazpacho Salad

Saucy Grilled Baby Back Ribs

Don't worry about the beer in this recipe. It's just root beer! It adds a subtle undertone to the yummy sauce.

—TERRI KANDELL ADDISON, MI

PREP: 2 HOURS • **GRILL:** 15 MIN.
MAKES: 8 SERVINGS

- 2 **cups ketchup**
- 2 **cups cider vinegar**
- 1 **cup corn syrup**
- ¼ **cup packed brown sugar**
- ¼ **cup root beer**
- ½ **teaspoon salt**
- ½ **teaspoon garlic powder**
- ½ **teaspoon onion powder**
- ½ **teaspoon hot pepper sauce**
- 4 **pounds pork baby back ribs**

1. In a large saucepan, combine first nine ingredients. Bring to a boil. Reduce heat; simmer, uncovered, 20-25 minutes or until slightly thickened, stirring occasionally.

2. Meanwhile, preheat oven to 325°. Set aside 3 cups of sauce for basting and serving.

3. Brush remaining sauce over ribs. Place bone side down on a rack in a large shallow roasting pan. Cover tightly with foil and bake 1½ to 2 hours or until tender.

4. Moisten a paper towel with cooking oil; using long-handled tongs, rub on grill rack to coat lightly. Grill ribs, covered, over medium heat 15-25 minutes or until browned, turning and brushing occasionally with some of the reserved sauce. Cut into serving-size pieces; serve with sauce.

NOTE *For tailgating, cook the ribs as directed and wrap and place in an insulated container to keep warm. Reheat on the grill just before serving.*

Saucy Grilled Baby Back Ribs

Meat Lovers' Snack Mix

BBQ Bacon Burgers

With a slice of bacon inside and a tasty barbecue-mayo sauce on top, these are definitely not ordinary burgers. I think you'll agree. Grill them up any time of year!

—**JOAN SCHOENHERR** EASTPOINTE, MI

START TO FINISH: 30 MIN. • **MAKES:** 4 SERVINGS

- ¼ cup mayonnaise
- ¼ cup barbecue sauce
- 4 bacon strips, cooked and crumbled
- 1½ teaspoons dried minced onion
- 1½ teaspoons steak seasoning
- 1 pound ground beef
- 4 slices Swiss cheese
- 4 hamburger buns, split
  Lettuce leaves and tomato slices

1. In a small bowl, combine mayonnaise and barbecue sauce. In another bowl, combine the bacon, 2 tablespoons of the mayonnaise mixture, onion and steak seasoning; crumble beef over mixture and mix well. Shape into four patties.

2. Grill burgers, covered, over medium heat for 5-7 minutes on each side or until a thermometer reads 160° and juices run clear. Top with cheese. Cover and cook 1-2 minutes longer or until cheese is melted. Spread remaining mayonnaise mixture over cut sides of bun bottoms. Layer with a lettuce, burger and tomato. Replace tops.

Meat Lovers' Snack Mix

Admittedly, this crunchy appetizer might skew toward dudes. But everyone will go wild for this go-to on game day! My husband loves that it features all of his favorite foods: salted meats, salted nuts and hot sauce.

—**GINA MYHILL-JONES** 100 MILE HOUSE, BC

PREP: 15 MIN. • **BAKE:** 50 MIN. + COOLING
MAKES: 6 CUPS

- 1¼ cups wasabi-coated green peas
- ¾ cup salted peanuts
- 3 pepperoni-flavored meat snack sticks (1½ ounces each), cut into bite-size pieces
- 2 ounces beef jerky, cut into bite-size pieces
- ½ cup corn nuts
- ½ cup Rice Chex
- ½ cup Multi Grain Cheerios
- ½ cup crunchy cheese puff snacks
- 2 tablespoons chopped sun-dried tomatoes (not packed in oil)
- ⅓ cup canola oil
- 1½ teaspoons chili powder
- 1½ teaspoons onion powder
- ½ teaspoon hot pepper sauce
- ½ teaspoon soy sauce
- ¼ teaspoon seasoned salt

1. Preheat oven to 250°. Combine first nine ingredients in a large bowl. In a small bowl, whisk oil, chili powder, onion powder, pepper sauce, soy sauce and seasoned salt. Drizzle over the cereal mixture and toss to coat.

2. Spread into a greased 15x10x1-in. baking pan. Bake 50 minutes, stirring every 10 minutes.

3. Cool completely on a wire rack. Store in an airtight container.

TOP TIP

Keep It Clean!

If you don't like getting your hands messy when mixing the meat mixture for burgers, put the ingredients in a large resealable plastic bag. Close up the bag and gently squeeze it to easily mix the ingredients. Or, if you do use your hands, first dampen them with water. This will help prevent the mixture from sticking to your skin.

Famous BBQ Chicken

This is a sticky, finger-lickin' sauce that everyone loves, including my kids. I make it in big batches now and give jars of it to family and friends.

—STACEY NERNESS SPENCER, IA

PREP: 45 MIN. • **GRILL:** 40 MIN.
MAKES: 4 SERVINGS PLUS 3 CUPS LEFTOVER SAUCE

- 2½ cups ketchup
- ½ cup packed brown sugar
- ½ cup honey
- ¼ cup liquid smoke
- ¼ cup molasses
- 1 serrano pepper, finely chopped
- 2 tablespoons prepared mustard
- 1 tablespoon white wine vinegar
- 1 tablespoon Worcestershire sauce
- 2 teaspoons onion powder
- 2 teaspoons garlic powder
- ¼ teaspoon cayenne pepper
- 4 chicken leg quarters
- ½ teaspoon salt
- ½ teaspoon pepper

1. In a large saucepan, combine the first 12 ingredients. Bring to a boil. Reduce heat; simmer, uncovered, for 30 minutes to allow flavors to blend. Set aside ½ cup sauce for basting; cover and refrigerate remaining sauce for later use.

2. Sprinkle chicken with salt and pepper. Moisten a paper towel with cooking oil; using long-handled tongs, rub on grill rack to coat lightly.

3. Prepare grill for indirect heat, using a drip pan. Place chicken skin side down over drip pan and grill, covered, over indirect medium heat for 20 minutes. Turn; grill 20-30 minutes longer or until a thermometer reads 170°-175°, basting occasionally with reserved sauce.

NOTE *Wear disposable gloves when cutting hot peppers; the oils can burn skin. Avoid touching your face.*

Molasses Steak Sandwiches

Molasses Steak Sandwiches

Molasses adds sweetness to this hearty sandwich. It's special enough to serve at any get-together.

—*TASTE OF HOME* TEST KITCHEN

PREP: 15 MIN. + MARINATING • **GRILL:** 15 MIN.
MAKES: 4 SERVINGS

- ¼ cup molasses
- 2 tablespoons brown sugar
- 2 tablespoons olive oil, divided
- 1 tablespoon Dijon mustard
- 4 beef tenderloin steaks (1 inch thick and 4 ounces each)
- 2 large portobello mushrooms, stems removed
- 4 kaiser rolls, split
- 4 slices Swiss cheese

1. In a large resealable plastic bag, mix molasses, brown sugar, 1 tablespoon oil and mustard. Add steaks; seal bag and turn to coat. Refrigerate up to 2 hours.

2. Drain beef, discarding marinade. Brush mushrooms with remaining oil. Grill steaks, covered, over medium heat 5-7 minutes on each side or until meat reaches desired doneness (for medium-rare, a thermometer should read 145°; medium, 160°; well-done, 170°).

3. Grill mushrooms, covered, for 8-10 minutes or until tender, turning occasionally. Remove steaks and mushrooms from grill; let stand 5 minutes.

4. Grill rolls, cut side down, for 2-3 minutes or until lightly toasted. Cut mushrooms and steaks into slices. Serve in rolls with cheese.

JAMIE FRANKLIN'S DIPPED BROWNIE POPS *PAGE 161*

Bake Sale Goodies

FUNDRAISERS ABOUND IN AUTUMN, AND BAKE SALES ARE A LONGTIME FAVORITE. WHETHER HELD AT THE SCHOOL, CHURCH OR COMMUNITY CENTER, THESE POPULAR EVENTS BRING OUT THE BAKER IN EVERYONE. TURN HERE THE NEXT TIME YOU NEED A SWEET SPECIALTY THAT'S SURE TO BRING IN THE SALES.

LANA WHITE'S RASPBERRY-ALMOND THUMBPRINT COOKIES *PAGE 163*

SANDY MCKENZIE'S BUTTERSCOTCH SHORTBREAD *PAGE 157*

CAROL HILLIER'S CALGARY NANAIMO BARS *PAGE 159*

Caramel Toffee Brownies

Caramel Toffee Brownies

I love to create recipes with foods I am craving, such as chocolate, toffee and caramel. Those favorites came together in this sensational treat. I frequently make the brownies to add to care packages for family and friends.

—**BRENDA CAUGHELL** DURHAM, NC

PREP: 30 MIN. • **BAKE:** 40 MIN. + COOLING
MAKES: 2 DOZEN

CARAMEL LAYER
- ½ **cup butter, softened**
- ⅓ **cup sugar**
- ⅓ **cup packed brown sugar**
- 1 **egg**
- ½ **teaspoon vanilla extract**
- 1 **cup all-purpose flour**
- ½ **teaspoon baking soda**
- ¼ **teaspoon salt**
- ½ **cup caramel ice cream topping**
- 2 **tablespoons 2% milk**
- 1 **cup toffee bits**

BROWNIE LAYER
- 1 **cup butter, cubed**
- 4 **ounces unsweetened chocolate**
- 4 **eggs, lightly beaten**
- 2 **cups sugar**
- 2 **teaspoons vanilla extract**
- 2 **cups all-purpose flour**

1. Preheat oven to 350°. In a large bowl, cream butter and sugars until light and fluffy; beat in egg and vanilla. Combine flour, baking soda and salt; gradually add to creamed mixture and mix well. In a small bowl, combine caramel topping and milk; add to batter and mix well. Fold in toffee bits; set aside.
2. In a microwave, melt the butter and chocolate. Beat in eggs, sugar and vanilla; gradually beat in flour.
3. Spread half of brownie batter into a greased 13x9-in. baking pan. Drop caramel batter by spoonfuls onto the brownie batter; swirl to combine. Drop remaining brownie batter on top.
4. Bake for 40-45 minutes or until a toothpick inserted in center comes out clean. Cool on a wire rack.

Oatmeal Surprise Cookies

Chocolate-covered raisins and the warming flavor of pumpkin pie spice turn these oatmeal cookies into prizewinning gourmet bites! Tuck a few into your child's lunch for a special surprise.

—**REBECCA CLARK** WARRIOR, AL

PREP: 20 MIN. • **BAKE:** 15 MIN./BATCH
MAKES: 3 DOZEN

- 1 **cup butter, softened**
- ¾ **cup packed brown sugar**
- ½ **cup sugar**
- 2 **eggs**
- 1½ **cups all-purpose flour**
- 1 **teaspoon baking soda**
- 1 **teaspoon pumpkin pie spice**
- 2¾ **cups quick-cooking oats**
- 1½ **cups chocolate-covered raisins**

1. Preheat oven to 350°. In a large bowl, cream butter and sugars until light and fluffy. Beat in eggs. Combine flour, baking soda and pumpkin pie spice; gradually add to creamed mixture and mix well. Stir in oats and raisins.
2. Drop by tablespoonfuls 2 in. apart onto greased baking sheets. Flatten slightly. Bake 13-15 minutes or until golden brown. Cool 5 minutes before removing to wire racks. Store in an airtight container.

Bacon Cinnamon Buns

I absolutely love bacon! I also love recipes that blend sweet and savory flavors, so I put chopped bacon in my cinnamon buns. The combination is finger-licking good.

—**DANIELLE WILLIAMS** NEWPORT, RI

PREP: 50 MIN. + RISING • **BAKE:** 20 MIN.
MAKES: 1 DOZEN

- 1 **package (¼ ounce) active dry yeast**
- 1 **cup warm whole milk (110° to 115°)**
- ¼ **cup sugar**
- ¼ **cup butter, softened**
- 1 **egg yolk**
- 1½ **teaspoons vanilla extract**
- ¾ **teaspoon salt**
- ½ **teaspoon ground nutmeg**
- 2¾ to 3 **cups all-purpose flour**

FILLING

- 5 **bacon strips, chopped**
- ½ **cup packed brown sugar**
- 1 **tablespoon maple syrup**
- 2 **teaspoons ground cinnamon**
- ½ **teaspoon ground nutmeg**

ICING

- 2 **cups confectioners' sugar**
- ½ **cup butter, softened**
- 2 **tablespoons whole milk**
- 1 **tablespoon maple syrup**

1. In a small bowl, dissolve yeast in warm milk. In a large bowl, combine sugar, butter, egg yolk, vanilla, salt, nutmeg, yeast mixture and 1 cup flour; beat on medium speed 2 minutes. Stir in enough remaining flour to form a soft dough (dough will be sticky).

2. Turn onto a floured surface; knead until smooth and elastic, 6-8 minutes. Place in a greased bowl, turning once to grease the top. Cover with plastic wrap and let rise in a warm place until doubled, about 1 hour.

3. In a small skillet, cook bacon over medium heat until crisp. Remove with a slotted spoon; drain the bacon on paper towels. Discard the drippings, reserving 2 tablespoons.

4. Wipe skillet clean if necessary. Combine brown sugar, syrup, cinnamon, nutmeg and reserved bacon drippings in skillet; cook and stir over medium heat until blended. Cool to room temperature.

5. Punch the dough down. Roll into an 18x12-in. rectangle. Spread the bacon mixture to within ½ in. of edges. Roll up jelly-roll style, starting with a short side; pinch seams to seal. Cut into 12 rolls.

6. Place rolls, cut side down, in a greased 13x9-in. baking dish. Cover and let rise in a warm place until doubled, about 45 minutes. Preheat oven to 400°. Bake 18-20 minutes or until golden brown.

7. In a small bowl, beat icing ingredients until smooth. Spread over warm rolls. Serve warm.

Bacon Cinnamon Buns

**Tart Cranberry
Quick Bread**

Tart Cranberry
Quick Bread

My mother used to make this bread. I usually stock up on cranberries when they're in season and freeze them so I can make this loaf year-round.

—**KAREN CZECHOWICZ** OCALA, FL

PREP: 20 MIN. • **BAKE:** 45 MIN. + COOLING
MAKES: 1 LOAF (12 SLICES)

- 1½ **cups all-purpose flour**
- ¾ **cup sugar**
- 1 **teaspoon baking powder**
- ¼ **teaspoon salt**
- ¼ **teaspoon baking soda**
- 1 **egg**
- ½ **cup orange juice**
- 2 **tablespoons butter, melted**
- 1 **tablespoon water**
- 1½ **cups fresh or frozen cranberries, halved**

1. Preheat the oven to 350°. In a large bowl, combine the first five ingredients. In a small bowl, whisk egg, orange juice, butter and water. Stir into dry ingredients just until moistened. Fold in cranberries.

2. Transfer to an 8x4-in. loaf pan coated with cooking spray and sprinkled with flour. Bake for 45-50 minutes or until a toothpick inserted near the center comes out clean. Cool for 10 minutes before removing from pan to a wire rack.

Chocolate Pear Hazelnut Tart

Chocolate Pear Hazelnut Tart

As a foreign exchange student in France, I was horribly homesick. My host family's grandmother asked if I'd like to help bake a tart. She made the trip unforgettable and inspired my passion for baking.

—**LEXI MCKEOWN** LOS ANGELES, CA

PREP: 45 MIN. + CHILLING
BAKE: 30 MIN. + COOLING
MAKES: 12 SERVINGS

- 1¼ cups all-purpose flour
- ⅓ cup ground hazelnuts
- ¼ cup packed brown sugar
  Dash salt
- ½ cup cold butter, cubed
- 3 to 5 tablespoons ice water

FILLING

- 3 eggs, separated
- ⅓ cup butter, softened
- ⅓ cup packed brown sugar
- 2 tablespoons amaretto or ½ teaspoon almond extract
- 1 cup ground hazelnuts
- 2 tablespoons baking cocoa
- 6 canned pear halves, drained, sliced and patted dry
- 2 tablespoons honey, warmed
  Confectioners' sugar

1. In a bowl, mix flour, hazelnuts, brown sugar and salt; cut in the butter until crumbly. Gradually add ice water, tossing with a fork until dough holds together when pressed. Shape into a disk; wrap in plastic wrap. Refrigerate for 30 minutes.
2. Place egg whites in a large bowl; let stand at room temperature 30 minutes.

Place oven rack in lowest position and preheat oven to 400°. On a lightly floured surface, roll dough to a ⅛-in.-thick circle; transfer to a 9-in. fluted tart pan with removable bottom. Trim pastry. Prick bottom of pastry with a fork. Refrigerate while preparing filling.
3. In a bowl, cream butter and brown sugar until blended. Beat in egg yolks and amaretto. Beat in hazelnuts and cocoa.
4. With clean beaters, beat egg whites on medium speed until stiff peaks form. Fold a third of the egg whites into the hazelnut mixture, then fold in remaining whites. Spread onto bottom of pastry shell. Arrange pears over top.
5. Bake tart on a lower oven rack for 30-35 minutes or until crust is golden brown. Brush pears with honey. Cool on a wire rack. Dust with confectioners' sugar.

Smackin' Good Snack Mix

This crunchy snack mix is perfect for bake sales, a party or tailgating. Everyone who has tried it likes it, and it even won a ribbon at my state fair.

—**LUCILE CLINE** WICHITA, KS

PREP: 15 MIN. • **BAKE:** 40 MIN. + COOLING
MAKES: 6 QUARTS

- 6 cups original Bugles
- 5 cups nacho cheese-flavored Bugles
- 4 cups miniature cheese crackers
- 1 package (6 ounces) miniature colored fish-shaped crackers
- 3 cups miniature pretzels
- 2 cups Crispix
- 2 cups lightly salted cashews
- ¾ cup butter-flavored popcorn oil
- 2 envelopes (1 ounce each) ranch salad dressing mix

1. Preheat oven to 250°. In a large bowl, combine first seven ingredients. Combine oil and dressing mix; pour over cracker mixture and toss to coat.
2. Transfer to three greased 15x10x1-in. baking pans. Bake 40-45 minutes or until crisp, stirring occasionally. Cool on wire racks. Store in an airtight container.

Halloween Chocolate Cookie Pops

Our children look forward to these cute cookies each year. They've become experts at making the silly faces with little candies.

—**KATHY STOCK** LEVAY, MO

PREP: 25 MIN. • **BAKE:** 10 MIN./BATCH + COOLING
MAKES: 2 DOZEN

- 1 cup butter, softened
- 2 cups sugar
- 2 eggs
- 3 teaspoons vanilla extract
- 3 cups all-purpose flour
- 1 cup baking cocoa
- ½ teaspoon baking powder
- ½ teaspoon baking soda
- ½ teaspoon salt
- 24 lollipop sticks
  Prepared vanilla frosting
  Food coloring
  Black decorating gel
  Optional decorations: candy corn, regular M&M's, M&M's minis and cinnamon hearts

1. Preheat oven to 350°. In a large bowl, beat butter and sugar until blended. Beat in eggs and vanilla. In a small bowl, whisk flour, cocoa, baking powder, baking soda and salt; gradually beat into sugar mixture. Shape dough into 1½-in. balls. Place 3 in. apart on greased baking sheets.
2. Insert a wooden stick into each cookie. Flatten with a glass dipped in sugar. Bake 10-12 minutes or until cookies are set. Remove from pans to wire racks to cool completely. Tint frosting; frost cookies. Decorate with gel and optional decorations as desired.

Halloween Chocolate Cookie Pops

Quadruple Chocolate Chunk Cookies

Apple Kuchen Bars

(5) INGREDIENTS

My mom made these classic treats, and now I bake them in my kitchen. I make double batches to pass on the love! The recipe is all about comfort and simplicity.

—**ELIZABETH MONFORT** CELINA, OH

PREP: 35 MIN. • **BAKE:** 1 HOUR + COOLING
MAKES: 2 DOZEN

- 3 **cups all-purpose flour, divided**
- ¼ **teaspoon salt**
- 1½ **cups cold butter, divided**
- 4 **to 5 tablespoons ice water**
- 8 **cups thinly sliced peeled tart apples (about 8 medium)**
- 2 **cups sugar, divided**
- 2 **teaspoons ground cinnamon**

1. Preheat oven to 350°. Place 2 cups flour and salt in a food processor; pulse until blended. Add 1 cup butter; pulse until butter is the size of peas. While pulsing, add just enough ice water to form moist crumbs. Press mixture into a greased 13x9-in. baking pan. Bake 20-25 minutes or until edges are lightly browned. Cool on a wire rack.

2. In a large bowl, combine apples, 1 cup sugar and cinnamon; toss to coat. Spoon over crust. Place remaining flour, butter and sugar in food processor; pulse until coarse crumbs form. Sprinkle over the apples. Bake 60-70 minutes or until golden brown and apples are tender. Cool completely on a wire rack. Cut into bars.

Apple Kuchen Bars

Quadruple Chocolate Chunk Cookies

Of all the recipes in my repertoire, I think my Quadruple Chocolate Chunk Cookies have the best shot at winning a cookie contest. When your cookies feature Oreos, candy bars and all the other goodies that go into a sweet treat, you're nearly guaranteed to turn out a winner.

—**JEFF KING** DULUTH, MN

PREP: 25 MIN. • **BAKE:** 10 MIN./BATCH
MAKES: 8 DOZEN

- 1 **cup butter, softened**
- 1 **cup sugar**
- 1 **cup packed brown sugar**
- 2 **eggs**
- 2 **teaspoons vanilla extract**
- 2½ **cups all-purpose flour**
- ¾ **cup Dutch-processed cocoa**
- 1 **teaspoon baking soda**
- ¼ **teaspoon salt**
- 1 **cup white baking chips, chopped**
- 1 **cup semisweet chocolate chips, chopped**
- 1 **cup chopped Oreo cookies (about 10 cookies)**
- 1 **Hershey's cookies and cream candy bar (1.55 ounces), chopped**

1. Preheat oven to 375°. In a large bowl, cream butter, sugar and brown sugar until light and fluffy. Beat in eggs and vanilla. In another bowl, whisk flour, cocoa, baking soda and salt; gradually beat into creamed mixture. Stir in the remaining ingredients.

2. Drop by tablespoonfuls 2 in. apart onto greased baking sheets. Bake for 6-8 minutes or until set. Cool on pans 1 minute. Remove to wire racks to cool completely. Store cookies in an airtight container.

❝ Excellent! Taste like a gooey brownie but in cookie form. ❞

—**COOKIEKRUMM** TASTEOFHOME.COM

Salted Caramel Cappuccino Cheesecake

I spent 16 years living in Seattle and became a coffee junkie! When I had to temporarily relocate across the country, I created this cheesecake with the flavors of salted caramel, coffee liqueur and espresso. I could always count on this luscious dessert to lift my spirits whenever I felt blue about leaving one of the great coffee destinations of the world.

—JULIE MERRIMAN SEATTLE, WA

PREP: 30 MIN. • **BAKE:** 55 MIN. + CHILLING
MAKES: 12 SERVINGS

- 1 package (9 ounces) chocolate wafers
- 1 cup (6 ounces) semisweet chocolate chips
- ½ cup packed brown sugar
- 2 tablespoons instant espresso powder
- ⅛ teaspoon ground nutmeg
- ½ cup butter, melted

FILLING

- 3 packages (8 ounces each) cream cheese, softened
- 1 cup packed brown sugar
- ½ cup sour cream
- ¼ cup Kahlua (coffee liqueur)
- 2 tablespoons all-purpose flour
- 2 tablespoons instant espresso powder
- 4 eggs, lightly beaten

TOPPING

- ½ cup hot caramel ice cream topping
- ½ teaspoon coarse sea salt

1. Preheat oven to 350°. Place a greased 9-in. springform pan on a double thickness of heavy-duty foil (about 18 in. square). Securely wrap foil around pan.
2. Place first five ingredients in a food processor; cover and pulse until fine crumbs form. Gradually add butter, pulsing until combined. Press onto the bottom and 2 in. up the sides of prepared pan; set aside.
3. In a large bowl, beat cream cheese and brown sugar until smooth. Beat in the sour cream, Kahlua, flour and espresso powder. Add eggs; beat on low speed just until combined. Pour into crust. Place springform pan in a large baking pan; add 1 in. of boiling water to larger pan.
4. Bake 55-65 minutes or until center is just set and top appears dull. Remove springform pan from water bath; remove foil. Cool cheesecake on a wire rack for 10 minutes; loosen edges from pan with a knife. Cool 1 hour longer. Refrigerate overnight.
5. Pour caramel topping over the cheesecake. Refrigerate for at least 15 minutes. Remove rim from pan. Just before serving, sprinkle sea salt over the caramel.

Butterscotch Shortbread

After sampling these tender cookies in a specialty store, I knew I had to duplicate them. My version has lots of toffee bits and butterscotch chips. I give away dozens as home-baked gifts.

—SANDY MCKENZIE BRAHAM, MN

PREP: 30 MIN. + CHILLING
BAKE: 10 MIN./BATCH + COOLING
MAKES: 4½ DOZEN

- 1 cup butter, softened
- ½ cup confectioners' sugar
- 1 teaspoon vanilla extract
- 1¾ cups all-purpose flour
- ½ cup cornstarch
- ¼ teaspoon salt
- ½ cup butterscotch chips, finely chopped
- ½ cup milk chocolate English toffee bits

1. In a large bowl, cream butter and confectioners' sugar until light and fluffy. Beat in vanilla. Combine flour, cornstarch and salt; gradually add to creamed mixture and mix well. Fold in butterscotch chips and toffee bits. Cover and refrigerate for 1 hour or until easy to handle.
2. Preheat oven to 350°. On a lightly floured surface, roll out dough to ¼-in. thickness. Cut with a floured 2-in. fluted round cookie cutter. Place 1 in. apart on ungreased baking sheets.
3. Bake 10-12 minutes or until lightly browned. Remove to wire racks.

Salted Caramel Cappuccino Cheesecake

Fun Caramel Apples

66 This is an awesome recipe that's great for the kids. 99
—JOYCE LAUHOFF
TASTEOFHOME.COM

Fun Caramel Apples

Charming designs and colorful candies make these caramel apples irresistible. Use apples at room temperature; if the apples are chilled, the caramel tends to slip off.
—DARLA WESTER MERIDEN, IA

PREP: 30 MIN. + CHILLING • **MAKES:** 8 SERVINGS

- 1 package (11½ ounces) milk chocolate chips
- 2 tablespoons shortening
- 1 package (14 ounces) vibrant green Wilton candy melts
- 1 package (14 ounces) white Wilton candy melts
- 2 packages (14 ounces each) caramels
- ¼ cup water
- 8 large tart apples, room temperature
- 8 lollipop sticks
  Assorted candies such as jimmies, M&M's and Reese's Pieces

1. In a microwave-safe bowl, melt the chocolate chips and shortening; stir until smooth and set aside. In another microwave-safe bowl, microwave and melt the green candy melts. Repeat with white candy melts.
2. In another microwave-safe bowl, microwave the caramels and water, uncovered, on high for 1 minute; stir. Heat 30-45 seconds longer or until caramels are melted; stir until smooth.
3. Line a baking sheet with waxed paper and grease the paper; set aside. Wash and thoroughly dry apples. Insert a stick into each; dip into caramel mixture, turning to coat. Place on prepared pan.
4. Drizzle with melted chocolate and candy melts. Decorate as desired with melted chocolate, candy melts and candies. Refrigerate until set.

Calgary Nanaimo Bars

This version may claim roots in Alberta, but the original was said to be dreamed up in a kitchen in Nanaimo, British Columbia. Either way, they feature three delicious layers of absolute Canadian goodness.

—**CAROL HILLIER** CALGARY, AB

PREP: 25 MIN. + CHILLING • **MAKES:** 3½ DOZEN

- ¼ **cup sugar**
- ¼ **cup baking cocoa**
- ¾ **cup butter, cubed**
- 2 **eggs, beaten**
- 2 **cups graham cracker crumbs**
- 1 **cup flaked coconut**
- ½ **cup chopped almonds, optional**

FILLING

- 2 **cups confectioners' sugar**
- 2 **tablespoons instant vanilla pudding mix**
- ¼ **cup butter, melted**
- 3 **tablespoons 2% milk**

GLAZE

- 3 **ounces semisweet chocolate, chopped**
- 1 **tablespoon butter**

1. Line an 8-in.-square baking pan with foil, letting ends extend over sides by 1 in. In a large heavy saucepan, combine sugar and cocoa; add butter. Cook and stir over medium-low heat until butter is melted.
2. Whisk a small amount of hot mixture into eggs. Return all to the pan, whisking constantly. Cook and stir until mixture reaches 160°. Remove from heat.
3. Stir in cracker crumbs, coconut and, if desired, almonds. Press into prepared pan. Refrigerate 30 minutes or until set.
4. For filling, in a small bowl, beat the confectioners' sugar, pudding mix, butter and milk until smooth; spread over crust.
5. In a microwave, melt chocolate and butter; stir until smooth. Spread over top. Refrigerate until set. Using foil, lift bars out of pan. Discard foil; cut into bars.

Apple Bavarian Torte

Apple Bavarian Torte

Layer a cream cheese filling, apples and almonds on a cookie-like crust for my picture-perfect torte. What a change of pace this would be at your next bake sale!

—**SHEILA SWIFT** DOBSON, NC

PREP: 20 MIN. • **BAKE:** 45 MIN. + COOLING
MAKES: 16 SERVINGS

- ½ **cup butter, softened**
- ⅓ **cup sugar**
- 1 **cup all-purpose flour**
- ¼ **teaspoon vanilla extract**

FILLING

- 1 **package (8 ounces) cream cheese, softened**
- ¼ **cup plus ⅓ cup sugar, divided**
- 1 **egg, lightly beaten**
- ½ **teaspoon vanilla extract**
- 5½ **cups thinly sliced peeled tart apples (about 6 medium)**
- ½ **teaspoon ground cinnamon**
- ¼ **cup sliced almonds**

1. Preheat oven to 450°. In a small bowl, cream the butter and sugar. Beat in the flour and vanilla until blended. Press onto the bottom of a greased 9-in. springform pan.
2. In a large bowl, beat cream cheese and ¼ cup sugar until fluffy. Beat in egg and vanilla. Pour over crust. In another large bowl, toss apples with cinnamon and remaining sugar. Spoon over cream cheese layer.
3. Bake 10 minutes. Reduce oven setting to 400°; bake 25 minutes. Sprinkle almonds over top; bake 10-15 minutes longer or until lightly browned and a toothpick inserted near the center comes out clean. Cool on a wire rack. Remove sides of pan before slicing. Store in the refrigerator.

Raspberry Breakfast Braid

Raspberry Breakfast Braid

We like using blackberries, marionberries or a mixture of berries in this quick and easy pastry. Best of all, it starts with a mix!

—TRESSA NICHOLLS SANDY, OR

PREP: 20 MIN. • **BAKE:** 15 MIN.
MAKES: 12 SERVINGS

- 2 cups biscuit/baking mix
- 1 package (3 ounces) cream cheese, cubed
- ¼ cup cold butter, cubed
- ⅓ cup 2% milk
- 1¼ cups fresh raspberries
- 3 tablespoons sugar
- ¼ cup vanilla frosting

1. Preheat oven to 425°. Place biscuit mix in a large bowl. Cut in cream cheese and butter until mixture resembles coarse crumbs. Stir in milk just until moistened. Turn onto a lightly floured surface; knead gently 8-10 times.
2. On a greased baking sheet, roll dough into an 18x12-in. rectangle. Spoon the raspberries down center third of dough; sprinkle with sugar.
3. On each long side, cut 1-in.-wide strips about 2½ in. into center. Starting at one end, fold alternating strips at an angle across raspberries; seal ends.
4. Bake 15-20 minutes or until golden brown. Remove pastry to a wire rack to cool slightly. In a microwave-safe dish, microwave frosting on high 5-10 seconds or until of desired consistency; drizzle over pastry.

Peter Peter Pumpkin Whoopies

When fall rolls around and it's time for a bake sale, this is the recipe I turn to. The whoopie pies go over wonderfully. The cream cheese filling is perked up with cinnamon and nutmeg, and it's perfect with the cakelike cookie.

—DAWN CONTE SICKLERVILLE, NJ

PREP: 35 MIN. + COOLING • **BAKE:** 10 MIN./BATCH
MAKES: 10 WHOOPIE PIES

- 1 package spice cake mix (regular size)
- 1¼ cups canned pumpkin
- 2 eggs
- ½ cup 2% milk
- ⅓ cup butter, softened

FILLING
- 2 packages (3 ounces each) cream cheese, softened
- ½ cup marshmallow creme
- ⅓ cup butter, softened
- 1½ cups confectioners' sugar
- ¾ teaspoon vanilla extract
- ½ teaspoon ground cinnamon
- ⅛ teaspoon ground nutmeg

1. Preheat oven to 375°. In a large bowl, combine first five ingredients; beat until well blended. Drop by ¼ cupfuls 3 in. apart onto lightly greased baking sheets. Bake 7-10 minutes or until set and edges are lightly browned. Remove to wire racks to cool completely.
2. For filling, in a small bowl, beat the cream cheese, marshmallow creme and butter. Beat in remaining ingredients. Spread on the bottoms of half of the cookies; top with remaining cookies. Store in the refrigerator.

TOP TIP

Marshmallow Ease

To easily remove marshmallow creme from a jar, place the jar in a pan of very hot water. Repeat this once or twice, and then spoon out the creme with a wooden spoon.

—MARY FRENCH PORT ORANGE, FL

Peter Peter Pumpkin Whoopies

Dipped Brownie Pops

I needed to host a quick fundraiser for a student organization, so I made these brownie pops. The kids loved them, and I sold more than 200 in an afternoon. Add crushed graham crackers to the dipped chocolate for a s'mores version.

—JAMIE FRANKLIN MURTAUGH, ID

PREP: 45 MIN. • **BAKE:** 35 MIN. + COOLING
MAKES: 16 BROWNIE POPS

- 1 package fudge brownie mix (13x9-inch pan size)
- 16 wooden pop sticks
- ⅔ cup semisweet chocolate chips
- 3 teaspoons shortening, divided
- ⅔ cup white baking chips
  Assorted sprinkles, chopped pecans and/or miniature marshmallows

1. Line a 8- or 9-in.-square baking pan with foil; grease the foil and set aside. Prepare and bake the brownie mix according to the package directions for the size baking pan used. Cool completely on a wire rack.

2. Using foil, lift brownie out of the pan; remove foil. Cut the brownie into sixteen squares. Gently insert a Popsicle stick into the side of each square. Cover and freeze 30 minutes.

3. In a microwave oven, melt the chocolate chips and 1½ teaspoons shortening; stir until smooth. Repeat with white baking chips and remaining shortening.

4. Dip eight brownies halfway into chocolate mixture; allow excess to drip off. Dip remaining brownies halfway into white chip mixture; allow excess to drip off. Sprinkle with toppings of your choice. Place on waxed paper; let stand until set. Place in bags and fasten with twist ties or ribbon if desired.

Dipped Brownie Pops

Gingersnap-Crusted Sweet Potato Cake

I like to bring one of these glazed sweet potato Bundt cakes as a special hostess gift during the holiday season. The icing looks pretty draping down the sides, and remains glossy even after it dries.

—CATHERINE WILKINSON DEWEY, AZ

PREP: 25 MIN. • **BAKE:** 65 MIN. + COOLING
MAKES: 12 SERVINGS

- 2 teaspoons plus 1 cup butter, softened, divided
- ⅓ cup finely crushed gingersnap cookies (about 6 cookies)
- 2 cups sugar
- 2 eggs
- 2 cans (15¾ ounces each) sweet potatoes, drained and pureed
- 3½ cups all-purpose flour
- 2 teaspoons baking soda
- 2 teaspoons ground ginger
- 1 teaspoon salt
- ½ teaspoon ground cloves
- 2¼ cups confectioners' sugar
- ½ cup maple syrup
- ¾ teaspoon vanilla extract

1. Preheat oven to 350°. Grease a 10-in. tube pan with 2 teaspoons butter and coat with crushed cookies; set aside.
2. In a large bowl, cream sugar and remaining butter until light and fluffy. Add eggs, one at a time, beating well after each addition. Beat in sweet potatoes. Combine the flour, baking soda, ginger, salt and cloves; gradually add to the creamed mixture.
3. Transfer mixture to prepared pan. Bake at 350° for 65-75 minutes or until a toothpick inserted near the center comes out clean. Cool for 10 minutes before removing from pan to a wire rack to cool completely.
4. For glaze, in a small bowl, combine the confectioners' sugar, maple syrup and vanilla. Pour over top of cake, allowing glaze to drape over sides.

Two-Chip Chocolate Chippers

Two-Chip Chocolate Chippers

When baking this chocolate chip cookie recipe, I am a stickler for using one stick of butter and one stick of margarine. That combination gives the cookies terrific texture. I also avoid using a scooper—the tool compacts the cookies too much.

—LEE ANN MILLER MILLERSBURG, OH

PREP: 20 MIN. • **BAKE:** 10 MIN./BATCH
MAKES: 5 DOZEN

- ½ cup butter, softened
- ½ cup stick margarine, softened
- ¾ cup packed brown sugar
- ¼ cup sugar
- 2 eggs
- 1½ teaspoons vanilla extract
- 2¼ cups all-purpose flour
- 1 package (3.4 ounces) instant vanilla pudding mix
- 1 teaspoon baking soda
- 1½ cups semisweet chocolate chips
- 1½ cups milk chocolate chips
- 1½ cups chopped pecans, optional

1. Preheat oven to 375°. In a large bowl, cream butter, margarine and sugars until light and fluffy. Beat in eggs and vanilla. Combine flour, pudding mix and baking soda; gradually add to creamed mixture and mix well. Stir in chocolate chips and, if desired, pecans.
2. Drop by rounded tablespoonfuls 1 in. apart onto ungreased baking sheets; flatten slightly with a glass. Bake for 8-10 minutes or until lightly browned. Remove to wire racks.

" These are the best cookies ever! Everyone just raves about them. "

—SNOWFALLN2
TASTEOFHOME.COM

Chocolate Ganache
Peanut Butter Cupcakes

I've been baking cakes for years and enjoy trying new combinations of flavors and textures. When I blended two popular flavors—peanut butter and chocolate—I knew I'd created something divine after just one bite. The cupcakes are definitely worth the time it takes to make them.

—RONDA SCHABES VICKSBURG, MI

PREP: 55 MIN. • **BAKE:** 20 MIN. + COOLING
MAKES: 2 DOZEN

- 2 cups sugar
- 1¾ cups all-purpose flour
- ¾ cup baking cocoa
- ½ teaspoon salt
- ½ teaspoon baking soda
- ½ teaspoon baking powder
- 1 cup buttermilk
- 1 cup strong brewed coffee, room temperature
- ½ cup canola oil
- 2 eggs
- 1 teaspoon vanilla extract

FILLING

- ½ cup creamy peanut butter
- 3 tablespoons unsalted butter, softened
- 1 cup confectioners' sugar
- 2 to 4 tablespoons 2% milk

**Chocolate Ganache
Peanut Butter Cupcakes**

GANACHE

- 2 cups (12 ounces) semisweet chocolate chips
- ½ cup heavy whipping cream

PEANUT BUTTER FROSTING

- 1 cup packed brown sugar
- 4 egg whites
- ¼ teaspoon salt
- ¼ teaspoon cream of tartar
- 1 teaspoon vanilla extract
- 2 cups unsalted butter, softened
- ⅓ cup creamy peanut butter

1. Preheat oven to 350°. In a large bowl, combine first six ingredients. Whisk buttermilk, coffee, oil, eggs and vanilla until blended; add to the dry ingredients until combined. (Batter will be very thin.) Fill paper-lined muffin cups two-thirds full.

2. Bake for 18-20 minutes or until a toothpick inserted near the center comes out clean. Cool for 10 minutes before removing from pans to wire racks to cool completely.

3. In a small bowl, cream peanut butter, butter, confectioners' sugar and enough milk to achieve piping consistency. Cut a small hole in the corner of a pastry or plastic bag; insert a small round tip. Fill with peanut butter filling. Insert tip into the top center of each cupcake; pipe about 1 tablespoon filling into each.

4. Place chocolate chips in a small bowl. In a small saucepan, bring cream just to a boil. Pour over chocolate; whisk until smooth. Dip the top of each cupcake into ganache; place on wire racks to set.

5. In a large heavy saucepan, combine brown sugar, egg whites, salt and cream of tartar over low heat. With a hand mixer, beat on low speed 1 minute. Continue beating on low over low heat until frosting reaches 160°, about 8-10 minutes. Pour into a large bowl; add vanilla. Beat on high until stiff peaks form, about 5 minutes.

6. Add butter, 1 tablespoon at a time, beating well after each addition. If mixture begins to look curdled, place frosting bowl in another bowl filled with hot water for a few seconds. Continue adding butter and beating until smooth. Beat in peanut butter for 1-2 minutes or until smooth.

7. Place frosting in a pastry or plastic bag with large star tip; pipe onto each cupcake. Store in an airtight container in the refrigerator. Let stand at room temperature before serving.

Raspberry-Almond
Thumbprint Cookies

These crisp, buttery thumbprints have a hint of almond and a touch of sweetness from the raspberry jam. A light drizzle of almond glaze makes the treats extra-special for bake sales.

—LANA WHITE ROY, WA

PREP: 40 MIN. + CHILLING
BAKE: 15 MIN./BATCH + COOLING
MAKES: 3½ DOZEN

- 1 cup butter, softened
- ⅔ cup sugar
- ½ teaspoon almond extract
- 2 cups all-purpose flour
- ½ cup seedless raspberry jam

GLAZE

- ⅓ cup confectioners' sugar
- ½ teaspoon almond extract
- 1 teaspoon water

1. In a large bowl, cream butter, sugar and extract until light and fluffy. Add flour and mix well. Chill for 1 hour.

2. Preheat oven to 350°. Roll into 1-in. balls. Place 2 in. apart on greased baking sheets. Using the end of a wooden spoon handle, make an indentation in the center of each; fill each with ¼ teaspoon of the jam.

3. Bake 13-16 minutes or until the edges are lightly browned. Remove to wire racks to cool completely.

4. For glaze, in a small bowl, combine confectioners' sugar, extract and water. Drizzle over cookies.

**POLLY COUMOS'
BOO-YA MINI PIZZAS** *PAGE 166*

Ghoulish Get-Togethers

PUT A SPELL ON FRIENDS AND FAMILY BY SERVING A "BOO-TIFUL" BUFFET FEATURING ANY OF THE SPOOKY SPECIALTIES FOUND HERE! WHETHER YOU'RE PLANNING SOME SILLY FUN FOR LITTLE GOBLINS OR HOSTING A CREEPY COCKTAIL PARTY FOR ADULTS, THE FOLLOWING BITES PROMISE TO TURN YOUR HOME INTO A DEVILISHLY PERFECT HALLOWEEN HAUNT.

ROSEMARY PACHA'S APPLE TRAIL MIX *PAGE 170*

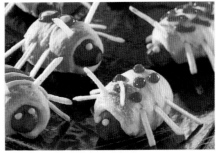

***TASTE OF HOME* TEST KITCHEN'S CREEPY-CRAWLY BUGS** *PAGE 174*

WENDY MYERS' WIGGLY WORM STIR-FRY *PAGE 174*

Mad Scientist Citrus Punch

Mad Scientist Citrus Punch

Serve this sweet concoction at your next Halloween party. What fun!
—**DIANNE CONWAY** LONDON, ON

PREP: 5 MIN. + CHILLING
MAKES: 8 SERVINGS (2 QUARTS)

- 2 **cups pineapple juice**
- 2 **cups orange juice**
- 1 **cup grapefruit juice**
- 1 **cup lemonade**
- 2 **cups ginger ale, chilled**
  Grenadine syrup

In a large pitcher, combine juices and lemonade. Refrigerate until chilled. Just before serving, stir in ginger ale. Pour into chilled glasses; slowly add grenadine to each.

Boo-Ya Mini Pizzas

These spooky pizzas are super-cute and made with simple ingredients. Now that's what I call party food!
—**POLLY COUMOS** MOGADORE, OH

START TO FINISH: 25 MIN.
MAKES: 20 MINI PIZZAS

- 2 **tubes (12 ounces each) refrigerated buttermilk biscuits**
- 1 **can (8 ounces) tomato sauce**
- 1½ **teaspoons dried minced onion**
- 1 **teaspoon dried oregano**
- 1 **teaspoon dried basil**
- ⅛ **teaspoon garlic powder**
- 20 **slices part-skim mozzarella cheese**
  Sliced ripe olives

1. Preheat oven to 400°. Roll or pat biscuits into 2½-in. circles. Place on greased baking sheets.
2. In a small bowl, combine tomato sauce, onion, oregano, basil and garlic powder; spread over biscuits. Bake for 8-10 minutes or until edges are lightly browned.
3. Meanwhile, using a small ghost-shape cookie cutter, cut a ghost out of each cheese slice. Immediately place a ghost over each warm pizza; add pieces of olives for faces.

Bone-Crunching Meatballs

Water chestnuts are the secret ingredient in these unique meatballs. Adults love the flavor, and kids enjoy the "bonelike" crunch the chestnuts add to each appetizer!

—*TASTE OF HOME* TEST KITCHEN

PREP: 30 MIN. • **BAKE:** 10 MIN. • **MAKES:** 5 DOZEN

- 1 can (8 ounces) sliced water chestnuts, drained
- 1 egg, lightly beaten
- 3 tablespoons reduced-sodium soy sauce
- ½ cup chopped green onions (green part only)
- ¼ cup dry bread crumbs
- 2 tablespoons minced fresh cilantro
- 1½ teaspoons grated lime peel
- 1½ teaspoons minced fresh gingerroot
- 1 garlic clove, minced
- ¼ teaspoon salt
- ¼ teaspoon pepper
- 1½ pounds lean ground turkey
- 2 tablespoons canola oil
  Plum sauce

1. Cut enough water chestnut slices in half to make 60 pieces; set aside. Save remaining water chestnuts slices for another use.

2. In a large bowl, combine the next 10 ingredients. Crumble turkey over mixture and mix well. Divide into 60 portions and shape each portion around a water chestnut piece.

3. Preheat oven to 350°. In a large nonstick skillet, saute meatballs in oil in batches 5 minutes or until browned. Transfer to a 13x9-in. baking dish.

4. Cover and bake 10-15 minutes or until meat is no longer pink; drain. Serve with plum sauce.

❝ These were a huge hit at my Halloween party! ❞

—KM2013
TASTEOFHOME.COM

Eyeball
Taco Salad

Eyeball Taco Salad

All eyes are on this tasty main-dish salad whenever it's out on the buffet. Topped with peepers, it's packed with beef, cheese, tomato and enough taco flavor to satisfy your entire crowd.

—**JOLENE YOUNG** UNION, IL

PREP: 35 MIN. • **BAKE:** 25 MIN.
MAKES: 10 SERVINGS

- 2½ pounds lean ground beef (90% lean)
- ¾ cup water
- 1 can (8 ounces) tomato sauce
- 1 envelope taco seasoning
- 1 package (12½ ounces) nacho tortilla chips, crushed
- 2 cups (8 ounces) shredded Monterey Jack cheese
- 2 cups (8 ounces) shredded cheddar cheese
- 4 cups torn iceberg lettuce
- 1 medium red onion, finely chopped
- 10 slices tomato, halved
- 1 cup (8 ounces) sour cream
- 10 whole pitted ripe olives, halved

1. In a Dutch oven, cook beef over medium heat until no longer pink; drain. Stir in water, tomato sauce and taco seasoning. Bring to a boil. Reduce heat; simmer, uncovered, for 15 minutes.

2. Meanwhile, preheat oven to 325°. Place the tortilla chips in a greased 15x10x1-in. baking pan; sprinkle with Monterey Jack cheese. Spread meat mixture over top; sprinkle with the cheddar cheese. Bake 25-30 minutes or until bubbly.

3. Top with lettuce and onion. Cut into ten 5x3-in. pieces. On each piece, arrange two tomato slices for eyes; top each with a dollop of sour cream and an olive half.

(5) INGREDIENTS
Bleeding Heart Brie

This impressive appetizer is simple to prepare with just a few ingredients. The cherries add a new twist to baked Brie and provide a sweet contrast to the salty cheese and golden pastry.

—*TASTE OF HOME* **TEST KITCHEN**

PREP: 15 MIN. • **BAKE:** 20 MIN.
MAKES: 10 SERVINGS

- 1 **tube (8 ounces) refrigerated crescent rolls**
- 1 **round (8 ounces) Brie cheese**
- ⅓ **cup cherry preserves**
- 1 **egg, lightly beaten**
   Assorted crackers

1. Preheat oven to 350°. Unroll crescent dough; divide into two squares. Seal the seams and perforations. Cut off corners from each square, forming two circles; discard scraps. Place one circle on a greased baking sheet; top with cheese. Spoon preserves over the top. Bring edges of dough up around sides of cheese. Top with remaining dough circle, pressing to seal edges. Brush top and sides with egg.
2. Bake 20-30 minutes or until golden brown. Cool 5 minutes before serving with crackers.

Chili Snack Mix

I remember my mother making chili mix in place of cookies for bake sales. Everyone loved it! It's also great for a snack at home, or to have on trips and at parties.
—**BARB GUSTISON** QUINCY, IL

PREP: 20 MIN. • **BAKE:** 10 MIN./BATCH + COOLING
MAKES: 6 QUARTS

- 1 **package (16 ounces) corn chips**
- 1 **can (11½ ounces) mixed nuts**
- 1 **package (11 ounces) pretzel sticks**
- 1 **package (6.6 ounces) miniature cheddar cheese fish-shaped crackers**
- 1 **cup butter, cubed**
- ½ **cup packed brown sugar**
- 1 **tablespoon garlic powder**
- 1 **tablespoon chili powder**
- ½ **teaspoon baking soda**

1. Preheat oven to 350°. In a large bowl, combine corn chips, nuts, pretzels and crackers. In a small saucepan, bring butter, brown sugar, garlic powder and chili powder to a boil. Remove from heat; stir in baking soda. Pour over the snack mixture and toss to coat.
2. Transfer to three greased 15x10x1-in. baking pans. Bake 10-12 minutes or until lightly toasted. Cool completely on wire racks. Store in airtight containers.

Li'l Lips

Li'l Lips

My kids just loved helping put the marshmallow "teeth" between the apple slices when I made these years ago. I usually made them with red apples but green apples would be a spooky alternative.
—**AGNES WARD** STRATFORD, ON

START TO FINISH: 20 MIN. • **MAKES:** 8 SERVINGS

- 1 **medium red apple**
- 1 **teaspoon lemon juice**
- ¼ **cup chunky peanut butter**
- 2 **tablespoons reduced-fat cream cheese**
- ⅛ **teaspoon ground cinnamon**
   Miniature marshmallows

1. Cut apple into 16 wedges; toss with lemon juice.
2. In a small bowl, mix peanut butter, cream cheese and cinnamon until blended. Spread about 2 teaspoons onto one side of half of the apple slices; top each with a second slice, pressing to form two lips.
3. Press marshmallows onto peanut butter for teeth. Cover and refrigerate until serving.

Bleeding Heart Brie

Haunted Potpie

Convenience items such as frozen hash browns, canned soup, frozen veggies and puff pastry make this savory potpie quick and easy...and creepy!

—*TASTE OF HOME* TEST KITCHEN

PREP: 30 MIN. • **BAKE:** 50 MIN.
MAKES: 12 SERVINGS

- 4 **cups cubed cooked chicken**
- 4 **cups frozen cubed hash brown potatoes, thawed**
- 1 **package (16 ounces) frozen mixed vegetables, thawed and drained**
- 1 **can (10¾ ounces) condensed cream of chicken soup, undiluted**
- 1 **can (10¾ ounces) condensed cream of onion soup, undiluted**
- 1 **cup (8 ounces) sour cream**
- ⅔ **cup milk**
- 2 **tablespoons all-purpose flour**
- ½ **teaspoon salt**
- ½ **teaspoon pepper**
- ¼ **teaspoon garlic powder**
- 3 **slices rye bread**
- 1 **sheet frozen puff pastry, thawed**

1. In a large bowl, combine the first 11 ingredients. Transfer to a greased 13x9-in. baking dish. Place bread in a food processor; cover and process to make crumbs. Sprinkle over chicken mixture. Bake at 350° for 40-45 minutes or until bubbly.

2. Meanwhile, on a lightly floured surface, unfold pastry sheet. Using a small floured ghost-shaped cookie cutter, cut out 12 ghosts. Place on an ungreased baking sheet. Remove potpie from the oven; set aside and keep warm.

3. Bake ghosts at 400° for 10 minutes or until puffy and golden brown. Top each serving with a ghost; serve immediately.

Slimy Red Goop Salad

⑤ INGREDIENTS

Slimy Red Goop Salad

This frightfully fun salad features cola, which adds to the bright, sparkling dish.

—JUDY NIX TOCCOA, GA

PREP: 20 MIN. + CHILLING • **MAKES:** 8 SERVINGS

- 1 **can (15 ounces) mandarin oranges**
- ½ **cup water**
- 2 **packages (3 ounces each) cherry gelatin**
- 1 **can (21 ounces) cherry pie filling**
- ¾ **cup cola**

1. Drain oranges, reserving juice; set fruit aside. In a large saucepan, bring mandarin orange juice and water to a boil; remove from the heat. Stir in gelatin until dissolved. Stir in pie filling and cola.

2. Pour into a 1½-qt. serving bowl. Refrigerate for 50 minutes or until slightly thickened. Fold in reserved oranges. Refrigerate 3 hours or until set.

❝Everyone LOVED this (salad) last year... kids and adults alike. It really does look CREEPY!❞

—MOMMAJAG
TASTEOFHOME.COM

Haunted Potpie

⑤ INGREDIENTS
S'mores-Dipped Apples

For me, the flavor combination of marshmallows, graham crackers and apples just can't be beat. Others must think the same thing. Any time I take these to an autumn bake sale, they sell out in a flash.
—**MARIA REGAKIS** SAUGUS, MA

PREP: 20 MIN. • **COOK:** 10 MIN. + CHILLING
MAKES: 8 SERVINGS

- 8 **large Granny Smith apples**
- 8 **wooden pop sticks**
- 2 **tablespoons butter**
- 2 **packages (16 ounces each) large marshmallows**
- 2 **cups coarsely crushed graham crackers**
- 1 **package (11½ ounces) milk chocolate chips**

1. Line a baking sheet with waxed paper; generously coat the waxed paper with cooking spray. Wash and dry the apples; remove stems. Insert pop sticks into apples.

2. In a large heavy saucepan, melt butter over medium heat. Add marshmallows; stir until melted. Dip apples, one at a time, into warm marshmallow mixture, allowing excess to drip off. Place on prepared baking sheet and refrigerate until set, about 15 minutes.

3. Place graham cracker crumbs in a shallow dish. In top of a double boiler or a metal bowl over barely simmering water, melt chocolate chips; stir until smooth. Dip bottom half of apples in chocolate; dip bottoms in cracker crumbs. Place on baking sheet. Refrigerate until set.

TOP TIP
Dipping Apples
Make sure the apples are at room temperature before dipping them. If the apples are too cold, ingredients may not stick particularly well and could slide off the apples.

Halloween Candy Bark

Halloween Candy Bark

My kids and I wanted to make a treat using beautiful fall colors and cute Halloween candies. Bring your own little ones into the kitchen to customize the bark with their favorite candies and cookies.
—**MARGARET BROTT** COLORADO SPRINGS, CO

PREP: 20 MIN. + STANDING • **MAKES:** 2¾ POUNDS

- 2 **teaspoons butter**
- 1½ **pounds white candy coating, coarsely chopped**
- 2 **cups pretzels, coarsely chopped**
- 10 **Oreo cookies, chopped**
- ¾ **cup candy corn**
- ¾ **cup dry roasted peanuts**
- ½ **cup milk chocolate M&M's**
- ½ **cup Reese's Pieces**

1. Line a 15x10x1-in. baking pan with foil; grease the foil with butter. In a microwave, melt candy coating; stir until smooth. Spread into prepared pan. Sprinkle with remaining ingredients; press into candy coating. Let stand about 1 hour.

2. Break or cut bark into pieces. Store in an airtight container.

Apple Trail Mix

With apple chips and cereal in fun shapes, this tasty mix makes a nutritious gift, bake sale item or Halloween party favor. Clear cone-shaped plastic bags and pretty ribbon make it look special.
—**ROSEMARY PACHA** BRIGHTON, IA

START TO FINISH: 15 MIN. • **MAKES:** 4 QUARTS

- 2 **packages (2½ ounces each) dried apple chips**
- 3 **cups Cinnamon Toast Crunch cereal**
- 2 **cups miniature pretzels**
- 2 **cups dry roasted peanuts**
- 1½ **cups Frosted Cheerios**
- 1½ **cups Apple Cinnamon Cheerios**
- 1½ **cups yogurt-covered raisins**
- 1½ **cups small apple-flavored green jelly beans**
- ⅔ **cup sunflower kernels**
  Ice cream waffle cones

In a large bowl, combine the first nine ingredients. Store in an airtight container. Serve the snack mix in waffle cones.

Dirt Balls

Looking for a showstopper on a Halloween buffet? Check out these dill-garlic cheese balls! They're easy to make, and you can simply omit the black sesame seeds for other holidays.

—KELLY YEAGER HAHNVILLE, LA

PREP: 20 MIN. + CHILLING
MAKES: 3 CHEESE BALLS (¾ CUP EACH)

- 2 **packages (8 ounces each) cream cheese, softened**
- 3 **tablespoons olive oil**
- 1 **cup (4 ounces) crumbled feta cheese**
- 5 **green onions, chopped**
- 3 **garlic cloves, minced**
- 1 **tablespoon dill weed**
- 2 **teaspoons dried oregano**
- ¾ **teaspoon coarsely ground pepper**
  Black sesame seeds
  Bagel chips

1. In a large bowl, beat cream cheese and oil until smooth. Stir in the feta cheese, onions, garlic, dill, oregano and pepper. Cover and refrigerate for at least 1 hour.

2. Shape cheese mixture into three balls and roll in sesame seeds. Wrap in plastic wrap; refrigerate for at least 1 hour. Serve with bagel chips.

Yummy Mummy with Veggie Dip

Yummy Mummy with Veggie Dip

I came up with this idea for dressing up a veggie tray for our annual Halloween party, and everyone got "wrapped up" in it. Frozen bread dough and dip mix make this a simple and easy appetizer that's as much fun to display as it is to eat!

—**HEATHER SNOW** SALT LAKE CITY, UT

PREP: 25 MIN. • **BAKE:** 20 MIN. + COOLING
MAKES: 16 SERVINGS (2 CUPS DIP)

- 1 loaf (1 pound) frozen bread dough, thawed
- 3 pieces string cheese
- 2 cups (16 ounces) sour cream
- 1 envelope fiesta ranch dip mix
- 1 pitted ripe olive
  Assorted crackers and fresh vegetables

1. Let dough rise according to package directions. Place dough on a greased baking sheet. For mummy, roll out dough into a 12-in. oval that is narrower at the bottom. For the mummy's neck, make an indentation on each side, about 1 in. down from the top. Let rise in a warm place for 20 minutes.
2. Preheat oven to 350°. Bake for 20-25 minutes or until golden brown. Arrange strips of string cheese over bread; bake 1-2 minutes longer or until cheese is melted. Remove from pan to a wire rack to cool.
3. Meanwhile, in a small bowl, combine the sour cream and dip mix. Chill dip until serving.
4. Cut mummy in half horizontally. Hollow out bottom half, leaving a ¾-in. shell. Cut removed bread into cubes; set aside. Place bread bottom on a serving plate. Spoon dip into shell. Replace top. For eyes, cut olive and position on head. Serve with crackers, vegetables and reserved bread.

Pumpkin Pie Martinis

This is an amazing treat! My girlfriends start asking me to make this drink in the fall and continue to request it through the holidays. Dessert martinis are always a great way to end a meal.

—**CATHLEEN BUSHMAN** GENEVA, IL

START TO FINISH: 5 MIN. • **MAKES:** 2 SERVINGS

- 1 vanilla wafer, crushed, optional
  Ice cubes
- 2 ounces vanilla-flavored vodka
- 2 ounces milk
- 2 ounces heavy whipping cream
- 1 ounce simple syrup
- 1 ounce hazelnut liqueur
- ⅛ teaspoon pumpkin pie spice
  Dash ground cinnamon

1. If a cookie-crumb rim is desired, moisten the rims of two cocktail glasses with water. Place cookie crumbs on a plate; dip rims in crumbs. Set aside.
2. Fill a mixing glass or tumbler three-fourths full with ice. Add the remaining ingredients; stir until condensation forms on outside of glass. Strain into two chilled cocktail glasses.
TO MAKE AHEAD *Prepare a martini mix of vodka, milk, cream, syrup and liqueur. Shake mix before using; pour 1 cup into the mixing glass for each batch of drinks. Add spices and proceed as directed.*

Pumpkin Pie Martinis

Pumpkin Spice Cake with Maple Glaze

Serve up some smiles with my delightful cake. This treat is a hit any time of the year, but it's especially nice during autumn. The traditional pumpkin flavor combined with spices and a delectable maple glaze give it real homemade flair.

—BARBARA ELLIOTT TYLER, TX

PREP: 20 MIN. • **BAKE:** 45 MIN. + COOLING
MAKES: 12 SERVINGS

- 1 **package yellow cake mix (regular size)**
- 1 **can (15 ounces) solid-pack pumpkin**
- 4 **eggs**
- ½ **cup canola oil**
- ⅓ **cup sugar**
- 2 **tablespoons ground cinnamon**
- 1 **teaspoon ground ginger**
- 1 **teaspoon ground allspice**
- 1 **teaspoon ground nutmeg**
- ¼ **teaspoon ground cloves**

GLAZE
- 2 **cups confectioners' sugar**
- 3 **to 4 tablespoons 2% milk**
- 2 **tablespoons maple syrup**
- ½ **teaspoon maple flavoring**
- ½ **cup chopped pecans, toasted**

1. Preheat oven to 350°. Place the first 10 ingredients in a large bowl; beat on low speed 30 seconds. Beat on medium for 2 minutes. Pour into a greased and floured 10-in. fluted tube pan.

2. Bake for 45-50 minutes or until a toothpick inserted near the center comes out clean. Cool 10 minutes before removing from pan to a wire rack to cool completely.

3. Whisk confectioners' sugar, milk, syrup and maple flavoring until smooth. Drizzle over cake and sprinkle with the pecans.

Pumpkin Spice Cake with Maple Glaze

Juicy Bat Wings

These wings are guaranteed to have your guests licking their fingers clean! If you'd like, you can replace the seasonings listed in the recipe with ¼ cup purchased blackened seasoning.

—COREY RUSSO ORONO, MN

START TO FINISH: 30 MIN.
MAKES: ABOUT 1 DOZEN

        Oil for deep-fat frying
2½ to 3 pounds chicken wings
½   cup cider vinegar
½   cup honey
1   tablespoon dried thyme
2   teaspoons sugar
1   teaspoon each salt, onion powder, garlic powder, paprika and pepper
½   teaspoon ground cumin
½   teaspoon dried oregano
½   teaspoon cayenne pepper
¼   teaspoon ground nutmeg

1. In an electric skillet or deep-fat fryer, heat oil to 375°. Fry chicken wings, a few at a time, for 3-4 minutes on each side or until juices run clear. Drain on paper towels; keep warm.

2. Meanwhile, in a small saucepan, combine the remaining ingredients. Bring to a boil; cook until liquid is syrupy and reduced by about half. (Keep face away from mixture as the odor is very strong.) Place chicken wings in a large bowl; drizzle with syrup and toss to coat.

⑤ INGREDIENTS

Creepy-Crawly Bugs

Who wouldn't want to eat our cute little bugs? Quick and easy prep and undeniable kid appeal make these a must-have for the buffet at a child's party.

—TASTE OF HOME TEST KITCHEN

START TO FINISH: 25 MIN. • **MAKES:** 8 SERVINGS

1   tube (11 ounces) refrigerated breadsticks
8   smoked sausage links or hot dogs
½   to ¾ cup potato sticks
    Ketchup and/or mustard

1. Preheat oven to 350°. Separate dough into strips. Unroll and cut eight strips in half widthwise; set remaining strips aside. Cut sausages in half widthwise. Wrap one piece of dough around each sausage, leaving the rounded end showing. Place seam side down on an ungreased baking sheet. Place reserved breadsticks on baking sheet.

2. Bake 15-17 minutes or until golden brown. Remove bugs to a serving plate and cool 2 minutes.

3. Insert potato sticks into baked dough to resemble legs and antennae. Decorate with ketchup and/or mustard. Serve warm. Save remaining breadsticks for another use.

NOTE *Refrigerated crescent rolls may be used in place of breadsticks. Follow the package directions for baking temperature and time.*

Wiggly Worm Stir-Fry

I love to cook with fresh vegetables, especially when they're from my garden. The ramen noodles look like worms, making this a fun dish for everyone.

—WENDY MYERS THOMPSON FALLS, MT

START TO FINISH: 20 MIN. • **MAKES:** 4 SERVINGS

1   small sweet red pepper, julienned
¾   cup cut fresh green beans
¾   cup thinly sliced fresh carrots
¼   cup chopped red onion
1   tablespoon canola oil
1   package (3 ounces) ramen noodles
1   yellow summer squash, sliced
1   medium zucchini, sliced
¼   cup chicken broth
1   tablespoon soy sauce
1   teaspoon fajita seasoning mix

1. In a large skillet or wok, stir-fry the pepper, green beans, carrots and onion in oil for 4 minutes. Meanwhile, cook noodles according to package directions (discard seasoning packet or save for another use).

2. Add the remaining ingredients to the vegetable mixture; cook and stir until vegetables are crisp-tender. Drain noodles; add to vegetables and stir until blended.

Juicy Bat Wings

Purple People-Eater

Purple People-Eater

This googly-eyed cupcake will get tongues wagging! Pretzels, marshmallows and candy help this monster come to life.

—KAREN TACK RIVERSIDE, CT

PREP: 45 MIN. + STANDING • **MAKES:** 6 CUPCAKES

- 6 **chocolate or vanilla cupcakes baked in black foil liners**
- 1 **can (16 ounces) vanilla frosting Neon purple food coloring**
- 9 **large marshmallows**
- 18 **thin pretzel sticks Black licorice laces**
- 12 **mini marshmallows**
- 6 **pink fruit chews**
- 18 **brown mini M&M's**

1. Spread tops of cupcakes with a mound of vanilla frosting. Spoon 1 tablespoon vanilla frosting into a small resealable bag. Tint the remaining vanilla frosting neon purple with the food coloring and place in a microwave-safe measuring cup.
2. Line a cookie sheet with waxed paper. Cut large marshmallows in half crosswise with scissors. Insert a pretzel stick into the side of each marshmallow to create eyes. Cut the black licorice laces into eighteen 2-in. pieces. Cut the mini marshmallows

in half on the diagonal to make the teeth. Soften pink fruit chews in the microwave for no more than 3 seconds.
3. Roll out each fruit chew into a 3-in. length. Cut into a long tongue with a rounded end. Press the back of a knife down the middle of the fruit chew to make the crease in the center of the tongue.
4. Place a wire rack over a cookie sheet lined with waxed paper. Heat the neon purple frosting in the microwave, stirring every 10 seconds, until the frosting is the consistency of slightly whipped cream, about 25 to 30 seconds total. Holding the frosted cupcakes by the foil liners, dip the cupcakes just up to the liners. Allow the excess frosting to drip off before inverting cupcake. Transfer to the wire rack to set.
5. Repeat with the remaining cupcakes. If the frosting becomes too thick, return it to the microwave and heat it for about 5 to 10 seconds longer, stirring well before dipping.
6. Holding the marshmallow eyes by the pretzel end, dip top half of marshmallows into the frosting to make the eyelids. Transfer the marshmallows to the waxed paper-lined cookie sheet. While frosting is still wet, add the black licorice lace along the dipped edge as the eyelid. Repeat with the remaining marshmallows. Snip a small corner from the bag with vanilla frosting. Pipe a dot of frosting on the marshmallow area and add the brown M&M as a pupil. Let eyes set for about 30 minutes before assembling cupcakes.
7. Spoon some of the remaining purple frosting on top of the dipped cupcakes and allow the frosting to drip over the sides.
8. While frosting is still wet, add three to four cut mini marshmallow pieces as the teeth along one edge of cupcakes. Insert three marshmallow eyes at different heights. Transfer to a serving platter and add the fruit chew tongue under the teeth.

People-Eater Cupcakes Are Eerily Easy!

Don't let the recipe for Purple People-Eater cupcakes scare you off! They're a cinch with a few no-fuss tips.

Making the Tongue:
Roll out each fruit chew into a 3-in. length. Cut into a long tongue with a rounded end. Press the back of a knife down the middle of the fruit chew to make the crease in the center of the monster's tongue.

Making the Eyes:
Holding the marshmallow eyes by the pretzel end, dip the top half of the marshmallows into the frosting to make the eyelids. While the frosting is still wet, add the black licorice lace along the dipped edge as the eyelid. Pipe a dot of frosting on the marshmallow area and add the brown candy as a pupil.
Don't be afraid to get creative. The above steps are simply ideas to get you started. Put your own spin on your kooky creations, and your adorable monster munchies will steal the spotlight at any Halloween get-together.

CATHY DOBBINS' GARLIC ROSEMARY TURKEY *PAGE 186*

Thanksgiving Gatherings

THANKSGIVING OFFERS FAMILIES MANY SPECIAL REASONS TO GATHER FOR A HEARTWARMING MEAL. AS YOUR LOVED ONES FLOCK TO THE DINNER TABLE, TREAT THEM TO THE FLAVORS OF HOME-STYLE COOKING WITH THE COMFORTING RECIPES YOU'VE LOOKED FORWARD TO ALL YEAR LONG.

GAYLEEN GROTE'S CREAMED PEAS AND CARROTS *PAGE 193*

COLLETTE GAUGLER'S BLUE-RIBBON APPLE PIE *PAGE 191*

JOANN KOERKENMEIER'S CREAMY MAKE-AHEAD MASHED POTATOES *PAGE 188*

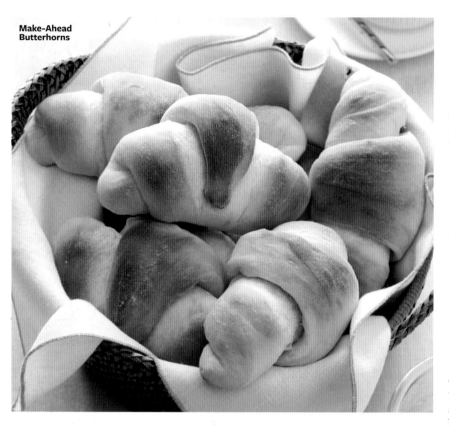

Make-Ahead Butterhorns

Brandied Apricot Tart

Canned apricots make this golden buttery tart a wonderful option any time of year. I brush on preserves and brandy, then sprinkle with almonds for a bit of crunch.

—**JOHNNA JOHNSON** SCOTTSDALE, AZ

PREP: 25 MIN. • **BAKE:** 20 MIN.
MAKES: 8 SERVINGS

- 1⅓ cups all-purpose flour
- 2 tablespoons sugar
- ½ cup cold butter
- 1 egg yolk
- 2 to 3 tablespoons 2% milk

FILLING
- ¾ cup apricot preserves
- 2 tablespoons apricot brandy
- 5 cans (15 ounces each) apricot halves, drained and halved
- 2 tablespoons slivered almonds, toasted
  Whipped cream, optional

1. Preheat oven to 450°. In a large bowl, combine flour and sugar. Cut in butter until crumbly. Add egg yolk. Gradually add the milk, tossing with a fork until a ball forms.
2. Press onto the bottom and up the sides of an ungreased 11-in. fluted tart pan with removable bottom. Bake for 8-10 minutes or until lightly browned. Cool on a wire rack. Reduce heat to 350°.
3. In a small saucepan, combine the preserves and brandy; cook and stir over low heat until melted. Brush 2 tablespoons over crust. Arrange half of the apricots over crust and brush with ⅓ cup of the preserve mixture; repeat. Sprinkle with almonds.
4. Bake 18-22 minutes longer or until crust is golden brown. Cool on a wire rack. Serve with the whipped cream if desired.

Make-Ahead Butterhorns

Mom loved to make these lightly sweet golden rolls. They're beautiful and impressive to serve with a big dinner. They also have a wonderful homemade flavor that makes them so memorable.
—**BERNICE MORRIS** MARSHFIELD, MO

PREP: 30 MIN. + RISING • **BAKE:** 15 MIN. + FREEZING
MAKES: 32 ROLLS

- 2 packages (¼ ounce each) active dry yeast
- ⅓ cup warm water (110° to 115°)
- 2 cups warm 2% milk (110° to 115°)
- 1 cup shortening
- 1 cup sugar
- 6 eggs
- 2 teaspoon salt
- 9 cups all-purpose flour, divided
- 3 to 4 tablespoons butter, melted

1. In a large bowl, dissolve yeast in water. Add milk, shortening, sugar,
eggs, salt and 4 cups flour; beat 3 minutes or until smooth. Add enough remaining flour to form a soft dough.
2. Turn onto a floured surface; knead lightly. Place in a greased bowl, turning once to grease top. Cover and let rise in a warm place until doubled, about 2 hours.
3. Punch dough down; divide into four equal parts. Roll each into a 9-in. circle; brush with butter. Cut each circle into eight pie-shaped wedges; roll up each wedge from wide edge to tip of dough and pinch to seal.
4. Place rolls with tip down on baking sheets; freeze. When frozen, place in freezer bags and seal. Store in freezer for up to 4 weeks.
5. Place on greased baking sheets; thaw 5 hours or until doubled in size. Preheat oven to 375°. Bake 12-15 minutes or until lightly browned. Remove from baking sheets; serve warm, or cool on wire rack.

Classic French Onion Soup

I hope you enjoy my signature soup the way my granddaughter does—in a French onion soup bowl complete with a homemade garlic crouton and gobs of melted Swiss cheese on top. If you haven't made French onion soup before, this is a good recipe to start with.

—LOU SANSEVERO FERRON, UT

PREP: 20 MIN. • **COOK:** 2 HOURS
MAKES: 12 SERVINGS

- 5 **tablespoons olive oil, divided**
- 1 **tablespoon butter**
- 8 **cups thinly sliced onions (about 3 pounds)**
- 3 **garlic cloves, minced**
- ½ **cup port wine**
- 2 **cartons (32 ounces each) beef broth**
- ½ **teaspoon pepper**
- ¼ **teaspoon salt**
- 24 **slices French bread baguette (½ inch thick)**
- 2 **large garlic cloves, peeled and halved**
- ¾ **cup shredded Gruyere or Swiss cheese**

1. In a Dutch oven, heat 2 tablespoons oil and butter over medium heat. Add onions; cook and stir for 10-13 minutes or until softened. Reduce heat to medium-low; cook for 30-40 minutes or until deep golden brown, stirring occasionally. Add minced garlic; cook 2 minutes longer.
2. Stir in wine. Bring to a boil; cook until liquid is reduced by half. Add the broth, pepper and salt; return to a boil. Reduce heat; simmer soup for 1 hour, stirring occasionally.
3. Meanwhile, place baguette slices on a baking sheet; brush both sides with remaining oil. Bake bread at 400° for 3-5 minutes on each side or until toasted. Rub toasts with halved garlic.
4. To serve, place twelve 8-oz. broiler-safe bowls or ramekins on baking sheets. Place two toasts in each. Ladle with soup; top with cheese. Broil 4 in. from heat until cheese is melted.

❝This was my first time making French onion soup. It was perfect.❞
—**MADRAVEN4** TASTEOFHOME.COM

Classic French Onion Soup

Roasted Garlic Butternut Soup

Roasted Garlic Butternut Soup

Why not start Thanksgiving with soup? My specialty celebrates autumn's flavors.

—**ROBIN HAAS** CRANSTON, RI

PREP: 35 MIN. • **COOK:** 20 MIN.
MAKES: 9 SERVINGS (2¼ QUARTS)

- 1 whole garlic bulb
- 1 teaspoon olive oil
- 1 medium butternut squash (3 pounds), peeled and cubed
- 1 medium sweet potato, peeled and cubed
- 1 large onion, chopped
- 2 tablespoons butter
- 3¼ cups water
- 1 can (14½ ounces) reduced-sodium chicken broth
- 1 teaspoon paprika
- ½ teaspoon pepper
- ¼ teaspoon salt
- 9 tablespoons crumbled blue cheese

1. Preheat oven to 425°. Remove papery outer skin from garlic (do not peel or separate cloves). Cut top off garlic bulb. Brush with oil; wrap in heavy-duty foil. Bake 30-35 minutes or until softened. Cool for 10-15 minutes.
2. Meanwhile, in a Dutch oven, saute squash, sweet potato and onion in butter until crisp-tender. Add water, broth, paprika, pepper and salt; squeeze the softened garlic into pan. Bring to a boil. Reduce heat; cover and simmer 20-25 minutes or until vegetables are tender. Cool slightly.
3. In a food processor, process soup in batches until smooth. Return all to pan and heat through. Ladle into bowls; top with blue cheese.

Holiday Green Bean Casserole

Try my perked-up green bean casserole this year and you'll never go back to the old stuff. No one will ever know it's light!

—**LAURA FALL-SUTTON** BUHL, ID

PREP: 40 MIN. • **BAKE:** 15 MIN.
MAKES: 12 SERVINGS

- 8 cups cut fresh green beans (about 2 pounds)
- ½ pound sliced fresh mushrooms
- 2 tablespoons butter
- 2 tablespoons all-purpose flour
- 1 teaspoon dried minced onion
- ½ teaspoon pepper
- ½ cup fat-free milk
- 1 cup reduced-fat sour cream
- 1 teaspoon Worcestershire sauce
- 1½ cups (6 ounces) shredded reduced-fat Swiss cheese

TOPPING
- ⅓ cup slivered almonds
- ⅓ cup crushed cornflakes
- 1 tablespoon butter, melted

1. Place beans in a Dutch oven and cover with water; bring to a boil. Cover and cook for 3-5 minutes or until crisp-tender; drain and set aside.
2. Preheat oven to 400°. In a large skillet, saute mushrooms in butter until tender. Stir in flour, onion and pepper until blended. Gradually stir in milk. Bring to a boil; cook and stir 1-2 minutes or until thickened. Remove from heat; stir in sour cream and Worcestershire sauce. Stir in beans and cheese until blended.
3. Transfer to an 11x7-in. baking dish coated with cooking spray (dish will be full). Combine topping ingredients; sprinkle over the top.
4. Bake, uncovered, 12-16 minutes or until bubbly and heated through.

Harvest Salad with Cherry Vinaigrette

Mixed greens and plenty of produce make this salad so satisfying, and it's gorgeous to serve for special holidays.

—**JAYE BEELER** GRAND RAPIDS, MI

PREP: 10 MIN. • **BAKE:** 50 MIN. + COOLING
MAKES: 10 SERVINGS (1 CUP EACH)

- 3 medium fresh beets (about 1 pound)
- 1 package (5 ounces) spring mix salad greens
- 2 medium apples, thinly sliced
- 1 medium carrot, shredded
- ½ cup grape tomatoes, halved
- ½ cup yellow grape tomatoes or pear tomatoes, halved
- ½ cup garbanzo beans or chickpeas, rinsed and drained
- ½ cup coarsely chopped walnuts, toasted
- 4 thick-sliced bacon strips, cooked and crumbled

CHERRY VINAIGRETTE
- ½ cup tart cherry preserves
- 3 tablespoons olive oil
- 2 tablespoons red wine vinegar
- 2 teaspoons Dijon mustard
- 1 garlic clove, minced
- ¼ teaspoon salt
- ⅛ teaspoon pepper

1. Preheat oven to 400°. Scrub beets and trim tops to 1 in. Wrap in foil; place on a baking sheet. Bake 50-60 minutes or until tender. Remove the foil; cool completely. Peel beets and cut into ½-in. pieces.
2. In a large bowl, combine salad greens, apples, carrot, tomatoes, beans, walnuts, bacon and cooled beets. In a small bowl, whisk the vinaigrette ingredients until blended. Serve with salad.

Harvest Salad with Cherry Vinaigrette

**Honey-Orange
Winter Vegetable Medley**

Honey-Orange Winter Vegetable Medley

A medley of vegetables coated with a sweet-savory sauce makes a lovely addition to any holiday dinner.

—JENNIFER CODUTO KENT, OH

PREP: 30 MIN. • **BAKE:** 1 HOUR
MAKES: 9 SERVINGS

- 3 cups fresh baby carrots
- 2 cups cubed red potatoes
- 2 cups pearl onions, peeled
- 2 cups cubed peeled sweet potatoes
- ¾ cup reduced-sodium chicken broth
- ½ cup orange marmalade
- ¼ cup honey
- 2 tablespoons lemon juice
- 1½ teaspoons poultry seasoning
- ¾ teaspoon salt
- ¾ teaspoon pepper
- 3 tablespoons butter, cubed

1. Preheat oven to 375°. Place the vegetables in a greased shallow 3-qt. baking dish. In a small bowl, combine broth, marmalade, honey, lemon juice and seasonings. Pour over vegetables and toss to coat. Dot with butter.
2. Cover and bake 30 minutes. Uncover and bake 30-40 minutes longer or until vegetables are tender.

Ginger-Streusel Pumpkin Pie

I love to bake and have spent a lot of time making goodies for my family and friends. I think the streusel topping gives this pie a special touch.

—SONIA PARVU SHERRILL, NY

PREP: 25 MIN. • **BAKE:** 55 MIN. + COOLING
MAKES: 8 SERVINGS

- 1 sheet refrigerated pie pastry
- 3 eggs
- 1 can (15 ounces) solid-pack pumpkin
- 1½ cups heavy whipping cream
- ½ cup sugar
- ¼ cup packed brown sugar
- 1½ teaspoons ground cinnamon
- ½ teaspoon salt
- ¼ teaspoon ground allspice
- ¼ teaspoon ground nutmeg
- ¼ teaspoon ground cloves

STREUSEL
- 1 cup all-purpose flour
- ½ cup packed brown sugar
- ½ cup cold butter, cubed
- ½ cup chopped walnuts
- ⅓ cup finely chopped crystallized ginger

1. Preheat oven to 350°. On a lightly floured surface, unroll pastry. Transfer pastry to a 9-in. pie plate. Trim pastry to ½ in. beyond edge of plate; flute edges.
2. In a large bowl, whisk eggs, pumpkin, cream, sugars, cinnamon, salt, allspice, nutmeg and cloves. Pour into pastry shell. Bake 40 minutes.
3. In a small bowl, combine flour and brown sugar; cut in butter until crumbly. Stir in the walnuts and ginger. Gently sprinkle over filling.
4. Bake 15-25 minutes longer or until a knife inserted near the center comes out clean. Cool on a wire rack. Refrigerate leftovers.

**Ginger-Streusel
Pumpkin Pie**

Mahogany-Glazed Cornish Hen

I make this for my husband and myself for Thanksgiving dinner. It's an elegant tradition that's perfect for two. Simply double or triple the recipe if you're expecting guests.
—**JEANNETTE SABO** LEXINGTON PARK, MD

PREP: 15 MIN. • **BAKE:** 20 MIN.
MAKES: 2 SERVINGS

- 1 **Cornish game hen (20 to 24 ounces), split lengthwise**
- 1 **tablespoon butter**
- ½ **teaspoon minced fresh gingerroot**
- ½ **teaspoon grated orange peel**
- 2 **tablespoons apricot preserves**
- 1 **tablespoon balsamic vinegar**
- 1 **tablespoon reduced-sodium soy sauce**
- 2 **teaspoons Dijon mustard**
- ¼ **teaspoon salt**
- ⅛ **teaspoon pepper**
- 1 **to 1½ cups chicken broth, divided**

1. Preheat oven to 450°. Place hen in a greased shallow roasting pan, skin side up. Combine butter, ginger and orange peel; rub under skin.
2. In a small bowl, whisk preserves, vinegar, soy sauce and mustard. Reserve half of the mixture for basting. Spoon remaining mixture over hen; sprinkle with salt and pepper. Pour ½ cup chicken broth into pan.
3. Roast 20-25 minutes or until a thermometer inserted in thigh reads 180°, adding broth to pan as necessary and basting with remaining glaze halfway through cooking. Serve with pan juices.

Pecan-Corn Bread Dressing

Pecan-Corn Bread Dressing

Plenty of pecans, bacon and butter give this dressing wonderfully rich flavor.
—*TASTE OF HOME* TEST KITCHEN

PREP: 25 MIN. • **BAKE:** 45 MIN.
MAKES: 10 SERVINGS

- 3 **cups water**
- ½ **cup butter**
- 1 **package (16 ounces) corn bread stuffing mix**
- 10 **bacon strips, diced**
- 1 **cup chopped celery**
- 1½ **cups chopped green onions**
- ½ **cup coarsely chopped pecans**
- ½ **teaspoon salt**
- ¼ **teaspoon pepper**

1. In a large saucepan, bring water and butter to a boil. Remove from heat and stir in stuffing mix; cover and set aside.
2. In a large skillet, cook bacon until crisp; remove with a slotted spoon to drain on paper towels. Discard all but 3 tablespoons of drippings; cook celery in drippings over medium heat for 5 minutes. Add onions and cook for 5 minutes or until celery is tender, stirring constantly. Add to corn bread mixture along with pecans, salt, pepper and bacon; mix well.
3. Transfer to a greased 2-qt. casserole. Cover and bake at 325° for 45 minutes or until heated through.

TOP TIP

To Chop or Not to Chop...That is the Question

Chopping an ingredient before or after measuring it can make a difference. Here's a trick that might help: If the word "chopped" comes before the ingredient when listed in a recipe, then chop the ingredient before measuring. If the word comes after the ingredient, then chop after measuring. For instance, "1 cup nuts, chopped" means you should measure 1 cup of nuts and then chop them. The phrase "1 cup chopped nuts" means you'd chop the nuts first and measure out 1 cup.

Sausage Stuffing Muffins

Oh-So-Good Creamy Mashed Potatoes

Yukon Golds are great for mashed potatoes because of their buttery flavor and low moisture content. They easily absorb the warm milk or melted butter you add to your spuds. Give my no-fuss recipe a try!

—**BRITTANY JACKSON** SEYMOUR, WI

PREP: 20 MIN. • **COOK:** 25 MIN.
MAKES: 18 SERVINGS (¾ CUP EACH)

- 8 large Yukon Gold potatoes, peeled and quartered (about 6 pounds)
- 2 teaspoons salt
- 2½ cups 2% milk
- ½ cup butter, cubed
- 3 teaspoons garlic salt
- 1 teaspoon pepper
- ¼ cup sour cream
  Additional 2% milk, optional
  Chopped fresh parsley

1. Place potatoes and salt in a stockpot; add water to cover. Bring to a boil. Reduce heat; cook, uncovered, for 20-25 minutes or until potatoes are tender. Meanwhile, in a large saucepan, heat milk, butter, garlic salt and pepper over medium heat until butter is melted.

2. Drain potatoes, then shake over low heat for 1-2 minutes to dry. Mash the potatoes with a potato masher or beat with a mixer; gradually add the milk mixture. Stir in sour cream. Stir in additional milk to thin if desired. Sprinkle with parsley.

FREEZE IT

Sausage Stuffing Muffins

When I made my first Thanksgiving dinner, I found that setting stuffing into a muffin tin makes for a special presentation. You can also bake the stuffing in a greased baking dish, if you'd rather.

—**TRICIA BIBB** HARTSELLE, AL

PREP: 45 MIN. • **BAKE:** 20 MIN.
MAKES: 1½ DOZEN

- 1 pound bulk pork sausage
- 4 celery ribs, chopped
- 2 medium onions, chopped
- ¼ cup butter, cubed
- 1 package (14 ounces) crushed corn bread stuffing
- 2 medium apples, peeled and chopped
- 1 package (5 ounces) dried cranberries
- 1 cup chopped pecans
- 1 teaspoon salt
- 1 teaspoon pepper
- 2 to 3 cups reduced-sodium chicken broth
- 2 eggs
- 2 teaspoons baking powder

1. Preheat oven to 375°. In a large skillet, cook sausage over medium heat until no longer pink; drain. Transfer to a large bowl; set aside.

2. In same skillet, saute the celery and onions in butter until tender. Transfer to bowl; add stuffing, apples, cranberries, pecans, salt and pepper. Stir in enough broth to reach desired moistness. Whisk eggs and baking powder; add to stuffing mixture.

3. Spoon into 18 greased muffin cups. Bake 20-25 minutes or until lightly browned. Cool 10 minutes. Run a knife around edges of muffin cups to loosen. Serve immediately.

FREEZE OPTION *Freeze cooled stuffing muffins in resealable plastic bags. To use, partially thaw in refrigerator overnight. Place muffins on greased baking sheets, cover with foil and reheat in a preheated 375° oven for 6-10 minutes or until heated through.*

“One of the best mashed potato recipes I ever made. Quick, easy and delicious.”

—**NOMARLOVER**
TASTEOFHOME.COM

Molasses-Bourbon Pecan Pie

Molasses-Bourbon Pecan Pie

Guests' mouths water when they see this Southern charmer. Its flaky crust perfectly complements the rich, nutty filling. What a treat for the holidays!

—**CHARLENE CHAMBERS**
ORMOND BEACH, FL

PREP: 35 MIN. + CHILLING
BAKE: 55 MIN. + COOLING
MAKES: 8 SERVINGS

- 1½ cups all-purpose flour
- ¾ teaspoon salt
- 6 tablespoons shortening
- 5 to 6 tablespoons ice water

FILLING

- ¾ cup packed brown sugar
- ¾ cup corn syrup
- ½ cup molasses
- 3 tablespoons butter
- ½ teaspoon salt
- 3 eggs, beaten
- 2 tablespoons bourbon
- 2 teaspoons vanilla extract
- 2 cups pecan halves
  Whipped cream

1. In a large bowl, combine flour and salt; cut in shortening until crumbly. Gradually add water, tossing with a fork until dough forms a ball. Wrap in plastic wrap. Refrigerate for 1 to 1½ hours or until easy to handle.

2. Roll out pastry to fit a 9-in. pie plate. Transfer pastry to pie plate. Trim pastry to ½ in. beyond edge of plate; flute edges. Refrigerate.

3. Meanwhile, in a large saucepan, combine the brown sugar, corn syrup, molasses, butter and salt; bring to a simmer over medium heat. Cover and stir for 2-3 minutes or until sugar is dissolved. Remove from the heat and cool to room temperature. (Mixture will be thick when cooled.)

4. Preheat oven to 350°. Stir the eggs, bourbon and vanilla into the molasses mixture. Stir in pecans. Pour into pastry shell. Bake 55-60 minutes or until a knife inserted near the center comes out clean. Cover the edges with foil during the last 30 minutes to prevent overbrowning if necessary.

5. Cool on a wire rack. Serve with whipped cream. Refrigerate leftovers.

Company Rice

This colorful side dish is a proven favorite with family and friends. One of my son's friends always requested "that rice" when he came over for dinner. It's delicious served with grilled salmon, beef, turkey, lamb roast or ham.

—**JAYNE SHILEY** CAMPBELLSPORT, WI

PREP: 10 MIN. • **COOK:** 55 MIN.
MAKES: 10 SERVINGS

- 1 celery rib, thinly sliced
- 1 large carrot, finely chopped
- 1 small onion, finely chopped
- 2 tablespoons butter
- 5 cups chicken broth
- 1 cup uncooked wild rice
- 1 cup uncooked long grain rice
- ⅔ cup dried cherries or cranberries
- ½ cup chopped pecans, toasted

1. In a saucepan, saute celery, carrot and onion in butter until tender. Stir in broth and wild rice. Bring to a boil. Reduce heat; cover and simmer for 25 minutes.

2. Add long grain rice; cover and simmer 20 minutes longer. Stir in cherries; cook 5 minutes longer or until the liquid is absorbed. Just before serving, stir in the pecans.

Taste-of-Fall Salad

My parents stayed with me at a friend's beautiful ranch for the holidays, and I made this great salad. We loved it so much, It turned into every night's first course.

—**KRISTIN KOSSAK** BOZEMAN, MT

START TO FINISH: 25 MIN. • **MAKES:** 6 SERVINGS

- ⅔ cup pecan halves
- ¼ cup balsamic vinegar, divided
  Dash cayenne pepper
  Dash ground cinnamon
- 3 tablespoons sugar, divided
- 1 package (5 ounces) spring mix salad greens
- ¼ cup olive oil
- 1 teaspoon Dijon mustard
- ⅛ teaspoon salt
- 1 medium pear, thinly sliced
- ¼ cup shredded Parmesan cheese

1. In a large heavy skillet, cook the pecans, 2 tablespoons vinegar, cayenne and cinnamon over medium heat until nuts are toasted, about 4 minutes. Sprinkle with 1 tablespoon sugar. Cook and stir for 2-4 minutes or until sugar is melted. Spread on foil to cool.

2. Place salad greens in a large bowl. In a small bowl, whisk the oil, mustard, salt and remaining vinegar and sugar; drizzle over greens and toss to coat. Arrange the greens, pear slices and pecans on six salad plates. Sprinkle with cheese.

Taste-of-Fall Salad

Turkey Pilgrim Cookies

These darling little gobblers are fun to make and will bring smiles to all of your Turkey Day guests.

—TASTE OF HOME TEST KITCHEN

START TO FINISH: 30 MIN. • **MAKES:** 1 DOZEN

- 84 **pieces candy corn**
- 24 **double-stuffed Oreo cookies**
- ¾ **cup canned chocolate frosting**
- 12 **miniature peanut butter cups**
- 12 **Hershey Kisses of your choice**
- ¾ **cup canned vanilla frosting**
  Orange food coloring
- 6 **miniature marshmallows, halved**
- 6 **mini Oreo cookies**
- 12 **Rolo candies**

1. Insert seven pieces of candy corn in a fan shape into half of the double-stuffed cookies. Position each cookie perpendicular to a remaining double-stuffed cookie; attach with chocolate frosting.

2. Using chocolate frosting, attach a peanut butter cup and a kiss to the front of each cookie. Tint vanilla frosting orange. For eyes, attach two marshmallow halves to each kiss with a small amount of orange frosting.

3. Twist mini cookies apart; remove and discard cream filling. Attach a Rolo to each mini cookie half with chocolate frosting and attach to tops of turkeys.

4. Using remaining frosting, pipe pupils, mouths and legs on turkeys. Let stand until set.

Turkey Pilgrim Cookies

Garlic Rosemary Turkey

⑤ INGREDIENTS

Garlic Rosemary Turkey

Our house smells incredible while the bird is roasting, and my family can hardly wait to eat. The garlic, herbs and lemon are such simple ingredients, but they're all you really need to make this holiday turkey shine.

—CATHY DOBBINS RIO RANCHO, NM

PREP: 10 MIN. • **BAKE:** 3 HOURS + STANDING
MAKES: 10 SERVINGS

- 1 **whole turkey (10 to 12 pounds)**
- 6 **to 8 garlic cloves, peeled**
- 2 **large lemons, halved**
- 2 **tablespoons olive oil**
- 2 **teaspoons dried rosemary, crushed**
- 1 **teaspoon rubbed sage**

1. Preheat oven to 325°. Cut six to eight small slits in turkey skin; insert garlic under the skin. Squeeze two lemon halves inside the turkey; squeeze remaining halves over outside of turkey. Place lemons in the cavity.

2. Tuck wings under the turkey; tie drumsticks together. Place on a rack in a shallow roasting pan, breast side up. Brush with oil; sprinkle with rosemary and sage. Roast 1 hour.

3. Cover turkey with foil; roast 2 to 2½ hours longer or until a thermometer inserted in thickest part of thigh reads 170°-175°. Baste occasionally with pan drippings.

4. Remove turkey from oven. Let stand 20 minutes before carving. If desired, skim fat and thicken pan drippings for gravy. Serve with turkey.

❝I made this for Thanksgiving. It was my first turkey, and it was fantastic and easy!❞
—THEHEAT01 TASTEOFHOME.COM

Cinnamon Raisin Bread

Cinnamon and raisins bring heartwarming flavor to this mildly sweet bread. It's ideal as a change-of-pace loaf for a special dinner.
—**FLO BURTNETT** GAGE, OK

PREP: 15 MIN. • **BAKE:** 55 MIN. + COOLING
MAKES: 2 LOAVES (12 SLICES EACH)

- 4 **cups all-purpose flour**
- 2 **cups sugar, divided**
- 2 **teaspoons baking soda**
- 1 **teaspoon salt**
- 2 **eggs**
- 2 **cups buttermilk**
- ½ **cup canola oil**
- ½ **cup raisins**
- 3 **teaspoons ground cinnamon**

1. Preheat oven to 350°. In a large bowl, combine flour, 1½ cups sugar, soda and salt. In a small bowl, whisk the eggs, buttermilk and oil. Stir into the dry ingredients just until moistened. Fold in raisins. Combine cinnamon and remaining sugar; set aside.

2. Spoon half the batter into two greased 8x4-in. loaf pans. Sprinkle with half of the reserved cinnamon-sugar; repeat layers. Gently cut through batter with a knife to swirl.

3. Bake 55-60 minutes or until a toothpick inserted in center comes out clean. Cool in pans 10 minutes before removing from pans to wire racks.

FREEZE OPTION *Wrap cooled bread in foil and freeze for up to 3 months. To use, thaw at room temperature.*

Cinnamon
Raisin Bread

Lemon Roasted Fingerlings
and Brussels Sprouts

Lemon Roasted Fingerlings and Brussels Sprouts

I've tried this recipe with other veggie combinations, too. The trick is choosing items that roast in about the same amount of time. Try skinny little green beans and thinly sliced onions, cauliflower florets and baby carrots, or okra and cherry tomatoes.
—**COURTNEY GAYLORD** COLUMBUS, IN

PREP: 15 MIN. • **BAKE:** 20 MIN.
MAKES: 8 SERVINGS

- 1 **pound fingerling potatoes, halved**
- 1 **pound Brussels sprouts, trimmed and halved**
- 6 **tablespoons olive oil, divided**
- ¾ **teaspoon salt, divided**
- ¼ **teaspoon pepper**
- 3 **tablespoons lemon juice**
- 1 **garlic clove, minced**
- 1 **teaspoon Dijon mustard**
- 1 **teaspoon honey**

1. Preheat oven to 425°. Place potatoes and Brussels sprouts in a greased 15x10x1-in. baking pan. Drizzle with 2 tablespoons oil; sprinkle with ½ teaspoon salt and pepper. Toss to coat. Roast 20-25 minutes or until tender, stirring once.

2. In a small bowl, whisk lemon juice, garlic, mustard, honey and remaining oil and salt until blended. Transfer the vegetables to a large bowl; drizzle with vinaigrette and toss to coat. Serve warm.

Moist Chocolate Cake

Creamy Make-Ahead Mashed Potatoes

Can mashed potatoes get any better? My answer is yes, particularly when you top them with cheese, onions and bacon.

—**JOANN KOERKENMEIER** DAMIANSVILLE, IL

PREP: 35 MIN. + CHILLING • **BAKE:** 40 MIN.
MAKES: 10 SERVINGS

- 3 **pounds potatoes (about 9 medium), peeled and cubed**
- 6 **bacon strips, chopped**
- 1 **package (8 ounces) cream cheese, softened**
- ½ **cup sour cream**
- ½ **cup butter, cubed**
- ¼ **cup 2% milk**
- 1½ **teaspoons onion powder**
- 1 **teaspoon salt**
- 1 **teaspoon garlic powder**
- ½ **teaspoon pepper**
- 1 **cup (4 ounces) shredded cheddar cheese**
- 3 **green onions, chopped**

1. Place potatoes in a Dutch oven; add water to cover. Bring to a boil. Reduce heat; cook, uncovered, 10-15 minutes or until tender.
2. Meanwhile, in a skillet, cook bacon over medium heat until crisp. Remove to paper towels with a slotted spoon; drain.
3. Drain potatoes; return to pan. Mash potatoes, gradually adding cream cheese, sour cream and butter. Stir in the milk and seasonings. Transfer to a greased 13x9-in. baking dish; sprinkle with the cheese, green onions and bacon. Refrigerate, covered, up to 1 day.
4. Preheat oven to 350°. Remove the potatoes from refrigerator and let stand while oven heats. Bake, uncovered, for 40-50 minutes or until heated through.

Moist Chocolate Cake

The cake reminds me of my grandmother, because it was one of her specialties. I bake it for family parties, and it always brings fond memories. It's light and airy with a delicious chocolate flavor.

—**PATRICIA KREITZ** RICHLAND, PA

PREP: 15 MIN. • **BAKE:** 25 MIN.
MAKES: 12 SERVINGS

- 2 **cups all-purpose flour**
- 1 **teaspoon salt**
- 1 **teaspoon baking powder**
- 2 **teaspoons baking soda**
- ¾ **cup baking cocoa**
- 2 **cups sugar**
- 1 **cup canola oil**
- 1 **cup brewed coffee**
- 1 **cup milk**
- 2 **eggs**
- 1 **teaspoon vanilla extract**

FAVORITE ICING
- 1 **cup milk**
- 5 **tablespoons all-purpose flour**
- ½ **cup butter, softened**
- ½ **cup shortening**
- 1 **cup sugar**
- 1 **teaspoon vanilla extract**

1. Preheat oven to 325°. Sift together dry ingredients in a bowl. Add oil, coffee and milk; mix at medium speed 1 minute. Add eggs and vanilla; beat 2 minutes longer. (Batter will be thin.)
2. Pour into two greased and floured 9-in. round baking pans, two 8-in. round baking pans or six muffin cups.
3. Bake 25-30 minutes. Cool 10 minutes before removing from pans. Cool on wire racks.
4. Meanwhile, for icing, combine milk and flour in a saucepan; cook until thick. Cover and refrigerate.
5. In a bowl, beat butter, shortening, sugar and vanilla until creamy. Add the chilled milk mixture and beat for 10 minutes. Frost cooled cake.

Triple Cranberry Sauce

Cranberry fans will ask for this sauce time and again. It's loaded with their favorite fruit—in fresh, dried and juice form. Orange and allspice make it simply awesome.

—**ARLENE SMULSKI** LYONS, IL

PREP: 10 MIN. • **COOK:** 15 MIN. + CHILLING
MAKES: 3 CUPS

- 1 **package (12 ounces) fresh or frozen cranberries**
- 1 **cup thawed cranberry juice concentrate**
- ½ **cup dried cranberries**
- ⅓ **cup sugar**
- 3 **tablespoons orange juice**
- 3 **tablespoons orange marmalade**
- 2 **teaspoons grated orange peel**
- ¼ **teaspoon ground allspice**

1. In a small saucepan, combine the cranberries, cranberry juice concentrate, dried cranberries and sugar. Cook over medium heat until the berries pop, about 15 minutes.

2. Remove from the heat; stir in the orange juice, marmalade, orange peel and allspice. Transfer to a small bowl; refrigerate until chilled.

Triple Cranberry Sauce

Rainbow Vegetable Skillet

Here's a skillet side dish to free up the oven when preparing holiday meals. It's pretty and absolutely scrumptious. Sometimes I turn it into a weeknight entree by stirring in pieces of cooked chicken.

—JENNIFER SCHMIDT DICKENS, TX

START TO FINISH: 30 MIN. • **MAKES:** 9 SERVINGS

- 1 **medium butternut squash (about 2 pounds)**
- ¼ **cup reduced-fat butter, melted**
- 2 **tablespoons brown sugar**
- 1 **tablespoon chili powder**
- 1 **tablespoon minced fresh cilantro**
- 1 **teaspoon salt**
- ½ **teaspoon pepper**
- ¼ **teaspoon ground cinnamon**
- 1 **medium green pepper, cut into 1-inch pieces**
- 1 **medium sweet yellow pepper, cut into 1-inch pieces**
- 1 **medium red onion, cut into wedges**
- 1 **tablespoon olive oil**
- 2 **cups grape tomatoes**

1. Cut squash in half; discard seeds. Place cut side down in a microwave-safe dish; add ½ in. water. Microwave, uncovered, on high for 10-12 minutes or until almost tender.

2. Meanwhile, in a small bowl, combine the butter, brown sugar, chili powder, cilantro, salt, pepper and cinnamon; set aside. When squash is cool enough to handle, peel and discard rind. Cut flesh into ½-in. pieces.

3. In a large skillet, saute peppers and onion in oil until tender. Add tomatoes and squash; heat through. Transfer to a large bowl; add butter mixture and toss to coat.

NOTE *This recipe was tested with Land O'Lakes light stick butter.*

⑤ INGREDIENTS
Honey-Apple Turkey Breast

We really like the honey flavor in this four-ingredient dish! The sweetness even comes through when I use the leftovers in casseroles and soups.

—RITA REINKE WAUWATOSA, WI

PREP: 10 MIN. • **BAKE:** 2 HOURS + STANDING
MAKES: 12-14 SERVINGS

- ¾ **cup thawed apple juice concentrate**
- ⅓ **cup honey**
- 1 **tablespoon ground mustard**
- 1 **bone-in turkey breast (6 to 7 pounds)**

1. Preheat oven to 325°. In a small saucepan, combine the apple juice concentrate, honey and mustard. Cook over low heat 2-3 minutes or just until blended, stirring occasionally.

2. Place turkey breast on a rack in a foil-lined shallow roasting pan; pour honey mixture over the top.

3. Bake, uncovered, 2 to 2½ hours or until a thermometer reads 170°, basting with pan juices every 30 minutes. (Cover loosely with foil if turkey browns too quickly.) Cover and let stand 15 minutes before carving.

TOP TIP

Cover It Up!

After baking a bone-in turkey, remove it from the oven and cover with foil. Let stand for 15 minutes before carving and you'll have a moister and juicier turkey.

Honey-Apple
Turkey Breast

Herbed Veggie Mix-Up

Herbed Veggie Mix-Up

A simple treatment of mixed herbs and seasonings brings out the best in this quick and colorful medley of vegetables.

—**MARIE FORTE** RARITAN, NJ

START TO FINISH: 25 MIN.
MAKES: 5 SERVINGS

- ½ **pound fresh green beans, cut into 1-inch pieces**
- 2 **medium carrots, julienned**
- ¼ **cup butter, cubed**
- ½ **pound sliced fresh mushrooms**
- 1 **medium onion, sliced**
- 2 **tablespoons minced fresh parsley**
- ½ **teaspoon salt**
- ½ **teaspoon dried oregano**
- ½ **teaspoon dried basil**
- ⅛ **teaspoon white pepper**

1. Place beans and carrots in a steamer basket; place in a large saucepan over 1 in. of water. Bring to a boil; cover and steam for 7-10 minutes or until crisp-tender.
2. Meanwhile, in a large skillet, melt butter. Add mushrooms and onion; saute until tender. Stir in the parsley, salt, oregano, basil, pepper, green beans and carrots; heat through.

Blue-Ribbon Apple Pie

This pie is special to me because I won a blue ribbon for it at the local fair and was able to compete at the state farm show.

—**COLLETTE GAUGLER** FOGELSVILLE, PA

PREP: 45 MIN. • **BAKE:** 55 MIN. + COOLING
MAKES: 8 SERVINGS

    Pastry for double-crust pie (9 inches)
WALNUT LAYER
- ¾ **cup ground walnuts**
- 2 **tablespoons brown sugar**
- 2 **tablespoons lightly beaten egg**
- 1 **tablespoon butter, melted**
- 1 **tablespoon 2% milk**
- ¼ **teaspoon lemon juice**
- ¼ **teaspoon vanilla extract**

FILLING
- 6 **cups sliced peeled tart apples (4-5 medium)**
- 2 **teaspoons lemon juice**
- ½ **teaspoon vanilla extract**
- ¾ **cup sugar**
- 3 **tablespoons all-purpose flour**
- 1¼ **teaspoons ground cinnamon**
- ¼ **teaspoon ground nutmeg**
- ⅛ **teaspoon salt**
- 3 **tablespoons butter, cubed**

TOPPING
- 1 **teaspoon 2% milk**
- 2 **teaspoons sugar**

1. Preheat oven to 375°. On a lightly floured surface, roll half of pastry dough to a ⅛-in.-thick circle; transfer to a 9-in. pie plate. Trim even with rim.
2. In a small bowl, mix walnut layer ingredients until blended. Spread onto bottom of pastry shell. Refrigerate while preparing filling.
3. For filling, in a large bowl, toss apples with lemon juice and vanilla. In a small bowl, mix the sugar, flour, cinnamon, nutmeg and salt; add to apple mixture and toss to coat.
4. Pour filling over walnut layer; dot with butter. Roll remaining pastry dough to a ⅛-in.-thick circle. Place over filling. Trim, seal and flute edge. Brush the top with milk; sprinkle with sugar. Cut slits in pastry.
5. Place pie on a baking sheet. Bake 55-65 minutes or until crust is golden brown and filling is bubbly. Cover the edge loosely with foil during the last 10 minutes if needed to prevent overbrowning. Remove foil. Cool on a wire rack.

PASTRY FOR DOUBLE-CRUST PIE (9 INCHES) *Combine 2½ cups of all-purpose flour and ½ tsp. salt; cut in 1 cup shortening until crumbly. Gradually add 4 to 5 tablespoons ice water, tossing with a fork until dough holds together when pressed. Divide dough in half and shape into disks; wrap in plastic wrap and refrigerate 1 hour.*

❝ I made this using my own pie crust. Definitely a hit, and I will be making it again. ❞
—**MRSJENB**
TASTEOFHOME.COM

Maple Walnut Cake

Maple Walnut Cake

This maple-flavored cake with candied walnuts honors my grandpa, who made maple syrup.
—**LORI FEE** MIDDLESEX, NY

PREP: 45 MIN. • **BAKE:** 15 MIN. + COOLING
MAKES: 16 SERVINGS

- ½ cup unsalted butter, softened
- 1½ cups packed light brown sugar
- 3 eggs
- 1 teaspoon maple flavoring or maple syrup
- 2 cups all-purpose flour
- 1 teaspoon baking powder
- 1 teaspoon baking soda
- ¼ teaspoon salt
- 1 cup buttermilk

CANDIED WALNUTS

- 1 tablespoon unsalted butter
- 1½ cups coarsely chopped walnuts
- 1 tablespoon maple syrup
- ¼ teaspoon salt

FROSTING

- 2 cups unsalted butter, softened
- 5 cups confectioners' sugar
- 1 teaspoon maple flavoring or maple syrup
- ¼ teaspoon salt
- ¼ to ½ cup half-and-half cream
- 3 tablespoons maple syrup, divided

1. Preheat oven to 350°. Line bottoms of three greased 9-in. round baking pans with parchment paper; grease paper.
2. In a large bowl, cream butter and brown sugar until blended. Add eggs, one at a time, beating well after each addition. Beat in maple flavoring. In another bowl, whisk flour, baking powder, baking soda and salt; add to the creamed mixture alternately with buttermilk, beating well after each addition.
3. Transfer to prepared pans. Bake for 11-13 minutes or until a toothpick inserted in center comes out clean. Cool in pans 10 minutes before removing to wire racks. Cool completely.
4. For candied walnuts, in a large skillet,

melt butter. Add walnuts; cook and stir over medium heat until nuts are toasted, about 5 minutes. Stir in maple syrup and salt; cook and stir 1 minute longer. Spread on foil to cool completely.

5. For frosting, in a large bowl, beat the butter until creamy. Beat in the confectioners' sugar, maple flavoring, salt and enough cream to reach desired consistency.

6. Place one cake layer on a serving plate; spread with 1 cup frosting. Sprinkle with ½ cup candied walnuts and drizzle with 1 tablespoon maple syrup. Repeat layers.

7. Top with remaining layer. Frost top and sides of cake. Top with remaining walnuts and syrup.

⑤ INGREDIENTS

Creamed Peas and Carrots

This comforting dish features a simply seasoned cream sauce that nicely complements the vegetables.
—**GAYLEEN GROTE** BATTLEVIEW, ND

START TO FINISH: 25 MIN. • **MAKES:** 4 SERVINGS

- 4 **medium carrots, sliced**
- 2 **cups frozen peas**
- 1 **tablespoon cornstarch**
- ¼ **teaspoon salt**
- ⅛ **teaspoon pepper**
- ½ **cup heavy whipping cream**

1. Place carrots in a large saucepan; add 1 in. of water. Bring to a boil. Reduce heat; cover and simmer for 5-8 minutes or until crisp-tender.

2. Add peas; return to a boil. Reduce heat; cover and simmer 5-10 minutes longer or until vegetables are tender. Drain, reserving ½ cup cooking liquid. Return vegetables and reserved liquid to the pan.

3. In a small bowl, combine the cornstarch, salt, pepper and cream until smooth. Stir into vegetables. Bring to a boil; cook and stir for 1-2 minutes or until thickened.

Crumb-Crusted Pork Roast with Root Vegetables

Crumb-Crusted Pork Roast with Root Vegetables

Not big on turkey? Perfect for fall, this hearty meal-in-one pork dish combines sweetly roasted veggies with a savory crumb coating.
—**TASTE OF HOME** TEST KITCHEN

PREP: 25 MIN. • **BAKE:** 1 HOUR + STANDING
MAKES: 8 SERVINGS

- 1 **boneless pork loin roast (2 to 3 pounds)**
- 4 **teaspoons honey**
- 1 **tablespoon molasses**
- 1½ **teaspoons spicy brown mustard**
- 2 **teaspoons rubbed sage**
- 1 **teaspoon dried thyme**
- 1 **teaspoon dried rosemary, crushed**
- ½ **cup soft whole wheat bread crumbs**
- 2 **tablespoons grated Parmesan cheese**
- 1 **large rutabaga, peeled and cubed**
- 1 **large sweet potato, peeled and cubed**
- 1 **large celery root, peeled and cubed**
- 1 **large onion, cut into wedges**
- 2 **tablespoons canola oil**
- ½ **teaspoon salt**
- ¼ **teaspoon pepper**

1. Preheat oven to 350°. Place roast on a rack in a shallow roasting pan coated with cooking spray. In a small bowl, mix the honey, molasses and mustard; brush over roast.

2. In a large bowl, mix sage, thyme and rosemary. In a small bowl, toss bread crumbs with Parmesan cheese and 2 teaspoons of the herb mixture; press onto roast.

3. Add vegetables, oil, salt and pepper to remaining herb mixture; toss to coat. Arrange vegetables around roast.

4. Roast for 1 to 1½ hours or until a thermometer reads 145°. Remove from pan; let stand 10 minutes before slicing. Serve with vegetables.

EULA FORBES' LEMON
SUGAR COOKIES *PAGE 200*

Afternoon Coffee & Tea

CALL FRIENDS FOR A CHEERY GET-TOGETHER BY HOSTING AN AFTERNOON COFFEE OR TEA. IN ADDITION TO HOT BEVERAGES, THIS CHAPTER OFFERS DELIGHTFUL FINGER FOODS IDEAL FOR A BOOK CLUB, SUNDAY LUNCHEON OR ANY COZY GATHERING.

JESSE ZIPURSKY'S CHOCOLATE-DIPPED BAKLAVA *PAGE 203*

KATHLEEN LARIMER'S SOUR CREAM BUNDT COFFEE CAKE *PAGE 198*

NAMRATA TELUGU'S MINT-CUCUMBER TOMATO SANDWICHES *PAGE 202*

Date-Walnut Pinwheels

Date-Walnut Pinwheels

Every time someone drops in for coffee, I bake up a batch of these quick fruit and nut cookies—I always keep the ingredients in my pantry. The recipe's a cinch to double, too, so it's good for parties and potlucks.
—**LORI MCLAIN** DENTON, TX

START TO FINISH: 25 MIN. • **MAKES:** 1 DOZEN

- 3 tablespoons sugar
- ½ teaspoon ground cinnamon
- 1 refrigerated pie pastry
- 1 tablespoon apricot preserves
- ⅔ cup finely chopped pitted dates
- ½ cup finely chopped walnuts

1. Preheat oven to 350°. Mix sugar and cinnamon. On a lightly floured surface, unroll pastry sheet; roll pastry into a 12-in. square. Spread preserves over top; sprinkle with dates, walnuts and cinnamon-sugar.
2. Roll up jelly-roll style; pinch seam to seal. Cut crosswise into 12 slices, about 1 in. thick. Place 1 in. apart on an ungreased baking sheet. Bake 12-14 minutes or until golden brown. Remove from pan to a wire rack to cool.

⑤INGREDIENTS

Apple Tea

When the weather outside is frightful, curl up indoors with this delightful brew.
—**EDNA JONES** ORLANDO, FL

START TO FINISH: 15 MIN. • **MAKES:** 2 SERVINGS

- 1 cup water
- 4 whole allspice
- 2 black tea bags
- 1 cup unsweetened apple juice or cider
- 2 tablespoons honey

In a small saucepan, bring water and allspice just to a boil; add tea bags. Remove from the heat; cover and steep for 3 minutes. Discard allspice and tea bags. Stir in apple juice and honey; heat through.

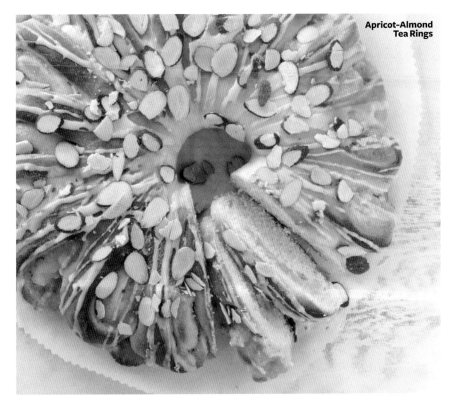

Apricot-Almond Tea Rings

Apricot-Almond Tea Rings

Apricots and almonds make the ideal pairing in this impressive iced ring. It's a perfect centerpiece for a coffee date with friends and a great breakfast treat for the family. Best of all, the recipe makes two rings!
—**ANN HILLMEYER** SANDIA PARK, NM

PREP: 45 MIN. + RISING
BAKE: 20 MIN. + COOLING
MAKES: 2 RINGS (8 SLICES EACH)

- **2 packages (¼ ounce each) active dry yeast**
- **¼ cup warm water (110° to 115°)**
- **1¼ cups warm 2% milk (110° to 115°)**
- **½ cup butter, softened**
- **⅓ cup sugar**
- **½ teaspoon salt**
- **½ cup mashed potato flakes**
- **2 eggs**
- **3½ to 4 cups all-purpose flour**

FILLING

- **1½ cups apricot preserves**
- **⅔ cup sugar**
- **5 ounces almond paste**
- **⅓ cup butter, softened**

ICING

- **1⅓ cups confectioners' sugar**
- **½ teaspoon vanilla extract**
- **2 to 3 tablespoons 2% milk**
- **⅓ cup sliced almonds, toasted**

1. In a large bowl, dissolve yeast in warm water. In another bowl, combine milk, butter, sugar, salt, potato flakes and eggs. Let stand 1 minute. Add milk mixture and 3 cups flour to yeast mixture; beat until smooth. Add enough remaining flour to form a soft dough.

2. Turn onto a floured surface; knead until smooth and elastic, about 6-8 minutes. Place in a greased bowl, turning once to grease the top. Cover and let rise in a warm place until doubled, about 1 hour.

3. Place preserves, sugar, almond paste and butter in a food processor; cover and process until blended. Punch dough down. Divide in half. On a lightly floured surface, roll each portion into 14x7-in. rectangle. Spread filling to within ½ in. of edges. Roll up jelly-roll style, starting with a long side; pinch seams to seal.

4. Place rolls, seam side down, on two parchment paper-lined baking sheets. Pinch ends together to form two rings. With scissors, cut from outside edge to two-thirds of the way toward center of rings at 1-in. intervals. Separate strips slightly; twist to allow filling to show. Let rise until doubled about 35-40 minutes.

5. Preheat oven to 375°. Bake for 18-22 minutes or until lightly browned. Remove from pans to wire racks to cool. Combine confectioners' sugar, vanilla and enough milk to achieve a drizzling consistency. Drizzle over warm tea rings and sprinkle with almonds.

Maple Hot Chocolate

When I first developed this version of hot chocolate, my husband was quite skeptical. But after one taste, he doubted me no more. It really hits the spot on a chilly afternoon, especially when served with cinnamon rolls or doughnuts.
—**DARLENE MILLER** LINN, MO

START TO FINISH: 15 MIN. • **MAKES:** 4 SERVINGS

- **¼ cup sugar**
- **1 tablespoon baking cocoa**
- **⅛ teaspoon salt**
- **¼ cup hot water**
- **1 tablespoon butter**
- **4 cups milk**
- **1 teaspoon maple flavoring**
- **1 teaspoon vanilla extract**
- **12 large marshmallows**

In a large saucepan, combine sugar, cocoa and salt. Stir in hot water and butter; bring to a boil. Add the milk, maple flavoring, vanilla and 8 marshmallows. Heat through, stirring occasionally, until marshmallows are melted. Ladle into mugs and top each with a marshmallow.

Sour Cream Bundt Coffee Cake

This yummy cake is so moist, you won't even need a cup of coffee! Be sure to make it for your next get-together. Your guests will thank you.

—**KATHLEEN LARIMER** DAYTON, OH

PREP: 40 MIN. • **BAKE:** 45 MIN. + COOLING
MAKES: 16 SERVINGS

- ⅔ cup chopped pecans
- 2 tablespoons brown sugar
- 1½ teaspoons ground cinnamon

BATTER

- 1 cup butter, softened
- 2 cups sugar
- 2 eggs
- ½ teaspoon vanilla extract
- 2 cups all-purpose flour
- 1 teaspoon baking powder
- ¼ teaspoon baking soda
- ¼ teaspoon salt
- 1 cup (8 ounces) sour cream
  Confectioners' sugar

1. Preheat oven to 350°. In a small bowl, combine pecans, brown sugar and cinnamon; set aside. In a large bowl, cream butter and sugar until light and fluffy. Add eggs, one at a time, beating well after each addition. Beat in vanilla.
2. Combine flour, baking powder, baking soda and salt; add to creamed mixture alternately with sour cream, beating well after each addition.
3. Pour half of the batter into a greased and floured 10-in. fluted tube pan; sprinkle with half of the pecan mixture. Gently top with remaining batter and pecan mixture.
4. Bake 45-50 minutes or until a toothpick inserted in center comes out clean. Cool for 10 minutes before removing from pan to a wire rack to cool completely. Sprinkle cooled cake with confectioners' sugar.

Cranberry Walnut Biscotti

Cranberry Walnut Biscotti

Here, a chocolate drizzle lends a little sweetness to biscotti loaded with walnuts and dried cranberries.

—**JOAN DUCKWORTH** LEE'S SUMMIT, MO

PREP: 25 MIN. • **BAKE:** 40 MIN. + COOLING
MAKES: ABOUT 1½ DOZEN

- 2 cups all-purpose flour
- ¾ cup sugar
- 1 teaspoon baking powder
- ⅛ teaspoon salt
- 3 eggs
- 1½ teaspoons vanilla extract
- 1 cup chopped walnuts, toasted
- 1 cup dried cranberries, chopped
- ½ cup milk chocolate chips
- 1 teaspoon shortening

1. Preheat oven to 350°. In a large bowl, combine the flour, sugar, baking powder and salt. In a small bowl, whisk eggs and vanilla; add to dry ingredients just until moistened. Fold in walnuts and cranberries (dough will be sticky).
2. Divide dough in half. On a greased baking sheet, with lightly floured hands, shape each half into a 10x2½-in. rectangle. Bake 20-25 minutes or until golden brown.
3. Carefully remove to wire racks; cool 10 minutes. Transfer to a cutting board; cut diagonally with a serrated knife into 1-in. slices. Place cut side down on ungreased baking sheets. Bake 8-10 minutes on each side or until lightly browned. Remove to wire racks to cool completely.
4. In a microwave, melt chocolate chips and shortening; stir until smooth. Drizzle over biscotti. Let stand until set. Store in an airtight container.

⑤ INGREDIENTS SLOW COOKER 🍲

Viennese Coffee

This isn't your regular cup of joe! I dress
it up with chocolate, whipped cream and
more, making it a drink to savor.

—SHARON DELANEY-CHRONIS
SOUTH MILWAUKEE, WI

PREP: 10 MIN. **• COOK:** 3 HOURS
MAKES: 4 SERVINGS

- 3 cups strong brewed coffee
- 3 tablespoons chocolate syrup
- 1 teaspoon sugar
- ⅓ cup heavy whipping cream
- ¼ cup creme de cacao or Irish cream liqueur
  Whipped cream and chocolate curls, optional

1. In a 1½-qt. slow cooker, combine
the coffee, chocolate syrup and sugar.
Cover and cook on low for 2½ hours.
2. Stir in heavy cream and creme de
cacao. Cover and cook 30 minutes
longer or until heated through.
3. Ladle coffee into mugs. Garnish
with whipped cream and chocolate
curls if desired.

Lemon Sugar Cookies

Lemon Sugar Cookies

These are my favorite sugar cookies. The lemon adds a unique flavor. They are great with coffee when company visits.
—**EULA FORBES** WAGONER, OK

PREP: 20 MIN. • **BAKE:** 10 MIN./BATCH
MAKES: ABOUT 11 DOZEN

- 1 cup butter, softened
- 1 cup sugar
- 1 cup confectioners' sugar
- 1 cup canola oil
- 2 eggs
- 1 teaspoon lemon extract
- 4½ cups all-purpose flour
- 1 teaspoon baking soda
- 1 teaspoon cream of tartar
  Additional sugar

1. Preheat oven to 350°. In a large bowl, beat butter, sugars and oil until blended. Beat in eggs and extract. Combine flour, baking soda and cream of tartar; stir into butter mixture (dough will be stiff).
2. Roll into 1-in. balls; place 2 in. apart on ungreased baking sheets. Press with bottom of a glass dipped in water, then in sugar. Bake 10 minutes or until edges are lightly browned.

Cardamom-Blackberry Linzer Cookies

Deeply spiced cardamom is the perfect match for the jam of your choice in this family favorite.
—**CHRISTIANNA GOZZI** ASTORIA, NY

PREP: 50 MIN. + CHILLING
BAKE: 10 MIN./BATCH + COOLING
MAKES: ABOUT 2 DOZEN

- 2 cups all-purpose flour
- 1 cup salted roasted almonds
- 2 to 3 teaspoons ground cardamom
- ¼ teaspoon salt
- 1 cup unsalted butter, softened
- ½ cup plus 1 teaspoon sugar, divided
- 1 egg
- 1 jar (10 ounces) seedless blackberry spreadable fruit
- 1 tablespoon lemon juice
- 3 tablespoons confectioners' sugar

1. In a food processor, combine ½ cup flour and almonds; pulse until almonds are finely ground. Add cardamom, salt and remaining flour; pulse until combined.
2. In a large bowl, cream butter and ½ cup sugar until light and fluffy. Beat in egg. Gradually beat in flour mixture. Divide dough in half. Shape each into a disk; wrap in plastic wrap. Refrigerate 1 hour or until firm enough to roll.
3. Preheat oven to 350°. On a lightly floured surface, roll each portion to ⅛-in. thickness. Cut with a floured 2-in. round cookie cutter. Using a floured 1-in. round cookie cutter, cut out the centers of half of the cookies. Place solid and window cookies 1 in. apart on greased baking sheets.
4. Bake 10-12 minutes or until light brown. Remove from pans to wire racks to cool completely.
5. In a small bowl, mix spreadable fruit, lemon juice and remaining sugar. Spread filling on bottoms of solid cookies; top with window cookies. Dust with confectioners' sugar.

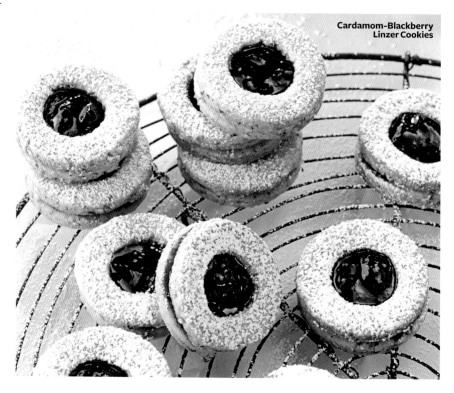

Cardamom-Blackberry Linzer Cookies

Chocolate-Raspberry Polka Dot Cake

Chocolate-Raspberry Polka Dot Cake

You'll have people requesting seconds on this tender cake. Chocolate cake layers are filled with a delightful raspberry whipped cream and silky ganache. It's all draped in a rich chocolate glaze. Then to add some whimsy, it's decorated with polka dots.

—**REBEKAH RADEWAHN** WAUWATOSA, WI

PREP: 1 HOUR + CHILLING
BAKE: 20 MIN. + COOLING • **MAKES:** 16 SERVINGS

- ¾ cup baking cocoa
- ¾ cup boiling water
- ¾ cup unsalted butter, softened
- 1½ cups sugar
- 1½ cups packed brown sugar
- 3 eggs
- 3 teaspoons vanilla extract
- ¾ cup buttermilk
- ¾ cup water
- 3 cups cake flour
- 1 teaspoon baking powder
- ½ teaspoon baking soda
- ¼ teaspoon plus ⅛ teaspoon salt

GANACHE
- 4 ounces semisweet chocolate, chopped
- 1 cup heavy whipping cream
- 1 teaspoon raspberry extract

RASPBERRY CREAM
- 1 package (10 ounces) frozen sweetened raspberries, thawed
- 1½ cups heavy whipping cream, whipped

GLAZE
- 1 pound semisweet chocolate, chopped
- 1½ cups unsalted butter, cubed
- 2 tablespoons corn syrup
- 2 teaspoons raspberry extract

GARNISH
- 2 ounces white candy coating, melted
- 1 ounce dark chocolate candy coating, melted
  Blue food coloring, optional

1. Line three 9-in. round baking pans with waxed paper; grease and flour the pans and paper. Set pans aside. Preheat oven to 350°.

2. Dissolve cocoa in boiling water; cool. In a large bowl, cream butter and sugars until light and fluffy. Add eggs, one at a time, beating well after each addition. Beat in cocoa mixture and vanilla. In a small bowl, combine buttermilk and water; set aside. Combine flour, baking powder, baking soda and salt; add to creamed mixture alternately with buttermilk mixture, beating well after each addition.

3. Transfer to prepared pans. Bake 20-25 minutes or until a toothpick inserted near the center comes out clean. Cool 10 minutes before removing from pans to wire racks to cool completely.

4. For ganache, place chocolate in a small bowl. In a small saucepan, bring cream just to a boil. Pour over chocolate; whisk until smooth. Stir in extract. Refrigerate until chilled. In a small bowl, beat chocolate mixture until soft peaks form, about 15 seconds.

5. For raspberry cream, place raspberries in a food processor, cover and process until blended. Strain raspberries, reserving juice. Discard seeds. Gently fold juice into whipped cream.

6. Cut each cake horizontally into two layers. Place one cake layer on a serving plate; spread with 1 cup raspberry cream. Top with another cake layer; spread with half of the ganache. Repeat raspberry and ganache layers. Top with another cake layer; spread with remaining raspberry cream. Top with remaining cake layer. Refrigerate for 1 hour or until set.

7. For glaze, in a microwave, melt chocolate, butter and corn syrup; stir until smooth. Stir in extract. Cool slightly, stirring occasionally. Pour over cake.

8. For garnish, in a microwave, melt candy coating in separate bowls; stir until smooth. Tint half of the white coating using blue coloring if desired. Pipe or spoon melted coating onto waxed paper in different sized circles; let stand until set. Press circles onto cake. Refrigerate cake until serving.

TOP TIP

Splitting Cakes Into Layers

From birthdays and graduations to Easter and Christmas, cakes are a celebratory standby. The next time you need to split a cake into layers, use a ruler to determine the center of the side of the cake and mark it with a toothpick. Continue inserting toothpicks around the cake. Using the toothpicks as a guide, cut the cake horizontally in half with a long serrated knife. Carefully remove the top half. Frost or fill the bottom half as the recipe instructs and replace the top. It's that easy!

Mint-Cucumber Tomato Sandwiches

I jazzed up the quintessential tea-time cucumber sandwich to suit my family's tastes. This was my absolute go-to sandwich when I was pregnant and it hit all the right spots!

—**NAMRATA TELUGU** TERRE HAUTE, IN

START TO FINISH: 15 MIN.
MAKES: 4 SANDWICHES

- 3 **tablespoons butter, softened**
- 8 **slices sourdough bread**
- 1 **large cucumber, thinly sliced**
- 2 **medium tomatoes, thinly sliced**
- ¼ **teaspoon salt**
- ⅛ **teaspoon pepper**
- ¼ **cup fresh mint leaves**

Spread butter over four slices of bread. Layer with cucumber and tomatoes; sprinkle with salt, pepper and mint. Top with remaining bread. If desired, cut each sandwich into quarters.

Mint-Cucumber Tomato Sandwiches

Chocolate-Dipped Baklava

Not only is this baklava a special addition to a cookie platter, but it makes a great gift.

—JESSE ZIPURSKY SAN RAMON, CA

PREP: 1 HOUR • **BAKE:** 30 MIN. + STANDING
MAKES: 3 DOZEN

- 1⅔ cups finely chopped pecans
- 1⅔ cups finely chopped walnuts
- ½ cup sugar
- 1½ teaspoons ground cinnamon
- ½ teaspoon ground allspice
- ½ teaspoon ground cloves
- 1 cup butter, melted
- 24 sheets phyllo dough (14x9-inch size)

SYRUP
- 1 cup water
- 1 cup honey
- ½ cup sugar
- 1 teaspoon ground cinnamon
- 1 teaspoon vanilla extract

DRIZZLE
- 1 cup (6 ounces) dark chocolate chips
- 1 teaspoon shortening

1. Preheat oven to 350°. In a large bowl, mix the first six ingredients. Brush a 13x9-in. baking pan with some of the butter. Unroll phyllo dough; trim to fit into pan.

2. Layer six sheets of phyllo in prepared pan, brushing each with butter. Keep remaining phyllo covered with plastic wrap and a damp towel to prevent it from drying out. Sprinkle with a third of the nut mixture. Repeat layers twice. Top with remaining phyllo sheets, brushing each with butter.

3. Using a sharp knife, cut into 1½-in. diamond shapes. Bake 30-35 minutes or until golden brown.

4. Meanwhile, in a saucepan, combine water, honey, sugar and cinnamon; bring to a boil. Reduce heat; simmer, uncovered, 10 minutes. Stir in vanilla.

5. Pour over warm baklava. Cool completely in pan on a wire rack. Cover and let stand for several hours or overnight.

6. In a microwave, melt chocolate chips and shortening; stir until smooth. Drizzle over baklava; let stand until set.

Dipped Lemon Spritz

Dipped Lemon Spritz

These refreshing cookies are sure to be a hit at parties. The chocolate will please your sweet tooth.

—LEE ROBERTS RACINE, WI

PREP: 50 MIN. • **BAKE:** 10 MIN./BATCH + COOLING
MAKES: 6 DOZEN

- ⅔ cup plus 2 tablespoons sugar
- 2 teaspoons grated lemon peel
- 1 cup unsalted butter, softened
- 1 egg
- 2 teaspoons lemon juice
- 1 teaspoon vanilla extract
- 2½ cups all-purpose flour
- ¼ teaspoon baking powder
  Dash salt
- 1 package (12 ounces) dark chocolate chips

1. Preheat oven to 350°. In a small food processor, combine sugar and lemon peel; cover and process until blended. In a large bowl, cream butter and ⅔ cup lemon-sugar until light and fluffy. Beat in egg, lemon juice and vanilla. Combine flour, baking powder and salt; gradually add to creamed mixture and mix well.

2. Using a cookie press fitted with a 1½-in. bar disk, form dough into long strips on ungreased baking sheets. Cut each strip into squares (there is no need to separate the pieces).

3. Bake 8-10 minutes or until set (do not brown). Remove to wire racks to cool completely.

4. In a microwave, melt chocolate; stir until smooth. Dip cookies diagonally in chocolate, allowing excess to drip off. Place on waxed paper; sprinkle chocolate with remaining lemon-sugar. Let stand until set. Store in an airtight container at room temperature, or freeze up to 3 months.

> ❝I made these for a cookie sale and got rave reviews.❞
> **—GRIMSHAWHAVEN**
> TASTEOFHOME.COM

Turtle Cookie Cups

Hazelnut Mocha Coffee

For special occasions, this chocolaty brew will be the talk of the town. You can make the mixture a few days in advance. When you're ready to serve it, simply brew the coffee and whip the chocolate.

—**MARY LEVERETTE** COLUMBIA, SC

PREP: 5 MIN. • **COOK:** 10 MIN. + CHILLING
MAKES: 6 SERVINGS

- 4 ounces semisweet chocolate, chopped
- 1 cup heavy whipping cream
- ⅓ cup sugar
- ½ teaspoon ground cinnamon
- 2 tablespoons hazelnut liqueur
- 4½ cups hot brewed coffee
  Sweetened whipped cream, optional

1. Place chocolate in a small bowl. In a small saucepan, bring cream just to a boil. Add sugar and cinnamon; cook and stir until sugar is dissolved. Pour over chocolate; stir with a whisk until smooth. Stir in liqueur.

2. Cool to room temperature, stirring occasionally. Refrigerate, covered, until cold. Beat just until soft peaks form, about 15 seconds (do not overbeat). For each serving, spoon ¼ cup into mugs. Top with ¾ cup coffee; stir to dissolve. Top with whipped cream if desired.

Turtle Cookie Cups

Gooey caramel pairs wonderfully with crunchy pecans in these sweet treats. For a twist, use white chocolate chips in the cups and drizzle with white chocolate.

—**HEATHER KING** FROSTBURG, MD

PREP: 35 MIN. + STANDING
BAKE: 10 MIN./BATCH + COOLING
MAKES: 4 DOZEN

- 1 cup butter, softened
- 1 cup packed brown sugar
- ½ cup sugar
- 2 eggs
- 1 teaspoon vanilla extract
- 2½ cups all-purpose flour
- 1 teaspoon baking soda
- ½ teaspoon salt
- 1¼ cups semisweet chocolate chips, divided
- ½ cup chopped pecans
- 1 cup Kraft caramel bits
- 3 tablespoons heavy whipping cream
- 48 pecan halves (about ¾ cup)

1. Preheat oven to 375°. In a large bowl, cream butter and sugars until light and fluffy. Beat in eggs and vanilla. In another bowl, whisk flour, baking soda and salt; gradually beat into creamed mixture.

2. Shape dough into 1-in. balls; place in greased mini-muffin cups. Press evenly onto bottoms and up the sides of cups. Bake 9-11 minutes or until edges are golden brown. With the back of measuring teaspoon, make an indentation in each cup. Immediately sprinkle with ¾ cup chocolate chips and chopped pecans. Cool in pans 10 minutes. Remove to wire racks to cool.

3. Meanwhile, in a small saucepan, melt caramel bits with cream; stir until smooth. Spoon into cups. Top each with a pecan half. In a microwave, melt remaining chocolate chips; stir until smooth. Drizzle over pecans.

Hazelnut Mocha Coffee

Caramel Apple Strudel

My father, who was born and raised in Austria, told stories about how his mother covered all of the kitchen counters with dough whenever she made apple strudel. This recipe is a modern, delicious way to carry on part of my family's heritage.

—**SARAH HAENGEL** BOWIE, MD

PREP: 35 MIN.+ COOLING • **BAKE:** 25 MIN.
MAKES: 8 SERVINGS

- 5 **medium apples, peeled and chopped (5 cups)**
- ¾ **cup apple cider or juice**
- ¼ **cup sugar**
- ½ **teaspoon ground cinnamon**
- ¼ **teaspoon ground allspice**
- ¼ **teaspoon ground cloves**
- 1 **frozen puff pastry sheet, thawed**
- ¼ **cup fat-free caramel ice cream topping**
- 1 **egg**
- 1 **tablespoon water**
- 1 **tablespoon coarse sugar**
  Sweetened whipped cream and additional caramel ice cream topping, optional

1. Preheat oven to 375°. In a large saucepan, combine the first six ingredients. Bring to a boil. Reduce heat; simmer, uncovered, 15-20 minutes or until apples are tender, stirring occasionally. Cool completely.

2. Unfold puff pastry onto a large sheet of parchment paper; roll into a 16x12-in. rectangle. Transfer paper and pastry to a baking sheet, placing a short side of the rectangle facing you. Using a slotted spoon, arrange apples on bottom half of pastry to within 1 in. of edges. Drizzle apples with caramel topping. Roll up jelly-roll style, starting with the bottom side. Pinch seams to seal and tuck the ends under.

3. In a small bowl, whisk egg with water; brush over pastry. Sprinkle with coarse sugar. Cut slits in top. Bake 25-30 minutes or until golden brown. If desired, serve with whipped cream and additional caramel topping.

Caramel Apple Strudel

66 So good! I made a couple of these babies and put them in the freezer to pull out for the holidays. 99

—**JMFORGACS** TASTEOFHOME.COM

**LANAEE O'NEILL'S SIMPLE
TOMATO SOUP** *PAGE 211*

Shopping Spree Eats

READY TO SHOP TILL YOU DROP? INVITE THE GANG OVER AFTER A BLACK FRIDAY SHOPPING SPREE AND RELAX WITH A FEW BITES. CONSIDER THE CHICKEN WITH APPLE-CHARDONNAY GRAVY THAT COOKS WHILE YOU'RE AT THE MALL OR THE MINESTRONE WITH TURKEY THAT'S READY IN HALF AN HOUR.

MARY WILHELM'S PUMPKIN BARS WITH BROWNED BUTTER FROSTING *PAGE 208*

JANE PASCHKE'S GARLIC KNOTS *PAGE 208*

MARCIA O'NEIL'S PUMPKIN HARVEST BEEF STEW *PAGE 213*

Pumpkin Bars with Browned Butter Frosting

I based this recipe on one my grandmother used to make, so sweet memories are baked into every bar. When preparing the frosting, carefully watch the butter and remove it from the heat as soon as it starts to brown. Do not use margarine.

—MARY WILHELM SPARTA, WI

PREP: 30 MIN. • **BAKE:** 20 MIN. + COOLING
MAKES: 2 DOZEN

- 1½ cups sugar
- 1 cup canned pumpkin
- ½ cup orange juice
- ½ cup canola oil
- 2 eggs
- 2 teaspoons grated orange peel
- 2 cups all-purpose flour
- 2 teaspoons baking powder
- 2 teaspoons pumpkin pie spice
- 1 teaspoon baking soda
- ¼ teaspoon salt

FROSTING

- ⅔ cup butter, cubed
- 4 cups confectioners' sugar
- 1 teaspoon vanilla extract
- 4 to 6 tablespoons 2% milk

1. Preheat oven to 350°. Grease a 15x10x1-in. baking pan. In a large bowl, beat the first six ingredients until well blended. In another bowl, whisk flour, baking powder, pie spice, baking soda and salt; gradually beat into pumpkin mixture.
2. Transfer to prepared pan. Bake for 18-22 minutes or until a toothpick inserted in center comes out clean. Cool completely in pan on a wire rack.
3. In a small heavy saucepan, melt butter over medium heat. Heat 5-7 minutes or until golden brown, stirring constantly. Transfer to a large bowl. Gradually beat in confectioners' sugar, vanilla and enough of the milk to reach desired consistency. Spread over bars; let stand until set.

Apple-Carrot Slaw with Pistachios

Apple-Carrot Slaw with Pistachios

Sweet, crunchy and colorful, a vibrant slaw like this will be an all-star at your next get-together. I prefer to use freshly julienned carrots but you could use the packaged variety if you like.

—LINDA SCHEND KENOSHA, WI

START TO FINISH: 20 MIN.
MAKES: 8 SERVINGS (1 CUP EACH)

- 6 cups julienned carrots (about 9 ounces)
- 4 medium Fuji, Gala or other sweet apples, julienned
- ¼ cup lemon juice
- 2 tablespoons sugar
- 1½ teaspoons ground cinnamon
- 1 cup chopped pistachios, divided
  Dash salt

In a large bowl, combine the first five ingredients. Add ½ cup pistachios; toss to combine. Season with salt to taste. Refrigerate, covered, until serving. Just before serving, sprinkle with remaining pistachios.

Garlic Knots

Here's a handy bread you can make in no time flat. Refrigerated biscuits make preparation simple. The Italian flavors complement a variety of meals.

—JANE PASCHKE UNIVERSITY PARK, FL

START TO FINISH: 30 MIN. • **MAKES:** 2½ DOZEN

- 1 tube (12 ounces) refrigerated buttermilk biscuits
- ¼ cup canola oil
- 3 tablespoons grated Parmesan cheese
- 1 teaspoon garlic powder
- 1 teaspoon dried oregano
- 1 teaspoon dried parsley flakes

1. Preheat oven to 400°. Cut each biscuit into thirds. Roll each piece into a 3-in. rope and tie into a knot; tuck ends under. Place 2 in. apart on a greased baking sheet. Bake for 8-10 minutes or until golden brown.
2. In a large bowl, combine remaining ingredients; add the warm knots and gently toss to coat.

Bruschetta Chicken Wrap

I absolutely love garlic, tomatoes and basil, all of which are required for good bruschetta. I took that favorite appetizer, added chicken and turned it all into these yummy wraps. They make a great lunch or no-fuss dinner.

—GINA RINE CANFIELD, OH

START TO FINISH: 30 MIN. • **MAKES:** 4 SERVINGS

- 2 plum tomatoes, finely chopped (about 1 cup)
- 1 cup fresh baby spinach, coarsely chopped
- ¼ cup finely chopped red onion
- 1 tablespoon shredded Parmesan or Romano cheese
- 1 tablespoon minced fresh basil
- 1 teaspoon olive oil
- 1 teaspoon balsamic vinegar
- ⅛ teaspoon plus ¼ teaspoon pepper, divided
  Dash garlic powder
- 4 boneless skinless chicken breast halves (4 ounces each)
- ½ teaspoon salt
- 2 ounces fresh mozzarella cheese, cut into 4 slices
- 4 whole wheat tortillas (8 inches)

1. In a small bowl, mix the tomatoes, spinach, onion, Parmesan cheese, basil, oil, vinegar, ⅛ teaspoon pepper and garlic powder.

2. Moisten a paper towel with cooking oil; using long-handled tongs, rub on grill rack to coat lightly. Sprinkle chicken with salt and remaining pepper; place on grill rack. Grill, covered, over medium heat 4-6 minutes on each side or until a thermometer reads 165°.

3. Top each chicken breast with one cheese slice; cover and grill 1-2 minutes longer or until cheese is melted. Grill the tortillas over medium heat for 20-30 seconds or until heated through.

4. Place chicken on center of each tortilla; top with about ¼ cup tomato mixture. Fold bottom of tortilla over filling; fold both sides to close.

Bruschetta
Chicken Wrap

Cranberry
Ambrosia Salad

Cranberry Ambrosia Salad

Here's a dish that is made a day ahead to make party planning easy. My paternal grandmother used to make it for Christmas dinner. I'm not sure how many batches she made, as there were nearly 50 aunts, uncles and cousins in our family. I still make the recipe in memory of her, and it's still as good as I remember.

—JANET HURLEY SHELL ROCK, IA

PREP: 20 MIN. + CHILLING • **MAKES:** 9 SERVINGS

- 1 pound fresh or frozen cranberries
- 1 can (20 ounces) crushed pineapple, drained
- 1 cup sugar
- 2 cups miniature marshmallows
- 1 cup heavy whipping cream, whipped
- ½ cup chopped pecans

1. In a food processor, cover and process cranberries until coarsely chopped.

2. Transfer to a large bowl; stir in the pineapple and sugar. Cover fruit mixture and refrigerate overnight.

3. Just before serving, fold in the marshmallows, whipped cream and pecans.

Minestrone with Turkey

Frozen Maple Mousse Pie

A homemade crust made with gingersnap cookie crumbs complements the maple flavor of my comforting treat.

—**DEIRDRE COX** KANSAS CITY, MO

PREP: 25 MIN. + FREEZING
BAKE: 10 MIN. + COOLING
MAKES: 8 SERVINGS

- 1½ cups gingersnap cookie crumbs (about 30 cookies)
- ¼ cup butter, melted
- 2 tablespoons confectioners' sugar

FILLING

- ½ cup maple syrup
- 4 egg yolks
- 2 tablespoons dark rum
- 1⅓ cups heavy whipping cream
  Additional gingersnap cookie crumbs

1. Preheat oven to 350°. Combine cookie crumbs, butter and confectioners' sugar; press onto the bottom and up the sides of a greased 9-in. pie plate. Bake crust for 8-10 minutes or until lightly browned. Cool on a wire rack.
2. In a double boiler or metal bowl over simmering water, constantly whisk the maple syrup and egg yolks until mixture reaches 160°. Remove from the heat; beat mixture for 5 minutes or until thickened. Stir in rum.
3. In a large bowl, beat cream until soft peaks form; fold into maple mixture. Spoon into prepared crust. Cover and freeze 4 hours or until set. Garnish with cookie crumbs if desired.

Frozen Maple Mousse Pie

Minestrone with Turkey

I have fond memories of my mom making this soup when I was young.

—**ANGELA GOODMAN** KANEOHE, HI

START TO FINISH: 30 MIN.
MAKES: 6 SERVINGS (2 QUARTS)

- 1 tablespoon olive oil
- 1 medium onion, chopped
- 1 medium carrot, sliced
- 1 celery rib, sliced
- 1 garlic clove, minced
- 4 cups chicken broth or homemade turkey stock
- 1 can (14½ ounces) diced tomatoes, undrained
- ⅔ cup each frozen peas, corn and cut green beans, thawed
- ½ cup uncooked elbow macaroni
- 1 teaspoon salt
- ¼ teaspoon dried basil
- ¼ teaspoon dried oregano
- ¼ teaspoon pepper
- 1 bay leaf
- 1 cup cubed cooked turkey
- 1 small zucchini, halved lengthwise and cut into ¼-inch slices
- ¼ cup grated Parmesan cheese, optional

1. In a Dutch oven, heat olive oil over medium-high heat. Add onion, carrot and celery; cook and stir until tender. Add garlic; cook 1 minute longer. Add broth, vegetables, macaroni and seasonings. Bring to a boil.
2. Reduce heat; simmer, uncovered, 5 minutes or until macaroni is al dente. Stir in turkey and zucchini; cook until zucchini is crisp-tender. Discard bay leaf. If desired, sprinkle servings with cheese.
FREEZE OPTION *Transfer cooled soup to freezer container and freeze up to 3 months. To use, thaw in the refrigerator overnight. Transfer to a saucepan. Cover and cook over medium heat until heated through. Serve with cheese if desired.*

Simple Tomato Soup

Simple Tomato Soup

I created this recipe on a bad-weather day. My husband and daughter now ask for it constantly. Whenever I send it with my daughter for lunch at school, I always send some for her friend, too. It is truly comfort food at its very best.

—LANAEE O'NEILL CHICO, CA

START TO FINISH: 30 MIN.
MAKES: 8 SERVINGS (2 QUARTS)

- 2 cans (14.5 ounces each) diced tomatoes with basil, oregano and garlic, undrained
- ¼ cup butter
- ½ cup finely chopped red onion
- 2 garlic cloves, minced
- 6 tablespoons all-purpose flour
- 1 carton (48 ounces) chicken broth
  Grated Parmesan cheese, optional

1. Place the tomatoes with juices in a blender; cover and process until pureed. In a large saucepan, heat butter over medium-high heat. Add onion; cook and stir until tender. Add garlic; cook 1 minute longer.
2. Remove from the heat; stir in the flour until smooth. Cook for 1 minute. Gradually whisk in broth. Add pureed tomatoes; bring to a boil over medium heat, stirring occasionally. Reduce heat and simmer for 20-25 minutes to allow the flavors to blend. If desired, sprinkle with cheese.

(5) INGREDIENTS

Savory Biscuit-Breadsticks

I love to experiment in the kitchen with simple ingredients like refrigerated biscuits. The results usually are a big hit, as these super-fast breadsticks are.

—BILLY HENSLEY MOUNT CARMEL, TN

START TO FINISH: 20 MIN.
MAKES: 10 BREADSTICKS

- ½ cup grated Parmesan cheese
- 2 teaspoons dried minced garlic
- ¼ teaspoon crushed red pepper flakes
- 1 tube (12 ounces) refrigerated buttermilk biscuits
- 2 tablespoons olive oil

Preheat oven to 400°. In a shallow bowl, mix cheese, garlic and pepper flakes. Roll each biscuit into a 6-in. rope. Brush lightly with oil; roll in cheese mixture. Place on a greased baking sheet. Bake 8-10 minutes or until golden brown.

(5) INGREDIENTS

Gingersnap Pear Trifles

Crystallized ginger adds both sweetness and spice to this easy trifle. Layer it with pears, crumbled gingersnap cookies and whipped cream, and you have autumn's flavors in a dish!

—TASTE OF HOME TEST KITCHEN

START TO FINISH: 10 MIN. • **MAKES:** 2 SERVINGS

- ½ cup heavy whipping cream
- ¼ cup lemon curd
- ½ cup crushed gingersnap cookies
- 1 cup chopped canned pears
- 2 tablespoons chopped crystallized ginger

1. In a small bowl, beat cream until soft peaks form. Fold in lemon curd.
2. Layer half of the crumbled cookies, pears and whipped cream in two dessert dishes. Repeat layers. Sprinkle with ginger. Serve immediately.

Savory Biscuit-Breadsticks

Chicken with Apple-Chardonnay Gravy

Chicken with Apple-Chardonnay Gravy

I create my own recipes by experimenting with various ingredients in the kitchen. I love this savory slow cooker chicken dish because it's easy, affordable and fills the house with awesome aromas that make your mouth water.

—**THERESA RETELLE** APPLETON, WI

PREP: 20 MIN. • **COOK:** 6 HOURS
MAKES: 6 SERVINGS

- **6 chicken leg quarters**
- **½ teaspoon salt**
- **¼ teaspoon pepper**
- **2 large sweet apples, peeled and cut into wedges**
- **1 large sweet onion, chopped**
- **2 celery ribs, chopped**
- **½ cup chardonnay**
- **1 envelope brown gravy mix**
- **2 large garlic cloves, minced**
- **1 teaspoon each minced fresh oregano, rosemary and thyme**
  Hot mashed potatoes

1. Sprinkle chicken with salt and pepper. Place half of the chicken in a 5-qt. slow cooker. In a bowl, combine the apples, onion and celery; spoon half of the mixture over chicken. Repeat layers.

2. In the same bowl, whisk wine, gravy mix, garlic and herbs until blended; pour over top. Cover and cook on low for 6-8 hours or until chicken is tender.

3. Remove chicken to a serving platter; keep warm. Cool apple mixture slightly; skim fat.

4. In a blender, cover and process the apple mixture in batches until smooth. Transfer to a saucepan and heat through over medium heat, stirring occasionally. Serve with chicken and mashed potatoes.

Snowy Raspberry Gelatin Mold

This mold is always on our holiday table. The raspberry layer makes an eye-catching base for the heavenly cream cheese layer.

—**LILY JULOW** LAWRENCEVILLE, GA

PREP: 30 MIN. + CHILLING
MAKES: 8 SERVINGS

- 1 envelope unflavored gelatin
- ½ cup cold water
- 1 cup half-and-half cream
- ½ cup sugar
- 1 package (8 ounces) cream cheese, softened
- 1 teaspoon vanilla extract
- 1 package (3 ounces) raspberry gelatin
- 1 cup boiling water
- 1 package (10 ounces) frozen sweetened raspberries, thawed
  Fresh raspberries, optional

1. In a small bowl, sprinkle unflavored gelatin over cold water; let stand for 1 minute. In a small saucepan, combine half-and-half and sugar. Cook and stir just until mixture comes to a simmer. Remove from the heat; stir into gelatin until dissolved.

2. In a large bowl, beat cream cheese until smooth. Fold in gelatin mixture. Stir in vanilla. Pour into a 6-cup mold coated with cooking spray. Refrigerate until set but not firm, about 45 minutes.

3. In a small bowl, dissolve raspberry gelatin in boiling water. Stir in the raspberries until blended. Carefully spoon over cream cheese layer. Cover and refrigerate for at least 4 hours.

4. Unmold onto a serving plate; garnish with fresh berries if desired.

SLOW COOKER
Pumpkin Harvest Beef Stew

By the time the stew is done simmering, the house smells absolutely wonderful.

—**MARCIA O'NEIL** CEDAR CREST, NM

PREP: 25 MIN. • **COOK:** 6½ HOURS
MAKES: 6 SERVINGS

- 1 tablespoon canola oil
- 1 beef top round steak (1½ pounds), cut into 1-inch cubes
- 1½ cups cubed peeled pie pumpkin or sweet potatoes
- 3 small red potatoes, peeled and cubed
- 1 cup cubed acorn squash
- 1 medium onion, chopped
- 2 cans (14½ ounces each) reduced-sodium beef broth
- 1 can (14½ ounces) diced tomatoes, undrained
- 2 bay leaves
- 2 garlic cloves, minced
- 2 teaspoons reduced-sodium beef bouillon granules
- ½ teaspoon chili powder
- ½ teaspoon pepper
- ¼ teaspoon ground allspice
- ¼ teaspoon ground cloves
- ¼ cup water
- 3 tablespoons all-purpose flour

1. In a large skillet, heat the oil over medium-high heat. Brown the beef in batches; remove with a slotted spoon to a 4- or 5-qt. slow cooker. Add pumpkin, potatoes, squash and onion. Stir in the broth, tomatoes and seasonings. Cover and cook on low for 6-8 hours or until meat is tender.

2. Remove bay leaves. In a small bowl, mix the water and flour until smooth; gradually stir into stew. Cover and cook on high for 30 minutes or until liquid is thickened.

Ultimate Panini

Ultimate Panini

I love caramelized onions, and I wanted to pair them with something special. This hearty sandwich is just that!

—**CHARLENE BROGAN** FALMOUTH, ME

PREP: 40 MIN. • **COOK:** 5 MIN./BATCH
MAKES: 4 SERVINGS

- 2 large onions, sliced
- 2 tablespoons canola oil
- 4 slices provolone cheese
- ½ pound thinly sliced deli ham
- 1 large tomato, sliced
- 8 garlic-flavored sandwich pickle slices
- 8 slices Italian bread (½ inch thick)
- 2 tablespoons butter, softened

1. In a large skillet, saute onions in oil until softened. Reduce heat to medium-low; cook, stirring occasionally, for 30 minutes or until deep golden brown.

2. Layer the cheese, ham, tomato, pickles and caramelized onions on four bread slices; top with remaining bread. Spread outsides of the sandwiches with butter.

3. Cook on a panini maker or indoor grill for 3-4 minutes or until bread is browned and cheese is melted.

TOP TIP

Paninis Made Simple

A panini is typically assembled with cheese, meat and vegetables. It's then grilled with a press until the interior is warm and the exterior is crispy. If you don't have a panini maker or indoor grill, simply grill the sandwich in a skillet over medium-high heat.

Mustard & Cranberry
Glazed Ham, page 281

Melting Snowmen,
page 238

Chocolate-Strawberry Cream
Cheese Tart, page 289

Benedictine Dip,
page 227

Winter

BABY, IT'S COLD OUTSIDE! WINTER IS THE
PERFECT SEASON TO GET COZY WITH FAMILY
AND FRIENDS. IT'S A TIME SO SHARE TRADITIONS,
MAKE MEMORIES AND SPREAD A LITTLE CHEER.
WHETHER YOU'RE BAKING CHRISTMAS COOKIES,
HOSTING AN OPEN HOUSE OR SERVING AN
UNFORGETTABLE HOLIDAY DINNER, TURN HERE
FOR DELICIOUS IDEAS SURE TO CREATE SOME
MAGIC IN YOUR HOME.

LISA SPEER'S MINI KEY LIME
AND COCONUT PIES *PAGE 220*

Yuletide Open House

HAPPY HOLIDAYS! COME IN AND JOIN THE FUN! AN OPEN HOUSE IS THE IDEAL WAY TO CELEBRATE. INVITE FRIENDS TO COME AND GO AS THEY PLEASE AND GET READY TO MAKE CHRISTMAS MERRY AND BRIGHT! TURN HERE FOR EASY APPETIZERS, HEARTY BITES AND MORE.

JANET EDWARDS' RASPBERRY-WALNUT BRIE *PAGE 225*

GRACIELA SANDVIGEN'S BLUE CHEESE SPINACH SALAD *PAGE 223*

CHERYL PERRY'S SMOKED GOUDA & BACON POTATOES *PAGE 222*

Cheddar-
Bacon Dip

Cheddar-Bacon Dip

Both children and adults enjoy this dip. I like it, too, since it's so quick and easy to prepare. I make it for special occasions, such as Christmas get-togethers.
—**CAROL WERKMAN** NEERLANDIA, AB

PREP: 15 MIN. + CHILLING
MAKES: 10-12 SERVINGS

- 1 **package (8 ounces) cream cheese, softened**
- 1 **cup (8 ounces) sour cream**
- 5 **green onions, thinly sliced**
- 4 **medium tomatoes, chopped**
- 1 **large green pepper, chopped**
- 1 **jar (16 ounces) taco sauce**
- 2 **cups (8 ounces) shredded cheddar cheese**
- 1 **pound sliced bacon, cooked and crumbled**
  Tortilla or nacho tortilla chips

1. In a bowl, beat cream cheese and sour cream. Spread in an ungreased 13x9-in. dish or on a 12-in. plate. Combine onions, tomatoes and green pepper; sprinkle over the cream cheese layer.
2. Pour taco sauce over the vegetables. Sprinkle with the cheddar cheese. Refrigerate. Just before serving, sprinkle with bacon. Serve dip with tortilla or taco chips.

TOP TIP

Distinctive Dippers

Potato chips, crackers and tortilla chips are longtime favorites when it comes to scooping up a serving of dip, but don't hesitate to get creative. Serve dips with pita wedges, crunchy breadsticks, pretzels or mini corn bread muffins. Carrots and celery sticks are fine, but why not mix it up with asparagus spears, green beans, mushrooms or even sliced pears?

Super Party Mix

Super Party Mix

It's hard to resist this spiced snack loaded with cereal, nuts and so much more. I keep some on hand for drop-in guests.
—**NANCY UPHAUS** TOPEKA, KS

PREP: 20 MIN. • **BAKE:** 1 HOUR + COOLING
MAKES: 3½ QUARTS

- 2 **cups cheddar-flavored snack crackers**
- 2 **cups thin pretzel sticks, broken**
- 2 **cups sesame snack sticks**
- 2 **cups Life cereal**
- 2 **cups Cheerios**
- 1 **cup Wheat Chex**
- 1 **cup Corn Chex**
- 1½ **cups unsalted dry roasted peanuts**
- ½ **cup butter, melted**
- ½ **cup canola oil**
- 2 **teaspoons seasoned salt**
- 1½ **teaspoons garlic powder**

1. In a large bowl, combine the crackers, pretzels, sesame sticks, cereals and nuts. In a small bowl, combine the remaining ingredients. Drizzle over cereal mixture; toss to coat.
2. Spread into two ungreased 15x10-in. baking pans. Bake at 250° for 1 hour, stirring every 15 minutes. Cool on wire racks. Store in airtight containers.

Mulled Wine

This mulled wine is soothing and satisfying with a delightful blend of spices warmed to perfection. Refrigerating the wine mixture overnight allows the flavors to blend, so don't omit this essential step.
—*TASTE OF HOME* TEST KITCHEN

PREP: 15 MIN. • **COOK:** 30 MIN. + CHILLING
MAKES: 5 SERVINGS

- 1 **bottle (750 milliliters) fruity red wine**
- 1 **cup brandy**
- 1 **medium orange, sliced**
- 1 **medium lemon, sliced**
- 1 **cup sugar**
- ⅛ **teaspoon ground nutmeg**
- 2 **cinnamon sticks (3 inches)**
- ½ **teaspoon whole allspice**
- ½ **teaspoon aniseed**
- ½ **teaspoon whole peppercorns**
- 3 **whole cloves**

GARNISH

    Cinnamon stick, star anise and orange twist

1. In a large saucepan, combine the wine, brandy, orange, lemon, sugar and nutmeg. Place remaining spices on a double thickness of cheesecloth; bring up corners of cloth and tie with string to form a bag. Add spice bag to wine mixture.
2. Bring to a boil, stirring occasionally. Reduce heat; cover and simmer gently for 20 minutes. Cool; cover and refrigerate overnight.
3. Strain; discard fruit and spice bag. Reheat wine; serve warm in mugs. Garnish as desired.
NOTE *This recipe was tested with Rioja wine. Merlot would also work well.*

British Tenderloin Crostini

I like to use an ovenproof skillet when searing the tenderloin for this special appetizer. This way, all the flavorful juices stay in the pan while the meat finishes cooking. It also makes for easy cleanup!
—**SHARON TIPTON** WINTER GARDEN, FL

PREP: 20 MIN. • **BAKE:** 30 MIN. + STANDING
MAKES: 3 DOZEN

- 1 **tablespoon olive oil**
- 1 **beef tenderloin roast (2 pounds)**
- 1 **teaspoon salt, divided**
- ½ **teaspoon coarsely ground pepper**
- 1 **cup (8 ounces) sour cream**
- ¼ **cup prepared horseradish**
- 2 **tablespoons lemon juice**
- ¼ **teaspoon paprika**
- 18 **slices pumpernickel bread, halved**
- 3 **tablespoons butter, melted**
- 1 **bunch watercress**

1. Rub oil over tenderloin; sprinkle with ¾ teaspoon salt and pepper. In a large skillet, brown beef on all sides. Place roast on a rack in a shallow roasting pan.
2. Bake, uncovered, at 425° for 25-35 minutes or until meat reaches desired doneness (for medium-rare, a meat thermometer should read 145°; medium, 160°; well-done, 170°). Let beef stand for 10 minutes before slicing thinly.
3. In a small bowl, combine the sour cream, horseradish, lemon juice, paprika and remaining salt. Chill until serving.
4. Brush both sides of bread with butter; place on baking sheets. Bake at 425° for 4-6 minutes or until toasted, turning slices once.
5. Spread with sauce; top with beef. Garnish with watercress sprigs.

Mini Key Lime and
Coconut Pies

Mini Key Lime and Coconut Pies

Savor the flavor of Key lime pie with these individual muffin-size treats. They're great when you need to serve a large group.

—LISA SPEER PALM BEACH, FL

PREP: 25 MIN. • **BAKE:** 10 MIN. + COOLING
MAKES: 1½ DOZEN

- 1 tube (16½ ounces) refrigerated sugar cookie dough
- 1 can (14 ounces) sweetened condensed milk
- ½ cup Key lime juice
- 3 egg yolks
- 2 teaspoons grated lime peel
- ½ cup heavy whipping cream
- ¼ cup confectioners' sugar
- ¼ teaspoon vanilla extract
- ⅛ teaspoon coconut extract
- ¼ cup flaked coconut, toasted

1. Slice cookie dough into 18 pieces. Press onto the bottom and ½ in. up the sides of greased muffin cups. Bake at 350° for 8-10 minutes or until edges are lightly browned.

2. Meanwhile, in a small bowl, combine the milk, lime juice, egg yolks and lime peel. Spoon into hot crusts. Bake 7-9 minutes longer or until filling is set. Cool completely in pans on wire racks. Cover and refrigerate until serving.

3. Just before serving, in a small bowl, beat cream until it begins to thicken. Add the confectioners' sugar and extracts; beat until soft peaks form. Remove pies from muffin cups. Top with whipped cream and sprinkle with coconut.

Pomegranate-Glazed Turkey Meatballs

A splash of pomegranate juice turns ordinary meatballs into something extraordinary. I love the sweet lightness of the glaze combined with the ground turkey, herbs and spices.

—DANIELLE D'AMBROSIO BRIGHTON, MA

PREP: 30 MIN. • **COOK:** 10 MIN.
MAKES: 3 DOZEN

- 1 egg, beaten
- ½ cup soft bread crumbs
- ½ cup minced fresh parsley
- 1 teaspoon salt
- 1 teaspoon smoked paprika
- 1 teaspoon coarsely ground pepper
- ¼ teaspoon garlic salt
- 1¼ pounds ground turkey
- 3 cups plus 1 tablespoon pomegranate juice, divided
- ½ cup sugar
- 1 tablespoon cornstarch

1. In a large bowl, combine the egg, bread crumbs, parsley, salt, paprika, pepper and garlic salt. Crumble turkey over mixture and mix well. Shape into 1-in. balls.

2. Divide between two ungreased 15x10x1-in. baking pans. Bake at 375° for 10-15 minutes or until a thermometer reads 165° and juices run clear.

3. Meanwhile, in a large skillet, combine 3 cups pomegranate juice and sugar. Bring to a boil; cook until liquid is reduced to about 1 cup. Combine the cornstarch and remaining juice; stir into skillet. Cook and stir for 1 minute or until sauce is thickened.

4. Gently stir in meatballs and heat through. Serve in a slow cooker or chafing dish.

Pomegranate-Glazed
Turkey Meatballs

Fireside Cheese Spread

Fireside Cheese Spread

When our family and friends get together for holidays, I serve my savory cheese spread. If you prefer, try a Swiss cheese spread instead of the cheddar. If you enjoy garlic, substitute a small clove of minced garlic for the garlic powder.

—DEBBIE TERENZINI-WILKERSON
LUSBY, MD

PREP: 10 MIN. + CHILLING
MAKES: ABOUT 3½ CUPS

- 1 **container (16 ounces) cheddar cheese spread, softened**
- 2 **packages (one 8 ounces, one 3 ounces) cream cheese, softened**
- 3 **tablespoons butter, softened**
- 1 **teaspoon Worcestershire sauce**
- ½ **teaspoon garlic powder**
  Paprika
  Snipped fresh parsley
  Assorted crackers

In a medium bowl, combine cheese spread, cream cheese, butter, Worcestershire sauce and garlic powder. Blend thoroughly. Chill at least 3 hours or overnight. Sprinkle with paprika and parsley. Serve with crackers.

Smoked Gouda & Bacon Potatoes

Here's a hearty, special appetizer you'll need to eat with a fork! Creme fraiche gives these bites a decadent flavor.

—CHERYL PERRY HERTFORD, NC

PREP: 50 MIN. • **BAKE:** 10 MIN.
MAKES: 2½ DOZEN (2 CUPS SAUCE)

- **2** whole garlic bulbs
- **1** tablespoon olive oil
- **15** small red potatoes, halved
- **15** bacon strips
- **2** cups (8 ounces) shredded smoked Gouda cheese
- **1** teaspoon coarsely ground pepper
- **2** cups creme fraiche or sour cream
- **¼** cup fresh cilantro leaves

1. Remove papery outer skin from garlic (do not peel or separate cloves). Cut tops off of garlic bulbs. Brush with oil. Wrap each bulb in heavy-duty foil. Bake at 425° for 30-35 minutes or until softened. Cool for 10-15 minutes.
2. Meanwhile, place potatoes in a large saucepan; cover with water. Bring to a boil. Reduce heat; cover and simmer for 8-10 minutes or just until tender. Cut bacon strips in half widthwise. In a large skillet, cook bacon over medium heat until partially cooked but not crisp. Remove to paper towels to drain; keep bacon warm.
3. Preheat oven to 375°. Place a tablespoonful of cheese on the cut side of a potato half. Wrap with a half-strip of bacon and secure with a toothpick. Place on an ungreased baking sheet. Repeat. Sprinkle appetizers with pepper. Bake 10-15 minutes or until bacon is crisp.
4. For sauce, squeeze softened garlic into a food processor. Add creme fraiche and cilantro; cover and process until blended. Serve with potatoes.

Green Beans with Yellow-Pepper Butter

⑤ INGREDIENTS

Green Beans with Yellow-Pepper Butter

Colorful, crunchy and buttery, these beans come together quickly and will be a hit on your holiday buffet. For variation, sprinkle toasted pine nuts over the top just before serving this colorful side dish.

—JUDIE WHITE FLORIEN, LA

START TO FINISH: 30 MIN. • **MAKES:** 12 SERVINGS

- **3** medium sweet yellow peppers, divided
- **2** tablespoons plus ½ cup butter, softened, divided
- **⅓** cup pine nuts
- **1** to 2 tablespoons lemon juice
- **½** teaspoon salt
- **¼** teaspoon pepper
- **2¼** pounds fresh green beans

1. Finely chop 1½ yellow peppers. In a large skillet, heat 2 tablespoons butter over medium-high heat. Add chopped peppers; cook and stir until tender.
2. Place pine nuts, lemon juice, salt, pepper and remaining butter in a food processor; process until blended. Add cooked peppers; process to blend.
3. Place beans in a Dutch oven and cover with water. Cut remaining 1½ peppers into thin strips; add to beans. Bring to a boil. Cook, covered, 5-7 minutes or until vegetables are crisp-tender; drain well and return to pot. Add butter mixture and toss to coat.

❝ I made these (potatoes) at Christmas...a big hit! After baking, I put some parsley flakes and melted butter on them. ❞
—PERMITCLERK TASTEOFHOME.COM

Chocolate Mallow Cake

Nothing compares to homemade cake, especially when gathering with friends and family for a special occasion. The young and young at heart love the pecan filling and the yummy marshmallow frosting.
—**EDNA HOFFMAN** HEBRON, IN

PREP: 1 HOUR • **BAKE:** 30 MIN. + CHILLING
MAKES: 15 SERVINGS

- ⅓ cup shortening
- 1 cup sugar
- ½ cup packed brown sugar
- 2 eggs
- 2 ounces unsweetened chocolate, melted and cooled
- 1 teaspoon vanilla extract
- 1 cup buttermilk
- ¼ cup water
- 1¾ cups cake flour
- 1½ teaspoons baking soda
- ¾ teaspoon salt

FILLING
- 1 cup packed brown sugar
- 3 tablespoons all-purpose flour
- 1 cup milk
- 2 egg yolks, beaten
- 2 tablespoons butter
- 1 teaspoon vanilla extract
- ½ cup chopped pecans

FROSTING
- 1½ cups sugar
- 2 egg whites
- ⅓ cup water
- 1 tablespoon light corn syrup
- ¼ teaspoon cream of tartar
- 2 cups miniature marshmallows
- 1 ounce unsweetened chocolate, melted

1. In a large bowl, cream shortening and sugars. Add eggs, one at a time, beating well after each. Beat in chocolate and vanilla. Combine buttermilk and water. Combine the cake flour, baking soda and salt; add to creamed mixture alternately with buttermilk mixture.

2. Pour into a greased and floured 13x9-in. baking pan. Bake at 350° for 30-35 minutes or until a toothpick inserted near the center comes out clean. Cool for 10 minutes before removing cake from pan to a wire rack.

3. For filling, in a small saucepan, combine brown sugar and all-purpose flour. Stir in milk until smooth. Cook and stir over medium-high heat until thickened and bubbly. Reduce heat; cook and stir 2 minutes longer. Remove from the heat. Stir a small amount of hot filling into egg yolks; return all to pan, stirring constantly. Bring to a gentle boil; cook and stir 2 minutes longer.

4. Remove from the heat. Gently stir in butter and vanilla. Cool to room temperature without stirring. Spread over cake to within ½ in. of edges; sprinkle with pecans. Refrigerate for 30 minutes or until set.

5. For frosting, in a heavy saucepan over low heat, combine the sugar, egg whites, water, corn syrup and cream of tartar. With a portable mixer, beat on low speed for 1 minute. Continue beating on low over low heat for 8-10 minutes or until frosting reaches 160°.

6. Pour into the large bowl of a heavy-duty stand mixer; add marshmallows. Beat on high for 7-9 minutes or until stiff peaks form. Carefully spread over cake. Pipe thin lines of melted chocolate over cake; gently pull a toothpick or sharp knife through lines in alternating directions. Store in the refrigerator.

Blue Cheese Spinach Salad

A simple dressing made of currant jelly and balsamic vinegar coats this colorful salad, sprinkled with crunchy pine nuts. If you like blue cheese, you'll love this refreshing toss. Best of all, it comes together in 15 minutes!
—**GRACIELA SANDVIGEN** ROCHESTER, NY

START TO FINISH: 15 MIN.
MAKES: 12 SERVINGS

- ½ cup red currant jelly
- 3 tablespoons balsamic vinegar
- 6 cups fresh baby spinach
- 2 pints fresh strawberries, quartered
- 1 cup mandarin oranges, drained
- ½ medium red onion, thinly sliced
- ½ cup crumbled blue cheese
- ½ cup pine nuts, toasted

1. Heat jelly in a small saucepan over low heat, stirring until smooth. Remove from heat; stir in vinegar.

2. In a large bowl, combine the spinach, strawberries, oranges, onion and blue cheese. Drizzle with dressing and toss to coat. Sprinkle with pine nuts.

Chocolate Mallow Cake

White Chocolate
Cranberry-Pecan Tart

White Chocolate Cranberry-Pecan Tart

The first time I tasted my friend's dessert was at a Christmas party that she was having. I got a copy of the recipe and now it's a yuletide tradition for my family. The white chips, cranberries and orange peel take pecan pie to a scrumptious new level.

—KAREN MOORE JACKSONVILLE, FL

PREP: 25 MIN. • **BAKE:** 40 MIN. + COOLING
MAKES: 16 SERVINGS

      Pastry for single-crust pie
      (9 inches)
  1   **cup fresh or frozen cranberries**
  1   **cup pecan halves**
  1   **cup white baking chips**
  3   **eggs**
  ¾   **cup packed brown sugar**
  ¾   **cup light corn syrup**
  2   **tablespoons all-purpose flour**
  1   **teaspoon grated orange peel**
      Whipped cream, optional

1. Preheat oven to 350°. Roll out pastry to fit an 11-in. tart pan with removable bottom; trim edges. Sprinkle with the cranberries, pecans and chips. In a small bowl, whisk the eggs, brown sugar, corn syrup, flour and orange peel; pour over chips.
2. Bake 40-45 minutes or until a knife inserted near the center comes out clean. Cool on a wire rack. Serve with whipped cream if desired.

Mostaccioli

Mostaccioli

Years ago, a friend shared her cheesy baked pasta recipe with me. I love to serve it with a salad and garlic bread. It's great for casually entertaining a large group.

—MARGARET MCNEIL GERMANTOWN, TN

PREP: 25 MIN. • **BAKE:** 25 MIN.
MAKES: 2 CASSEROLES (6 SERVINGS EACH)

- 1 package (16 ounces) mostaccioli
- 1½ pounds ground beef
- 1¼ cups chopped green pepper
- 1 cup chopped onion
- 1 jar (26 ounces) spaghetti sauce
- 1 can (10¾ ounces) condensed cheddar cheese soup, undiluted
- 1½ teaspoons Italian seasoning
- ¾ teaspoon pepper
- 2 cups (8 ounces) shredded part-skim mozzarella cheese, divided

1. Preheat oven to 350°. Cook mostaccioli according to package directions. Meanwhile, in a large skillet, cook beef, green pepper and onion over medium heat until meat is no longer pink; drain. Stir in spaghetti sauce, soup, Italian seasoning and pepper.
2. Drain mostaccioli. Add mostaccioli and 1½ cups cheese to beef mixture. Transfer to two greased 11 x 7-in. baking dishes. Sprinkle with remaining cheese.
3. Cover and bake 20 minutes. Uncover; bake 5-10 minutes longer or until bubbly and cheese is melted.

---

⑤ INGREDIENTS
Crab Crescents

Good and quick are two ways to describe this appetizer. These little bites are delicious and decadent!

—STEPHANIE HOWARD OAKLAND, CA

START TO FINISH: 25 MIN.
MAKES: 16 APPETIZERS

- 1 tube (8 ounces) refrigerated crescent rolls
- 3 tablespoons prepared pesto
- ½ cup fresh crabmeat

1. Unroll crescent dough; separate into eight triangles. Cut each triangle in half lengthwise, forming two triangles. Spread ½ teaspoon pesto over each triangle; place 1 rounded teaspoonful of crab along the wide end of each triangle.
2. Roll up triangles from the wide ends and place point side down 1 in. apart on an ungreased baking sheet.
3. Bake at 375° for 10-12 minutes or until golden brown. Serve warm.

---

⑤ INGREDIENTS
Raspberry-Walnut Brie

Only a few ingredients are needed to make this creamy and elegant appetizer. It's perfect for an evening with friends or a cozy movie night with the family.

—JANET EDWARDS BEAVERTON, OR

START TO FINISH: 10 MIN. • **MAKES:** 16 SERVINGS

- ¼ cup seedless raspberry jam
- 2 rounds (8 ounces each) Brie cheese
- 1 package (11½ ounces) stone ground wheat crackers, divided
- ½ cup finely chopped walnuts
- 1 tablespoon butter, melted

1. In a small microwave-safe bowl, microwave jam on high for 15-20 seconds or until melted; brush over the Brie.
2. Crush nine crackers. In a small bowl, combine the cracker crumbs, nuts and butter; press into the jam. Serve with remaining crackers.

Mashed Potatoes with Garlic-Olive Oil

Garlic mashed potatoes are high on our "love it" list. To intensify the flavor, I combine garlic and olive oil in the food processor and drizzle it on top of the potatoes right before serving.

—EMORY DOTY JASPER, GA

START TO FINISH: 30 MIN.
MAKES: 12 SERVINGS (¾ CUP EACH)

- 4 pounds red potatoes, quartered
- ½ cup olive oil
- 2 garlic cloves
- ⅔ cup heavy whipping cream
- ¼ cup butter, softened
- 2 teaspoons salt
- ½ teaspoon pepper
- ⅔ to ¾ cup whole milk
- 3 green onions, chopped
- ¾ cup grated Parmesan cheese, optional

1. Place potatoes in a Dutch oven; add water to cover. Bring to a boil. Reduce heat; cook, uncovered, for 15-20 minutes or until tender. Meanwhile, place oil and garlic in a small food processor; process until blended.
2. Drain potatoes; return to pan. Mash potatoes, gradually adding cream, butter, salt, pepper and enough milk to reach desired consistency. Stir in green onions. Serve with garlic olive oil and, if desired, grated cheese.
NOTE *For food safety purposes, prepare garlic olive oil just before serving; do not store leftover oil mixture.*

Mashed Potatoes with Garlic-Olive Oil

Mushroom and
Bacon Cheesecake

Mushroom and Bacon Cheesecake

My family loves anything with cream cheese, so I knew this savory cheesecake appetizer would go down as an all-time favorite. Add mushrooms, bacon, red peppers and parsley for a pretty garnish on top. This is a great recipe to make ahead for when you're in need of a dish to pass.

—MACEY ALLEN GREEN FOREST, AR

PREP: 50 MIN. • **BAKE:** 55 MIN. + CHILLING
MAKES: 16 SERVINGS

- 1¾ cups soft bread crumbs
- 1 cup grated Parmesan cheese
- 6 tablespoons butter, melted

FILLING
- 1 cup finely chopped onion
- 1 cup finely chopped sweet red pepper
- 1 tablespoon olive oil
- 4 cups assorted chopped fresh mushrooms
- 3 packages (8 ounces each) cream cheese, softened
- 1 teaspoon salt
- 1 teaspoon pepper
- ½ cup sour cream
- 4 eggs, lightly beaten
- 12 bacon strips, cooked and crumbled
- 1 cup (4 ounces) crumbled feta cheese
- ½ cup minced fresh parsley
  Roasted sliced mushrooms, fresh parsley and additional cooked bacon strips, optional
  Assorted crackers

1. Place a greased 9-in. springform pan on a double thickness of heavy-duty foil (about 18 in. square). Securely wrap foil around pan.

2. In a small bowl, combine the bread crumbs, Parmesan cheese and butter. Press onto the bottom of a greased 9-in. springform pan. Place pan on a baking sheet. Bake at 350° for 10-15 minutes or until golden brown. Cool on a wire rack.

3. Meanwhile, in a large skillet, saute onion and red pepper in oil for 2 minutes. Add the mushrooms; cook and stir for 10 minutes or until liquid has evaporated. Set aside to cool.

4. In a large bowl, beat the cream cheese, salt and pepper until light and fluffy. Beat in sour cream. Add eggs; beat on low speed just until combined. Fold in the bacon, feta cheese, parsley and mushroom mixture. Pour into crust. Place springform pan in a large baking pan; add 1 in. of hot water to larger pan.

5. Bake at 350° for 55-65 minutes or until center is just set and top appears dull. Remove springform pan from water bath. Cool on a wire rack for 10 minutes. Carefully run a knife around edge of pan to loosen; cool 1 hour longer. Refrigerate overnight.

6. Remove sides of pan. Top with mushrooms, parsley and additional bacon if desired. Serve with crackers.

Shrimp Cocktail

During the '60s, shrimp cocktail was one of the most popular party foods around—and it's still a crowd favorite. It's the one appetizer that I serve for every special occasion.

—PEGGY ALLEN PASADENA, CA

PREP: 30 MIN. + CHILLING
MAKES: ABOUT 6 DOZEN (1¼ CUPS SAUCE)

- 3 quarts water
- 1 small onion, sliced
- ½ medium lemon, sliced
- 2 sprigs fresh parsley
- 1 tablespoon salt
- 5 whole peppercorns
- 1 bay leaf
- ¼ teaspoon dried thyme
- 3 pounds uncooked large shrimp, peeled and deveined (tails on)

SAUCE
- 1 cup chili sauce
- 2 tablespoons lemon juice
- 2 tablespoons prepared horseradish
- 4 teaspoons Worcestershire sauce
- ½ teaspoon salt
  Dash cayenne pepper

1. In a Dutch oven, combine the first eight ingredients; bring to a boil. Add shrimp. Reduce heat; simmer, uncovered, for 4-5 minutes or until the shrimp turn pink.

2. Drain shrimp and immediately rinse in cold water. Refrigerate for 2-3 hours or until cold. In a small bowl, combine the sauce ingredients. Refrigerate until serving.

3. Arrange shrimp on a serving platter; serve with sauce.

TOP TIP

Savory Cheesecakes Strike a Chord with Busy Hostesses

Savory cheesecakes are great change-of-pace appetizers for busy cooks. Loaded with everything from herbs and veggies to meats and cheeses, these party starters serve a crowd, can be made ahead of time and bake on their own once the prep work is done. Cooks can also get creative with the recipes, putting their own spin on the cheesecake with various seasonings, cheeses and more.

Benedictine Dip

Benedictine Dip

Benedictine is a creamy spread studded with chopped cucumbers. It was named in honor of Jennie Carter Benedict, a chef and restaurateur from Louisville who created the condiment at the turn of the 20th century. Originally used for cucumber sandwiches, Benedictine is now commonly enjoyed as a dip for chips or crackers.
—*TASTE OF HOME* TEST KITCHEN

START TO FINISH: 15 MIN. • **MAKES:** 1¾ CUPS

- 4 ounces cream cheese, softened
- 1 log (4 ounces) fresh goat cheese
- 2 tablespoons minced fresh parsley
- 1 tablespoon mayonnaise
- ¼ teaspoon salt
- ⅛ teaspoon cayenne pepper
- ⅛ teaspoon pepper
- 1 drop green food coloring, optional
- ¾ cup finely chopped peeled cucumber, patted dry
- ¼ cup finely chopped green onions
  Assorted crackers

In a small bowl, combine the cheeses, parsley, mayonnaise, salt, cayenne, pepper and food coloring if desired; beat until smooth. Stir in cucumber and onion. Chill until serving. Serve with crackers.

⑤INGREDIENTS
Pink Party Punch

Here's a fun beverage that will be the highlight of any party. The fruity flavors blend perfectly together, making it impossible to have just one glass.
—**CAROL GARNETT** BELLEVUE, WA

START TO FINISH: 10 MIN.
MAKES: 32 SERVINGS (6 QUARTS)

- 2 bottles (46 ounces each) white grape juice, chilled
- 1 bottle (48 ounces) cranberry juice, chilled
- 2 cans (12 ounces each) frozen lemonade concentrate, thawed
- 1 bottle (1 liter) club soda, chilled
- 1 pint lemon sherbet

1. In two pitchers, combine juices and lemonade concentrate; refrigerate until serving.
2. Just before serving, stir in club soda and top with scoops of sherbet.

Baked Ham with Orange Glaze

This ham has a wonderful orange glaze that makes it special for any holiday gathering or even a nice family dinner. You can also insert whole cloves into the ham for added color and flavor. Enjoy it by serving extra glaze on the side.
—*TASTE OF HOME* TEST KITCHEN

PREP: 5 MIN. • **BAKE:** 1 HOUR 50 MIN. + STANDING
MAKES: 12 SERVINGS

- 1 fully cooked bone-in ham (6 to 7 pounds)
- 2 cups apple cider or apple juice
- 2 cups orange juice
- ⅓ cup orange marmalade
- ¼ cup packed brown sugar
- ¼ cup Dijon mustard
- ¼ teaspoon ground ginger

1. Preheat oven to 325°. Place ham on a rack in a shallow roasting pan. Trim fat; score surface of ham, making diamond shapes ¼ in. deep. Add cider and orange juice to pan. Loosely cover ham with foil; bake 1 hour.
2. Combine remaining ingredients; brush some glaze over ham. Bake, uncovered, 50-60 minutes longer or until a thermometer reads 140° and ham is heated through, brushing occasionally with glaze.
3. Let stand 15 minutes before slicing. Serve with remaining glaze.

Cookie Exchange

CUTE GINGERBREAD MEN, JAM-FILLED COOKIES, ENTICING SQUARES OF CHOCOLATY FUDGE... WHAT WHIMSICAL SWEETS WILL APPEAR ON YOUR COOKIE PLATTER THIS YEAR? WHETHER YOU ARE HOSTING A COOKIE EXCHANGE, BAKING A FEW GIFTS OR SIMPLY GETTING READY FOR SANTA'S VISIT, THESE TREATS SATISFY EVERYONE'S SWEET TOOTH.

SUSAN WESTERFIELD'S CHERRY NUT COOKIES *PAGE 241*

LORRAINE CALAND'S HONEY-PECAN SQUARES *PAGE 237*

JEANNINE SCHNEIDER'S REINDEER BROWNIES *PAGE 234*

Triple-Ginger
Gingersnaps

Triple-Ginger Gingersnaps

Ginger cookies are holiday standbys. I tuck
them into clean, recycled coffee cans
wrapped in decorative paper. I add ribbon
or trim for a pretty presentation.
—**JESSICA FOLLEN** WAUNAKEE, WI

PREP: 35 MIN. + CHILLING • **BAKE:** 10 MIN./BATCH
MAKES: 4 DOZEN

- ⅔ **cup butter, softened**
- 1 **cup packed brown sugar**
- ¼ **cup molasses**
- 1 **egg**
- 2 **teaspoons minced fresh gingerroot**
- 1 **cup all-purpose flour**
- ¾ **cup whole wheat flour**
- 3 **teaspoons ground ginger**
- 1½ **teaspoons baking soda**
- ½ **teaspoon fine sea salt or kosher salt**
- ½ **teaspoon ground nutmeg**
- ¼ **teaspoon ground cloves**
- 3 **tablespoons finely chopped crystallized ginger**
- ¼ **cup sugar**
- 1½ **teaspoons ground cinnamon**

1. In a large bowl, cream butter and
brown sugar until light and fluffy. Beat in
molasses, egg and fresh ginger.
2. Combine flours, ground ginger,
baking soda, salt, nutmeg and cloves;
gradually add to creamed mixture and
mix well. Stir in crystallized ginger.
Cover and refrigerate 1 hour or until easy
to handle.

3. Preheat oven to 350°. In a small bowl,
combine sugar and cinnamon. Shape
dough into 1-in. balls; roll in sugar
mixture. Place 3 in. apart on parchment
paper-lined baking sheets.
4. Bake 10-12 minutes or until set. Cool
2 minutes before removing from pans to
wire racks. Store in an airtight container.

Pfeffernusse Cookies

A German tradition, these fragrant cookies
pack a warm rush of spices in every
bite. Also called pepper nuts, they go
wonderfully with coffee or tea.
—**JOANNE NELSON** EAST STROUDSBURG, PA

PREP: 35 MIN. + CHILLING • **BAKE:** 15 MIN./BATCH
MAKES: 10 DOZEN

- ½ **cup molasses**
- ¼ **cup honey**
- ¼ **cup butter, cubed**
- ¼ **cup shortening**
- 2 **eggs**
- 1½ **teaspoons anise extract**
- 4 **cups all-purpose flour**
- ¾ **cup sugar**
- ½ **cup packed brown sugar**
- 2 **teaspoons ground cinnamon**
- 1½ **teaspoons baking soda**
- 1 **teaspoon ground ginger**
- 1 **teaspoon ground cardamom**
- 1 **teaspoon ground nutmeg**
- 1 **teaspoon ground cloves**
- ¾ **teaspoon coarsely ground pepper**
- ½ **teaspoon salt**
- 1 **cup confectioners' sugar**

1. In a small saucepan, combine
molasses, honey, butter and shortening.
Cook and stir over medium heat until
melted. Remove from heat; cool to room
temperature. Stir in eggs and extract.
2. Combine flour, sugar, brown sugar,
cinnamon, baking soda, ginger,
cardamom, nutmeg, cloves, pepper and
salt. Gradually add molasses mixture and
mix well. Cover and refrigerate at least
2 hours or overnight.
3. Preheat oven to 325°. Roll dough into
1-in. balls. Place 1 in. apart on greased
baking sheets. Bake 12-15 minutes or
until golden brown. Remove cookies to
wire racks. Roll warm cookies in
confectioners' sugar. Cool completely.
Store in an airtight container.

Pfeffernusse
Cookies

Caramel Pretzel Bites

Caramel Pretzel Bites

I created this recipe wanting to make my own version of a pretzel log dipped in caramel, chocolate and nuts from a popular candy store. These are smothered with homemade caramel.

—MICHILENE KLAVER
GRAND RAPIDS, MI

PREP: 45 MIN. + COOLING
MAKES: 6 DOZEN

- 2 teaspoons butter, softened
- 4 cups pretzel sticks
- 2½ cups pecan halves, toasted
- 2¼ cups packed brown sugar
- 1 cup butter, cubed
- 1 cup corn syrup
- 1 can (14 ounces) sweetened condensed milk
- ⅛ teaspoon salt
- 1 teaspoon vanilla extract
- 1 package (11½ ounces) milk chocolate chips
- 1 tablespoon plus 1 teaspoon shortening, divided
- ⅓ cup white baking chips

1. Line a 13x9-in. pan with foil; grease foil with softened butter. Spread pretzels and pecans on bottom of prepared pan.
2. In a large heavy saucepan, combine brown sugar, cubed butter, corn syrup, milk and salt; cook and stir over medium heat until a candy thermometer reads 240°(soft-ball stage). Remove from heat. Stir in vanilla. Pour over pretzel mixture.
3. In a microwave, melt chocolate chips and 1 tablespoon shortening; stir until smooth. Spread over caramel layer. In microwave, melt baking chips and remaining shortening; stir until smooth. Drizzle over top. Let stand until set.
4. Using foil, lift candy out of pan; remove foil. Using a buttered knife, cut candy into bite-size pieces.

Folded Hazelnut Cookies

We made these cookies when my boys were small. The boys were covered in flour, with aprons wrapped around them and Nutella on their faces.

—PAULA MARCHESI LENHARTSVILLE, PA

PREP: 30 MIN. • **BAKE:** 10 MIN./BATCH
MAKES: ABOUT 2 DOZEN

- 1 tablespoon finely chopped hazelnuts
- 1 tablespoon sugar
- 1½ cups all-purpose flour
- ½ cup confectioners' sugar
- ¼ cup cornstarch
- ¾ cup cold butter, cubed
- 2 tablespoons Nutella
- 1 egg, lightly beaten

1. Preheat oven to 350°. In a small bowl, mix hazelnuts and sugar. In a large bowl, whisk flour, confectioners' sugar and cornstarch. Cut in butter until crumbly. Transfer to a clean work surface. Knead gently until mixture forms a smooth dough, about 2 minutes (dough will be crumbly but will come together).
2. Divide dough in half. On a lightly floured surface, roll each portion to ⅛-in. thickness. Cut with a floured 2-in. round cookie cutter. Place ¼ teaspoon Nutella in center. Fold dough partially in half, just enough to cover filling.
3. Place 1 in. apart on greased baking sheets. Brush with beaten egg; sprinkle with hazelnut mixture. Bake 10-12 minutes or until bottoms are light brown. Remove from pans to wire racks to cool.

Folded Hazelnut Cookies

White Chocolate Cranberry Biscotti

White Chocolate Cranberry Biscotti

Over the years, I've adapted my most-requested biscotti recipe to add some of my favorite ingredients: cranberries, white chocolate and pistachios. This biscotti keeps and freezes well, so you can make it in advance for the holidays.
—**SUSAN NELSON** NEWBURY PARK, CA

PREP: 25 MIN. • **BAKE:** 35 MIN.
MAKES: 2½ DOZEN

- ¾ cup sugar
- ½ cup canola oil
- 2 eggs
- 1 teaspoon vanilla extract
- 1¾ cups all-purpose flour
- 1½ teaspoons baking powder
- ½ teaspoon salt
- ¾ cup white baking chips
- ¾ cup dried cranberries
- ¾ cup pistachios

1. Preheat oven to 325°. In a small bowl, beat sugar and oil until blended. Beat in eggs and vanilla. Combine the flour, baking powder and salt; gradually add to sugar mixture and mix well. Stir in the chips, cranberries and pistachios.
2. Divide dough in half. With lightly floured hands, shape each half into a 10x1½-in. rectangle on a parchment paper-lined baking sheet. Bake 30-35 minutes or until lightly browned.
3. Place pans on wire racks. When cool enough to handle, transfer to a cutting board; cut diagonally with a serrated knife into ½-in. slices. Place cut side down on baking sheets.
4. Bake 6-7 minutes on each side or until golden brown. Remove to wire racks to cool completely. Store in an airtight container.

Pumpkin Pie Spiced Blondies

Pumpkin Pie Spiced Blondies

My family loves pumpkin pie at holiday time and craves brownies all year long. So everyone's doubly happy when I bring out a platter of my spiced blondies.
—**AMY ANDREWS** MAPLE VALLEY, WA

PREP: 25 MIN. • **BAKE:** 25 MIN. + COOLING
MAKES: 16 SERVINGS

- ¾ cup butter, softened
- ¾ cup packed brown sugar
- 2 eggs
- 4 teaspoons light corn syrup
- 1½ teaspoons rum extract
- 1⅓ cups all-purpose flour
- 2 teaspoons pumpkin pie spice
- ½ teaspoon baking powder
- ¼ teaspoon salt
- 1 cup white baking chips
- ¾ cup chopped pecans, optional

FROSTING

- 1¼ cups confectioners' sugar
- 3 tablespoons cream cheese, softened
- ⅛ teaspoon vanilla extract
- 1½ to 2 teaspoons orange juice

1. Preheat oven to 350°. In a large bowl, cream butter and brown sugar until light and fluffy. Beat in eggs, corn syrup and extract. In another bowl, whisk flour, pie spice, baking powder and salt; gradually beat into creamed mixture. Stir in baking chips and, if desired, pecans.
2. Spread into a greased 8-in.-square baking pan. Bake 25-30 minutes or until a toothpick inserted in center comes out clean (do not overbake). Cool completely in pan on a wire rack.
3. In a small bowl, beat confectioners' sugar, cream cheese, vanilla and enough orange juice to reach a spreading consistency. Spread over top; cut into bars. Refrigerate leftovers.

Raspberry & Chocolate Shortbread Bars

When I was a child, I decided that the combination of chocolate and raspberries was made in heaven, and that any treat made with these two delicious ingredients would be at the top of my holiday list. That said, this recipe is a longtime favorite. Try it with any preserves you like.
—**LILY JULOW** LAWRENCEVILLE, GA

PREP: 25 MIN. • **BAKE:** 30 MIN. + COOLING
MAKES: 2 DOZEN

- 1 cup unsalted butter, softened
- 1 cup sugar
- 2 egg yolks
- ½ teaspoon vanilla extract
- 2 cups all-purpose flour
- 1 teaspoon baking powder
- ¼ teaspoon salt
- 1 jar (10 ounces) seedless raspberry spreadable fruit
- 4 ounces bittersweet chocolate, finely chopped
- ⅓ cup heavy whipping cream

1. Preheat oven to 350°. In a large bowl, cream butter and sugar until light and fluffy. Beat in egg yolks and vanilla. In a small bowl, mix flour, baking powder and salt; gradually add to creamed mixture, mixing well.
2. Press half of the dough onto bottom of a greased 11x7-in. baking dish. Top with spreadable fruit. Crumble remaining dough over fruit. Bake on lowest oven rack 30-40 minutes or until golden brown. Cool completely on a wire rack.
3. Place chocolate in a small bowl. In a small saucepan, bring cream just to a boil. Pour over chocolate; whisk until smooth. Drizzle over top of shortbread; let stand until set. Cut into bars.

Raspberry & Chocolate Shortbread Bars

Reindeer Brownies

Reindeer Brownies

My son, Jeremy, is 36 but acts as if he's 5 when he sees these brownies—I've been making them for more than 30 years! My daughter, Jayme, and my four grandchildren love them, too. If you're short on time, a boxed mix works just fine.
—JEANNINE SCHNEIDER FREMONT, CA

PREP: 30 MIN. • **BAKE:** 25 MIN. + COOLING
MAKES: 2 DOZEN

- ¾ **cup butter, cubed**
- 4 **ounces unsweetened chocolate, chopped**
- 3 **eggs**
- 2 **cups sugar**
- ¼ **teaspoon salt**
- 1 **teaspoon vanilla extract**
- 1 **cup all-purpose flour**
- 1 **can (16 ounces) chocolate frosting**
- 48 **candy eyeballs**
- 24 **Red Hots**
- 48 **miniature pretzels**

1. Preheat oven to 350°. Line a 13x9-in. baking pan with foil, letting ends extend up sides; grease foil. In a microwave, melt butter and chocolate; stir until smooth. Cool slightly.
2. In a large bowl, beat eggs, sugar and salt. Stir in vanilla and the chocolate mixture. Gradually add flour, mixing thoroughly.

3. Spread into prepared pan. Bake 25-30 minutes or until brownie begins to pull away from sides of pan. Cool completely in pan on a wire rack.
4. Lifting with foil, remove brownie from pan. Spread frosting over top. Cut into 12 squares; cut squares into triangles. Attach candies and pretzels to make reindeer faces.

Chocolate-Dipped Orange Cookies

With orange peel and extract, these tender cookies are bursting with fresh citrus flavor. Dipping them in chocolate adds a special touch that folks adore.
—JOANNE BURKERT BEECHER, IL

PREP: 30 MIN. • **BAKE:** 10 MIN./BATCH + COOLING
MAKES: 3 DOZEN

- 1 **cup butter, softened**
- ½ **cup confectioners' sugar**
- 1 **teaspoon grated orange peel**
- 1 **teaspoon orange extract**
- 2 **cups all-purpose flour**
- ¼ **teaspoon salt**
- 6 **ounces dark chocolate candy coating**
- ½ **cup chopped almonds, toasted**

1. Preheat oven to 350°. In a large bowl, cream butter and confectioners' sugar until light and fluffy. Beat in orange peel and extract. Combine flour and salt; gradually add to creamed mixture and mix well.
2. Divide dough into 36 pieces; shape each into a 2½-in. rope. Place 2 in. apart on ungreased baking sheets. Bake 10-12 minutes or until set. Cool 2 minutes before removing from pans to wire racks to cool completely.
3. In a microwave, melt candy coating; stir until smooth. Dip ends of cookies in coating; allow excess to drip off. Sprinkle with almonds. Place on waxed paper; let stand until set. Store in an airtight container.

Chocolate Angel Food Candy

You might want to hide this candy until Christmas. Often called fairy food or sponge candy, it is a honeycombed, crunchy, chocolate-covered delight that's simply irresistible.
—GERALYN EMMERICH HUBERTUS, WI

PREP: 20 MIN. • **COOK:** 20 MIN. + COOLING
MAKES: ABOUT 1¼ POUNDS

- 1 **teaspoon butter**
- 1 **cup sugar**
- 1 **cup dark corn syrup**
- 1 **tablespoon white vinegar**
- 1 **tablespoon baking soda**
- ½ **pound dark chocolate candy coating, coarsely chopped**
- 1 **teaspoon shortening, divided**
- ½ **pound milk chocolate candy coating, coarsely chopped**

1. Line a 9-in.-square pan with foil and grease foil with butter; set aside. In a large heavy saucepan, combine sugar, corn syrup and vinegar. Cook and stir over medium heat until sugar is dissolved. Bring to a boil. Cook, without stirring, until a candy thermometer reads 300° (hard-crack stage).
2. Remove from heat; stir in baking soda. Immediately pour into prepared pan. Do not spread candy. Cool; then using foil, lift candy out of pan. Gently peel off foil; break candy into pieces.
3. In a microwave, melt dark chocolate coating and ½ teaspoon shortening; stir until smooth. Dip half the candies in the melted dark chocolate mixture, allowing excess to drip off. Place on waxed paper; let stand until set. Repeat with milk chocolate coating and remaining shortening and candies. Store in an airtight container.
NOTE *We recommend that you test your candy thermometer before each use by bringing water to a boil; the thermometer should read 212°. Adjust your recipe temperature up or down based on your test.*

Tiger Butter Candy

Tiger Butter Candy

Fans of tiger butter fudge will revel in this version that's very similar to bark candy. The chocolate swirls are pleasing to the eye, and the creamy peanut butter flavor is a treat for the taste buds.

—**PHILIP JONES** LUBBOCK, TX

PREP: 15 MIN. + CHILLING
MAKES: ABOUT 1¼ POUNDS

- 1 **pound white candy coating, coarsely chopped**
- ½ **cup chunky peanut butter**
- ½ **cup semisweet chocolate chips**
- ½ **teaspoon shortening**

Line a 15x10x1-in. pan with foil; set aside. In a microwave-safe bowl, melt candy coating and peanut butter; stir until smooth. Spread into prepared pan. In another microwave-safe bowl, melt chocolate chips and shortening; stir until smooth. Drizzle over top; cut through with a knife to swirl. Chill until firm. Break into pieces. Store in an airtight container.

Chocolate Gingerbread Cookies

My mother, Esther, created this recipe, and I've been making the cookies in her honor every Christmas since then. People can't get enough of the homey combination of molasses and chocolate.

—KAREN SUE GARBACK-PRISTERA
ALBANY, NY

PREP: 40 MIN. + CHILLING
BAKE: 10 MIN./BATCH + COOLING
MAKES: 3 DOZEN

- ½ cup butter, softened
- ¾ cup sugar
- 1 egg
- ½ cup molasses
- 3 cups all-purpose flour
- 2 tablespoons plus 1½ teaspoons baking cocoa
- 1 teaspoon baking soda
- 1 teaspoon ground cinnamon
- ½ teaspoon baking powder
- ½ teaspoon salt
  Icing and decorations of your choice

1. In a large bowl, cream butter and sugar until light and fluffy. Beat in egg and molasses. Combine flour, cocoa, baking soda, cinnamon, baking powder and salt; gradually add to creamed mixture and mix well. Cover and refrigerate 1 hour or until easy to handle.
2. Preheat oven to 350°. On a lightly floured surface, roll dough to ⅛-in. thickness.
3. Cut dough with a floured 3½-in. gingerbread boy cookie cutter; place 1 in. apart on ungreased baking sheets. Repeat with remaining dough; chill and reroll scraps.
4. Bake 6-8 minutes or until edges are firm. Remove to wire racks to cool. Ice and decorate as desired.

Fudge Bonbon Cookies

Fudge Bonbon Cookies

These fudgy favorites are double delights because the cookies are flavored with both chocolate chips and chocolate kisses. Drizzled with white chocolate on top, they make a great addition to a cookie platter.

—JANICE SMITH CYNTHIANA, KY

PREP: 25 MIN. • **BAKE:** 10 MIN./BATCH + COOLING
MAKES: ABOUT 5½ DOZEN

- 2 cups all-purpose flour
- ½ cup finely chopped pecans
- 2 cups (12 ounces) semisweet chocolate chips
- ¼ cup butter, cubed
- 1 can (14 ounces) sweetened condensed milk
- 1 teaspoon vanilla extract
- 1 package (12 ounces) milk chocolate kisses
- 2 ounces white baking chocolate
- 1 teaspoon canola oil

1. In a large bowl, combine flour and pecans; set aside.
2. In a microwave-safe bowl, melt chocolate chips and butter; stir until smooth. Stir in milk and vanilla until blended. Add to the flour mixture and mix well.
3. Preheat oven to 350°. When dough is cool enough to handle, shape a tablespoonful around each chocolate kiss. Place 1 in. apart on ungreased baking sheets. Bake 7-9 minutes or until tops begin to crack. Cool on wire racks.
4. In a microwave, melt white chocolate and oil; stir until smooth. Drizzle over the cookies.

Chocolate-Citrus Spritz

Tired of your usual spritz cookies? Add a burst of tangy orange flavor with this two-tone, chocolate-dipped variation. They look extra-special on a Christmas tray.

—ALISSA STEHR
GAU-ODERNHEIM, GERMANY

PREP: 20 MIN. • **BAKE:** 10 MIN./BATCH + COOLING
MAKES: 4 DOZEN

- ¾ cup butter, softened
- 1 cup sugar
- 1 egg
- 2 tablespoons orange juice
- 4 teaspoons grated orange peel
- 2¾ cups all-purpose flour
- 1 teaspoon baking powder
- ¼ teaspoon salt
- ½ cup ground walnuts
- 1 cup (6 ounces) semisweet chocolate chips
- 1 tablespoon shortening

1. Preheat oven to 350°. In a bowl, cream butter and sugar until light and fluffy. Gradually beat in egg, orange juice and peel. In another bowl, whisk flour, baking powder and salt; gradually add to creamed mixture, mixing well.

2. Using a cookie press fitted with a bar disk, press long strips of dough onto ungreased baking sheets; cut ends to release from disk. Cut each strip into 3-in. lengths (no need to separate them).

3. Bake 8-10 minutes or until set (do not brown). Re-cut cookies if necessary. Remove from pans to wire racks to cool completely.

4. Place walnuts in a shallow bowl. In a microwave, melt chocolate chips and shortening; stir until smooth. Dip each cookie halfway in chocolate; allow excess to drip off. Sprinkle with walnuts. Place on waxed paper; let stand until set.

Honey-Pecan Squares

When we left Texas to head north, a neighbor gave me pecans from his trees. I'm happy to send these nutty squares back to him, and he's happy to get them.

—LORRAINE CALAND SHUNIAH, ON

PREP: 15 MIN. • **BAKE:** 30 MIN.
MAKES: 2 DOZEN

- 1 cup unsalted butter, softened
- ¾ cup packed dark brown sugar
- ½ teaspoon salt
- 3 cups all-purpose flour

FILLING

- ½ cup unsalted butter, cubed
- ½ cup packed dark brown sugar
- ⅓ cup honey
- 2 tablespoons sugar
- 2 tablespoons heavy whipping cream
- ¼ teaspoon salt
- 2 cups chopped pecans, toasted
- ½ teaspoon maple flavoring or vanilla extract

1. Preheat oven to 350°. Line a 13x9-in. baking pan with parchment paper, letting ends extend up sides of pan. In a large bowl, cream the butter, brown sugar and salt until light and fluffy. Gradually beat in flour. Press into prepared pan. Bake 16-20 minutes or until lightly browned.

2. In a small saucepan, combine the first six filling ingredients; bring to a boil. Cook 1 minute. Remove from the heat; stir in pecans and maple flavoring. Pour over crust.

3. Bake 10-15 minutes or until bubbly. Cool in pan on a wire rack. Lifting with parchment paper, transfer to a cutting board; cut into bars.

NOTE *To toast nuts, spread in a 15x10x1-in. baking pan. Bake at 350° for 5-10 minutes or until nuts are lightly browned, stirring occasionally. Or, spread in a dry nonstick skillet and heat over low heat until lightly browned, stirring occasionally.*

Chocolate-Citrus Spritz

Melting Snowmen

Melting Snowmen

The cute minty characters are sure to melt hearts. Feel free to experiment with different candies for the decorations.

—*TASTE OF HOME* TEST KITCHEN

PREP: 1½ HOURS + STANDING • **MAKES:** 2 DOZEN

- ¾ **cup sweetened condensed milk**
- 1½ **teaspoons peppermint extract**
- 2¼ **cups confectioners' sugar**
- ½ **cup baking cocoa**
- 1 **pound white candy coating, chopped, divided**
- 7 **to 8 Starburst candies (orange for noses and colors of your choice for earmuffs)**
- ⅓ **cup dark chocolate chips**

1. In a small bowl, combine milk and extract. Stir in 2 cups confectioners' sugar and cocoa to form a stiff dough. Turn onto a surface lightly sprinkled with confectioners' sugar. Knead in enough remaining confectioners' sugar to form a very stiff dough (dough should not be sticky).

2. Divide into thirds. Shape one portion into twenty-four ½-in. balls. Shape remaining portions of dough into twenty-four 1-in. balls. On waxed paper-lined baking sheets, flatten each 1-in. ball into an irregular 1½-in. circle.

3. In a microwave-safe bowl, melt 2 oz. white candy coating. Using melted coating, attach a ½-in. ball near an edge of each circle. Let dry 1 hour.

4. Using Starburst candies, cut out noses and earmuffs as desired. Melt remaining white candy coating; cool slightly. Working in batches of six, spoon candy coating over snowmen, allowing coating to drape over each until completely covered. Immediately attach noses and earmuffs. Let stand at room temperature until dry to the touch, about 1 hour.

5. In a microwave, melt chocolate chips; stir until smooth. Using a toothpick and melted chocolate, form eyes, mouths, buttons and tops of earmuffs.

Vanilla Crescents

My vanilla cookies are especially cozy at Christmastime, but they are wonderful all year long. Enjoy them with hot tea or coffee.

—**CARA MCDONALD** WINTER PARK, CO

PREP: 20 MIN. • **BAKE:** 10 MIN./BATCH
MAKES: 4 DOZEN

- 1 **cup unsalted butter, softened**
- ½ **cup sugar**
- 1 **teaspoon vanilla extract**
- ⅛ **teaspoon almond extract**
- 2 **cups all-purpose flour**
- 1¼ **cups ground almonds**
- ½ **teaspoon salt**
  Confectioners' sugar

1. Preheat oven to 350°. In a large bowl, cream butter and sugar until light and fluffy. Beat in extracts. In another bowl, whisk flour, almonds and salt; gradually beat into creamed mixture.

2. Divide dough into four portions. On a lightly floured surface, roll each portion into a 24-in. rope. Cut crosswise into twelve 2-in. logs; shape each into a crescent. Place 1½ in. apart on ungreased baking sheets.

3. Bake 10-12 minutes or until set. Cool on pans 2 minutes before removing to a wire rack. Dust warm cookies with confectioners' sugar.

Vanilla Crescents

⑤INGREDIENTS

Chocolate-Topped Marshmallow Sticks

I like to use all sorts of shapes and flavors of marshmallows to mix things up. The sticks are always a hit at local bake sales and make fun additions to cookie exchanges.

—**TERI RASEY** CADILLAC, MI

PREP: 20 MIN. + STANDING • **COOK:** 10 MIN.
MAKES: 3 DOZEN

- 2 **cups (12 ounces) semisweet chocolate chips**
- 3 **teaspoons shortening, divided**
- 36 **lollipop sticks**
- 1 **package (10 ounces) large marshmallows (about 36)**
- ½ **cup white baking chips**
  Optional toppings: assorted nonpareils, colored sugars, small or crushed candies and flaked coconut

1. In a microwave, melt chocolate chips and 2 teaspoons shortening; stir until mixture is smooth.
2. Insert one lollipop stick into each marshmallow. Dip marshmallows in melted chocolate, turning to coat; allow excess to drip off. Place on waxed paper.
3. In a microwave, melt white baking chips with remaining shortening; drizzle over chocolate. Decorate with toppings if desired. Let stand until set.
4. Use to stir servings of hot cocoa. Store in an airtight container.

Make It Special

The marshmallow sticks are great for Christmas, particularly when featuring red and green sprinkles or white and blue nonpareils. Keep the recipe handy for other holidays as well. Use pastel jimmies for spring celebrations or jazz up the marshmallows with school colors for summer graduation parties.

Chocolate-Topped Marshmallow Sticks

Candy Land Garland

Sweeten up your holiday trimmings with garlands starring everyone's favorite cookies and other chocolate-covered treats.

Bake up your own cookies or buy some from the grocery store. Then, simply thread the snacks with ribbon of your choice for a scene-stealing specialty guests are sure to adore.

The best part? Taking the garland down! Mmm!

Chai Chocolate Chip Shortbread

Chai Chocolate Chip Shortbread

I've always loved the taste of chai tea, and decided to incorporate it into one of my recipes. Everyone who samples my shortbread can't believe how delicious it is. I hope you feel the same!

—**PAULA MARCHESI** LENHARTSVILLE, PA

PREP: 35 MIN. + CHILLING
BAKE: 15 MIN./BATCH + COOLING
MAKES: 4 DOZEN

- 1¾ cups all-purpose flour
- ½ cup sugar
- ⅓ cup cornstarch
- ¼ cup vanilla chai tea latte mix
- 1 cup cold butter, cubed
- ½ teaspoon vanilla extract
- ¾ cup finely chopped almonds
- ⅓ cup miniature semisweet chocolate chips
- 4 ounces semisweet chocolate, melted

1. Place flour, sugar, cornstarch and latte mix in a food processor; pulse until blended. Add butter and vanilla; pulse until butter is the size of peas. Add almonds and chocolate chips; pulse until mixture is blended.
2. Transfer to a lightly floured surface; knead until dough forms a ball. Divide dough into six portions; wrap each in plastic wrap. Refrigerate at least 30 minutes or until firm enough to roll.
3. Preheat oven to 375°. On a lightly floured surface, roll each portion of dough into a 5-in. circle. Cut into eight wedges. Place 2 in. apart on ungreased baking sheets.
4. Bake 15-18 minutes or until edges begin to brown. Cool 1 minute before removing from pans to wire racks. Drizzle with melted chocolate; let stand until set. Store in airtight containers.

Cherry Nut Cookies

So pretty with a dusting of powdered sugar, these cookies are fabulous!

—SUSAN WESTERFIELD ALBUQUERQUE, NM

PREP: 25 MIN. • **BAKE:** 20 MIN./BATCH
MAKES: 25 COOKIES

- 1 package (6 ounces) golden raisins and cherries
- ¼ cup sugar
- 3 tablespoons cherry juice blend
  Dash ground cinnamon
- ½ cup butter, softened
- 1 package (3 ounces) cream cheese, softened
- 1¼ cups all-purpose flour
- 1 white chocolate Toblerone candy bar (3.52 ounces), finely chopped
- ¼ cup finely chopped walnuts, toasted
- 2 teaspoons water
- ¼ cup confectioners' sugar

1. In a small saucepan, combine first four ingredients. Bring to a boil. Reduce heat; simmer, uncovered, 6-8 minutes or until most of the liquid is absorbed, stirring occasionally. Cool.

2. Meanwhile, preheat oven to 350°. In a large bowl, beat butter and cream cheese until smooth. Gradually add flour.

3. Turn dough onto a lightly floured surface; knead until smooth, about 3 minutes. Roll into a 12½-in. square; cut into 2½-in. squares.

4. Stir candy and walnuts into fruit mixture. Drop filling by tablespoonfuls onto center of each square. Bring two opposite corners to center; moisten edges with water and pinch together.

5. Place 1 in. apart on lightly greased baking sheets. Bake 16-18 minutes or until lightly browned. Remove to wire racks to cool.

6. Sprinkle with confectioners' sugar. Store in an airtight container.

Almond Crunch Toffee

Since I was 14 years old, this toffee has been my claim to fame. One bite and you won't be able to stop eating it!

—ANNA GINSBERG AUSTIN, TX

PREP: 30 MIN. • **COOK:** 30 MIN. + CHILLING
MAKES: ABOUT 2 POUNDS

- 1½ teaspoons plus 1 cup butter, softened, divided
- 1 cup sugar
- ½ cup water
- ¼ teaspoon salt
- 1 cup sliced almonds
- ½ teaspoon baking soda
- 8 ounces dark chocolate candy bars, chopped
- 1 cup chopped pecans, toasted
- ¼ cup dry roasted peanuts, chopped
- 3 tablespoons chocolate-covered coffee beans, halved
- 4 ounces white baking chocolate, chopped

1. Line a 13x9-in. pan with foil. Grease the foil with 1½ teaspoons butter; set aside. In a heavy 3-qt. saucepan, melt remaining butter. Stir in the sugar, water and salt. Cook over medium heat until a candy thermometer reads 240° (soft-ball stage), stirring occasionally.

2. Stir in almonds. Cook until candy thermometer reads 300° (hard-crack stage), stirring occasionally. Remove from the heat; stir in baking soda until light and foamy. Pour into prepared pan. Sprinkle with chocolate; let stand for 5 minutes. Carefully spread chocolate; sprinkle with pecans and peanuts. Cool on a wire rack for 30 minutes.

3. Sprinkle with coffee beans; press down lightly. Chill for 1 hour or until chocolate is firm.

4. In a microwave, melt white chocolate; stir until smooth. Drizzle over candy. Chill 30 minutes longer or until firm.

5. Using foil, lift candy out of pan; discard foil. Break candy into pieces. Store in an airtight container.

NOTE *We recommend that you test your candy thermometer before each use by bringing water to a boil; the thermometer should read 212°. Adjust your recipe temperature up or down based on your test.*

Cherry Nut Cookies

“ The toffee is like a really good potato chip—you can't have just one. ”

—TBAZ
TASTEOFHOME.COM

My Christmas Fudge

My fudge is virtually foolproof and so creamy you won't believe it. I've searched for years for the richest fudge, and this one does it for me. You can add just about anything you like to customize it.

—BARB MILLER OAKDALE, MN

PREP: 15 MIN. • **COOK:** 10 MIN. + COOLING
MAKES: 5¾ POUNDS (96 PIECES)

- 4½ cups sugar
- 1 can (12 ounces) evaporated milk
- ½ cup butter, cubed
- 2 packages (11½ ounces each) milk chocolate chips
- 4½ cups miniature marshmallows
- 2 ounces unsweetened chocolate, chopped
- 3 cups chopped walnuts, toasted
- 2 teaspoons vanilla extract
- 4 ounces white baking chocolate, melted

1. Line a 13x9-in. pan with foil; coat with cooking spray.

2. In a heavy Dutch oven, combine sugar, milk and butter. Bring to a rapid boil over medium heat, stirring constantly. Cook and stir 5 minutes. Remove from heat.

3. Stir in chocolate chips, marshmallows and chopped chocolate until melted. Fold in walnuts and vanilla. Immediately spread into the prepared pan. Drizzle with melted white baking chocolate; cool completely.

4. Using foil, lift fudge out of pan. Remove foil; cut fudge into 96 squares. Store between layers of waxed paper in airtight containers.

NOTE *To toast nuts, spread in a 15x10x1-in. baking pan. Bake at 350° for 5-10 minutes or until lightly browned, stirring occasionally. Or, spread in a dry nonstick skillet and heat over low heat until lightly browned, stirring occasionally.*

My Christmas Fudge

Snow-Puffed Meringues

(5) INGREDIENTS

Snow-Puffed Meringues

My family and friends like a nice pick-me-up dessert after a big holiday meal. These feather-light morsels fit the bill perfectly. To make a double batch, or to make them easier to ship, skip the Nutella and dust with cocoa instead.

—LORRAINE CALAND SHUNIAH, ON

PREP: 20 MIN. • **BAKE:** 45 MIN. + COOLING
MAKES: ABOUT 3 DOZEN

- 4 egg whites
- ½ teaspoon vanilla extract
- ¼ teaspoon salt
- ½ cup sugar
- 1 cup confectioners' sugar
- ⅓ cup Nutella

1. Place egg whites in a large bowl; let stand at room temperature 30 minutes.
2. Preheat oven to 225°. Add vanilla and salt to egg whites; beat on medium speed until foamy. Gradually add sugar, a tablespoon at a time, beating on high after each addition until sugar is dissolved. Continue beating until stiff, glossy peaks form. Fold in confectioners' sugar.
3. Cut a small hole in the tip of a pastry bag or in a corner of a food-safe plastic bag; insert a #96 star tip. Transfer meringue to the bag. Pipe 1½-in.-diameter cookies 2 in. apart onto parchment paper-lined baking sheets.
4. Bake 45-50 minutes or until firm to the touch. Turn oven off (do not open oven door); leave meringues in oven for 1½ hours. Remove from oven; cool completely on baking sheets.
5. Remove meringues from paper. Spread Nutella on the bottoms of half the cookies; cover with remaining cookies. Store in airtight containers at room temperature.

Cranberry-Raspberry Window Cookies

For dainty little treats, try these lovely bites with a tart filling and buttery cookie. Try to keep the filling and cookies separate until ready to assemble to prevent the final products from becoming soggy.

—DEIRDRE COX KANSAS CITY, MO

PREP: 50 MIN. + CHILLING
BAKE: 15 MIN./BATCH + COOLING
MAKES: ABOUT 2½ DOZEN

- 1⅓ cups all-purpose flour
- ⅓ cup confectioners' sugar
- 2 tablespoons sugar
- ¼ teaspoon salt
- ¾ cup cold unsalted butter, cubed
- 1½ teaspoons lime juice

FILLING
- 1 cup fresh or frozen cranberries, thawed
- ¾ cup seedless black raspberry spreadable fruit
- ⅓ cup sugar
- 1 tablespoon lime juice
  Confectioners' sugar

1. Place flour, confectioners' sugar, sugar and salt in a food processor; pulse until blended. Add butter; pulse until butter is the size of peas. Drizzle with lime juice and pulse just until moist crumbs form. Shape dough into a disk; wrap in plastic wrap. Refrigerate about 1 hour or until firm enough to roll.
2. For filling, in a small saucepan, combine cranberries, spreadable fruit, sugar and lime juice. Bring to a boil, stirring to dissolve sugar. Reduce heat to medium; cook, uncovered, 10-12 minutes or until berries pop and mixture is thickened, stirring occasionally. Remove from heat; cool slightly. Process in a food processor until blended; cool completely.
3. Preheat oven to 325°. On a lightly floured surface, roll dough to ⅛-in. thickness. Cut with a floured 1¾-in. scalloped round cookie cutter.
4. Using a floured ¾-in. round cookie cutter, cut out the centers of half of the cookies. Place solid and window cookies 1 in. apart on greased baking sheets. Bake 12-15 minutes or until golden brown. Remove from pans to wire racks to cool completely.
5. Spread filling on bottoms of solid cookies; top with window cookies. Dust with confectioners' sugar.

TOP TIP

Sandwich Cookies Made Simple

Sandwich cookies may seem like a lot of work, but they're really quite simple—and the results are impressive. To save time, bake the cookies one day, and assemble them the next. You can also bring little ones into the kitchen to spread the filling over the bottoms of half of the cookies or to set the top half in place.

STEPHANIE TEWELL'S
S'MORES CANDY *PAGE 255*

Gifts from the Kitchen

NOTHING WARMS HEARTS QUICKER THAN A HOME-BAKED SURPRISE. IDEAL FOR NEIGHBORS, TEACHERS, CO-WORKERS AND OTHERS, THESE YUMMY IDEAS ARE SURE TO BE CHERISHED BY ALL. BAKE UP A FEW COOKIES OR CANDIES TODAY AND SHARE THE SPIRIT OF THE HOLIDAY WITH EVERYONE ON YOUR LIST.

IDA HILTY'S EASY HOLIDAY FUDGE *PAGE 256*

THERESA RYAN'S CHOCOLATE-FILLED SPRITZ *PAGE 251*

PATTI MAURER'S MINT CHOCOLATE BARK *PAGE 249*

Double-Chocolate Espresso Cookies

Anyone who is a chocolate and espresso fan is sure to love these snacks. Coffee enhances the flavor of chocolate in my tender, chewy cookies. They are guaranteed to wake up your taste buds.

—CINDI DECLUE ANCHORAGE, AK

PREP: 30 MIN. • **BAKE:** 10 MIN./BATCH
MAKES: 3 DOZEN

- 3 ounces unsweetened chocolate, chopped
- 2 cups (12 ounces) semisweet chocolate chips, divided
- ½ cup butter, cubed
- 1 tablespoon instant coffee granules
- 1 cup plus 2 tablespoons sugar
- 3 eggs
- ¾ cup all-purpose flour
- ½ teaspoon baking powder
- ¼ teaspoon salt

1. In a small heavy saucepan, melt unsweetened chocolate, 1 cup chocolate chips and butter with coffee granules; stir until smooth. Remove from the heat; set aside to cool.

2. Preheat oven to 350°. In a small bowl, beat sugar and eggs 3 minutes or until thick and lemon-colored. Beat in chocolate mixture. Combine flour, baking powder and salt; add to chocolate mixture. Stir in remaining chips.

3. Drop by rounded teaspoonfuls 2 in. apart onto greased baking sheets. Bake 10-12 minutes or until puffed and tops are cracked. Cool 5 minutes before removing to wire racks.

Double-Chocolate Espresso Cookies

Double-Crust Strawberry Pie

The first time I made this pie it was delectable, so I wanted to share it. Fresh strawberries sprinkled with cinnamon make it a delicious dessert, whether it's served warm or slightly chilled.

—**PATRICIA KUTCHINS** LAKE ZURICH, IL

PREP: 25 MIN. • **BAKE:** 35 MIN. + COOLING
MAKES: 8 SERVINGS

- ½ cup plus 1 tablespoon sugar, divided
- ¼ cup all-purpose flour
- ½ teaspoon ground cinnamon
- 4 cups fresh strawberries (about 1¼ pounds), sliced
  Pastry for double-crust pie (9 inches)
- 2 tablespoons 2% milk

1. Preheat oven to 425°. In a large bowl, mix ½ cup sugar, flour and cinnamon; add strawberries and toss to coat.
2. On a lightly floured surface, roll one half of pastry dough to a ⅛-in.-thick circle; transfer to a 9-in. pie plate. Trim pastry even with rim. Add filling.
3. Roll remaining dough to a ⅛-in.-thick circle. Place over filling. Trim, seal and flute edge. Cut slits in top. Brush with milk; sprinkle with remaining sugar.
4. Bake 35-40 minutes or until crust is golden brown and filling is bubbly. Cover edge loosely with foil during the last 20 minutes if needed to prevent overbrowning.
5. Remove foil. Cool on a wire rack for 1 hour before serving.

Almond Bonbon Cookies

Almond paste is wrapped in cookie dough for these bite-sized treats. Dip the bonbons in vanilla or chocolate icing—or a little of both! Top with holiday sprinkles for an easy yet impressive touch.

—**TERI RASEY** CADILLAC, MI

PREP: 20 MIN. • **BAKE:** 10 MIN./BATCH
MAKES: 4 DOZEN

- 1 cup butter, softened
- ⅔ cup confectioners' sugar
- ¼ cup 2% milk
- 1 teaspoon vanilla extract
- 3 cups all-purpose flour
- 1 package (7 ounces) almond paste

VANILLA ICING
- 1 cup confectioners' sugar
- 4½ teaspoons 2% milk
- 1 teaspoon vanilla extract

Almond Bonbon Cookies

CHOCOLATE ICING
- 1 cup confectioners' sugar
- 1 ounce unsweetened chocolate, melted and cooled
- 3 tablespoons 2% milk
- 1 teaspoon vanilla extract
  Assorted sprinkles

1. Preheat oven to 375°. In a large bowl, cream butter and confectioners' sugar until light and fluffy. Beat in milk and vanilla. Gradually beat in flour.
2. Cut almond paste into 12 slices (about ¼ in. thick); cut each into quarters. Shape into balls. Wrap tablespoons of cookie dough around almond paste to cover completely. Place 2 in. apart on ungreased baking sheets.
3. Bake 10-12 minutes or until golden brown. Remove to wire racks to cool completely.
4. In a small bowl, mix vanilla icing ingredients until smooth. For chocolate icing, mix confectioners' sugar, cooled chocolate, milk and vanilla until smooth.
5. Dip cookies in icings as desired; allow excess to drip off. Decorate with sprinkles. Place on waxed paper; let stand until set. Store in airtight containers.

Double-Crust Strawberry Pie

Iced Coconut Crescents

Iced Coconut Crescents

Cookie crescents get a tropical twist when you add refreshing orange juice and coconut. Bake these goodies any time of year and decorate them to suit the season or occasion.

—MARIA BENBROOK PORT MONMOUTH, NJ

PREP: 15 MIN. • **BAKE:** 10 MIN./BATCH
MAKES: 4 DOZEN

- ½ cup butter, softened
- ¾ cup sugar
- 3 eggs
- ½ cup orange juice
- 1½ teaspoons vanilla extract
- 3 cups all-purpose flour
- 3 teaspoons baking powder
- 1⅔ cups flaked coconut

ICING

- 2 cups confectioners' sugar
- ¼ cup 2% milk
  Assorted sprinkles of your choice

1. Preheat oven to 350°. In a large bowl, cream butter and sugar until light and fluffy. Beat in eggs, orange juice and vanilla. Combine flour and baking powder; gradually add to creamed mixture and mix well. Stir in coconut.

2. Shape tablespoonfuls of dough into crescent shapes. Place 2 in. apart on ungreased baking sheets. Bake 8-10 minutes or until edges are lightly browned. Cool 1 minute before removing to wire racks to cool.

3. In a small bowl, combine the confectioners' sugar and milk. Decorate as desired with icing and sprinkles. Let stand until set.

Spicy Bavarian Beer Mustard

Here's a gift that has a little bite! Include a festive tag that lists serving suggestions. For example, "Happy holidays! This spicy beer mustard is great with pretzels or as a condiment for bratwurst."

—*TASTE OF HOME* TEST KITCHEN

PREP: 15 MIN. + CHILLING • **PROCESS:** 15 MIN.
MAKES: 7 HALF-PINTS

- 2 cups dark beer
- 2 cups brown mustard seeds
- 2 cups ground mustard
- 1½ cups packed brown sugar
- 1½ cups malt vinegar
- ½ cup balsamic vinegar
- 3 teaspoons salt
- 2 teaspoons ground allspice
- ½ teaspoon ground cloves
- 2 teaspoons vanilla extract

1. In a small bowl, combine beer and mustard seeds. Cover and refrigerate overnight.

2. Place seed mixture in a blender. Cover and process until chopped and slightly grainy. Transfer to a Dutch oven. Add the ground mustard, brown sugar, vinegars, salt, allspice and cloves. Bring just to a boil. Remove from heat; stir in vanilla.

3. Ladle hot liquid into seven hot half-pint jars, leaving ½-in. headspace. Wipe rims. Center lids on jars; screw on bands until fingertip tight.

4. Place jars into canner with simmering water, ensuring that they are completely covered with water. Bring to a boil; process for 10 minutes. Remove the jars and cool.

NOTE *The processing time listed is for altitudes of 1,000 feet or less. For altitudes up to 3,000 feet, add 5 minutes; 6,000 feet, add 10 minutes; 8,000 feet, add 15 minutes; 10,000 feet, add 20 minutes.*

Spicy Bavarian Beer Mustard

Mint Chocolate Bark

After sampling peppermint bark candy from an upscale store, I thought, "I can make that!" Using four ingredients, I came up with a simple version that won over my friends and family.

—**PATTI MAURER** WISE, VA

PREP: 15 MIN. + CHILLING • **MAKES:** 1½ POUNDS

- 1 teaspoon plus 3 tablespoons shortening, divided
- 1 package (10 ounces) Andes creme de menthe baking chips
- 2 cups white baking chips
- ½ cup crushed peppermint candies

1. Line a 13x9-in. pan with foil; grease foil with 1 teaspoon shortening.
2. In a microwave, melt Andes baking chips and 1 tablespoon shortening; stir until smooth. Pour into prepared pan. Refrigerate 10 minutes or until set.
3. In top of a double boiler or a metal bowl over barely simmering water, melt baking chips with remaining shortening; stir until smooth. Spread over chocolate layer; sprinkle with crushed candies. Cool. Refrigerate 2 hours or until firm.
4. Break into small pieces. Store in an airtight container.

Raspberry-Cream Cheese Ladder Loaves

My friend Debbie created this delicious coffee cake-like delight. You can sprinkle the bread with granulated sugar before baking if desired. What a great gift!

—**CHAR OUELLETTE** COLTON, OR

PREP: 45 MIN. + RISING
BAKE: 15 MIN. + COOLING
MAKES: 2 LOAVES (8 SLICES EACH)

- 3¾ to 4¼ cups all-purpose flour, divided
- ¼ cup sugar
- 1 package (¼ ounce) quick-rise yeast
- 1¼ teaspoons salt
- 1 teaspoon baking powder
- ½ cup buttermilk
- ½ cup sour cream
- ¼ cup butter, cubed

Raspberry-Cream Cheese Ladder Loaves

- ¼ cup water
- 1 egg
- ½ teaspoon almond extract

FILLING

- 1 package (8 ounces) cream cheese, softened
- ¼ cup sugar
- 3 tablespoons all-purpose flour
- 1 egg yolk
- ⅓ cup seedless raspberry jam

1. In a large bowl, combine 2 cups flour, sugar, yeast, salt and baking powder. In a small saucepan, heat buttermilk, sour cream, butter and water to 120°-130°; add to dry ingredients. Beat on medium speed 2 minutes. Add egg, extract and ½ cup flour; beat 2 minutes longer. Stir in enough remaining flour to form a soft dough.
2. Turn dough onto a floured surface; knead until smooth and elastic, about 6-8 minutes. Cover and let rest 10 minutes.
3. Meanwhile, in a small bowl, beat the cream cheese, sugar, flour and egg yolk until smooth; set aside.
4. Divide dough in half. Roll each piece into a 12x10-in. rectangle; place on greased baking sheets. Spread cheese mixture down the center of each rectangle. Stir the jam; spoon over the cheese mixture.
5. On each long side, cut ¾-in.-wide strips about 2½ in. into center. Starting at one end, fold alternating strips at an angle across the filling; pinch ends to seal. Cover and let rise until doubled, about 1 hour.
6. Preheat oven to 350°. Bake 15-19 minutes or until golden brown. Cool on wire racks. Store leftovers in refrigerator.

HOW-TO

Braid Dough

Place three ropes of dough, almost touching, on a baking sheet. Starting in the middle, loosely bring left rope under center rope. Bring the right rope under the new center rope and repeat until you reach the end.

Chocolate-Covered Almond Butter Brickle

Chocolate-Covered Almond Butter Brickle

I love this soft brittle because the texture is wonderfully different, and the flavors remind me of a favorite candy bar.
—**JOANN BELACK** BRADENTON, FL

PREP: 10 MIN. • **COOK:** 20 MIN. + CHILLING
MAKES: ABOUT 1¾ POUNDS

- 1½ **teaspoons plus 2 tablespoons unsalted butter, divided**
- 1 **cup crunchy almond butter**
- ½ **teaspoon baking soda**
- 1 **teaspoon plus 2 tablespoons water, divided**
- ¾ **cup sugar**
- ¾ **cup light corn syrup**
- 1 **teaspoon almond extract**
- 1 **cup 60% cacao bittersweet chocolate baking chips**
- ⅓ **cup chopped almonds, toasted**
- ¾ **cup flaked coconut**

1. Grease a 15x10x1-in. pan with 1½ teaspoons butter. Place the almond butter in a microwave-safe bowl; microwave, covered, at 50% power for 30-60 seconds or until softened, stirring once. In a small bowl, dissolve baking soda in 1 teaspoon water. Set aside almond butter and baking soda mixture.
2. In a large heavy saucepan, combine sugar, corn syrup and 2 tablespoons water. Bring to a boil over medium heat, stirring constantly. Using a pastry brush dipped in water, wash down sides of the pan to eliminate sugar crystals. Cook until a candy thermometer reads 240° (soft-ball stage), stirring occasionally, about 10 minutes. Add remaining butter; cook until candy thermometer reads 300° (hard-crack stage), stirring frequently, about 5 minutes longer.
3. Remove from heat; stir in the softened almond butter, almond extract and dissolved baking soda. (Candy will foam.) Immediately pour into prepared pan. Spread to ¼-in. thickness.
4. Sprinkle with chocolate chips; let stand until chocolate begins to melt. Spread evenly; sprinkle with almonds

and coconut, pressing slightly to adhere. Cool slightly. Refrigerate 1 hour or until chocolate is set.

5. Break candy into pieces. Store between layers of waxed paper in an airtight container.

NOTE *To toast nuts, spread in a 15x10x1-in. baking pan. Bake at 350° for 5-10 minutes or until lightly browned, stirring occasionally. Or, spread in a dry nonstick skillet and heat over low heat until lightly browned, stirring occasionally.*

Chocolate-Filled Spritz

I found this delicious cookie recipe years ago. Over time, I decided to liven the spritz up with a creamy chocolate filling.

—THERESA RYAN
WHITE RIVER JUNCTION, VT

PREP: 20 MIN. • **BAKE:** 10 MIN./BATCH + COOLING
MAKES: ABOUT 3 DOZEN

- 1 cup butter, softened
- ⅔ cup sugar
- 1 egg
- ½ teaspoon vanilla extract
- ½ teaspoon lemon or orange extract
- 2¼ cups all-purpose flour
- ¼ teaspoon baking powder
- ¼ teaspoon salt
- 4 ounces unsweetened chocolate, chopped

1. Preheat oven to 350°. In a large bowl, cream butter and sugar until light and fluffy. Beat in egg and extracts. Combine dry ingredients; gradually add to the creamed mixture and mix well.

2. Using a cookie press fitted with the disk of your choice, press dough 2 in. apart onto ungreased baking sheets. Bake 10-12 minutes or until set (do not brown). Remove to wire racks to cool.

3. In a microwave, melt the chocolate; stir until smooth. Spread over bottom of half of the cookies; top with the remaining cookies.

Candy Cane Rolls

Candy Cane Rolls

These fun and lightly sweet rolls make a cute gift to share. They're also great for a holiday brunch, an evening snack or any time, really!

—JANICE PETERSON HURON, SD

PREP: 30 MIN. + RISING • **BAKE:** 15 MIN.
MAKES: 2 DOZEN

- 1 package (¼ ounce) active dry yeast
- ¼ cup warm water (110° to 115°)
- ¾ cup warm milk (110° to 115°)
- ¼ cup sugar
- ¼ cup shortening
- 1 egg
- 1 teaspoon salt
- 3¼ to 3¾ cups all-purpose flour
- 1 cup red candied cherries, quartered
- 1 cup confectioners' sugar
- 1 to 2 tablespoons milk

1. In a small bowl, dissolve yeast in warm water. In a large bowl, combine warm milk, sugar, shortening, egg, salt, yeast mixture and 2 cups flour; beat until smooth. Add cherries. Stir in enough remaining flour to form a soft dough (dough will be sticky).

2. Turn dough onto a floured surface; knead until smooth and elastic, about 6-8 minutes. Place in a greased bowl, turning once to grease the top. Cover with plastic wrap and let rise in a warm place until doubled, about 1 hour.

3. Punch down dough; let rest for 10 minutes. Turn dough onto a lightly floured surface; divide in half. Roll each half into a 12x7-in. rectangle. Cut each into twelve 1-in.-wide strips. Twist each strip and place 2 in. apart on greased baking sheets, curving one end like a cane. Cover with a kitchen towel; let rise in a warm place until doubled, about 45 minutes.

4. Preheat oven to 375°. Bake 12-15 minutes or until golden brown. Remove from pans to wire racks to cool. In a small bowl, mix confectioners' sugar and enough milk to reach the desired consistency. Drizzle over rolls.

Hazelnut
Macarons

Hazelnut Macarons

Julia Child had a love of life and French cooking as described by her and Alex Prud'homme in *My Life in France*. The woman who introduced Americans to the delights of French cuisine would find these crisp, chewy French-style macaron cookies a delight, too!

—*TASTE OF HOME* **TEST KITCHEN**

PREP: 30 MIN. • **BAKE:** 10 MIN./BATCH
MAKES: 5 DOZEN

- 6 egg whites
- 1½ cups hazelnuts
- 2½ cups confectioners' sugar
  Dash salt
- ½ cup superfine sugar

ESPRESSO FILLING
- 1 cup sugar
- 6 tablespoons water
- 6 egg yolks
- 4 teaspoons instant espresso powder
- 1 teaspoon vanilla extract
- 1½ cups butter, softened
- 6 tablespoons confectioners' sugar

1. Place egg whites in a small bowl; let stand at room temperature for 30 minutes.
2. Preheat oven to 350°. Place hazelnuts in a 15x10x1-in. baking pan. Bake 7-10 minutes or until lightly toasted and fragrant. Transfer to a clean kitchen towel; cool. Rub briskly with towel to remove the skins.
3. Place the confectioners' sugar and hazelnuts in a food processor. Cover and process until hazelnuts are ground.
4. Add salt to egg whites; beat on medium speed until soft peaks form. Gradually add the superfine sugar, 1 tablespoon at a time, beating on high until stiff peaks form. Fold in hazelnut mixture.
5. Place mixture in a heavy-duty resealable plastic bag; cut a small hole in a corner of the bag. Pipe 1-in.-diameter cookies 2 in. apart onto parchment paper-lined baking sheets. Bake at 350° 9-12 minutes or until lightly browned and firm to the touch. Cool completely on pans on wire racks.
6. For filling, in a heavy saucepan, bring sugar and water to a boil; cook over medium-high heat until the sugar is dissolved. Remove from the heat. Add a small amount of hot mixture to egg yolks; return all to the pan, stirring constantly. Cook 2-3 minutes or until mixture thickens, stirring constantly. Remove from the heat; stir in espresso powder and vanilla. Cool to room temperature.
7. In a stand mixer with the whisk attachment, beat butter until creamy, about 3 minutes. Gradually beat in cooked sugar mixture. Beat in the confectioners' sugar until fluffy. Refrigerate filling until it reaches spreading consistency, about 10 minutes.
8. Spread on the bottoms of half of the cookies; top with remaining cookies. Store in the refrigerator.

FREEZE IT
Ginger Pear Freezer Jam
At dinner with friends one evening, the hostess served us some pears she had preserved with ginger and lemon. The flavor was so heavenly, I decided to use the fresh pears she gave us to try my hand at a ginger and lemon freezer jam.
—**JENI PITTARD** STATHAM, GA

PREP: 30 MIN. • **COOK:** 10 MIN. + STANDING
MAKES: 7 CUPS

- 5½ cups finely chopped peeled fresh pears (about 10 medium)
- 1 package (1¾ ounces) pectin for lower sugar recipes
- 2 tablespoons lemon juice
- 1½ teaspoons grated lemon peel
- 1 teaspoon minced fresh gingerroot
- 4 cups sugar
- 1 teaspoon vanilla extract

1. Rinse seven 1-cup plastic containers and lids with boiling water. Dry thoroughly. In a Dutch oven, combine pears, pectin, lemon juice, lemon peel and ginger. Bring to a full rolling boil over high heat, stirring constantly. Stir in sugar. Boil for 1 minute, stirring constantly. Stir in vanilla.
2. Remove from heat; skim off foam. Immediately fill all containers to within ½ in. of tops. Wipe off top edges of containers; immediately cover with lids. Let stand at room temperature 24 hours.
3. Jam is now ready to use. Refrigerate up to 3 weeks or freeze extra containers up to 12 months. Thaw frozen jam in refrigerator before serving.

Sparkling Cider Pound Cake

This pound cake is incredible, and reminds me of fall and winter with every bite. Using sparkling apple cider in the batter and the glaze gives it a delicious and unique flavor. I love everything about it!

—NIKKI BARTON PROVIDENCE, UT

PREP: 20 MIN. • **BAKE:** 40 MIN. + COOLING
MAKES: 12 SERVINGS

- ¾ cup butter, softened
- 1½ cups sugar
- 3 eggs
- 1½ cups all-purpose flour
- ¼ teaspoon baking powder
- ¼ teaspoon salt
- ½ cup sparkling apple cider

GLAZE
- ¾ cup confectioners' sugar
- 3 to 4 teaspoons sparkling apple cider

1. Preheat oven to 350°. Line bottom of a greased 9x5-in. loaf pan with parchment paper; grease paper.

2. In a large bowl, cream butter and sugar until light and fluffy. Add eggs, one at a time, beating well after each addition. In another bowl, whisk flour, baking powder and salt; add to creamed mixture alternately with cider, beating well after each addition.

3. Transfer to prepared pan. Bake 40-50 minutes or until a toothpick inserted into center comes out clean. Cool in pan for 10 minutes before removing to a wire rack to cool completely.

4. In a small bowl, mix glaze ingredients until smooth; spoon over top of cake, allowing it to flow over sides.

❝I made this cake for our family, and it was a great success.❞

—EMMANUELLEB
TASTEOFHOME.COM

Sparkling Cider
Pound Cake

**Butter
Snowmen
Cookie**

Butter Snowmen Cookie

These snowmen literally melt in your mouth, but they're almost too cute to eat. If you're looking for a fun cookie for a gift, bake sale or cookie exchange, this is it!

—**KATHLEEN TAUGHER** EAST TROY, WI

PREP: 40 MIN. • **BAKE:** 15 MIN./BATCH
MAKES: 1 DOZEN

- 1 **cup butter, softened**
- ½ **cup sugar**
- 1 **tablespoon milk**
- 1 **teaspoon vanilla extract**
- 2¼ **cups all-purpose flour**
  Blue and orange paste food coloring
  Miniature chocolate chips

1. Preheat oven to 325°. In a large bowl, cream butter and sugar until light and fluffy. Add milk and vanilla; mix well. Gradually add flour. Remove ⅔ cup dough to a small bowl; tint blue. Repeat with 1 tablespoon of dough and orange food coloring; set aside.

2. For snowmen, shape white dough into 12 balls, 1¼ in. each; 12 balls, about ½ in. each; and 12 balls, about ⅛ in. each. For bodies, place large balls on two ungreased baking sheets; flatten to ⅜-in. thickness. Place ½-in. balls above bodies for heads; flatten.

3. Shape half of blue dough into 12 triangles. Place triangles above heads for hats; attach ⅛-in. white balls for tassels. Shape orange dough into noses; place on

heads. Divide the remaining blue dough into 12 pieces; shape into scarves and position on snowmen. Add chocolate chip eyes and buttons.

4. Bake 13-16 minutes or until set. Cool 2 minutes before carefully removing to wire racks.

Salted Caramel Fudge Drops

These cookies, which start with a mix, are unbelievably decadent! It's nice dough to make ahead, roll into balls and freeze for up to three months. Then just bake the cookies as you need them. I like to use caramel-filled Dove chocolates for the surprise centers.

—**CAROLE HOLT** MENDOTA HEIGHTS, MN

PREP: 20 MIN. • **BAKE:** 10 MIN./BATCH
MAKES: 4 DOZEN

- 6 **ounces unsweetened chocolate**
- ⅓ **cup butter, cubed**
- 1 **package (17½ ounces) sugar cookie mix**
- 1 **egg**
- 1 **can (14 ounces) sweetened condensed milk**
- 1 **teaspoon vanilla extract**
- 48 **caramel-filled chocolate candies**
  Coarsely ground sea salt

1. Preheat oven to 350°. Melt the unsweetened chocolate and butter in a microwave; stir until smooth. Cool slightly. In a large bowl, beat cookie mix, egg, milk, vanilla and chocolate mixture. Drop by tablespoonfuls 2 in. apart on ungreased baking sheets.

2. Bake 8-10 minutes or until edges are set. Press a candy into the center of each cookie. Let stand 2 minutes. Sprinkle with salt. Remove from pans to wire racks to cool completely.

TO MAKE AHEAD *Cookies can be stored for 1 week in an airtight container at room temperature.*

**Salted Caramel
Fudge Drops**

Marvelous Maple Fudge

Use this delicious, easy recipe for gift-giving, potlucks, large family gatherings or bake sales. Line your pan with foil to make removing the fudge a breeze.

—JEANNIE GALLANT CHARLOTTETOWN, PE

PREP: 10 MIN. • **COOK:** 20 MIN. + COOLING
MAKES: 1¾ POUNDS (64 PIECES)

- 1 teaspoon plus 1 cup butter, divided
- 2 cups packed brown sugar
- 1 can (5 ounces) evaporated milk
- 1 teaspoon maple flavoring
- ½ teaspoon vanilla extract
- ⅛ teaspoon salt
- 2 cups confectioners' sugar

1. Line an 8-in.-square pan with foil; grease foil with 1 teaspoon butter.
2. Cube remaining butter. In a large saucepan, combine cubed butter, brown sugar and milk. Bring to a full boil over medium heat, stirring constantly. Cook 10 minutes, stirring frequently. Remove from heat.
3. Stir in maple flavoring, vanilla and salt. Add confectioners' sugar; beat on medium speed 2 minutes or until smooth. Immediately spread mixture into prepared pan. Cool completely.
4. Using foil, lift the fudge out of pan. Remove foil; cut into 1-in. squares. Store in an airtight container.

**Marvelous
Maple Fudge**

**Candy Cane
Hot Cocoa Mix**

Candy Cane Hot Cocoa Mix

We make batches of this minty, malted milk-flavored hot chocolate to give as gifts. Be prepared—friends will return the jars, asking for refills!

—SARA TATHAM PLYMOUTH, NH

PREP TIME: 30 MIN.
MAKES: 20 SERVINGS (6⅔ CUPS HOT COCOA MIX)

- 1⅓ cups instant chocolate drink mix
- 1⅓ cups chocolate malted milk powder
- ⅓ cup baking cocoa
- 1 cup confectioners' sugar
- 6 tablespoons powdered nondairy creamer
- 3 cups nonfat dry milk powder
- 1½ cups miniature semisweet chocolate chips
- 1 cup crushed candy canes (about 40 mini candy canes)

EACH SERVING
- ¾ cup hot water

1. In a large bowl, mix chocolate drink mix, malted milk powder and baking cocoa. In another bowl, mix confectioners' sugar and creamer.
2. In each of four 1-pint canning jars, layer ¾ cup nonfat dry milk powder, ¾ cup chocolate mixture, 3 tablespoons chocolate chips, ⅓ cup confectioners' sugar mixture, 3 tablespoons chocolate chips and ¼ cup candy canes, pouring ingredients through a large funnel or a waxed-paper cone. Press candy canes down to fit if needed.
3. Cover and store in a cool dry place up to 2 months (mixture will settle). To use, transfer contents of jar to a covered container or large resealable plastic bag; mix well.
TO PREPARE HOT COCOA *Place ⅓ cup combined mix in a mug; stir in ¾ cup hot water until blended.*

S'mores Candy

Miss s'mores in the winter? Here's the solution! Combine marshmallow creme, chocolate, graham crackers and more for a summery delight in the middle of winter.

—STEPHANIE TEWELL ELIZABETH, IL

PREP: 1 HOUR • **COOK:** 5 MIN. + STANDING
MAKES: 4 DOZEN

- 2 cups milk chocolate chips
- ½ cup heavy whipping cream
- 1 package (14.4 ounces) whole graham crackers, quartered
- 1 cup marshmallow creme
- 2 cartons (7 ounces each) milk chocolate for dipping
- 4 ounces white candy coating, coarsely chopped

1. Place chocolate chips in a small bowl. In a small saucepan, bring cream just to a boil. Pour over chocolate chips; whisk until smooth. Cool, stirring occasionally, to room temperature or until chocolate mixture reaches a spreading consistency, about 10 minutes.
2. Spread chocolate mixture over half of the graham crackers; spread the marshmallow creme over remaining graham crackers and press together.
3. Melt dipping chocolate according to package directions; dip half of each cracker in melted chocolate and allow excess to drip off. Place on waxed paper; let stand until set.
4. In a microwave, melt candy coating; stir until smooth. Drizzle over tops; let stand until set. Store in an airtight container in the refrigerator.

Orange-Marmalade Linzer Tarts

Orange-Marmalade Linzer Tarts

These little cutout tarts are almost too pretty to eat! The golden sandwich Christmas cookies dusted with confectioners' sugar reveal a colorful, citrusy center of orange marmalade.

—**TRISHA KRUSE** EAGLE, ID

PREP: 25 MIN. + CHILLING • **BAKE:** 10 MIN./BATCH
MAKES: 2½ DOZEN

- 1½ cups all-purpose flour, divided
- 1 cup chopped almonds, toasted
- ½ teaspoon baking powder
- ¼ teaspoon salt
- ½ cup unsalted butter, softened
- ⅔ cup sugar
- 4 egg yolks
- ½ teaspoon almond extract
- ½ teaspoon grated lemon peel
- ¾ cup orange marmalade
- 2 teaspoons confectioners' sugar

1. In a food processor, combine ½ cup flour and almonds; cover and pulse until almonds are finely ground. Add baking powder, salt and remaining flour; cover and process just until combined.
2. In a small bowl, cream butter and sugar until light and fluffy. Beat in egg yolks, extract and lemon peel. Gradually add almond mixture to creamed mixture and mix well.
3. Divide dough in half. Shape each into a ball, then flatten into a disk. Wrap in plastic wrap and refrigerate 1 hour.
4. Preheat oven to 350°. On a floured surface, roll out one portion of dough to ⅛-in. thickness. Cut with a floured 2-in. round cookie cutter. Using a floured 1-in. round cookie cutter, cut out the centers of half the cookies. Place solid and cutout cookies 1 in. apart on greased baking sheets.
5. Bake 6-8 minutes or until edges are lightly browned. Cool 5 minutes before removing cookies to wire racks to cool completely. Repeat with remaining cookie dough.
6. Spread 1 teaspoon marmalade on bottoms of solid cookies. Sprinkle cutout cookies with confectioners' sugar; place on top of the marmalade. Store in an airtight container.

Easy Holiday Fudge

A friend shared this quick and easy candy recipe with me. The holidays just wouldn't be the same without it.

—**IDA HILTY** AMITY, OR

PREP: 10 MIN. + CHILLING
MAKES: ABOUT 2½ POUNDS

- 1 teaspoon butter
- 1 can (14 ounces) sweetened condensed milk
- 2 cups (12 ounces) semisweet chocolate chips
- 1 cup butterscotch chips
- 1 cup chopped pecans
- ½ cup raisins
- 1 teaspoon vanilla extract

Line a 9-in.-square baking pan with foil. Grease foil with butter; set aside. Combine milk and chips in a large microwave-safe bowl. Microwave, uncovered, on high for 1 minute; stir. Cook 30-60 seconds longer, stirring every 30 seconds, or until chips are melted. Stir in the pecans, raisins and vanilla. Transfer to prepared pan. Cover and refrigerate for 2 hours or until firm. Using foil, lift fudge out of pan. Gently peel off foil; cut fudge into 1-in. squares. Store in an airtight container.

Cranberry-Pistachio Sticky Buns

Looking for a fantastic hostess gift for brunch? Try these gooey sticky buns. They use frozen yeast roll dough and couldn't be simpler to make. The buns rise overnight in the refrigerator, so you just need to bake them the next morning.

—**ATHENA RUSSELL** FLORENCE, SC

PREP: 20 MIN. + CHILLING • **BAKE:** 30 MIN.
MAKES: 2 DOZEN

- 1 cup chopped pistachios
- ½ cup dried cranberries
- 1 teaspoon ground cinnamon
- 24 frozen bread dough dinner rolls, thawed
- ½ cup butter, cubed
- 1 cup packed brown sugar
- 1 package (4.6 ounces) cook-and-serve vanilla pudding mix
- 2 tablespoons 2% milk
- ½ teaspoon orange extract

1. Sprinkle pistachios, cranberries and cinnamon in a greased 13x9-in. baking dish. Arrange the rolls in a single layer on top.
2. In a small saucepan over low heat, melt butter. Remove from the heat; stir in the brown sugar, pudding mix, milk and extract until smooth. Pour over dough. Cover and refrigerate overnight.
3. Remove from the refrigerator 30 minutes before baking. Preheat oven to 350°. Bake 30-35 minutes or until golden brown. (Cover loosely with foil if top browns too quickly.) Cool 1 minute before inverting onto a serving platter.

Cranberry-Pistachio Sticky Buns

Peppermint S'more Tassies

Graham cracker cookie cups brim with a luscious peppermint-milk chocolate filling, sweet marshmallow creme and crushed peppermint candies. Santa and his elves will look forward to these!

—**EDWINA GADSBY** HAYDEN, ID

PREP: 25 MIN. • **BAKE:** 10 MIN./BATCH + COOLING
MAKES: 3 DOZEN

- 1 **package (17½ ounces) sugar cookie mix**
- ½ **cup graham cracker crumbs**
- ½ **cup butter, softened**
- 1 **egg**
- 1 **cup milk chocolate chips**
- ⅓ **cup heavy whipping cream**
- ½ **teaspoon peppermint extract**
- ½ **cup marshmallow creme**
- ¼ **cup crushed peppermint candies**

1. Preheat oven to 375°. Place cookie mix, cracker crumbs, butter and egg in a large bowl; beat until well mixed. Shape into 36 balls; press onto bottoms and up sides of greased miniature muffin cups.

2. Bake 9-10 minutes or until golden brown. Cool 30 minutes before removing from pans to wire racks.

3. Meanwhile, place chocolate chips in a small bowl. In a small saucepan, bring cream just to a boil. Pour over chocolate; whisk until smooth. Stir in extract. Let stand 15 minutes or until cooled. Spoon 2 teaspoons of the chocolate mixture into each cup.

4. Place marshmallow creme in a small microwave-safe bowl. Microwave at 50% power 15 seconds or just until softened. Spoon a dollop of marshmallow cream onto each cup; sprinkle with candies.

TO MAKE AHEAD *Bake and cool cookie cups as directed. Freeze for up to 1 month. Several hours before serving, proceed with finishing cookies as directed.*

Peppermint S'more Tassies

“ The filling was delicious, even without the pretty peppermint sprinkles! ”
—**KATTASSAH** TASTEOFHOME.COM

JANE ROSSEN'S
SCALLOPS IN SHELLS *PAGE 263*

Christmas Eve Buffet

THE BIG DAY IS ALMOST HERE! LET'S CELEBRATE WITH FAMILY, FRIENDS AND FOOD! NO MATTER HOW YOU ENJOY CHRISTMAS EVE, MAKE IT A NIGHT TO REMEMBER WITH THESE MUST-TRY RECIPES. IN ADDITION TO CLASSIC TASTES, YOU MIGHT ALSO FIND SOME NEW FAVORITES TO ADD TO YOUR HOLIDAY LINEUP.

CINDY CASAZZA'S ITALIAN RAINBOW COOKIES *PAGE 263*

DEBBIE SHANNON'S CHICKEN MARSALA LASAGNA *PAGE 265*

BETH BURGMEIER'S SICILIAN SALAD *PAGE 264*

Frozen Peppermint Torte

I first made this peppermint torte for a ladies meeting at our church. Feel free to use chopped Oreos instead of candy canes on top, and replace the red food coloring with green for a Frozen Grasshopper Torte.

—**ELMA PENNER** OAK BLUFF, MB

PREP: 25 MIN. + FREEZING • **MAKES:** 12 SERVINGS

- 4 **cups crushed Oreo cookies (about 40 cookies)**
- ¼ **cup butter, melted**
- 1 **pint (2 cups) vanilla ice cream, softened if necessary**
- 2 **cups heavy whipping cream**
- 1 **jar (7 ounces) marshmallow creme**
- ¼ **cup 2% milk**
- ¼ **to ½ teaspoon peppermint extract**
- 2 **drops red food coloring, optional**
  Chopped candy canes, optional

1. In a bowl, combine crushed cookies and melted butter; toss until coated. Reserve ¼ cup mixture for topping. Press remaining mixture onto bottom of a 9-in. springform pan or 13x9-in. dish. Freeze 10 minutes. Spread ice cream over crust. Freeze, covered, until firm.
2. In a bowl, beat cream until soft peaks form. In a bowl, mix marshmallow creme, milk, extract and, if desired, food coloring. Fold in whipped cream.
3. Spread over ice cream. Sprinkle with chopped candy canes. Freeze, covered, until firm.

Frozen Peppermint Torte

Spinach Dip-Stuffed Mushrooms

Spinach Dip-Stuffed Mushrooms

Hosting a holiday party? Consider this light version of classic spinach dip. It's stuffed inside juicy mushroom caps instead of a bread bowl, so you don't need crackers or other dippers. The bites are always a real crowd pleaser!

—**ASHLEY PIERCE** BRANTFORD, ON

PREP: 25 MIN. • **BAKE:** 15 MIN.
MAKES: 16 APPETIZERS

- 16 **large fresh mushrooms**
- 2 **cups fresh baby spinach, coarsely chopped**
- 1 **tablespoon olive oil**
- 2 **garlic cloves, minced**
- ½ **cup reduced-fat sour cream**
- 3 **ounces reduced-fat cream cheese**
- ⅓ **cup shredded part-skim mozzarella cheese**
- 3 **tablespoons grated Parmesan cheese**
- ¼ **teaspoon salt**
- ¼ **teaspoon cayenne pepper**
- ¼ **teaspoon pepper**

1. Preheat oven to 400°. Remove stems from mushrooms and set caps aside; discard stems or save for another use. In a small skillet, saute spinach in oil until wilted. Add garlic; cook 1 minute longer.
2. In a small bowl, combine sour cream, cream cheese, mozzarella, Parmesan, salt, cayenne, pepper and spinach mixture. Stuff into mushroom caps.
3. Place in a 15x10x1-in. baking pan coated with cooking spray. Bake, uncovered, 12-15 minutes or until mushrooms are tender.

❝ My neighbor made these mushrooms for a Christmas party, and I was impressed. We are now making them for Christmas Eve dinner! ❞

—**BUFFY269** TASTEOFHOME.COM

Antipasto Appetizer

Serve this with a slotted spoon as an appetizer or over torn romaine lettuce as a salad. I like to serve it on a buffet with toasted baguette slices on the side.
—**TAMRA DUNCAN** LINCOLN, AR

PREP: 10 MIN. + CHILLING • **MAKES:** 6 CUPS

- 1 jar (16 ounces) roasted sweet red pepper strips, drained
- ½ pound part-skim mozzarella cheese, cubed
- 1 cup grape tomatoes
- 1 jar (7½ ounces) marinated quartered artichoke hearts, undrained
- 1 jar (7 ounces) pimiento-stuffed olives, drained
- 1 can (6 ounces) pitted ripe olives, drained
- 1 teaspoon dried basil
- 1 teaspoon dried parsley flakes
  Pepper to taste
  Toasted baguette slices or romaine lettuce, torn

1. In a large bowl, combine the first nine ingredients; toss to coat. Cover and refrigerate for at least 4 hours before serving.
2. Serve antipasto with baguette slices or over lettuce.
NOTE *This recipe was tested with Vlasic roasted red pepper strips.*

Antipasto Appetizer

Mediterranean Eggplant Dip

I love Mediterranean food, and the flavors in this change-of-pace dip are so vibrant.
—**STACY MULLENS** GRESHAM, OR

PREP: 20 MIN. • **BAKE:** 40 MIN.
MAKES: 16 SERVINGS (¼ CUP DIP EACH)

- 1 large eggplant (about 1½ pounds), peeled
- 1 small onion, coarsely chopped
- 6 garlic cloves, peeled
- 3 tablespoons olive oil
- 2 cups (16 ounces) reduced-fat sour cream
- 4 teaspoons lemon juice
- ¾ teaspoon salt
- ½ teaspoon pepper
- 10 drops liquid smoke, optional
  Minced fresh parsley
  Optional ingredients: naan flatbread wedges or miniature pitas, cherry tomatoes, celery sticks, julienned red pepper, baby carrots and Greek olives

1. Preheat oven to 400°. Cut eggplant crosswise into 1-in. slices; place on a greased 15x10x1-in. baking pan. Top with onion and garlic cloves. Drizzle with oil.
2. Roast 40-45 minutes or until eggplant is very soft, turning and stirring the vegetables once. Cool slightly.
3. Place eggplant mixture in a food processor; process until blended.

Transfer to a large bowl; stir in sour cream, lemon juice, salt, pepper and, if desired, liquid smoke.
4. Sprinkle with parsley. Serve with flatbread and vegetables as desired.

Cranberry Catch of the Day

Most folks may not think of serving fish during the holidays, but a colorful cranberry sauce and pleasant pecan dressing make this entree very elegant.
—**LINDA PATRICK** HOUSTON, TX

PREP: 20 MIN. • **BAKE:** 25 MIN.
MAKES: 6 SERVINGS

- 1½ cups chopped celery
- ½ cup chopped onion
- 9 tablespoons butter, divided
- 6 cups cubed bread
- ¾ cup chopped pecans
- ⅓ cup orange juice
- 1½ teaspoons grated orange peel
- 1 teaspoon salt, divided
- 6 haddock, cod or halibut fillets (6 ounces each)

ORANGE-CRANBERRY SAUCE

- ½ cup sugar
- 2 teaspoons cornstarch
- ½ cup water
- ½ cup orange juice
- 1 cup fresh or frozen cranberries
- 2 teaspoons grated orange peel

1. Preheat oven to 350°. In a large skillet over medium heat, cook and stir celery and onion in 6 tablespoons butter until tender. Stir in bread cubes, pecans, orange juice, peel and ½ teaspoon salt. Transfer to a greased 13x9-in. baking dish. Arrange fillets over the stuffing.
2. Melt remaining butter; drizzle over fillets. Sprinkle with remaining salt. Bake, uncovered, 25-28 minutes or until fish flakes easily with a fork.
3. In a small saucepan, combine sugar and cornstarch; whisk in water and orange juice until smooth. Bring to a boil, stirring constantly. Add cranberries; cook 5 minutes or until berries pop. Stir in orange peel. Serve with fish and stuffing.

**Bruschetta
with Prosciutto**

Bruschetta with Prosciutto

A crowd-pleaser any time of year, this savory-tasting appetizer is perfect for holiday get-togethers.

—**DEBBIE MANNO** FORT MILL, SC

START TO FINISH: 25 MIN.
MAKES: ABOUT 6½ DOZEN

- 8 plum tomatoes, seeded and chopped
- 1 cup chopped sweet onion
- ¼ cup grated Romano cheese
- ¼ cup minced fresh basil
- 2 ounces thinly sliced prosciutto, finely chopped
- 1 shallot, finely chopped
- 3 garlic cloves, minced
- ⅓ cup olive oil
- ⅓ cup balsamic vinegar
- 1 teaspoon minced fresh rosemary
- ¼ teaspoon pepper
- ⅛ teaspoon hot pepper sauce, optional
- 1 French bread baguette (10½ ounces), cut into ¼-inch slices

1. In a large bowl, combine the first seven ingredients. In another bowl, whisk the oil, vinegar, rosemary, pepper and pepper sauce if desired. Pour over tomato mixture; toss to coat.

2. Place bread slices on an ungreased baking sheet. Broil 3-4 in. from the heat for 1-2 minutes or until golden brown. With a slotted spoon, top each slice with tomato mixture.

TOP TIP

Balsamic Makes It Better

Balsamic vinegar is made from sweet white grapes and aged in wooden barrels for at least 10 years. You can substitute cider vinegar or a mild red wine vinegar. White wine vinegar is much stronger and sharper and should be used sparingly if it's all you have in the pantry.

Scallops in Shells

My elegant recipe makes an excellent first course. The buttery scallops are served in a rich, creamy sauce.
—**JANE ROSSEN** BINGHAMTON, NY

PREP: 35 MIN. • **BAKE:** 10 MIN.
MAKES: 8 SERVINGS

- 2 cups water
- 16 sea scallops (about 2 pounds)
- 1 teaspoon salt
- 1½ cups thinly sliced fresh mushrooms
- 2 shallots, finely chopped
- ¼ cup butter, cubed

SAUCE

- 2 tablespoons butter
- 2 tablespoons all-purpose flour
- ¾ cup 2% milk
- 2 tablespoons grated Parmesan cheese
- 2 tablespoons sherry
- ½ teaspoon salt
- ¼ teaspoon lemon juice
- ¼ teaspoon pepper
- ⅛ teaspoon grated lemon peel
- 8 scallop shells
- ⅓ cup dry bread crumbs
- 2 tablespoons butter, melted

1. Place water in a large saucepan. Bring to a boil. Reduce heat; add scallops and poach, uncovered, 6 minutes or until firm and opaque. Drain scallops, reserving 1 cup liquid.

2. Sprinkle scallops with salt. In a large skillet, saute mushrooms and shallots in butter until tender. Add scallops; cook 2 minutes longer. Remove scallops from heat and set aside.

3. For sauce, in a small saucepan, melt butter. Stir in flour until smooth; gradually add milk and reserved poaching liquid. Bring to a boil; cook and stir 2 minutes or until thickened. Stir in cheese, sherry, salt, lemon juice, pepper and lemon peel; add to the skillet.

4. Preheat oven to 375°. Divide scallop mixture among eight scallop shells. Combine bread crumbs and melted butter; sprinkle over tops. Place on an ungreased 15x10x1-in. baking pan. Bake 8-12 minutes or until crumbs are golden brown.

Italian Rainbow Cookies

My family has made these cookies for generations. They are always a special treat!
—**CINDY CASAZZA** HOPEWELL, NJ

PREP: 35 MIN. + CHILLING • **BAKE:** 10 MIN./BATCH
MAKES: 11 DOZEN

- 4 eggs
- 1 cup sugar
- 3½ ounces almond paste, cut into small pieces
- 1 cup all-purpose flour
- 1 cup butter, melted and cooled
- ½ teaspoon salt
- ½ teaspoon almond extract
- 6 to 8 drops red food coloring
- 6 to 8 drops green food coloring
- ¼ cup seedless raspberry jam

GLAZE

- 1 cup (6 ounces) semisweet chocolate chips
- 1 teaspoon shortening

1. Preheat oven to 375°. In a large bowl, beat eggs and sugar 2-3 minutes or until thick and lemon-colored. Gradually add almond paste; mix well. Gradually add flour, butter, salt and extract.

2. Divide batter into thirds. Tint one portion red and one portion green; leave remaining portion plain. Spread one portion into each of three well-greased 11x7-in. baking dishes.

3. Bake 7-11 minutes or until a toothpick inserted into center comes out clean and edges begin to brown. Cool 10 minutes before removing from pans to wire racks to cool completely.

4. Place red layer on waxed paper; spread with 2 tablespoons jam. Top with plain layer and remaining jam. Add green layer; press down gently.

5. For glaze, in a microwave, melt chocolate chips and shortening; stir until smooth. Spread half over green layer. Refrigerate 20 minutes or until set. Turn over; spread remaining glaze over red layer. Refrigerate 20 minutes or until set.

6. With a sharp knife, trim edges. Cut rectangle lengthwise into fourths. Cut each portion into ¼-in. slices.

Chive and Cheese Breadsticks

No Italian supper would be complete without bread. With two types of cheese, garlic and minced chives, these tasty twists go above and beyond.
—**REBEKAH BEYER** SABETHA, KS

PREP: 15 MIN. + RISING • **BAKE:** 15 MIN.
MAKES: 16 BREADSTICKS

- 1 loaf (1 pound) frozen bread dough, thawed
- ⅓ cup butter, softened
- 2 tablespoons minced chives
- 1 garlic clove, minced
- ¾ cup shredded part-skim mozzarella cheese
- ½ cup shredded Parmesan cheese, divided

1. On a lightly floured surface, roll dough into a 12-in. square. In a small bowl, combine butter, chives and garlic; spread over dough. Sprinkle with mozzarella cheese and ¼ cup Parmesan.

2. Fold dough in half; seal edges. Cut into sixteen ¾-in.-wide strips. Twist each strip 2-3 times; pinch ends.

3. Place 2 in. apart in a greased 15x10x 1-in. baking pan. Cover and let rise until nearly doubled, about 40 minutes.

4. Preheat oven to 375°. Sprinkle dough with remaining Parmesan cheese. Bake 13-15 minutes or until golden brown.

Chive and Cheese Breadsticks

FREEZE IT

Beef en Croute Appetizers

Here, flaky pastry, savory beef tenderloin and a tangy cream sauce come together for a holiday-worthy hors d'oeuvre.
—**JOAN COOPER** SUSSEX, WI

PREP: 45 MIN. • **BAKE:** 15 MIN.
MAKES: 16 APPETIZERS (1½ CUPS SAUCE)

- 2 **beef tenderloin steaks (8 ounces each), cut into ½-inch cubes**
- 2 **tablespoons olive oil, divided**
- 1¼ **cups chopped fresh mushrooms**
- 2 **shallots, chopped**
- 2 **garlic cloves, minced**
- ⅓ **cup sherry or chicken broth**
- ⅓ **cup heavy whipping cream**
- ½ **teaspoon salt**
- ⅛ **teaspoon pepper**
- 1 **tablespoon minced fresh parsley**
- 1 **package (17.3 ounces) frozen puff pastry, thawed**
- 1 **egg, beaten**

HORSERADISH CREAM

- 1 **cup sour cream**
- ½ **cup mayonnaise**
- 2 **tablespoons prepared horseradish**
- 1 **tablespoon minced chives**
- ¼ **teaspoon pepper**
  Additional minced chives, optional

1. In a large skillet, brown beef in 1 tablespoon oil. Remove and keep warm.
2. In same skillet, saute mushrooms and shallots in remaining oil until tender. Add garlic; cook 1 minute longer. Add sherry, stirring to loosen browned bits from pan. Stir in cream, salt and pepper. Bring to a boil; cook until liquid is almost evaporated, about 7 minutes. Stir in beef and parsley; set aside and keep warm.
3. Preheat oven to 400°. On a lightly floured surface, unfold puff pastry. Roll each sheet into a 12-in. square. Cut each into 16 squares.
4. Place 2 tablespoonfuls of beef mixture in center of half of squares. Top with remaining squares; press edges with a fork to seal. Place on parchment paper-lined baking sheets. Cut slits in top; brush with egg. Bake 14-16 minutes or until golden brown.
5. In a small bowl, combine horseradish cream ingredients; serve with appetizers. Garnish with additional chives if desired.
TO MAKE AHEAD *Freeze unbaked pastries on baking sheets until firm, then wrap and store in the freezer for up to 2 months. When ready to use, bake frozen appetizers at 400° for 16-18 minutes or until golden brown.*

Sicilian Salad

Loaded with fabulous flavor, this hearty salad tosses up in no time. Chop the tomatoes and celery and cube the cheese before guests arrive, and you'll have it ready in moments.
—**BETH BURGMEIER** EAST DUBUQUE, IL

START TO FINISH: 15 MIN. • **MAKES:** 10 SERVINGS

- 1 **package (9 ounces) iceberg lettuce blend**
- 1 **jar (16 ounces) pickled banana peppers, drained and sliced**
- 1 **jar (5¾ ounces) sliced green olives with pimientos, drained**
- 3 **plum tomatoes, chopped**
- 4 **celery ribs, chopped**
- 1 **cup chopped pepperoni**
- ½ **cup cubed part-skim mozzarella cheese**
- ½ **cup Italian salad dressing**

In a large bowl, combine the first seven ingredients. Drizzle with dressing and toss to coat.

(5) INGREDIENTS

Sparkling Cranberry Kiss

I love the tartness of cranberries in cold beverages. This recipe is easily doubled, tripled or even quadrupled.
—**SHANNON ARTHUR** WHEELERSBURG, OH

START TO FINISH: 5 MIN.
MAKES: 14 SERVINGS (¾ CUP EACH)

- 6 **cups cranberry juice**
- 1½ **cups orange juice**
- 3 **cups ginger ale**
  Ice cubes
  Orange slices, optional

In a pitcher, combine cranberry juice and orange juice. Just before serving, stir in ginger ale; serve over ice. If desired, serve with orange slices.

Beef en Croute Appetizers

Chicken Marsala Lasagna

Chicken Marsala Lasagna

I love chicken Marsala, but most recipes do not serve a crowd. This is a version I developed to serve 12, and it's just perfect for a winter dinner.

—DEBBIE SHANNON RINGGOLD, GA

PREP: 50 MIN. • **BAKE:** 50 MIN. + STANDING
MAKES: 12 SERVINGS

- 4 teaspoons Italian seasoning, divided
- 1 teaspoon salt
- ¾ pound boneless skinless chicken breasts, cubed
- 1 tablespoon olive oil
- ¼ cup finely chopped onion
- ½ cup butter, cubed
- 12 garlic cloves, minced
- ½ pound sliced baby portobello mushrooms
- 1½ cups beef broth
- ¾ cup Marsala wine, divided
- ¼ teaspoon coarsely ground pepper
- 3 tablespoons cornstarch
- ½ cup finely chopped fully cooked ham
- 1 carton (15 ounces) ricotta cheese
- 1 package (10 ounces) frozen chopped spinach, thawed and squeezed dry
- 2 cups (8 ounces) shredded Italian cheese blend
- 1 cup grated Parmesan cheese, divided
- 2 eggs, lightly beaten
- 12 lasagna noodles, cooked, rinsed and drained

1. Combine 2 teaspoons Italian seasoning and salt; sprinkle over chicken. In a large skillet, saute chicken in oil until no longer pink. Remove and keep warm.
2. In same skillet, cook onion in butter over medium heat 2 minutes. Add garlic; cook 2 minutes. Stir in mushrooms; cook 4-5 minutes longer or until tender.
3. Stir in broth, ½ cup wine and pepper; bring to a boil. Combine cornstarch and remaining wine until smooth; stir into pan. Bring to a boil; cook and stir for 2 minutes or until thickened. Stir in ham and chicken.
4. Preheat oven to 350°. In a large bowl, combine ricotta cheese, spinach, Italian cheese blend, ¾ cup Parmesan cheese, eggs and remaining Italian seasoning. Spread 1 cup chicken mixture into a greased 13x9-in. baking dish. Layer with three noodles, about ¾ cup chicken mixture and about 1 cup ricotta mixture. Repeat layers three times.
5. Cover and bake 40 minutes. Sprinkle with remaining Parmesan cheese. Bake, uncovered, for 10-15 minutes or until bubbly and cheese is melted. Let stand 10 minutes before cutting.

Italian Cream Cheese Cake

Buttermilk makes every bite of this awesome dessert moist and flavorful. I rely on this recipe year-round.

—JOYCE LUTZ CENTERVIEW, MO

PREP: 40 MIN. • **BAKE:** 20 MIN. + COOLING
MAKES: 12 SERVINGS

- ½ cup butter, softened
- ½ cup shortening
- 2 cups sugar
- 5 eggs, separated
- 1 teaspoon vanilla extract
- 2 cups all-purpose flour
- 1 teaspoon baking soda
- 1 cup buttermilk
- 1½ cups flaked coconut
- 1 cup chopped pecans
CREAM CHEESE FROSTING
- 2 packages (one 8 ounces, one 3 ounces) cream cheese, softened
- ¾ cup butter, softened
- 6 cups confectioners' sugar
- 1½ teaspoons vanilla extract
- ¾ cup chopped pecans

1. Preheat oven to 350°. In a large bowl, cream butter, shortening and sugar until light and fluffy. Beat in egg yolks and vanilla. Combine flour and baking soda; add to creamed mixture alternately with buttermilk. Beat just until combined. Stir in coconut and pecans.
2. In a small bowl, beat egg whites until stiff peaks form. Fold a fourth of the egg whites into batter, then fold in remaining whites. Pour into three greased and floured 9-in. round baking pans.
3. Bake 20-25 minutes or until a toothpick inserted into center comes out clean. Cool 10 minutes before removing from the pans to wire racks to cool completely.
4. In a large bowl, beat cream cheese and butter until smooth. Beat in the confectioners' sugar and vanilla until fluffy. Stir in pecans. Spread frosting between layers and over top and sides of cake. Store in the refrigerator.

❝ My daughter made this cake for Thanksgiving and it is DELICIOUS! I am going to make it for our Christmas dinner. ❞

—MELINDASIMONE TASTEOFHOME.COM

KELLEY WINSHIP'S CANDY CANE COFFEE CAKES *PAGE 274*

Christmas Day Brunch

THE STOCKINGS ARE STUFFED...THE GIFTS ARE WRAPPED...CHRISTMAS IS HERE! ENJOY THE DAY WITH A SPIRITED BRUNCH. FROM COMFORTING FRENCH TOAST AND OVERNIGHT EGG BAKES TO EYE-OPENING CINNAMON ROLLS AND CLASSIC COFFEE CAKES, YOU'LL FIND EVERYTHING YOU NEED TO MAKE THIS SPECIAL MORNING JUST PERFECT.

SUZANNE FRANCIS' MUSHROOM-ARTICHOKE BRUNCH BAKE *PAGE 275*

SHARON DELANEY-CHRONIS' RICH HAZELNUT COFFEE *PAGE 277*

CHRIS O'CONNELL'S OVERNIGHT REINDEER ROLLS *PAGE 273*

Ultimate Bacon-Maple
French Toast

Ultimate Bacon-Maple French Toast

A savory update on baked French toast, this is an easy make-ahead dish that is excellent for brunch, showers or even a change-of-pace dinner. The combination of maple syrup, bacon and nuts makes it so satisfying.
—**JOHN WHITEHEAD** GREENVILLE, SC

PREP: 30 MIN. + CHILLING
BAKE: 40 MIN. + STANDING
MAKES: 10 SERVINGS

- 8 eggs
- 2 cups half-and-half cream
- 1 cup 2% milk
- 1 tablespoon sugar
- 1 tablespoon brown sugar
- 1 teaspoon vanilla extract
- ½ teaspoon ground cinnamon
- ¼ teaspoon ground nutmeg
  Dash salt
  Dash cayenne pepper
- 1 loaf (1 pound) French bread, cut into 1-inch slices

TOPPING

- 6 thick-sliced bacon strips, cooked and crumbled
- 1 cup butter, melted
- 1 cup packed brown sugar
- ½ cup chopped pecans, toasted
- 2 tablespoons corn syrup

- 1 teaspoon ground cinnamon
- ½ teaspoon ground nutmeg
- ¼ teaspoon ground cloves
  Maple syrup

1. Grease a 13x9-in. baking dish and set aside.
2. In a large shallow bowl, whisk first 10 ingredients. Dip each slice of bread into egg mixture. Arrange slices in prepared dish. Pour remaining egg mixture over top. Cover and refrigerate overnight.
3. Remove from refrigerator 30 minutes before baking. Preheat oven to 350°. In a small bowl, combine the topping ingredients. Spread over top.
4. Bake, uncovered, 40-45 minutes or until a knife inserted near center comes out clean. Let stand 10 minutes before serving. Drizzle with syrup.

Hot Malted Chocolate

Here, malted milk powder adds a nice touch to a yummy favorite.
—**CHRISTY MEINECKE** MANSFIELD, TX

START TO FINISH: 20 MIN. • **MAKES:** 5 SERVINGS

- 4 cups 2% milk
- 1 cup heavy whipping cream
- ½ cup sugar
- 1 cup milk chocolate chips
- ⅓ cup malted milk powder
- 2 teaspoons vanilla extract

1. In a saucepan, heat milk over medium heat until bubbles form around sides of pan. Meanwhile, in a small bowl, beat cream until it begins to thicken. Add sugar; beat until soft peaks form.
2. Whisk chocolate chips and milk powder into milk until chocolate is melted. Remove from the heat; whisk in vanilla. Pour into mugs. Spoon whipped cream over the top.

Chive Horseradish Sauce

Smoked salmon gets a delicious treatment when piled on pumpernickel or cocktail rye and dolloped with this sauce.
—**CONNIE FICKES** YORK, PA

START TO FINISH: 5 MIN. • **MAKES:** 1½ CUPS

- 1½ cups sour cream
- 3 tablespoons prepared horseradish
- 2 tablespoons minced chives
- 2 teaspoons lemon juice
- ¼ teaspoon salt
  Pumpernickel bread slices
  Smoked salmon or lox

In a bowl, combine the sour cream, horseradish, chives, lemon juice and salt. Refrigerate until serving. Serve with pumpernickel and salmon.

Chive Horseradish Sauce

Pumpkin Cheesecake Muffins

My mother-in-law came up with these tender treats by combining a few of her favorite muffin recipes. Chock-full of pumpkin, they feature both a sweet cream cheese filling and crunchy praline topping.

—LISA POWELSON SCOTT CITY, KS

PREP: 25 MIN. • **BAKE:** 15 MIN. • **MAKES:** 2 DOZEN

- 3 cups all-purpose flour
- 2 cups sugar
- 2 teaspoons baking soda
- 2 teaspoons baking powder
- 1 teaspoon salt
- 1 teaspoon ground cinnamon
- 4 eggs
- 1 can (15 ounces) solid-pack pumpkin
- 1½ cups canola oil

CREAM CHEESE FILLING

- 1 package (8 ounces) cream cheese, softened
- ½ cup sugar
- 1 egg
- 1 tablespoon all-purpose flour

PRALINE TOPPING

- ⅔ cup chopped pecans
- ⅓ cup packed brown sugar
- 2 tablespoons sour cream

1. Preheat oven to 400°. In a large bowl, combine first six ingredients. In another bowl, whisk eggs, pumpkin and oil. Stir into dry ingredients just until moistened. Fill greased or paper-lined muffin cups one-third full.

2. For filling, beat cream cheese, sugar, egg and flour until smooth. Drop by tablespoonfuls into center of each muffin. Top with remaining batter.

3. For topping, in a small bowl, combine pecans, brown sugar and sour cream; spoon over batter. Bake 15-18 minutes or until a toothpick inserted into a muffin comes out clean. Cool 5 minutes before removing from pans to wire racks. Serve warm. Refrigerate leftovers.

Pumpkin Cheesecake Muffins

Southwest Tortilla Scramble

Southwest Tortilla Scramble

Here's my version of a deconstructed breakfast burrito that's actually good for you. Go for hefty corn tortillas in this recipe. Flour ones can get lost in the scramble.

—**CHRISTINE SCHENHER** EXETER, CA

START TO FINISH: 15 MIN.
MAKES: 2 SERVINGS

- 4 **egg whites**
- 2 **eggs**
- ¼ **teaspoon pepper**
- 2 **corn tortillas (6 inches), halved and cut into strips**
- ¼ **cup chopped fresh spinach**
- 2 **tablespoons shredded reduced-fat cheddar cheese**
- ¼ **cup salsa**

1. In a large bowl, whisk egg whites, eggs and pepper. Stir in tortillas, spinach and cheese.
2. Heat a large skillet coated with cooking spray over medium heat. Pour in egg mixture; cook and stir until eggs are thickened and no liquid egg remains. Top with salsa.

66 **Excellent! So easy and quick.** 99
—MHICKIEAZ
TASTEOFHOME.COM

Gingerbread Belgian Waffles

Crumb-Topped Cranberry Cake

This dessert has a little something for everyone—moist yellow cake, cream cheese filling and a cranberry-coconut topping. Serve it at brunch or dinner!

—**DARLENE BRENDEN** SALEM, OR

PREP: 40 MIN. • **BAKE:** 50 MIN. + COOLING
MAKES: 12 SERVINGS

- 2 cups plus 2 tablespoons all-purpose flour
- ⅔ cup sugar
- ½ teaspoon baking powder
- ½ teaspoon baking soda
- 1 package (8 ounces) cream cheese, divided
- 2 eggs
- ¾ cup 2% milk
- 2 tablespoons canola oil
- 1 teaspoon vanilla extract
- ½ cup flaked coconut
- 1 cup whole-berry cranberry sauce

TOPPING

- 6 tablespoons all-purpose flour
- 2 tablespoons sugar
- 2 tablespoons cold butter

1. Preheat oven to 350°. In a large bowl, combine flour, sugar, baking powder and baking soda; cut in 3 ounces of cream cheese until mixture resembles fine crumbs.

2. In another bowl, whisk 1 egg, milk and oil; stir into crumb mixture just until moistened. Spread batter into a greased and floured 9-in. springform pan; set aside.

3. In a small bowl, beat remaining cream cheese until fluffy. Beat in vanilla and remaining egg; carefully spread over batter. Sprinkle with coconut. Dollop with cranberry sauce. In a small bowl, combine flour and sugar; cut in butter until crumbly. Sprinkle over the top.

4. Bake 50-55 minutes or until golden brown. Cool on a wire rack 15 minutes. Carefully run a knife around edge of pan to loosen. Remove sides of pan. Cool completely. Store in the refrigerator.

Gingerbread Belgian Waffles

I like to combine the sweet and spicy flavor of gingerbread with cool and creamy cream cheese frosting. It's a heavenly way to start a wintry day!

—**JANNINE FISK** MALDEN, MA

PREP: 25 MIN. • **COOK:** 5 MIN./BATCH
MAKES: 6 ROUND WAFFLES (1½ CUPS ICING)

- 2 cups all-purpose flour
- ¼ cup packed brown sugar
- 3 teaspoons baking powder
- 1½ teaspoons ground ginger
- 1 teaspoon baking soda
- 1 teaspoon ground cinnamon
- ½ teaspoon salt
- ¼ teaspoon ground nutmeg
- 4 eggs, separated
- 2 cups buttermilk
- ½ cup butter, melted
- ½ cup molasses
- 2 teaspoons vanilla extract

ICING

- 1½ cups confectioners' sugar
- ½ cup butter, softened
- ¼ cup cream cheese, softened
- 2 tablespoons 2% milk
- ½ teaspoon vanilla extract
- ⅛ teaspoon salt

1. In a large bowl, combine the first eight ingredients. In another bowl, whisk egg yolks, buttermilk, butter, molasses and vanilla. Add to dry ingredients; stir just until combined.

2. In a small bowl, beat egg whites until stiff. Gently fold into batter.

3. Bake in a preheated round Belgian waffle iron according to manufacturer's directions until golden brown.

4. Meanwhile, in a small bowl, combine all icing ingredients; beat until smooth. Serve with waffles.

(5) INGREDIENTS

Maple-Bacon Grits Puff

Bacon and maple add salty sweetness to an impressive grits dish that tastes as good as it looks.

—LOTTE WASHBURN SEBRING, FL

PREP: 20 MIN. • **BAKE:** 1 HOUR
MAKES: 8 SERVINGS

- 8 **bacon strips, chopped**
- 2 **cups 2% milk**
- 1¼ **cups water**
- ½ **teaspoon salt**
- 1 **cup quick-cooking grits**
- ½ **cup maple syrup**
- 4 **eggs, lightly beaten**
  Minced fresh chives, optional

1. Preheat oven to 350°. In a large skillet, cook bacon over medium heat until crisp, stirring occasionally. Remove with a slotted spoon; drain on paper towels. Reserve 2 tablespoons drippings.

2. In a large saucepan, bring milk, water and salt to a boil. Slowly stir in grits. Reduce heat to medium-low; cook, covered, 5-7 minutes or until thickened, stirring occasionally. Remove from heat; stir in maple syrup, half of the cooked bacon and reserved drippings.

3. In a small bowl, whisk a small amount of hot grits into eggs until blended; return all to pan, mixing well. Transfer to a greased 8-in.-square baking dish.

4. Bake, uncovered, 1 hour or until a knife inserted near the center comes out clean. Sprinkle with remaining bacon and, if desired, chives; let stand 5 minutes before serving.

Maple-Bacon Grits Puff

Brunch Beignets

Brunch Beignets

Enjoy breakfast the New Orleans way with these warm, crispy bites. Topped with powdered sugar, they are a delight!

—LOIS RUTHERFORD ELKTON, FL

PREP: 20 MIN. • **COOK:** 5 MIN./BATCH
MAKES: ABOUT 2 DOZEN

- 2 **eggs, separated**
- 1 **cup all-purpose flour**
- 1 **teaspoon baking powder**
- ⅛ **teaspoon salt**
- ½ **cup sugar**
- ¼ **cup water**
- 1 **tablespoon butter, melted**
- 2 **teaspoons grated lemon peel**
- 1 **teaspoon vanilla extract**
- 1 **teaspoon brandy, optional**
  Oil for deep-fat frying

1. Place egg whites in a small bowl; let stand at room temperature for 30 minutes.

2. Meanwhile, in a large bowl, combine the flour, baking powder and salt. Combine the egg yolks, sugar, water, butter, lemon peel, vanilla and brandy if desired; stir into dry ingredients just until combined. Beat egg whites on medium speed until soft peaks form; fold into batter.

3. In an electric skillet or deep-fat fryer, heat oil to 375°. Drop batter by teaspoonfuls, a few at a time, into the hot oil. Fry until golden brown, about 1½ minutes on each side. Drain on paper towels. Dust with confectioners' sugar. Serve warm.

Overnight Reindeer Rolls

Have fun making these reindeer-shaped rolls with the kids. And make sure to take pictures of the final product because they'll be gone before you know it!

—CHRIS O'CONNELL SAN ANTONIO, TX

PREP: 50 MIN. + RISING • **BAKE:** 10 MIN.
MAKES: 3 DOZEN

- 2 **packages (¼ ounce each) active dry yeast**
- 1½ **cups warm water (110° to 115°)**
- 2 **eggs**
- ½ **cup butter, softened**
- ½ **cup sugar**
- 2 **teaspoons salt**
- 5¾ to 6¼ **cups all-purpose flour**

DECORATIONS
- 1 **egg**
- 2 **teaspoons water**
- 36 **raisins (about 2 tablespoons), halved**
- 18 **red candied cherries, halved**

1. In a small bowl, dissolve yeast in warm water. In a large bowl, combine eggs, butter, sugar, salt, yeast mixture and 3 cups flour; beat on medium speed until smooth. Stir in enough remaining flour to form a very soft dough (dough will be sticky). Do not knead. Cover with plastic wrap; refrigerate overnight.
2. Turn dough onto a floured surface; divide and shape into 36 balls. Roll each into a 5-in. log. Cut each log halfway down the center. Pull the cut sections apart for antlers. Using kitchen shears, snip ½-in. cuts along outer sides for antler points. Flatten uncut half of log for the reindeer face.
3. Place 2 in. apart on greased baking sheets. Cover with kitchen towels; let rise in a warm place until doubled, about 30 minutes. Preheat oven to 400°.
4. In a small bowl, whisk egg and water until blended; brush over rolls. Press raisin halves into dough for eyes; press the cherry halves into dough for noses. Bake 8-10 minutes or until golden brown. Serve warm.

Overnight Cinnamon Rolls

Packed with cinnamon flavor, these soft from-scratch rolls are definitely worth the wait. Preparing them the night before makes them an ideal addition to holiday breakfasts and brunches.

—CHRIS O'CONNELL SAN ANTONIO, TX

PREP: 35 MIN. + RISING • **BAKE:** 20 MIN.
MAKES: 2 DOZEN

- 2 **packages (¼ ounce each) active dry yeast**
- 1½ **cups warm water (110° to 115°)**
- 2 **eggs**
- ½ **cup butter, softened**
- ½ **cup sugar**
- 2 **teaspoons salt**
- 5¾ to 6¼ **cups all-purpose flour**

FILLING
- 1 **cup packed brown sugar**
- 4 **teaspoons ground cinnamon**
- ½ **cup softened butter, divided**

GLAZE
- 2 **cups confectioners' sugar**
- ¼ **cup half-and-half cream**
- 2 **teaspoons vanilla extract**

1. In a small bowl, dissolve yeast in warm water. In a large bowl, combine eggs, butter, sugar, salt, yeast mixture and 3 cups flour; beat on medium speed until smooth. Stir in enough remaining flour to form a very soft dough (dough will be sticky). Do not knead. Cover with plastic wrap; refrigerate overnight.
2. In a small bowl, mix brown sugar and cinnamon. Turn dough onto a floured surface; divide dough in half. Roll one portion into an 18x12-in. rectangle. Spread with ¼ cup butter to within ½ in. of edges; sprinkle evenly with half of the brown sugar mixture.
3. Roll up jelly-roll style, starting with a long side; pinch seam to seal. Cut into 12 slices. Place in a greased 13x9-in. baking pan, cut side down. Repeat with remaining dough and filling.
4. Cover with kitchen towels; let rise in a warm place until doubled, about 1 hour. Preheat oven to 375°.
5. Bake 20-25 minutes or until lightly browned. In a bowl, mix confectioners' sugar, cream and vanilla; spread over warm rolls.

Overnight Reindeer Rolls

Overnight Cinnamon Rolls

Candy Cane Coffee Cakes

Candy Cane Coffee Cakes

I make my festive-looking coffee cakes at Christmas and for winter breakfasts. The recipe makes three cakes, so it's perfect if you plan to hand out a few gifts as brunch guest leave. Feel free to experiment with the dried fruits if you'd like.

—KELLEY WINSHIP
WEST RUTLAND, VT

PREP: 40 MIN. + RISING • **BAKE:** 15 MIN.
MAKES: 3 COFFEE CAKES

- 2 **cups (16 ounces) sour cream**
- 2 **packages (¼ ounce each) active dry yeast**
- ½ **cup warm water (110° to 115°)**
- ¼ **cup butter, softened**
- ⅓ **cup sugar**
- 2 **teaspoons salt**
- 2 **eggs, beaten**
- 5¼ **to 6 cups all-purpose flour, divided**
- 1½ **cups (12 ounces) finely chopped dried apricots**
- 1½ **cups finely chopped maraschino cherries**
- 2 **tablespoons butter, melted**

ICING
- 2 **cups confectioners' sugar**
- 2 **to 3 tablespoons water**

1. In a saucepan, heat sour cream until lukewarm. Set aside. In a large bowl, dissolve yeast in warm water; add sour cream, softened butter, sugar, salt, eggs and 2 cups flour. With an electric mixer, beat until smooth. Stir in just enough of the remaining flour to form a soft dough.
2. Turn out onto a floured surface and knead until smooth and elastic. Place in a greased bowl, turning once to grease top. Cover and let rise in a warm place until doubled, about 1 hour.
3. Punch dough down; divide into three equal parts. On a lightly floured surface, roll each part into a 15x6-in. rectangle. Place on greased baking sheets.
4. With a scissors, make 2-in. cuts at ½-in. intervals on the long sides of rectangle. Combine apricots and

cherries; spread one-third of the mixture down the center of each rectangle.

5. Crisscross strips over filling. Stretch dough to 22 in. and curve to form cane. Let rise until doubled, about 45 minutes.

6. Preheat oven to 375°. Bake 15-20 minutes. While warm, brush canes with melted butter. Combine icing ingredients and drizzle over tops.

Cinnamon-Chip Scones

Paper bakery boxes lined with creatively cut tissue paper give these coffeehouse favorites a casual look. Dress up a box with polka-dot ribbon and a trio of fresh cinnamon sticks tied within a bow.

—BONNIE BUCKLEY KANSAS CITY, MO

PREP: 25 MIN. • **BAKE:** 15 MIN.
MAKES: 1 DOZEN

- 2½ **cups all-purpose flour**
- ⅓ **cup sugar**
- 3 **teaspoons baking powder**
- 1 **teaspoon ground cinnamon, divided**
- ½ **cup cold butter**
- ⅔ **cup cinnamon baking chips**
- 1 **cup plus 1 tablespoon heavy whipping cream, divided**
- 1 **egg**
- 1 **tablespoon coarse sugar**

1. Preheat oven to 400°. In a large bowl, combine flour, sugar, baking powder and ½ teaspoon cinnamon. Cut in butter until mixture resembles coarse crumbs. Stir in baking chips. Whisk 1 cup cream and egg; stir into crumb mixture just until moistened.

2. Turn dough onto a floured surface; knead 10 times. Pat into a 9-in. circle. Cut into 12 wedges. Separate wedges and place on a greased baking sheet. Brush with remaining cream. Combine coarse sugar and remaining cinnamon; sprinkle over the tops.

3. Bake 14-16 minutes or until golden brown. Serve warm.

Mushroom-Artichoke
Brunch Bake

Mushroom-Artichoke Brunch Bake

This is a lovely meatless egg bake, but you can also add a layer of cooked and sliced smoked sausages or cooked and crumbled bacon over the layer of artichokes, just under the cheese.

—SUZANNE FRANCIS MARYSVILLE, WA

PREP: 30 MIN. • **BAKE:** 40 MIN.
MAKES: 12 SERVINGS

- 3 **cups frozen shredded hash brown potatoes, thawed**
- 2 **tablespoons butter, melted, divided**
- ½ **teaspoon salt**
- 2½ **cups sliced fresh mushrooms**
- 1 **can (14 ounces) water-packed artichoke hearts, rinsed, drained and quartered**
- 3 **cups (12 ounces) shredded cheddar cheese**
- 12 **eggs**
- 1¾ **cups 2% milk**
- 1 **can (4 ounces) chopped green chilies, drained**

1. Preheat oven to 350°. Place potatoes in a greased 13x9-in. baking dish; drizzle with 1 tablespoon butter and sprinkle with salt. Bake 20-25 minutes or until lightly browned.

2. Meanwhile, in a small skillet, saute mushrooms in remaining butter until

tender. Place artichokes on paper towels; pat dry. Sprinkle mushrooms, artichokes and cheese over the potatoes. In a large bowl, whisk the eggs, milk and green chilies; pour over cheese.

3. Bake, uncovered, 40-45 minutes or until a knife inserted near the center comes out clean. Let stand 5 minutes before serving.

⑤INGREDIENTS

Cran-Grape Cooler

You're just a few ingredients away from refreshment with this colorful cooler that keeps the holidays merry and bright!

—DIDI DESJARDINS DARTMOUTH, MA

START TO FINISH: 10 MIN.
MAKES: 9 SERVINGS (2¼ QUARTS)

- 6 **cups cranberry-grape juice, chilled**
- 3 **cups lemon-lime soda, chilled**
- 2 **tablespoons lime juice**
  Ice cubes
  Lime slices and maraschino cherries, optional

In a large pitcher, combine the cranberry-grape juice, soda and lime juice. Serve over ice; garnish servings with lime slices and cherries if desired.

Apple Streusel Muffins

A pretty glaze makes these coffee cake-like muffins special enough for company. My family enjoys them for sit-down breakfasts and snacks alike.

—DULCY GRACE ROARING SPRING, PA

PREP: 20 MIN. • **BAKE:** 15 MIN. + COOLING
MAKES: 1 DOZEN

- 2 **cups all-purpose flour**
- 1 **cup sugar**
- 1 **teaspoon baking powder**
- ½ **teaspoon baking soda**
- ½ **teaspoon salt**
- 2 **eggs**
- ½ **cup butter, melted**
- 1¼ **teaspoons vanilla extract**
- 1½ **cups chopped peeled tart apples**

STREUSEL TOPPING

- ⅓ **cup packed brown sugar**
- 1 **tablespoon all-purpose flour**
- ⅛ **teaspoon ground cinnamon**
- 1 **tablespoon cold butter**

GLAZE

- 1½ **cups confectioners' sugar**
- 1 **to 2 tablespoons milk**
- 1 **teaspoon butter, melted**
- ¼ **teaspoon vanilla extract**
- ⅛ **teaspoon salt**

1. Preheat oven to 375°. In a large bowl, combine flour, sugar, baking powder, baking soda and salt. In another bowl, combine eggs, butter and vanilla; stir into dry ingredients just until moistened (batter will be stiff). Fold in apples.
2. Fill greased or paper-lined muffin cups three-fourths full. In a small bowl, combine the brown sugar, flour and cinnamon; cut in butter until crumbly. Sprinkle over batter.
3. Bake 15-20 minutes or until a toothpick inserted into muffin center comes out clean. Cool 5 minutes before removing from pan to a wire rack to cool completely. Combine glaze ingredients; drizzle over muffins.

Brunch Egg Bake

Brunch Egg Bake

This colorful egg casserole makes entertaining easy. It comes together in just 15 minutes and the oven does the rest of the work for you!

—GLORIA ROHLFING YORK, PA

PREP: 15 MIN. • **BAKE:** 35 MIN. + STANDING
MAKES: 12 SERVINGS

- 3 **cups (12 ounces) shredded cheddar cheese**
- 3 **cups (12 ounces) shredded part-skim mozzarella cheese**
- 1 **jar (4½ ounces) sliced mushrooms, drained**
- ½ **cup chopped sweet red pepper**
- ⅓ **cup sliced green onions**
- 2 **tablespoons butter**
- 2 **cups diced fully cooked ham**
- ½ **cup all-purpose flour**
- 1¾ **cups milk**
- 8 **eggs, lightly beaten**
- 2 **tablespoons minced fresh parsley**
- ½ **teaspoon salt**
- ½ **teaspoon dried basil**
- ¼ **teaspoon pepper**

1. Preheat oven to 350°. Combine cheeses; place 3 cups in an ungreased 13x9-in. baking dish and set aside.
2. In a large skillet, saute mushrooms, red pepper and onions in butter until tender; drain. Spoon into baking dish. Sprinkle with ham and remaining cheese mixture.
3. In a large bowl, whisk flour and milk until smooth; stir in eggs, parsley, salt, basil and pepper until blended. Slowly pour over cheeses.
4. Bake, uncovered, 35-40 minutes or until a knife inserted near the center comes out clean. Let stand 10 minutes before cutting.

> ❝This is my favorite brunch recipe. I took this casserole to brunch at church and received several compliments.❞
>
> —VIKINGSFANSWIFE TASTEOFHOME.COM

Breakfast Sausage Patties

Buttermilk is the secret ingredient that keeps these pork patties moist, while a blend of seasonings creates a wonderful flavor guests love.

—**HARVEY KEENEY** MANDAN, ND

PREP: 30 MIN. • **COOK:** 10 MIN./BATCH
MAKES: 20 PATTIES

- ¾ **cup buttermilk**
- 2¼ **teaspoons kosher salt**
- 1½ **teaspoons rubbed sage**
- 1½ **teaspoons brown sugar**
- 1½ **teaspoons pepper**
- ¾ **teaspoon dried marjoram**
- ¾ **teaspoon dried savory**
- ¾ **teaspoon cayenne pepper**
- ¼ **teaspoon ground nutmeg**
- 2½ **pounds ground pork**

1. In a large bowl, combine buttermilk and seasonings. Add pork; mix lightly but thoroughly. Shape into twenty 3-in. patties.
2. In a large skillet coated with cooking spray, cook patties in batches over medium heat 5-6 minutes on each side or until a thermometer reads 160°. Remove to paper towels to drain.

Rich Hazelnut Coffee

I love to try new recipes and entertain friends and relatives. This adult beverage couldn't be more perfect for doing just that. Coffee lovers, rejoice! Your favorite drink just got better.

—**SHARON DELANEY-CHRONIS** SOUTH MILWAUKEE, WI

START TO FINISH: 15 MIN. • **MAKES:** 4 SERVINGS

- 3 **cups hot brewed coffee**
- ½ **cup packed brown sugar**
- 2 **tablespoons butter**
- ¾ **cup half-and-half cream**
- ¼ **cup hazelnut liqueur or ¼ teaspoon almond extract**
  Whipped cream and instant espresso powder, optional

1. In a large saucepan, combine the coffee, brown sugar and butter. Cook and stir over medium heat until sugar is dissolved. Stir in cream; heat through.
2. Remove from the heat; stir in hazelnut liqueur. Ladle into mugs. Garnish with whipped cream and dust with espresso powder if desired.

Any-Season Fruit Bowl

Any-Season Fruit Bowl

A refreshing fruit salad like this one is a welcome addition to a winter brunch. A hint of anise gives it real holiday flavor...and it looks gorgeous on a buffet table.

—**FRANCES STEVENSON** MCRAE, GA

PREP: 5 MIN. + CHILLING
COOK: 25 MIN. + CHILLING
MAKES: 16-18 SERVINGS

- 2 **cups water**
- 1½ **cups sugar**
- ⅓ **cup lime or lemon juice**
- 1 **teaspoon anise extract**
- ½ **teaspoon salt**
- 3 **oranges, peeled and sectioned**
- 3 **kiwifruit, peeled and sliced**
- 2 **grapefruit, peeled and sectioned**
- 2 **large apples, cubed**
- 1 **pint strawberries, sliced**
- 1 **pound green grapes**
- 1 **can (20 ounces) pineapple chunks, drained**

1. In a medium saucepan, combine water, sugar, lime juice, anise and salt. Bring to a boil over medium heat; cook for 20 minutes, stirring occasionally. Remove from the heat; cover and refrigerate for 6 hours or overnight.
2. Combine fruit in a large bowl; add dressing and toss to coat. Cover and chill for at least 1 hour.

Breakfast Sausage Patties

ROGER BOWLDS'
SALT-ENCRUSTED PRIME RIB *PAGE 292*

Christmas Dinner

RAISE A GLASS AND MAKE A TOAST OVER AN IMPRESSIVE HOLIDAY MEAL GUESTS WON'T SOON FORGET. FROM INCREDIBLE ENTREES TO DECADENT DESSERTS, THE SPECIAL RECIPES IN THIS CHAPTER PROMISE TO MAKE MEMORIES THAT WILL LAST ALL YEAR LONG. WHAT AN INCREDIBLE WAY TO CELEBRATE CHRISTMAS!

GRETCHEN FARR'S MIXED GREEN SALAD WITH CRANBERRY VINAIGRETTE *PAGE 287*

KATHY HARDING'S GARLIC KNOTTED ROLLS *PAGE 293*

DEANN ALEVA'S CHOCOLATE TRUFFLES *PAGE 281*

Ranch Green Beans

Ranch Green Beans

Years ago, I discovered this handwritten recipe on a note card and decided to give it a try. It's deliciously different from the usual green bean casserole and quickly became a favorite with my gang.
—**CAROL CONN** AURORA, CO

PREP: 15 MIN. • **COOK:** 20 MIN.
MAKES: 6 SERVINGS

- 1¼ **pounds fresh green beans, trimmed**
- 2 **tablespoons butter**
- 1½ **cups sliced fresh mushrooms**
- 1 **medium onion, chopped**
- 2 **garlic cloves, minced**
- 2 **tablespoons all-purpose flour**
- 1½ **cups 2% milk**
- 2 **tablespoons ranch salad dressing mix**
- ¼ **teaspoon white pepper**
- ¼ **cup soft bread crumbs, toasted**

1. Place green beans in a Dutch oven; add water to cover. Bring to a boil. Cook, uncovered, 3-4 minutes or just until tender. Drain.

2. Meanwhile, in a large skillet, heat butter over medium-high heat. Add the mushrooms and onion; cook and stir 3-4 minutes or until tender. Add garlic; cook 1 minute longer.

3. In a small bowl, whisk flour and 2 tablespoons milk until smooth. Whisk in remaining milk; stir into mushroom mixture. Bring to a boil, stirring constantly. Cook and stir for 2 minutes. Stir in salad dressing mix and pepper. Add beans; heat through. Transfer to a serving bowl; sprinkle with toasted bread crumbs.

> " Nice alternative to a traditional green bean casserole. "
> —**MJLOUK**
> TASTEOFHOME.COM

Chocolate Truffles

Perfect for entertaining, these chocolaty, silky candies are hard to resist! I like to keep a few on hand for a quick treat.
—**DEANN ALEVA** HUDSON, WI

PREP: 25 MIN. + CHILLING • **MAKES:** 3 DOZEN

- 14 ounces semisweet chocolate, divided
- 1 cup heavy whipping cream
- ⅓ cup butter, softened
- 1 teaspoon rum extract
- ½ cup finely chopped pecans or walnuts, toasted

1. Coarsely chop 12 ounces of chocolate; set aside. In a saucepan, heat cream over low heat until bubbles form around sides of the pan. Remove from the heat; add chopped chocolate, stirring until melted and smooth.

2. Cool to room temperature. Stir in butter and extract. Cover tightly and refrigerate mixture for at least 6 hours or until firm.

3. Grate remaining chocolate; place in a shallow dish. Add nuts; set aside. Shape tablespoonfuls of chilled chocolate mixture into balls. Place on waxed paper-lined baking sheets. (If truffles are soft, refrigerate until easy to handle.) Roll truffles in chocolate-nut mixture. Store in an airtight container in the refrigerator.

Chocolate Truffles

Mustard & Cranberry Glazed Ham

This glaze is a simple way to ensure your ham will be the showstopper on your holiday table. Best of all, it only calls for four basic ingredients.
—**NELLA PARKER** HERSEY, MI

PREP: 15 MIN. • **BAKE:** 1 HOUR 50 MIN. + STANDING
MAKES: 12 SERVINGS (4 CUPS SAUCE)

- 1 fully cooked bone-in ham (6 to 8 pounds)
  Whole cloves
- 3 cans (14 ounces each) jellied or whole-berry cranberry sauce
- 1½ cups packed brown sugar
- 1½ cups dry red wine or chicken broth
- 3 tablespoons Dijon mustard

1. Preheat oven to 325°. Place ham on a rack in a shallow roasting pan. If desired, score the surface of the ham, making diamond shapes ½ in. deep. Insert cloves into the surface. Loosely cover ham with foil; bake 1½ hours.

2. In a large saucepan, combine the cranberry sauce, brown sugar and wine. Bring to a boil. Reduce heat; simmer, uncovered, 10 minutes or until slightly thickened. Remove from the heat; whisk in mustard.

3. Pour 2 cups cranberry mixture over ham. Bake 20-30 minutes longer or until a thermometer reads 140°. Let stand for 10 minutes before slicing. Serve with remaining sauce.

Mustard & Cranberry Glazed Ham

Brussels Sprouts & Kale Saute

In an effort to add more greens to our meals, I created this side dish, and my kids eat it up. The crispy salami is the "hook."

—JENNIFER MCNABB BRENTWOOD, TN

START TO FINISH: 30 MIN.
MAKES: 12 SERVINGS (½ CUP EACH)

- ¼ pound thinly sliced hard salami, cut into ¼-inch strips
- 1½ teaspoons olive oil
- 2 tablespoons butter
- 2 pounds fresh Brussels sprouts, thinly sliced
- 2 cups shredded fresh kale
- 1 large onion, finely chopped
- ½ teaspoon kosher salt
- ⅛ teaspoon cayenne pepper
- ¼ teaspoon coarsely ground pepper
- 1 garlic clove, minced
- ½ cup chicken broth
- ½ cup chopped walnuts
- 1 tablespoon balsamic vinegar

1. In a Dutch oven, cook and stir the salami in oil over medium-high heat for 3-5 minutes or until crisp. Remove to paper towels with a slotted spoon; reserve drippings in pan.
2. Add butter to drippings; heat over medium-high heat. Add the Brussels sprouts, kale, onion, salt, cayenne and pepper; cook and stir until vegetables are crisp-tender. Add garlic; cook 1 minute longer.
3. Stir in broth; bring to a boil. Reduce heat; cover and cook for 4-5 minutes or until the Brussels sprouts are tender. Stir in walnuts and vinegar. Serve with salami strips.

> **"**I was asked to bring this to Christmas dinner as a repeat side dish.**"**

—SAV0808
TASTEOFHOME.COM

Artichoke & Green Bean Penne

Artichoke & Green Bean Penne

This pretty side dish goes well with just about any main course...and it even makes a fantastic meatless entree! Featuring colorful produce, toasted almonds and a creamy sauce, it's sure to satisfy.

—SARAH PIERCE SANTA MONICA, CA

PREP: 25 MIN. • **COOK:** 15 MIN.
MAKES: 9 SERVINGS

- 3 cups uncooked penne pasta
- ¾ pound fresh green beans, trimmed and cut into 1-inch pieces
- 1 cup sliced fresh mushrooms
- 1 medium sweet red pepper, chopped
- 3 tablespoons butter, cubed
- 1 package (8 ounces) frozen artichoke hearts, thawed and quartered
- 1 carton (8 ounces) Mascarpone cheese
- ¼ cup heavy whipping cream
- ¾ teaspoon salt
- ½ teaspoon pepper
- ¼ cup slivered almonds, toasted
- ¼ cup grated Parmesan cheese

1. In a large saucepan, cook pasta according to package directions, adding the green beans during the last 5 minutes of cooking.
2. In a Dutch oven, saute mushrooms and red pepper in butter until tender. Reduce heat; stir in the artichokes, Mascarpone cheese, cream, salt and pepper. Heat through (do not boil).
3. Drain beans and pasta; stir into artichoke mixture. Add almonds and toss to coat. Sprinkle with Parmesan cheese.

Beef Tenderloin with Mushroom-Wine Sauce

This succulent roast takes a little extra time to prepare, but it's worth it for holidays and special occasions. It's one of my top dinner requests.

—TONYA BURKHARD DAVIS, IL

PREP: 15 MIN. • **BAKE:** 50 MIN. + STANDING
MAKES: 12 SERVINGS (ABOUT 3½ CUPS SAUCE)

- 2 teaspoons dried thyme
- 2 teaspoons seasoned salt
- 1 beef tenderloin roast (5 pounds)
- 9 bacon strips, finely chopped
- 3 cups sliced fresh mushrooms
- 4 tablespoons butter, divided
- 4 medium onions, chopped (about 3 cups)
- 9 garlic cloves, minced
- ⅓ cup tomato paste
- 6 cups beef stock
- 2¼ cups dry red wine
- 3 tablespoons all-purpose flour
- ¼ teaspoon salt
- ¼ teaspoon pepper

1. Preheat oven to 425°. Rub thyme and seasoned salt onto all sides of roast. Place tenderloin on a rack in a shallow roasting pan. Roast 50-60 minutes or until meat reaches desired doneness (for medium-rare, a thermometer should read 145°; medium, 160°; well-done, 170°).

2. Meanwhile, in a Dutch oven, cook bacon over medium heat until crisp, stirring occasionally. Remove with a slotted spoon; drain on paper towels. Discard drippings, reserving 2 tablespoons in pan. Add mushrooms to drippings; cook and stir 4-5 minutes or until tender. Remove from pan.

3. Place 1 tablespoon butter in pan. Add onions; cook and stir over medium heat 6-8 minutes or until tender. Stir in garlic; cook 1 minute longer. Add tomato paste, stock and wine, stirring to loosen browned bits from pan. Bring to a boil; cook 20-25 minutes or until liquid is reduced almost by half.

4. In a microwave, melt remaining butter. Mix flour with butter until smooth; gradually whisk into sauce. Return to a boil, stirring constantly; cook and stir 1-2 minutes or until thickened. Stir in bacon, mushrooms, salt and pepper; heat through.

5. Remove roast from oven; tent with foil. Let stand 15 minutes before slicing. Serve with sauce.

Chocolate Chunk Pecan Pie

Our family hosts an annual party for our close friends, complete with a pie bake-off. A few years ago, this recipe won first prize! It's a wonderful dessert.

—JANICE SCHNEIDER KANSAS CITY, MO

PREP: 35 MIN. + CHILLING
BAKE: 55 MIN. + CHILLING • **MAKES:** 10 SERVINGS

- 1¼ cups all-purpose flour
- ⅛ teaspoon salt
- 1 package (3 ounces) cold cream cheese, cubed
- ¼ cup cold butter, cubed
- 2 to 3 tablespoons ice water

FILLING
- ⅓ cup sugar
- 3 tablespoons butter
- 2 cups coarsely chopped semisweet chocolate, divided
- 4 eggs
- 1 cup dark corn syrup
- 2 teaspoons vanilla extract
  Dash salt
- 2½ cups pecan halves, toasted

1. In a small bowl, mix flour and salt; cut in cream cheese and butter until crumbly. Gradually add ice water, tossing with a fork until dough holds together when pressed. Shape into a disk; wrap in plastic wrap. Refrigerate 30 minutes or overnight.

2. Preheat oven to 350°. On a lightly floured surface, roll dough to a ⅛-in.-thick circle; transfer to a 9-in. pie plate. Trim pastry to ½ in. beyond rim; flute edge. Refrigerate while making filling.

3. In a small saucepan, combine sugar, butter and 1 cup chopped chocolate; stir over low heat until smooth. Cool slightly.

4. In a large bowl, whisk eggs, corn syrup, vanilla and salt until blended. Stir in chocolate mixture. Layer pecans and remaining chopped chocolate in pastry shell; pour chocolate mixture over top.

5. Bake 55-60 minutes or until set. Cool 1 hour on a wire rack. Refrigerate 2 hours or until cold.

Beef Tenderloin with Mushroom-Wine Sauce

Smoked Gouda and Ham Appetizer Tarts

I call these "Star of the Party" tarts because they have that "I want more" appeal. They're so easy to make, too!

—MARY HAWKES PRESCOTT, AZ

START TO FINISH: 30 MIN. • **MAKES:** 2 DOZEN

- 1 egg, lightly beaten
- 2 tablespoons chopped fresh chives
- 1 tablespoon minced shallot
- 1 tablespoon mayonnaise
- 2 teaspoons honey mustard
- 1 teaspoon seasoned pepper
- 1¼ cups (5 ounces) shredded smoked Gouda cheese
- ½ cup finely chopped fully cooked smoked ham
- 2 tablespoons chopped dried cranberries
- 24 wonton wrappers
  Cooking spray
  Additional minced fresh chives, optional

1. Preheat oven to 350°. In a large bowl, combine first six ingredients. Stir in cheese, ham and cranberries. Spritz one side of each wonton wrapper with cooking spray. Gently press wrappers into miniature muffin cups, coated side up. Spoon 1 tablespoon cheese mixture into each.

2. Bake 10-14 minutes or until crusts are golden brown. Sprinkle with fresh chives if desired; serve warm. Refrigerate any leftovers.

Smoked Gouda and Ham Appetizer Tarts

Pancetta-Wrapped Shrimp with Honey-Lime Glaze

⑤ INGREDIENTS

Pancetta-Wrapped Shrimp with Honey-Lime Glaze

Requested every year by my family during the holidays, these shrimp appetizers feature a wonderful honey-lime cilantro glaze. The pancetta offers a great change from appetizers with bacon.

—JENNIFER TIDWELL FAIR OAKS, CA

START TO FINISH: 25 MIN. • **MAKES:** 1½ DOZEN

- 6 thin slices pancetta
- 18 uncooked large shrimp, peeled and deveined
- ¼ cup honey
- 2 tablespoons lime juice
- 1 teaspoon hot water
- 1 tablespoon minced fresh cilantro

1. Preheat oven to 375°. Cut each slice of pancetta into three strips. Wrap one strip around each shrimp; secure with a toothpick. Place shrimp in a foil-lined 15x10x1-in. baking pan. In a small bowl, whisk honey, lime juice and water until blended; reserve 2 tablespoons for brushing cooked shrimp.

2. Brush half the remaining honey mixture over shrimp. Bake 5 minutes. Turn shrimp; brush with remaining half of the honey mixture. Bake 4-6 minutes

longer or until pancetta is crisp and shrimp turn pink.

3. Remove from oven; brush with reserved 2 tablespoons honey mixture. Sprinkle with cilantro.

⑤ INGREDIENTS SLOW COOKER 🍲

Make-Ahead Eggnog

Homemade eggnog is a tradition in many families during the Christmas season. This slow-cooker version of the classic beverage shaves off preparation time.

—TASTE OF HOME TEST KITCHEN

PREP: 10 MIN. • **COOK:** 2 HOURS
MAKES: 9 SERVINGS (¾ CUP EACH)

- 6 cups whole milk
- 1 cup egg substitute
- ⅔ cup sugar
- 2 teaspoons rum extract
- 1½ teaspoons pumpkin pie spice
  French vanilla whipped topping, optional

In a 3-qt. slow cooker, combine the first five ingredients. Cover and cook on low for 2-3 hours or until heated through. Serve in mugs; dollop with whipped topping if desired.

Christmas Goose with Orange Glaze

A holiday goose is an impressive centerpiece. The orange sauce makes this a bird even Scrooge would love.

—**TERRI DRAPER** COLUMBUS, MT

PREP: 15 MIN. • **BAKE:** 2¾ HOURS + STANDING
MAKES: 10 SERVINGS

- 1 **domestic goose (10 to 12 pounds)**
- 1 **teaspoon salt**
- ½ **teaspoon rubbed sage**
- ¼ **teaspoon pepper**
- 6 **small navel oranges, divided**
- ⅓ **cup light corn syrup**
- 2 **tablespoons sugar**

1. Sprinkle goose with salt, sage and pepper; prick skin well with a fork. Cut three oranges into quarters; place in goose cavity. Tuck wings under; tie drumsticks together. Place breast side up on a rack in a roasting pan.

2. Bake, uncovered, at 350° for 2¾ to 3¼ hours or until a meat thermometer reads 180°. (Cover loosely with foil if goose browns too quickly). If necessary, drain fat from pan as it accumulates.

3. Cut peel from remaining oranges into long thin strips; cut oranges into sections, discarding membranes. Set orange sections aside.

4. Place goose on a serving platter; cover and let stand for 15 minutes. Meanwhile, in a small skillet over medium heat, cook and stir corn syrup and sugar until sugar is dissolved. Stir in orange sections and peel; heat through.

5. Brush glaze over goose. Spoon orange sections and peel around goose for garnishes if desired.

**Christmas Goose
with Orange Glaze**

Cherry-Walnut Cake Roll

Fit for a Christmas-dinner finale, this fruity old-world cake roll is simply luscious.

—*TASTE OF HOME* TEST KITCHEN

PREP: 45 MIN. • **BAKE:** 10 MIN. + COOLING
MAKES: 12 SERVINGS

- ½ cup dried cherries
- ¼ cup cherry brandy
- 4 eggs, separated
- 2 tablespoons plus ⅓ cup sugar, divided
- 2 tablespoons canola oil
- 1 teaspoon vanilla extract
- ½ teaspoon lemon extract
- ½ cup all-purpose flour
- ¼ cup ground walnuts
- 1 teaspoon ground cinnamon
- ¾ teaspoon baking powder

FILLING/FROSTING

- 2 packages (one 8 ounces, one 3 ounces) cream cheese, softened
- 1 cup confectioners' sugar
- 1 cup heavy whipping cream, whipped
  Semisweet chocolate, optional

1. Combine cherries and cherry brandy; cover and let stand overnight.
2. Place egg whites in a small bowl; let stand at room temperature 30 minutes. Line a greased 15x10x1-in. baking pan with waxed paper; grease the paper and set aside.
3. Preheat oven to 375°. In a large bowl, beat egg yolks until slightly thickened. Gradually add 2 tablespoons sugar, beating on high speed until thick and lemon-colored, about 5 minutes. Beat in oil, vanilla and lemon extract.
4. With clean beaters, beat egg whites on medium speed until soft peaks form. Gradually beat in remaining sugar, 1 tablespoon at a time, on high until stiff peaks form; fold into yolk mixture. Combine flour, walnuts, cinnamon and baking powder; gradually fold into egg mixture. Spread into prepared pan.
5. Bake 10-12 minutes or until cake springs back when lightly touched. Cool 2 minutes. Invert onto a kitchen towel dusted with confectioners' sugar. Gently peel off waxed paper. Roll up cake in the towel jelly-roll style, starting with a short side. Cool completely on a wire rack.
6. In a large bowl, beat cream cheese until smooth. Beat in confectioners' sugar. Fold in whipped cream. Unroll cake; spread with 1¼ cups filling to within ½ in. of edges.
7. Drain cherries and pat dry with paper towels. Arrange cherries over filling. Starting at the short side, roll up cake; place seam side down on a serving platter. Frost cake with remaining filling. Melt chocolate and drizzle over frosting if desired. Cover and refrigerate cake until serving.

Golden Gouda Mushroom Soup

A rich and creamy soup makes a good first impression as a formal first course. Sherry and smoked Gouda with a hint of holiday spice make every sip better than the last.

—**CHARLOTTE ROGERS** VIRGINIA BEACH, VA

START TO FINISH: 30 MIN. • **MAKES:** 6 SERVINGS

- ½ cup butter, cubed
- ½ cup all-purpose flour
- ½ teaspoon pepper
- ½ teaspoon ground allspice
- 1 carton (32 ounces) chicken broth
- ½ cup sherry or additional chicken broth
- ½ cup heavy whipping cream
- ½ pound sliced fresh mushrooms
- 4 garlic cloves, minced
- 2 cups (8 ounces) shredded smoked Gouda cheese
  Chives and smoked paprika

1. In a large saucepan, melt butter. Stir in the flour, pepper and allspice until smooth; gradually add the broth, sherry and cream. Bring to a boil. Add the mushrooms and garlic. Reduce heat; cover and simmer for 5-6 minutes or until mushrooms are tender.
2. Add cheese; cook and stir until melted. Garnish individual servings with chives and paprika.

Cherry-Walnut Cake Roll

Mixed Green Salad with Cranberry Vinaigrette

This colorful salad is a bright and tasty introduction to a special meal. Dried cranberries and tart apples along with glazed walnuts and rich blue cheese add interest to the mix.

—GRETCHEN FARR PORT ORFORD, OR

START TO FINISH: 25 MIN. • **MAKES:** 8 SERVINGS

- 1 cup fresh or frozen cranberries
- ⅓ cup sugar
- ⅓ cup water
- ½ cup cider vinegar
- 1½ teaspoons Dijon mustard
- 3 tablespoons olive oil

SALAD

- 2 packages (5 ounces each) spring mix salad greens
- 1 medium tart apple, chopped
- ⅔ cup dried cranberries
- ⅔ cup glazed walnuts
- ⅔ cup crumbled blue cheese

1. In a small saucepan, combine the cranberries, sugar and water. Cook over medium heat until berries pop, about 10 minutes.

2. Cool slightly. Place the cranberry mixture, vinegar and mustard in a blender; cover and process until pureed.

3. While processing, gradually add oil in a steady stream. Refrigerate mixture until serving.

4. Just before serving, in a large bowl, combine the salad greens, apple, cranberries and walnuts.

5. Drizzle with 1 cup vinaigrette and toss to coat. Sprinkle with blue cheese. Serve with remaining vinaigrette.

Supreme Stuffed Crown Roast

Supreme Stuffed Crown Roast

I've made crown roasts for many years, but was only satisfied with the results when I combined a few recipes to come up with this guest-pleasing version. It is beautifully roasted with an apricot glaze and a nicely browned stuffing.

—ISABELL COOPER CAMBRIDGE, NS

PREP: 20 MIN. • **BAKE:** 2½ HOURS + STANDING
MAKES: 12 SERVINGS

- 1 pork crown roast (12 ribs and about 8 pounds)
- ½ teaspoon seasoned salt
- ⅓ cup apricot preserves

APRICOT DRESSING

- ¼ cup butter, cubed
- 1 cup sliced fresh mushrooms
- 1 medium onion, finely chopped
- 1 celery rib, finely chopped
- 1 cup chopped dried apricots
- ½ teaspoon dried savory
- ½ teaspoon dried thyme
- ¼ teaspoon salt
- ¼ teaspoon pepper
- 3 cups soft bread crumbs

1. Preheat oven to 350°. Place roast, rib ends up, in a large shallow roasting pan; sprinkle with seasoned salt. Bake, uncovered, 1 hour.

2. Brush sides of roast with preserves. Bake 1½ to 2 hours longer or until meat reaches desired doneness (for medium-rare, a thermometer should read 145°; medium, 160°). Transfer roast to a serving platter. Let stand 20 minutes before carving.

3. For dressing, in a large skillet, heat butter over medium-high heat. Add mushrooms, onion and celery; cook and stir 6-8 minutes until tender. Stir in apricots and seasonings. Add bread crumbs; toss to coat. Transfer to a greased 8-in.-square baking dish.

4. Bake 15-20 minutes or until lightly browned. Spoon stuffing into center of roast; carve roast between ribs to serve.

Duchess Potatoes

Present potatoes in an attractive new way! Guests will love this pretty take on a classic side dish.

—*TASTE OF HOME* TEST KITCHEN

PREP: 35 MIN. • **BAKE:** 20 MIN.
MAKES: 6 SERVINGS

- 2 **pounds russet potatoes, peeled and quartered**
- 3 **egg yolks**
- 3 **tablespoons fat-free milk**
- 2 **tablespoons butter**
- 1 **teaspoon salt**
- ¼ **teaspoon pepper**
- ⅛ **teaspoon ground nutmeg**
- 1 **egg, lightly beaten**

1. Place potatoes in a large saucepan and cover with water. Bring to a boil. Reduce heat; cover and simmer 15-20 minutes or until tender. Drain. Over very low heat, stir potatoes 1-2 minutes or until steam has evaporated. Remove from heat.

2. Preheat oven to 400°. Press through a potato ricer or strainer into a large bowl. Stir in the egg yolks, milk, butter, salt, pepper and nutmeg.

3. Using a pastry bag or heavy-duty resealable plastic bag and a large star tip, pipe potatoes into six mounds on a parchment paper-lined baking sheet. Brush with beaten egg. Bake 20-25 minutes or until golden brown.

Duchess
Potatoes

Chocolate-Strawberry Cream Cheese Tart

Chocolate-Strawberry Cream Cheese Tart

Bound to impress, this dessert features velvety cream cheese, fresh red strawberries and a drizzle of fudge atop a crunchy chocolate almond crust. It's too gorgeous to resist!

—PRISCILLA YEE CONCORD, CA

PREP: 20 MIN. • **BAKE:** 15 MIN. + CHILLING
MAKES: 12 SERVINGS

- ¾ cup all-purpose flour
- ½ cup finely chopped almonds, toasted
- 6 tablespoons butter, melted
- ⅓ cup baking cocoa
- ¼ cup packed brown sugar

FILLING

- 2 packages (8 ounces each) cream cheese, softened
- 1 cup confectioners' sugar
- 1 teaspoon vanilla extract
- 3 cups halved fresh strawberries
- 3 tablespoons hot fudge ice cream topping

1. Preheat oven to 375°. In a small bowl, combine the first five ingredients; press onto the bottom and up the sides of an ungreased 9-in. fluted tart pan with removable bottom. Bake 12-15 minutes or until crust is set. Cool on a wire rack.
2. In another small bowl, beat cream cheese, confectioners' sugar and vanilla until smooth. Spread over bottom of prepared crust. Arrange strawberry halves, cut side down, over filling. Cover and refrigerate at least 1 hour.
3. Just before serving, drizzle fudge topping over tart. Refrigerate leftovers.

Marmalade Candied Carrots

This is my favorite carrot recipe. Crisp-tender carrots have a citrusy sweet flavor that's perfect for any special occasion.
—HEATHER CLEMMONS SUPPLY, NC

START TO FINISH: 30 MIN. • **MAKES:** 8 SERVINGS

- 2 pounds fresh baby carrots
- ⅔ cup orange marmalade
- 3 tablespoons brown sugar
- 2 tablespoons butter
- ½ cup chopped pecans, toasted
- 1 teaspoon rum extract

1. In a large saucepan, place steamer basket over 1 in. of water. Place carrots in basket. Bring water to a boil. Reduce heat to maintain a low boil; steam, covered, 12-15 minutes or until carrots are crisp-tender.
2. Meanwhile, in a small saucepan, combine marmalade, brown sugar and butter; cook and stir over medium heat until mixture is thickened and reduced to about ½ cup. Stir in pecans and rum extract.
3. Place carrots in a large bowl. Add the marmalade mixture and toss gently to coat.

Marmalade Candied Carrots

Save Time with a Pinch of Planning

The night before your holiday feast, dig out your best serving pieces and utensils. Decide which platters, bowls and trays will feature which foods, and set those pieces on the table or buffet. Many busy hostesses label the dishes with the foods that will occupy them to best streamline dinner prep on the big day.

Gingerbread Ice Cream Sandwiches

the bottom of half of the cookies; top with remaining cookies. Wrap each in plastic wrap; freeze on a baking sheet at least 1 hour.

Jeweled Fruitcake

I promise that this fruitcake is simply fantastic. Even my friends and family members who would ordinarily avoid fruitcake say they love it! It's wonderful after dinner.

—**SHARON HOFFMAN** DONNA, TX

PREP: 30 MIN. • **BAKE:** 1 HOUR + COOLING
MAKES: 4 MINI LOAVES (6 SLICES EACH)

- 2 packages (8 ounces each) pitted dates, chopped
- ½ pound pecan halves
- ½ pound Brazil nuts
- 1 jar (10 ounces) red maraschino cherries, well drained
- 1 jar (10 ounces) green maraschino cherries, well drained
- ½ cup flaked coconut
- 1½ cups all-purpose flour
- 1½ cups sugar
- 1 teaspoon baking powder
- 1 teaspoon salt
- 3 eggs
- 2 teaspoons vanilla extract

1. Preheat oven to 300°. Line four greased and floured 5¾x3x2-in. loaf pans with waxed paper and grease the paper; set aside.
2. In a large bowl, combine dates, nuts, cherries and coconut. Combine flour, sugar, baking powder and salt; stir into fruit mixture until well coated.
3. In a small bowl, beat eggs and vanilla until foamy. Fold into fruit mixture and mix well. Pour into prepared pans.
4. Bake 60-70 minutes or until a toothpick inserted near the center comes out clean. Cool 10 minutes before removing from pans to wire racks to cool completely. Wrap tightly and store in a cool, dry place. Cut with a serrated knife.

FREEZE IT
Gingerbread Ice Cream Sandwiches

When it comes to making an ice cream sandwich, not all gingerbread men are created equal. Some are too crispy; others too soft, but these thin yet sturdy boys hold up nice in the freezer and make for a whimsical make-ahead dessert.

—*TASTE OF HOME* TEST KITCHEN

PREP: 30 MIN. + CHILLING • **BAKE:** 10 MIN./BATCH + FREEZING
MAKES: 1 DOZEN

- 3 cups vanilla ice cream
- ¾ teaspoon ground cinnamon

COOKIES
- ⅓ cup butter, softened
- ½ cup packed brown sugar
- 1 egg
- ⅓ cup molasses
- 2 cups all-purpose flour
- 1 teaspoon ground ginger
- ¾ teaspoon baking soda
- ¾ teaspoon ground cinnamon
- ½ teaspoon ground cloves
- ¼ teaspoon salt

1. In a blender, combine ice cream and cinnamon. Transfer to a freezer container; freeze for at least 2 hours.
2. Meanwhile, in a large bowl, cream butter and brown sugar until light and fluffy. Add egg, then molasses. Combine flour, ginger, baking soda, cinnamon, cloves and salt; gradually add to creamed mixture and mix well. Cover and refrigerate 2 hours or until easy to handle.
3. Preheat oven to 350°. On a lightly floured surface, roll dough to ⅛-in. thickness. Cut with a floured 3½-in. gingerbread-shaped cookie cutter. Place 1 in. apart on ungreased baking sheets. Bake 8-10 minutes or until edges are firm. Remove to wire racks to cool. To make ice cream sandwiches, spread ¼ cup softened ice cream over

Festive Fall Tortellini Toss

I love mushrooms, squash, apples and walnuts. I combined these ingredients with pasta to make a delicious side dish; the recipe can easily be doubled and can be served either warm or at room temperature.

—ROXANNE CHAN ALBANY, CA

PREP: 25 MIN. • **COOK:** 10 MIN.
MAKES: 12 SERVINGS (⅔ CUP EACH)

- 1 **package (9 ounces) refrigerated cheese tortellini**
- 2 **tablespoons olive oil**
- ½ **pound sliced baby portobello mushrooms**
- 1¾ **cups cubed peeled butternut squash (about ¼-inch cubes)**
- ½ **teaspoon poultry seasoning**
- 1 **medium tart apple, chopped**
- 3 **tablespoons thawed apple juice concentrate**
- 3 **tablespoons cider vinegar**
- 1 **green onion, thinly sliced**
- ⅓ **cup chopped walnuts, toasted**
- ⅓ **cup cubed smoked Gouda cheese (about ¼-inch cubes)**
- 2 **tablespoons minced fresh parsley**

1. Cook tortellini according to package directions. In a large skillet, heat oil over medium-high heat. Add mushrooms, squash and poultry seasoning; cook and stir 6-8 minutes or until mushrooms are tender. Add apple, apple juice concentrate, vinegar and onion; cook 2-3 minutes longer or until squash is tender.

2. Drain tortellini; rinse with cold water and place in a large bowl. Add squash mixture, walnuts, cheese and parsley; toss gently to coat.

Festive Fall Tortellini Toss

Nutty Wild Rice

Here's a fantastic side dish for poultry meals. You'll go nuts for it and its hearty crunch. It truly packs a zesty bite.

—HEATHER WEBB CHANNELVIEW, TX

PREP: 15 MIN. • **COOK:** 50 MIN.
MAKES: 5 SERVINGS

- 2½ cups water
- ½ cup uncooked wild rice
- 1 tablespoon reduced-sodium soy sauce
- 6 green onions, sliced
- 1 tablespoon butter
- ⅔ cup sliced almonds, toasted
- ¼ cup sunflower kernels
- 3 tablespoons sesame seeds, toasted
- ¼ teaspoon salt

1. In a large saucepan, bring the water, rice and soy sauce to a boil. Reduce heat; cover and simmer for 45-60 minutes or until rice is tender.

2. Meanwhile, in a small skillet, saute onions in butter until tender. Stir in the remaining ingredients; heat through. Remove from the heat.

3. Drain rice if necessary. Stir in onion mixture.

Nutty Wild Rice

Cardamom Twist

This golden holiday loaf has a soft, tender texture and the perfect amount of cardamom flavor in every bite. Slices are especially good with a cream cheese spread or fresh honey butter.

—CARLA MILLER PASCO, WA

PREP: 40 MIN. + RISING
BAKE: 25 MIN. + COOLING
MAKES: 1 LOAF (18 SLICES)

- ½ cup sliced fresh carrots
- 2 packages (¼ ounce each) active dry yeast
- 1¾ cups warm water (110° to 115°)
- 4½ teaspoons cardamom pods (about 40)
- ¾ cup sugar
- ⅓ cup canola oil
- 2 teaspoons salt
- 4¾ to 5¼ cups all-purpose flour
- 1 egg white
- 1 tablespoon water
- 2 teaspoons coarse sugar

1. Place 1 in. of water in a small saucepan; add carrots. Bring to a boil. Reduce heat; cover and simmer for 6-8 minutes or until tender. Drain, reserving ¼ cup water. Transfer carrots and reserved water to a small food processor; cover and process until smooth.

2. In a large bowl, dissolve yeast in warm water. Remove seeds from cardamom pods; coarsely crush seeds. Add the seeds, sugar, oil, salt, pureed carrots and 2½ cups flour to yeast mixture. Beat until smooth. Stir in enough remaining flour to form a firm dough (dough will be sticky).

3. Turn dough onto a floured surface; knead until smooth and elastic, about 6-8 minutes. Place in a greased bowl, turning once to grease the top. Cover and let rise in a warm place until doubled, about 1 hour.

4. Punch dough down; turn onto a lightly floured surface. Divide into thirds; shape each into a 25-in. rope. Place ropes on a greased baking sheet and braid; pinch ends together, forming a round loaf. Cover and let rise until doubled, about 30 minutes.

5. Preheat oven to 350°. Beat egg white and water; brush over loaf. Sprinkle with coarse sugar. Bake 25-35 minutes or until golden brown. Remove to a wire rack.

⑤ INGREDIENTS

Salt-Encrusted Prime Rib

Restaurants have nothing on this recipe. For a true meat lover, it's very easy to prepare. The results are beyond belief.

—ROGER BOWLDS BAKERSFIELD, CA

PREP: 15 MIN. • **BAKE:** 2¼ HOURS + STANDING
MAKES: 10 SERVINGS

- 1 box (3 pounds) kosher salt (about 6 cups), divided
- 1 bone-in beef rib roast (6 to 8 pounds)
- 3 tablespoons Worcestershire sauce
- 2 tablespoons cracked black pepper
- 2 teaspoons garlic powder
- ½ cup water

1. Preheat oven to 450°. Line a shallow roasting pan with heavy-duty foil. Place 3 cups salt on foil, spreading evenly to form a ½-in. layer.

2. Brush roast with Worcestershire sauce; sprinkle with pepper and garlic powder. Place roast on layer of salt, fat side up. In a small bowl, mix water and remaining salt (mixture should be just moist enough to pack). Beginning at the base of the roast, press salt mixture onto the sides and top of roast.

3. Roast 15 minutes. Reduce oven setting to 325°. Roast 2 to 2¼ hours or until a thermometer reaches 130° for medium-rare; 145° for medium. (Temperature of roast will continue to rise about 15° upon standing.) Let stand 20 minutes.

4. Remove and discard salt crust; brush away any remaining salt. Carve the roast into slices.

German Black Forest Cake

German Black Forest Cake

As far as I know, this cake recipe can be traced back to my German great-grandma. When I got married, my mother gave me a copy, and I hope to someday pass it down to my children, too.
—**STEPHANIE TRAVIS** FALLON, NV

PREP: 45 MIN. + COOLING
BAKE: 30 MIN. + COOLING • **MAKES:** 12 SERVINGS

- 1 **cup whole milk**
- 3 **eggs**
- ½ **cup canola oil**
- 3 **teaspoons vanilla extract**
- 2 **cups plus 2 tablespoons all-purpose flour**
- 2 **cups sugar**
- ¾ **cup baking cocoa**
- 1½ **teaspoons baking powder**
- ¾ **teaspoon baking soda**
- ¾ **teaspoon salt**
- FILLING
- 2 **cans (14½ ounces each) pitted tart cherries**
- 1 **cup sugar**
- ¼ **cup cornstarch**
- 3 **tablespoons cherry brandy or 2 teaspoons vanilla extract**
- WHIPPED CREAM
- 3 **cups heavy whipping cream**
- ⅓ **cup confectioners' sugar**

1. Preheat oven to 350°. Line bottoms of two greased 9-in. round baking pans with waxed paper; grease paper.
2. In a large bowl, beat milk, eggs, oil and vanilla until well blended. In another bowl, whisk flour, sugar, cocoa, baking powder, baking soda and salt; gradually beat into milk mixture.
3. Transfer to prepared pans. Bake for 30-35 minutes or until a toothpick inserted into center comes out clean. Cool cake in pans 10 minutes before removing to wire racks; remove paper. Cool completely.
4. Meanwhile, for filling, drain cherries, reserving ½ cup juice. In a small saucepan, whisk sugar, cornstarch and reserved juice; add cherries. Cook and stir over low heat 10-12 minutes or until thickened and bubbly. Remove from heat; stir in brandy. Cool completely.
5. In a large bowl, beat cream until it begins to thicken. Add confectioners' sugar; beat until stiff peaks form.
6. Using a long serrated knife, cut each cake horizontally in half. Place one cake layer on a serving plate. Top with 1½ cups whipped cream. Spread ¾ cup filling to within 1 in. of edge. Repeat twice. Top with remaining cake layer. Frost top and sides of cake with remaining whipped cream, reserving some to pipe decorations, if desired. Spoon remaining filling onto top of cake. Refrigerate until serving.

Garlic Knotted Rolls

Using frozen yeast dough is an easy way to make homemade rolls. These cute knots add a special touch to any menu.
—**KATHY HARDING** RICHMOND, MO

PREP: 15 MIN. + RISING • **BAKE:** 15 MIN.
MAKES: 10 ROLLS

- 1 **loaf (1 pound) frozen bread dough, thawed**
- 1½ **teaspoons dried minced onion**
- 3 **tablespoons butter**
- 4 **garlic cloves, minced**
- ⅛ **teaspoon salt**
- 1 **egg, beaten**
- 1 **teaspoon poppy seeds**

1. Pat out dough on a work surface; sprinkle with minced onion and knead until combined. Divide dough in half. Shape each piece into five balls. To form knots, roll each ball into a 10-in. rope; tie into a knot. Tuck ends under. Place rolls 2 in. apart on a greased baking sheet.
2. In a small skillet over medium heat, melt butter. Add garlic and salt; cook and stir 1-2 minutes. Brush over rolls. Cover and let rise until doubled, about 30 minutes.
3. Preheat oven to 375°. Brush tops of rolls with egg; sprinkle with poppy seeds. Bake 15-20 minutes or until golden brown.

LINDA STEMEN'S CAPPUCCINO CHEESECAKE *PAGE 305*
TASTE OF HOME TEST KITCHEN'S VANILLA BEAN FIZZ *PAGE 305*

New Year's Party

HAPPY NEW YEAR! HOW DO YOU CELEBRATE THE ARRIVAL OF THE BABY NEW YEAR? CHAMPAGNE AT MIDNIGHT? A SPECIAL DINNER? MAYBE YOU ENJOY A CASUAL BRUNCH ON NEW YEAR'S DAY OR SPEND THE AFTERNOON ON THE COUCH WATCHING THE BIG GAME. MIX-AND-MATCH THE RECIPES THAT FOLLOW TO CREATE YOUR IDEAL CELEBRATION TO RING IN THE YEAR.

ANNMARIE LUCENTE'S CRUMB-TOPPED CLAMS *PAGE 306*

TASTE OF HOME **TEST KITCHEN'S LAYERED PEPPERMINT ICEBOX CAKE** *PAGE 300*

JACKIE PRICE'S FETTUCCINE SEAFOOD ALFREDO *PAGE 299*

Poached Egg Salads with Pancetta Vinaigrette

New Year's Bloody Mary

While I was cleaning out my fridge, a lot of the ingredients for a Bloody Mary just jumped out at me. I couldn't resist combining them into a spicy Mary.
—**JIMMY CABABA** WEST ALLIS, WI

START TO FINISH: 10 MIN. • **MAKES:** 2 SERVINGS

- 1½ cups tomato juice
- 2 ounces vodka
- 3 tablespoons beef broth
- 2 teaspoons dill pickle juice
- 2 teaspoons stone-ground mustard
- 1 teaspoon lemon juice
- 1 teaspoon lime juice
- ½ teaspoon hot pepper sauce
- ½ teaspoon Worcestershire sauce
- ½ teaspoon prepared horseradish
- ¼ teaspoon garlic powder
- ¼ teaspoon pepper
  Ice cubes

In a small pitcher, mix first 12 ingredients; serve over ice.

Poached Egg Salads with Pancetta Vinaigrette

Nothing is better than when the yolk breaks over this salad's rustic flavors of shiitake mushrooms, pancetta and arugula.
—**CINDIE HARAS** JUPITER, FL

PREP: 40 MIN. • **MAKES:** 8 SERVINGS

- 1 can (14 ounces) water-packed quartered artichoke hearts, rinsed and drained
- 1½ cups whole fresh shiitake mushrooms
- 2 tablespoons olive oil
- 1 teaspoon minced fresh rosemary
- ½ teaspoon salt
- ¼ teaspoon coarsely ground pepper

DRESSING

- 2 ounces pancetta or bacon strips, chopped
- 1 shallot, finely chopped
- ¼ cup sherry vinegar
- 1 tablespoon Dijon mustard
- 1 teaspoon sugar
- ¼ cup olive oil

SALADS

- 1 tablespoon white vinegar
- 8 eggs
- 2 cups fresh arugula

1. In a large bowl, combine the artichokes, mushrooms, oil, rosemary, salt and pepper; transfer to an ungreased baking sheet. Bake at 425° for 10-15 minutes or until mushrooms are tender.

2. Meanwhile, in a large skillet, cook pancetta and shallot over medium heat until pancetta is crisp. Stir in the sherry vinegar, mustard and sugar; heat through. Transfer mixture to a small bowl; gradually whisk in oil. Set aside.

3. Place 2-3 in. of water in a large skillet with high sides; add white vinegar. Bring to a boil; reduce heat and simmer gently. Break cold eggs, one at a time, into a custard cup or saucer; holding the cup close to the surface of the water, slip each egg into water.

4. Cook, uncovered, until whites are completely set and yolks are still soft, about 4 minutes. With a slotted spoon, lift eggs out of water.

5. Divide arugula among eight salad plates. Top each with artichoke mixture and a poached egg; drizzle with the vinaigrette.

New Year's Bloody Mary

Stuffed Shrimp Appetizers

Here's a trick: Double this stuffing and use the excess for stuffing button mushrooms. Then bake them alongside the shrimp. Two easy appetizers at once!

—**SHIRLEY LEASOCK** ROCKWOOD, PA

PREP: 25 MIN. • **BAKE:** 10 MIN.
MAKES: 20 APPETIZERS

- 20 uncooked large shrimp
  (about 1 pound)
- 1 egg, beaten
- ½ cup soft bread crumbs
- 1 tablespoon mayonnaise
- ½ teaspoon lemon juice
- ¼ teaspoon salt-free seasoning blend
- ¼ teaspoon pepper
- ⅛ teaspoon dried oregano
  Dash cayenne pepper
- 1 can (6 ounces) lump crabmeat, drained
- 2 tablespoons grated Parmesan cheese
- 1 teaspoon paprika

1. Peel and devein shrimp, leaving the tails on. Butterfly each shrimp along the outside curve. Open shrimp flat and place butterflied side down in an ungreased 15x10x1-in. baking pan.
2. In a small bowl, combine the egg, bread crumbs, mayonnaise, lemon juice and seasonings. Stir in crab. Place 1 tablespoonful of mixture over each shrimp; sprinkle with Parmesan and paprika. Bake at 350° for 9-11 minutes or until shrimp turn pink. Serve warm.

Stuffed Shrimp Appetizers

Brie Toasts with Cranberry Compote

Brie Toasts with Cranberry Compote

Just seven ingredients are all I need to create an elegant appetizer perfect for entertaining. The tart cranberry compote pairs well with creamy Brie cheese.

—**KATHERINE WATSON** OMAHA, NE

PREP: 30 MIN. • **BAKE:** 5 MIN.
MAKES: ABOUT 2 DOZEN

- 1 cup dried cranberries
- 1 cup balsamic vinegar
- ½ cup jellied cranberry sauce
- 1 tablespoon sugar
- 1 loaf (1 pound) French bread, cut into ½-inch slices
- 3 tablespoons butter, melted
- ½ pound Brie cheese, thinly sliced

1. In a small saucepan, combine the cranberries, vinegar, cranberry sauce and sugar. Cook and stir over medium heat until thickened, about 12 minutes.
2. Brush bottoms of bread with butter; place on ungreased baking sheets. Bake at 350° for 1-2 minutes or until lightly toasted. Top bread with Brie. Bake for 4-6 minutes or until cheese is melted. Spoon cranberry mixture over cheese, about 1 tablespoon on each.

TOP TIP

Brie Basics

Lots of hosts rely on Brie for fast and easy appetizers. Brie is a soft cows' milk cheese, named after the French region of Brie. It's pale in color with a grayish-white edible rind. The interior has a soft, spreadable consistency when served at room temperature. It's perfect for use on cheese trays or melted in sandwiches, soups or fondues.

Smoked Salmon Bites with Shallot Sauce

Smoked Salmon Bites with Shallot Sauce

Tangy Dijon-mayo sauce adds zip to puff pastry and layers of crisp arugula, smoked salmon and shaved Asiago cheese. I make these a couple of times a year.
—**JAMIE BROWN-MILLER** NAPA, CA

START TO FINISH: 30 MIN.
MAKES: 25 APPETIZERS

- 1　sheet frozen puff pastry, thawed

SAUCE
- 2　shallots
- 2　tablespoons Dijon mustard
- 1　tablespoon mayonnaise
- 1　tablespoon red wine vinegar
- ¼　cup olive oil

FINISHING
- 1　cup fresh arugula or baby spinach, coarsely chopped
- 4½　ounces smoked salmon or lox, thinly sliced
- ½　cup shaved Asiago cheese

1. Preheat oven to 400°. Unfold puff pastry; cut into 25 squares. Transfer to greased baking sheets. Bake 11-13 minutes or until golden brown.
2. Meanwhile, grate one shallot and finely chop the other. In a small bowl, combine shallots, mustard, mayonnaise and vinegar. While whisking, gradually add oil in a steady stream. Spoon a small amount of sauce onto each pastry; layer with arugula and salmon. Drizzle with remaining sauce and sprinkle with Asiago cheese.

Portobello-Stuffed Pork Roast

Tart cherries and earthy mushrooms come together in a savory stuffing for pork tenderloin. The sauce—prepared with port wine and balsamic vinegar—makes every bite even better.
—**LINDA MONACH** CHESTNUT HILL, MA

PREP: 35 MIN. • **BAKE:** 2 HOURS + STANDING
MAKES: 8 SERVINGS (1 CUP SAUCE)

- 1　package (6 ounces) dried cherries
- ¾　cup ruby port wine or grape juice, warmed, divided
- 3　large portobello mushrooms, divided
- 1　medium onion, finely chopped
- 3　tablespoons olive oil
- 6　garlic cloves, minced
- 1½　cups soft bread crumbs
- ⅓　cup chopped pecans
- ½　teaspoon salt
- ¼　teaspoon pepper
- 3　tablespoons plus ¼ cup balsamic vinegar, divided
- 1　boneless pork loin roast (3 to 4 pounds)

CHERRY PORT WINE SAUCE
- ½　cup ruby port wine or grape juice
- ½　cup balsamic vinegar
- ¼　cup chicken broth
- 3　garlic cloves, minced
- ½　cup heavy whipping cream

1. In a small bowl, combine cherries and ½ cup wine. Let stand 5 minutes. Drain cherries, reserving wine; set side.
2. Chop one mushroom. In a large skillet, saute onion in oil until tender. Add garlic; cook 1 minute longer. Remove from heat. Add bread crumbs, pecans, salt, pepper, 3 tablespoons balsamic vinegar, ½ cup cherries and chopped mushroom.
3. Preheat oven to 350°. Starting about a third in from one side, make a lengthwise slit in the roast to within ½ in. of bottom. Turn roast over and make another lengthwise slit, starting from about a third in from the opposite side. Open roast so it lies flat; cover with plastic wrap. Flatten to ¾-in. thickness; remove plastic. Spread stuffing mixture over meat.

4. Roll up jelly-roll style, starting with a long side. Tie pork at 2-in. intervals with kitchen string. Place on a rack in a shallow roasting pan. Slice remaining mushrooms; brush with 1 tablespoon vinegar. Arrange around pork.
5. Bake 1 hour. In a small bowl, combine remaining vinegar and reserved wine; brush over pork. Bake 1 to 1½ hours longer or until a thermometer reads 160°. Let stand 10 minutes before slicing.
6. For sauce, in a small saucepan, combine wine, vinegar, broth, garlic and remaining cherries. Bring to a boil; cook until liquid is reduced by half. Stir in cream; simmer 5 minutes. Serve with pork and mushrooms.

SLOW COOKER

Hot Wing Dip

Since I usually have all the ingredients on hand, this is a great go-to snack for entertaining friends and family.
—**COLEEN CORNER** GROVE CITY, PA

PREP: 10 MIN. • **COOK:** 1 HOUR
MAKES: 18 SERVINGS (¼ CUP EACH)

- 2　cups shredded cooked chicken
- 1　package (8 ounces) cream cheese, cubed
- 2　cups (8 ounces) shredded cheddar cheese
- 1　cup ranch salad dressing
- ½　cup Louisiana-style hot sauce
　　Tortilla chips and celery sticks
　　Minced fresh parsley, optional

In a 3-qt. slow cooker, mix the first five ingredients. Cook, covered, on low for 1-2 hours or until cheese is melted. Serve with chips and celery. If desired, sprinkle with parsley.

❝ This dip is so good, I could have eaten it all myself! ❞
—ANITAMM
TASTEOFHOME.COM

Champagne Party Punch

Because a New Year's party wouldn't be complete without a little bubbly, this Champagne-spiked cocktail is a perfect addition to the menu.

—*TASTE OF HOME* **TEST KITCHEN**

PREP: 15 MIN. + CHILLING
MAKES: 18 SERVINGS (¾ CUP EACH)

- 1 **cup sugar**
- 1 **cup water**
- 2 **cups unsweetened apple juice**
- 2 **cups unsweetened pineapple juice**
- ½ **cup lemon juice**
- ⅓ **cup thawed orange juice concentrate**
- ¼ **cup lime juice**
- 2 **cups ice cubes**
- 1 **quart ginger ale, chilled**
- 1 **bottle (750 ml) Champagne, chilled**

1. In a large pitcher, combine sugar and water; stir until sugar is dissolved. Add the apple juice, pineapple juice, lemon juice, orange juice concentrate and lime juice. Refrigerate until serving.

2. Just before serving, pour into a punch bowl and add ice cubes. Slowly add ginger ale and Champagne.

Champagne Party Punch

Fettuccine Seafood Alfredo

Fettuccine Seafood Alfredo

I started making this Alfredo for special occasions because it's a delicious meal that's great for entertaining.

—**JACKIE PRICE** TRENTON, MO

START TO FINISH: 25 MIN.
MAKES: 5 SERVINGS

- 12 **ounces uncooked fettuccine**
- 2 **tablespoons olive oil, divided**
- 1 **pound uncooked jumbo shrimp, peeled and deveined**
- 6 **garlic cloves, minced**
- 1 **can (12 ounces) evaporated milk**
- ½ **teaspoon salt**
- ¼ **cup grated Parmesan cheese**
- ¼ **cup sour cream**
- ½ **pound lump crabmeat, drained**
- ¼ **cup minced fresh basil**

1. Cook fettuccine according to package directions.

2. Meanwhile, in a large skillet, heat 1 tablespoon oil over medium-high heat. Add shrimp; cook and stir 4 minutes or until shrimp turn pink. Remove and keep warm.

3. In same pan, heat remaining oil over medium heat. Add garlic; cook and stir 1-2 minutes. Add milk and salt. Bring just to a boil, stirring constantly.

4. Remove from heat; stir in cheese until melted. Whisk in sour cream. Drain fettuccine; add to skillet with shrimp and crab. Heat through. Stir in basil.

Beer-Cheese Appetizers

It's hard to stop eating these irresistible bites that feature a classic pairing of beer and hot melted cheese. They disappear fast on game day.

—**KRISTY WILSHIRE** PITTSBURGH, PA

PREP: 25 MIN. • **BAKE:** 5 MIN./BATCH
MAKES: 80 APPETIZERS (1¾ CUPS SAUCE)

- 2 **cups biscuit/baking mix**
- ½ **cup shredded cheddar cheese**
- ½ **cup beer or nonalcoholic beer**
- 2 **tablespoons butter, melted**
  Sesame and/or poppy seeds

CHEESE SAUCE
- 1 **package (8 ounces) process cheese (Velveeta), cubed**
- ½ **cup refried beans**
- 2 **jalapeno peppers, seeded and chopped**
- ¼ **cup sour cream**
- ¼ **cup salsa**

1. Preheat oven to 450°. Combine biscuit mix and cheese in a large bowl. Stir in beer until a soft dough forms. Turn onto a floured surface; knead five times. Roll into a 16x10-in. rectangle. Cut into 2-in. squares; cut each square in half diagonally.

2. Place 1 in. apart on greased baking sheets. Brush with butter; sprinkle with seeds. Bake 6-8 minutes or until lightly browned. Remove to wire racks to cool.

3. For sauce, combine remaining ingredients in a small saucepan. Cook and stir over medium heat until cheese is melted. Serve immediately with triangles for dipping.

NOTE *Wear disposable gloves when cutting hot peppers; the oils can burn skin. Avoid touching your face.*

Layered Peppermint Icebox Cake

(5) INGREDIENTS

Layered Peppermint Icebox Cake

Take four ingredients and turn them into an impressive, no-bake cake. What could be easier?

—**TASTE OF HOME** TEST KITCHEN

PREP: 20 MIN. + CHILLING • **MAKES:** 8 SERVINGS

- 3 **cups heavy whipping cream**
- 3 **tablespoons sugar**
- 1 **teaspoon peppermint extract**
- 2 **packages (9 ounces each) chocolate wafers**
  Edible flowers of your choice, chocolate curls and crushed candy canes, optional

1. In a large bowl, beat the cream, sugar and peppermint extract on high until stiff peaks form. Cut a small hole in the corner of a pastry or plastic bag. Fill with whipped cream.

2. On a serving plate, arrange seven cookies in a circle, using one cookie in the center. Pipe ⅔ cup whipped cream over cookies. Repeat layers nine times. Refrigerate overnight.

3. Garnish with flowers, chocolate curls and crushed candy if desired.

Herb & Roasted Pepper Cheesecake

Savory cheesecakes offer make-ahead convenience and are a great way to serve a crowd. Here, roasted red peppers and fresh herbs create a lovely spread for pita chips. Bacon and garlic add a savory finish.

—LAURA JULIAN AMANDA, OH

PREP: 20 MIN. • **BAKE:** 35 MIN. + CHILLING
MAKES: 24 SERVINGS

- 3 packages (8 ounces each) cream cheese, softened
- ¾ cup whole-milk ricotta cheese
- 1½ teaspoons salt
- ¾ teaspoon pepper
- 3 eggs, lightly beaten
- 1½ cups roasted sweet red peppers, drained and finely chopped
- ¾ cup minced fresh basil
- ⅓ cup minced fresh chives
- 3 tablespoons minced fresh thyme
- 3 tablespoons crumbled cooked bacon
- 3 garlic cloves, minced
- 1 tablespoon olive oil
  Roasted sweet red pepper strips and additional minced chives, optional
  Baked pita chips

1. Preheat oven to 350°. Place a greased 9-in. springform pan on a double thickness of heavy-duty foil (about 18 in. square). Securely wrap foil around pan.
2. Place cream cheese, ricotta cheese, salt and pepper in a food processor; cover and process until smooth. Add eggs; pulse just until combined. Add red peppers, herbs, bacon and garlic; cover and pulse just until blended. Pour filling into prepared pan. Place springform pan in a large baking pan; add 1 in. of boiling water to larger pan.
3. Bake 35-45 minutes or until center is just set and top appears dull. Remove springform pan from water bath; remove foil. Cool cheesecake on a wire rack for 10 minutes; loosen edges from pan with a knife. Cool 1 hour longer. Refrigerate overnight.
4. Remove rim from pan. Just before serving, drizzle cheesecake with oil; top with red pepper strips and chives if desired. Serve with pita chips.

Portobello & Green Bean Saute

Portobello & Green Bean Saute

I think the key to tasty veggies is simplicity. That is the way I like to cook: simple everyday ingredients combined to be fantastic. Be careful with the salt—the bouillon may have enough for most tastes. If portobello mushrooms are not available, white button mushrooms work equally well.

—ELAINE SHOEMAKE SEDGEWICKVILLE, MO

START TO FINISH: 20 MIN. • **MAKES:** 10 SERVINGS

- 1 pound fresh green beans, trimmed and halved
- 1 pound baby portobello mushrooms, quartered
- 1 medium onion, finely chopped
- ¼ cup butter, cubed
- 2 garlic cloves, minced
- 1 teaspoon chicken bouillon granules
- 4 plum tomatoes, peeled and chopped
- 1 teaspoon dried marjoram
- ¼ teaspoon pepper
- ¼ cup minced fresh parsley

1. Place the beans in a large saucepan and cover with water; bring to a boil. Cover and cook for 3-5 minutes or until crisp-tender.
2. Meanwhile, in a large skillet, saute mushrooms and onion in butter until tender. Add garlic and bouillon; cook 1 minute longer. Drain green beans; add to skillet and toss to coat. Remove from the heat. Stir in the tomatoes, marjoram and pepper. Sprinkle with parsley.

Herb & Roasted Pepper Cheesecake

Chunky Garlic Mashed Potatoes

Sweet 'n' Spicy Snack Mix

Most snack mixes contain either peanuts or nuts of some kind. This one, with Chex cereal, cheesy snack crackers and mini pretzels, is tasty and delicious without the nuts. It's sure to spice up your next party.
—TASTE OF HOME TEST KITCHEN

PREP: 10 MIN. • **BAKE:** 45 MIN. • **MAKES:** 10 CUPS

- 4 cups miniature pretzels
- 2⅓ cups reduced-fat cheese-flavored baked snack crackers
- 2 cups Wheat Chex
- 3 tablespoons butter, melted
- 1 tablespoon reduced-sodium soy sauce
- 2 teaspoons chili powder
- 1 teaspoon barbecue seasoning
- 3 cups Corn Pops

1. Preheat oven to 250°. In a large bowl, combine pretzels, crackers and cereal. In a small bowl, combine butter, soy sauce, chili powder and barbecue seasoning; pour over cereal mixture and toss to coat.
2. Transfer to a 15x10x1-in. baking pan coated with cooking spray. Bake for 45 minutes, stirring every 15 minutes. Stir in Corn Pops. Store in airtight containers.

NOTE *Read all ingredient labels for possible nut content prior to use. Ingredient formulas can change, and production facilities vary among brands. If you're concerned that your brand may contain nuts, contact the company.*

⑤ INGREDIENTS
Chunky Garlic Mashed Potatoes

I like to dress up these mashed spuds with a whole bulb of roasted garlic. It may seem like overkill, but once cooked, the garlic mellows out and you're left with a sweet and delicate flavor.
—JACKIE GREGSTON HALLSVILLE, TX

START TO FINISH: 30 MIN. • **MAKES:** 9 SERVINGS

- 3 pounds Yukon Gold potatoes, cut into quarters
- 1 whole garlic bulb, cloves separated and peeled
- ½ cup butter, cubed
- ½ cup half-and-half cream
- 2 tablespoons prepared horseradish
- ¾ teaspoon salt
- ¾ teaspoon pepper
  Fresh thyme leaves, optional

1. Place potatoes and garlic cloves in a large saucepan; cover with water. Bring to a boil. Reduce heat; cover and cook for 15-20 minutes or until the potatoes are tender.
2. In a small saucepan, heat butter and cream; keep warm. Drain potatoes and garlic; return to pan. Add horseradish, salt, pepper and butter mixture; mash. Garnish with thyme if desired.

TOP TIP

Hosting an Appetizer Party for the New Year?

When planning an appetizer buffet, offer a variety of tastes, textures and colors to please your guests' palates. Choose snacks that can be picked up and eaten without utensils, such as cubed sausage and cheese, skewered meatballs, kabobs and cut veggies. Set out bowls of nuts and snack mixes in other rooms.

Herb-Roasted Olives & Tomatoes

Serve these roasted veggies with slices from crunchy baguettes. You can also double or triple the amounts and have leftovers to toss with spaghetti the next day.

—ANNDREA BAILEY
HUNTINGTON BEACH, CA

START TO FINISH: 20 MIN. • **MAKES:** 4 CUPS

- 2 cups cherry tomatoes
- 1 cup garlic-stuffed olives
- 1 cup Greek olives
- 1 cup pitted ripe olives
- 8 garlic cloves, peeled
- 3 tablespoons olive oil
- 1 tablespoon herbes de Provence
- ¼ teaspoon pepper

Preheat oven to 425°. Combine the first five ingredients on a greased 15x10x1-in. baking pan. Add oil and seasonings; toss to coat. Roast for 15-20 minutes or until tomatoes are softened, stirring occasionally.

NOTE *Look for herbes de Provence in the spice aisle.*

Pomegranate Champagne Cocktail

Toast the one your heart adores with this slightly tart and daringly different sparkling pomegranate cocktail.

—TASTE OF HOME TEST KITCHEN

START TO FINISH: 5 MIN. • **MAKES:** 1 SERVING

- 1 sugar cube or 1 teaspoon sugar
- 2 to 4 dashes bitters, optional
- 1 ounce pomegranate juice
- ½ ounce brandy
- ½ ounce pomegranate liqueur
- ⅓ cup Champagne

GARNISH
- Pomegranate seeds

Place sugar in a champagne flute; sprinkle with bitters if desired. Pour the juice, brandy and liqueur into the glass. Top with Champagne. Garnish with pomegranate seeds.

Herb-Roasted Olives & Tomatoes

(5) INGREDIENTS

Garbanzo-Stuffed Mini Peppers

Pretty mini peppers are the right size for a two-bite snack. They have all the crunch of a pita chip but offer great color for an appetizer buffet.

—CHRISTINE HANOVER
LEWISTON, CA

START TO FINISH: 20 MIN.
MAKES: 32 APPETIZERS

- 1 teaspoon cumin seeds
- 1 can (15 ounces) garbanzo beans or chickpeas, rinsed and drained
- ¼ cup fresh cilantro leaves
- 3 tablespoons water
- 3 tablespoons cider vinegar
- ¼ teaspoon salt
- 16 miniature sweet peppers, halved lengthwise
  Additional fresh cilantro leaves

1. In a dry small skillet, toast cumin seeds over medium heat for 1-2 minutes or until aromatic, stirring frequently. Transfer to a food processor. Add garbanzo beans, cilantro, water, vinegar and salt; pulse until blended.

2. Spoon into pepper halves. Top with additional cilantro. Keep refrigerated until serving.

Garbanzo-Stuffed
Mini Peppers

Cappuccino Cheesecake

Vanilla Bean Fizz

boil. Pour over chocolate; whisk until smooth. Stir in liqueur. Pour 1¾ cups over crust. Freeze for 30 minutes or until firm. For garnishes, drop remaining ganache by teaspoonfuls onto waxed paper-lined sheets; cover and refrigerate.

3. Dissolve coffee granules in rum. In a large bowl, beat cream cheese and sugar until smooth. Beat in the flour, ground coffee, vanilla, molasses and rum mixture. Add eggs; beat on low speed just until combined. Pour over ganache. Place pan on a baking sheet.

4. Bake at 350° for 1 to 1¼ hours or until center is almost set. Let stand for 5 minutes. Combine the sour cream, sugar and vanilla; spread over top of cheesecake. Bake 5 minutes longer. Cool on a wire rack for 10 minutes. Carefully run a knife around edge of pan to loosen; cool 1 hour longer. Refrigerate overnight.

5. Remove sides of pan. Just before serving, arrange garnishes over top.

⑤ INGREDIENTS

Vanilla Bean Fizz

Here, a homemade vanilla bean syrup fabulously flavors Champagne. The bubbly beverage is ideal for holidays throughout the year.

—**TASTE OF HOME** TEST KITCHEN

PREP: 10 MIN. + COOLING
MAKES: 8 SERVINGS

- 2 **cups water**
- 1 **cup sugar**
- 4 **vanilla beans, split**
- 4 **cups Champagne, chilled**

1. In a small saucepan, bring water and sugar to a boil. Add vanilla beans. Reduce heat; simmer, uncovered, for 10 minutes. Remove from the heat; cool to room temperature. Discard beans.

2. For each serving, pour ¼ cup vanilla syrup into a champagne flute; add ½ cup Champagne.

Cappuccino Cheesecake

This is the perfect dessert on a holiday spread. Instead of pouring the decadent ganache over the top of this coffee-flavored cheesecake, I use most of it to cover the chocolate crust.

—**LINDA STEMEN** MONROEVILLE, IN

PREP: 40 MIN. • **BAKE:** 65 MIN. + CHILLING
MAKES: 16 SERVINGS

- 24 **Oreo cookies**
- ⅓ **cup butter, melted**

GANACHE

- 1 **package (10 ounces) 60% cacao bittersweet chocolate baking chips**
- 1 **cup heavy whipping cream**
- ⅓ **cup coffee liqueur**

FILLING

- 1 **tablespoon instant coffee granules**
- 2 **tablespoons dark rum**
- 4 **packages (8 ounces each) cream cheese, softened**
- 1⅓ **cups sugar**
- 2 **tablespoons all-purpose flour**
- 2 **tablespoons ground coffee**
- 3 **teaspoons vanilla extract**
- 2 **teaspoons molasses**
- 4 **eggs, lightly beaten**

TOPPING

- 1½ **cups (12 ounces) sour cream**
- ⅓ **cup sugar**
- 2 **teaspoons vanilla extract**

1. Place cookies in a food processor. Cover and pulse until fine crumbs form. Transfer to a bowl and stir in butter. Press onto the bottom of a greased 10-in. springform pan; set aside.

2. Place chocolate in a small bowl. In a small saucepan, bring cream just to a

Antipasto Braid

We're fans of Mediterranean food, so this play on antipasto is a favorite in my family. Meat and cheese make it a nice, hearty appetizer. Give it a try this year!

—PATRICIA HARMON BADEN, PA

PREP: 25 MIN. • **BAKE:** 30 MIN. + STANDING
MAKES: 12 SERVINGS

- ⅓ cup pitted Greek olives, chopped
- ¼ cup marinated quartered artichoke hearts, drained and chopped
- ¼ cup julienned oil-packed sun-dried tomatoes
- 2 tablespoons plus 2 teaspoons grated Parmesan cheese, divided
- 3 tablespoons olive oil, divided
- 1 tablespoon chopped fresh basil or 1 teaspoon dried basil
- 1 tube (11 ounces) refrigerated crusty French loaf
- 6 thin slices prosciutto or deli ham
- 4 slices provolone cheese
- ¾ cup julienned roasted sweet red peppers

1. Preheat oven to 350°. In a small bowl, toss olives, artichoke hearts, tomatoes, 2 tablespoons Parmesan, 2 tablespoons oil and basil until combined.
2. On a lightly floured surface, carefully unroll French loaf dough; roll into a 15x10-in. rectangle. Transfer to a greased 15x10x1-in. baking pan. Layer prosciutto, provolone cheese and red peppers lengthwise down center third of rectangle. Top with olive mixture.
3. On each long side, cut 10 strips about 3½ in. into the center. Starting at one end, fold alternating strips at an angle across filling, pinching ends to seal. Brush with remaining oil and sprinkle with remaining Parmesan cheese.
4. Bake 30-35 minutes or until golden brown. Let stand 10 minutes before cutting. Serve warm.

Crumb-Topped Clams

Crumb-Topped Clams

In my family, it wouldn't be Christmas Eve without baked clams. However, they make a special bite for New Year's Eve or any other occasion. They're an easy hit.

—ANNMARIE LUCENTE MONROE, NY

PREP: 35 MIN. • **BROIL:** 10 MIN.
MAKES: 2 DOZEN

- 2 pounds kosher salt
- 2 dozen fresh littleneck clams
- ½ cup dry bread crumbs
- ¼ cup chicken broth
- 1 tablespoon minced fresh parsley
- 2 tablespoons olive oil
- 2 garlic cloves, minced
- ¼ teaspoon dried oregano
  Dash pepper
- 1 tablespoon panko (Japanese) bread crumbs
  Lemon wedges

1. Spread salt into an ovenproof metal serving platter or a 15x10x1-in. baking pan. Shuck clams, leaving clams and juices in bottom shells. Arrange in prepared platter; divide the juices among clamshells.
2. In a small bowl, mix dry bread crumbs, chicken broth, parsley, oil, garlic, oregano and pepper; spoon over clams. Sprinkle with bread crumbs.
3. Broil 4-6 in. from heat 6-8 minutes or until clams are firm and crumb mixture is crisp and golden brown. Serve immediately with lemon wedges.

⑤ INGREDIENTS

Glazed Spiral-Sliced Ham

In my mind, few foods in a holiday spread are as tempting as a big baked ham. I always hope for leftovers so we can have ham sandwiches in the following days.

—EDIE DESPAIN LOGAN, UT

PREP: 10 MIN. • **BAKE:** 1 HOUR 35 MIN.
MAKES: 12 SERVINGS

- 1 spiral-sliced fully cooked bone-in ham (7 to 9 pounds)
- ½ cup pineapple preserves
- ½ cup seedless raspberry jam
- ¼ cup packed brown sugar
- ¼ teaspoon ground cloves

1. Preheat oven to 300°. Place ham directly on roasting pan, cut side down. Bake, covered, 1¼ to 1¾ hours.
2. In a bowl, mix remaining ingredients. Spread over ham. Bake, uncovered, for 20-30 minutes longer or until a meat thermometer reads 140° (do not overcook).

Sicilian Overstuffed Sandwich Wedges

For a casual New Year's lunch or dinner, you'll have a guaranteed winner with this stacked-high, Italian-style sandwich. I like the convenience of assembling it a day in advance. Enjoy!

—**PAT POWELL** WOOSTER, OH

PREP: 30 MIN. + CHILLING • **MAKES:** 8 SERVINGS

- 1 round loaf (1 pound) unsliced Italian bread
- ½ cup pitted Greek olives, sliced
- ½ cup chopped pimiento-stuffed olives
- ¼ cup minced fresh parsley
- ¼ cup olive oil
- 1 tablespoon fresh oregano leaves
- 1 tablespoon balsamic vinegar
- 1 teaspoon minced garlic
- ½ teaspoon coarsely ground pepper
- ¼ teaspoon crushed red pepper flakes
- ½ cup sliced pepperoncini
- ¼ pound thinly sliced hard salami
- ¼ pound sliced provolone cheese
- 1 jar (16 ounces) roasted sweet red pepper strips, drained
- ¼ pound sliced pepperoni

1. Cut loaf of bread in half; hollow out top and bottom, leaving a ¾-in. shell (discard removed bread or save for another use).

2. In a small bowl, combine the olives, parsley, oil, oregano, vinegar, garlic, pepper and pepper flakes. Spoon half into bread shell. Layer with pepperoncini, salami, cheese, roasted peppers, pepperoni and remaining olive mixture. Replace bread top.

3. Wrap in plastic wrap; refrigerate for 2-3 hours or overnight. Cut into eight wedges.

NOTE *This recipe was tested with Vlasic roasted red pepper strips. Look for pepperoncini (pickled peppers) in the pickle and olive section of your grocery store.*

TOP TIP

All Greek to You?

Also known as kalamata olives, Greek olives are almond-shaped and have a dark eggplant color.

Black-Eyed Peas & Ham

SLOW COOKER

Black-Eyed Peas & Ham

We have slow-cooked black-eyed peas regularly at our house. They're supposed to bring good luck in the new year.

—**DAWN FRIHAUF** FORT MORGAN, CO

PREP: 20 MIN. • **COOK:** 6 HOURS
MAKES: 12 SERVINGS (¾ CUP EACH)

- 1 package (16 ounces) dried black-eyed peas, rinsed and sorted
- ½ pound fully cooked boneless ham, finely chopped
- 1 medium onion, finely chopped
- 1 medium sweet red pepper, finely chopped
- 5 bacon strips, cooked and crumbled
- 1 large jalapeno pepper, seeded and finely chopped
- 2 garlic cloves, minced
- 1½ teaspoons ground cumin
- 1 teaspoon reduced-sodium chicken bouillon granules
- ½ teaspoon salt
- ½ teaspoon cayenne pepper
- ¼ teaspoon pepper
- 6 cups water
    Minced fresh cilantro, optional
    Hot cooked rice

In a 6-qt. slow cooker, combine the first 13 ingredients. Cover and cook on low for 6-8 hours or until peas are tender. Sprinkle with cilantro if desired. Serve with rice.

NOTE *Wear disposable gloves when cutting hot peppers; the oils can burn skin. Avoid touching your face.*

Sicilian Overstuffed Sandwich Wedges

30-MINUTE RECIPE INDEX

These recipes can be prepared, start to finish, in just 30 minutes or less.